INSIGHT GUIDES

Created and Directed by Hans Höfer

InDIa

Edited by Andrew Eames
Project Editors: Samuel Israel and Bikram Grewal
Updated by Jan McGirk

Editorial Director: Brian Bell

APA PUBLICATIONS

Part of the Langenscheidt Publishing Group

ABOUT THIS BOOK

Höfer

ndia is whatever you want it to be, but never what you expect it to be. This seemingly nonsensical paradox is just another in a nation of paradoxes. It is a nation that is both drippingly lush and blazingly arid, a nation which plasters its walls with cow-dung and its roofs with satellite dishes, a nation which values spiritualism above everything, but barely notices the passing of human life. It is a nation of world-famous cities, where everyone lives in villages.

Such a complex destination lends itself perfectly to the approach taken by the 190-title award-winning Insight Guides series, created in 1970 by **Hans Höfer**, founder of Apa Publications and still the company's driving force. Each book encourages readers to celebrate the essence of the place rather than try to tailor it to their expectations, and is edited in the belief that, without insight into a people's character and culture, travel is more likely to narrow the mind than broaden it.

Insight Guide: India is carefully structured: the first section covers the country's history, and then analyses its culture in a series of magazine-style essays. The main Places section provides a comprehensive run-down on the things worth seeing and doing in each region. Finally, a fact-packed listings section contains all the information you'll need on travel, hotels, shops, restaurants and opening times. Complementing the text, remarkable photography sets out to communicate directly and provocatively life as it is lived by the locals.

Itzkovitz

Grewal

he engine behind the original edition of this book was a Harvard law student, now a California-based lawyer, **Jay Itzkowitz**, who travelled widely in India and put together the editorial team in New Delhi. Leading the way were **Samuel Israel**, the doyen of India's book-publishing editors and former director of the National Book Trust, and **Bikram Grewal**, managing director of Dass Media. These two co-wrote the chapter about Bombay, and Grewal wrote on Madras.

The chapter about India's land and climate was the work of **Dr Kamala Seshan**, geographer and lecturer at the National Council of Educational Research and Training, New Delhi. The several chapters on the subject of Indian history were produced by **Professor Harbans Mukhia**, who teaches history at Jawaharlal Nehru University in Delhi.

Mukhia

The broad picture of the peoples of India was presented by **Radhika Chopra**, who supplemented her PhD in sociology by spending a year in a Punjabi village. Meanwhile, the complex subject of religion in India was explored by **Professor V. S. Naravané**, who divides his time between writing books in India and teaching as a visiting professor at a US university.

Naravané

Royina Grewal, a writer on travel and culture, dealt both with India's numerous festivals and its food. Music and dance were described by **Leela Samson**, herself a talented performer of Bharata Natyam. **Dr Geeti Sen**, an art historian and editor of the India International Centre Quarterly, contributed the essay on Indian art. The rich variety of India's handicrafts was covered by **Laila Tyabji**, a consultant on Indian crafts for the Metropolitan Museum of Art, New York.

Sen

In the Places section, **M. C. Joshi**, a director in the Archaeological Survey of India, covered Delhi and Uttar Pradesh. The mountain state of Himachal Pradesh was described by **Vijay Parmar**, a young assistant

hushwant Singh

director in the Centre for Cultural Resources and Training, New Delhi.

Jammu and Kashmir were covered by **Jeffrey Young Campbell**, an American born in India who works at the Ford Foundation in community forestry. **Sardar Khushwant Singh**, MP, one of India's most widely syndicated political commentators, wrote about Punjab and Haryana. For Rajasthan, the editors turned to **Francis Wacziarg**, in collaboration with copywriter **Aman Nath**. Covering eastern and northeastern India, including Calcutta and the Andamans, was a Frenchman, **Michel Vatin**.

M. M. Buch, who wrote about Madhya Pradesh, was a senior civil servant until he resigned to devote himself to ecological studies and conservation. Maharashtra is covered by **Anil Dharkar**, former editor of the magazine *Debonair*.

Dharkar

Usha Albuquerque, who contributed the section about Goa, was born of Goan parents in north India. She has lived all over the nation, but always returns to the land of her parents.

Jaya Jaitly, who wrote about Gujarat, is a consultant to the Gujarat State Handicraft Corporation. For Andhra Pradesh, the editors recruited **Dr K. V. Soundararajan**, retired director of the Archaeological Survey of India and author of a dozen learned books.

Soundararajan

M. V. Kamath, a veteran journalist, covered his home state of Karnataka, while Englishwoman **Pepita Noble** documented the increasingly popular destination of Kerala.

T his book has been through several editions. Under the supervision of London-based editor **Andrew Eames**, Delhi-based journalist **Jan McGirk** worked on this latest edition, writing new chapters about Indian wildlife and use of English, and commissioning new pieces. McGirk, who is originally from California, has been in India since 1990, and has enjoyed life as a new-age memsahib.

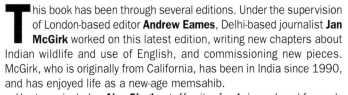

Singh

McGirk

Her team includes **Ajay Singh**, staff writer for *Asiaweek* and formerly a journalist with Associated Press in Delhi. Singh, who has lived in both Japan and the US, penned the excellent essay on India Today. **Amrita Shah**, a shrewd observer of India's media world, about which she writes in this book, has a colourful career both in the mainstream as an ex-stringer for *Time* magazine, creator of a top magazine in Bombay, and as an author of romantic fiction under the pseudonym Nikki Pasha.

Shah

Bill Aitken, a Scot who hitch-hiked to India in 1959, has worked as a cook in a Himalayan ashram and as a private secretary to a maharani. Along the way he has written four books, two about railways, about which he writes in this volume. Also at work in this new edition are **Lea Terhune** (writing about Ashrams), an American writer and long-time student of Tibetan Buddhism, who has collaborated on two books on the subject; and **Vikram Sundarji** (a new chapter on Tamil Nadu), a Tamilian Brahmin who has at times been newspaper columnist, author, screenwriter, teacher, social worker, house husband and media consultant.

Sundarji

The new and exhaustive Travel Tips section at the back of the book was compiled by **Farah Singha** and collated by **Jane Hutchings**.

New photographs come from one of Apa's star photographers, **Lyle Lawson**, the **Dinodia Press Agency** in Bombay, and from one of India's best-known names, **Ashvin Mehta**.

CONTENTS

CONTENTS

TRAVEL TIPS

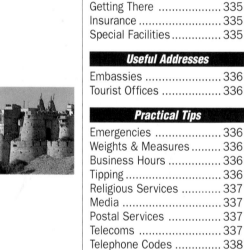

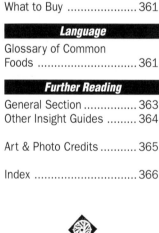

THE ALLURE OF INDIA

India has always welcomed and intrigued the traveller. In 1897, Mark Twain described it as "the land of dreams and romance, of fabulous wealth and fabulous poverty, of splendour and rags, of palaces and hovels, of famine and pestilence, of genii and giants and Aladdin lamps, of tigers and elephants, the cobra and the jungle, the country of a hundred nations and a hundred tongues, of a thousand religions and two million gods…" Today's visitors, from the moment they step off the plane, are assaulted by contradictions no less vivid and paradoxes no less puzzling than they ever were.

There is evidence, from earliest historical times, of great movements of peoples across the subcontinent, sometimes replacing existing populations, sometimes integrating with them. The Indo-Aryans themselves came in massive sweeps through the lofty passes in the northwest, bringing with them the rudiments of the Hindu faith, later to be developed on Indian soil into one of the most philosophically subtle and complex of all religions.

While it is in only recent years that Hinduism is again having a major influence outside the Indian subcontinent, Buddhism, which grew out of Hinduism, is a major world religion. But India has also received the gifts of Islam, Christianity, Zoroastrianism, and, on a very small scale but very significantly, Judaism. India has been the proverbial sponge, and not only in matters religious.

With various races and religions came a variety of ethnic types, their art, architecture, culture, languages, customs, literature, style of music and dance, administrative structures, systems of thought, science, technology and medicine. Few of these have entirely lost their identity, all have had their influence, and many have found a permanent place in India's intricate mosaic.

While it is this variety and complexity that makes India attractive for the traveller, it is also the source of many of India's difficulties, past and contemporary. It is just this heterogeneity that makes it one of the most difficult of countries to govern. And that difficulty will not diminish, as India's population threatens to exceed China's one billion well before the end of the century.

But, despite its problems, India retains its allure for visitors eager to understand rather than judge on first acquaintance. Everyone's perception is different, but the English journalist James Cameron, one of India's greatest advocates, summed up the subcontinent's appeal wonderfully well when he wrote: "I like the evening in India, the one magic moment when the sun balances on the rim of the world, and the hush descends, and ten thousand civil servants drift homeward on a river of bicycles, brooding on the Lord Krishna and the cost of living."

Preceding pages: Orissan appliqué work; Kathakali dancer; Lambadi woman. Himalayan landscape; palace (Hawa Mahal) in Jaipur; camel fair at Pushkar, Rajasthan; Gujarati folk dance. **Left**, a welcoming Rajasthani.

LAND AND CLIMATE

Beneath its distinctive bulge, India narrows like an elephant's trunk to drink from the Indian Ocean, Bay of Bengal, and Arabian Sea. Such thirst is understandable. The greatest deserts of the world – the Mexican, the Sahara, and the Arabian – lie at the same latitude. But India extends far beyond the Thar desert, and extra altitude provides rainforests, alpine meadows and glaciers.

A cool rainy season follows the monsoon trail from June to September, and when these winds retreat in October a fierce heat follows. The eastern and southeastern coasts, however, get rain and cyclonic squalls. In November, when the sun crosses south of the Equator, the winter season starts in the northern plain. Until February the weather remains cold (below 5°C/41°F) in the Himalaya and its foothills, where skiing is possible, pleasant in the plains (between 15°C/59°F and 20°C/68°F) and warm (above 20°C/68°F) in South India, except in the Nilgiri Hills and the Ghats.

India's summer, which runs from March to May, is hot and dry, with flurries of wind raising a dusty curtain over the northern plain and temperatures averaging 40°C (104°F). Tempered by the sea breezes, South India is sultry and hot but temperatures are usually bearable, between 27°C (80°F) and 29°C (84°F).

Come June, the intense heat of the northern plain causes the upper air currents to move north of the Himalaya and draw the monsoon across the entire country. Starting from the southwestern coast, it branches eastward and northward, and on reaching the Ganga delta follows the wide river valleys bounded by the Himalaya with its heavily forested foothills.

The most luxuriant rainforests, however, lie on the southwest coast, in Kerala, where the lagoons are canopied by coconut trees. The coast stretches north to the estuarine plains of Goa with its wide sunny beaches lapped by the gentle waves of the Arabian Sea. The rest of the coast is mostly rocky, rising to the low red lateritic plateaus and then steeply to the black, forest-covered slopes of the Western Ghats. Farther north, in Kathiawar, the coast becomes dry and salt-encrusted with marshy lowlands rich with flamingo.

Inland, the open country covered with cotton and sunflower fields merges into the rocky

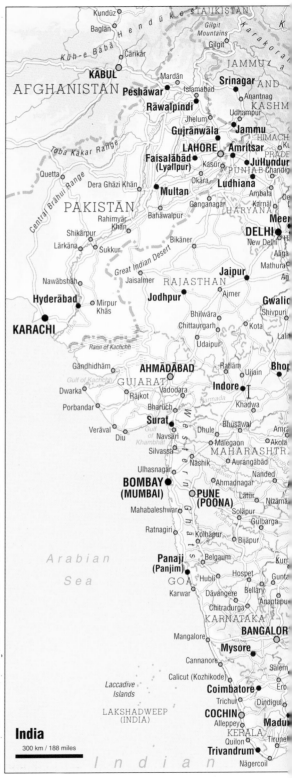

India
300 km / 188 miles

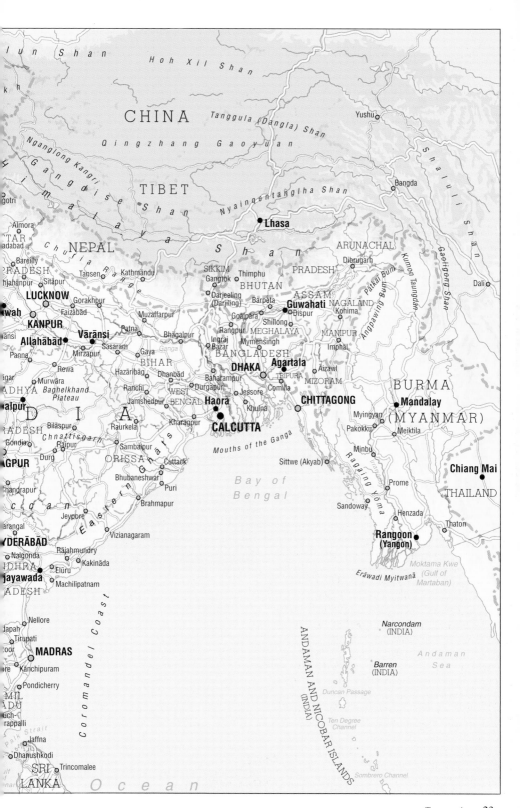

desert. From the Rann (saline marshlands) of Kutch in the west to the Luni River is the Great Desert, and farther north between Jaisalmer and Jodhpur is the Little Desert. Here is open scrub country with rocky hills often capped by the forts of the Rajput kings. Wandering herds of sheep and goats, and camels carrying cotton and marble, are seen in this area.

Separating the desert from the Gangetic plain and the Deccan lava tableland are the rugged plateaus of Malwa, Bundelkhand and Rewa. Stony, harsh and covered with only a thin layer of soil, the plateau is drained by the Chambal, Ken and Betwa Rivers. Bandits hide in the ravines made by the rivers, and fields of mustard and wheat form a patchwork of green and gold.

On the west, steeply rising from the plain to the lava plateau, is the Vindhya range. The Narmada, flowing through a narrow gorge, and the Tapi, through a broad valley, are separated by the Satpura range. South of the Tapi are the hills where Buddhist monks carved and painted in the caves at Ajanta and Ellora. At the mouth of the Tapi is the ancient port city of Surat, famous for its gold and silver brocade *(zari)*. It was here that the British East India Company set up its first "factory", as its trading centres were called.

By 15 June, the eastward moving monsoon winds reach the Chhotanagpur plateau which is drained by the Damodar. It is a wide plateau with conical and dome-shaped hills which look like gigantic bubbles.

During the three long monsoon months the brown forests of sal, bamboo and teak turn green and the tribesmen collect lac (the secretion of a forest insect) and mahua flowers. The steel city of Jamshedpur and the coal and iron-ore mines introduce a veneer of urban culture here. The plateau is flanked by the Rajmahal Hills which descend steeply to the Ganga plain where the river takes a sharp bend to the sea.

Distinct from these plateaus is the black lava-covered Deccan where streams meander among hills that seem to have had their tops neatly sliced off. It was on the "table-tops" of steep-sided hills that the Marathas built a series of impregnable fortresses.

Deccan peninsula: South Deccan is the dry heartland of the peninsula, the Telengana and Karnataka plateaus. Cut across by the Krishna, Godavari and Kaveri flowing east, the wet Karnataka plateau has dense sandal, teak and sisoo forests, where elephants roam wild. The Telengana plateau, just adjacent, has in con-trast a thin cover of red lateritic soils with rocky humps between. Thorny scrub and wild Indian date palms grow on this soil. The landscape has a scarred and wounded appearance because of the dried river channels in which tanks have been built to hold water when the rivers are briefly in flood. Here is the erstwhile princely state of Hyderabad, the pearl city, surrounded by vineyards.

Southwest of the plateau, separated from Kerala by the blue Nilgiris, with its coffee plantations and the cloud-covered Palni Hills, in the rain shadow, is the Coimbatore plateau which extends east to the coast near Madras. The Kaveri which rises here flows into the

Tamilnad plains. The Kaveri delta is the ricebowl of Tamil Nadu, its prosperity reflected in the lofty temple towers of Thanjavur.

India's stony east coast, with vast bare spaces scattered over with aloes and palm trees and swampy alluvial shores, merges northwards into the fertile deltaic lowlands of the Krishna, Godavari and Mahanadi Rivers. Wooded forests replace the open fields of surgarcane and tobacco in places reached by the summer monsoon.

Replenishing itself in its passage over the Bay of Bengal, the southwest monsoon continues westwards along the wide Ganga plain and eastward along the Brahmaputra gorge.

Eastwards, the Brahmaputra Valley cuts across the Shillong plateau, by the Garo, Khasi and Jaintia Hills, through the Assam-Burma range. The Brahmaputra swings across its wide valley which is encased in an immense rocky corridor. On the rises and levees of the river tiny hamlets are surrounded by rice fields and tea plantations. On the slopes tussar silkworms are bred on the mulberry trees, and pineapple plantations are seen.

Mangrove delta: The Brahmaputra reaches the wet Ganga delta which is dominated by the port of Calcutta. Criss-crossed by the distributaries of an ever-growing delta, the mangrove forests offer excellent opportunities for boat-

ing among their roots. Farther inland, patches of jungle have been cleared to grow barley and pulses.

Following the monsoon winds westwards comes the Middle Ganga plain in which tract the annual rainfall decreases from 55 inches (140cm) to 31 inches (80cm) near Delhi. North of this plain are the foothills of the Himalaya across which the tributaries of the Ganga flow, through steep reed-filled courses in sal forests. Here, as in the Duars of Bengal, the Terai has jungles of sisoo and tamarisk which afford excellent hideouts for tigers.

Left, lush Nilgiri Hills. **Above**, Kerala backwater.

When the now comparatively dry monsoon winds reach the upper course of the Ganga, the fields are ready for sowing. The canal-irrigated wheat plains of Punjab merge into the dry land of Haryana to the southwest. Delhi, the gateway to the Ganga plain, is located here.

Northward the foothill ridges of the Shiwaliks and the gravel vales rise through ridges and valleys to the snowcapped peaks of the Himalaya. The ascent is from some 980–1,960 ft (300–600 metres) above the plain to 15,750 ft (4,800 metres) in the middle Himalaya in which are Nanda Devi and Annapurna peaks rising up to 22,970 ft (7,000 metres).

The Tista Valley in the Eastern Himalaya lies opposite the Ganga delta at the head of which is Sikkim. Orchids and rhododendrons grow wild here and the musk deer and rhinoceros are found in these dense forests. The valleys are a patchwork of paddy fields, and on the terraced slopes are yellow maize and millet fields.

Largely deforested, but excellent for trekking and fishing, the Central Himalaya lies wholly in the state of Himachal Pradesh. The golden, snowcapped Dhola Dhar ranges of the lesser Himalaya separate the river Beas from the Ravi. At the head of the Beas is apple-land and the Kulu Valley. The most striking feature of this area is the Sutlej River which emerges suddenly from the earth, some 19 miles (30km) from the Mansarowar Lake in Tibet, and descends across the mighty Himalaya.

The chir and deodar jungles of the upper slopes enclose broad sloping river terraces covered with fields of potato and rice enclosed by thick hedges. From the Kulu Valley, traditional routes of the Bhotiya shepherds enter the upland pastures of Ladakh.

From the lofty glacier-garlanded heights of Badrinath, the Alakananda and Baghirathi, tributaries of the Ganga, flow across the Kumaon Himalaya.

The lowest valleys of the Himalayan foothills, the Terai, are hot and sultry in summer and get heavy rainfall in July. The nomadic ways of the Bhotiyas are replaced by a settled pastoral economy on the forest edge, and farming is done in the valleys.

The lofty Himalaya of the north, dipping to the vast Ganga-Yamuna plain which is hemmed in by the rocky massif of the plateau in the south, suggest powerful and conflicting forces beneath the earth which have moulded the features of this unique subcontinent. In this setting are India's fields and villages.

The strikingly complex society that today comprises India, Pakistan and Bangladesh, but was until 1947 a single unit, India, evokes the vision of a very long process of evolution. Many facets of human existence contributed to this process: ecology, human skills and labour, social divisions and the ensuing frictions, and not least culture and religion.

Basic factors: A cardinal feature of the Indian ecology, which exercised a considerable influence on the historical development of the subcontinent, was the very high fertility of its land. The topsoil in the river basins was renewed annually with the inundations caused by the summer monsoons which deposited enormous quantities of fertile silt from the mountains. The Indus and Ganga alone are estimated to bring down a million tons of suspended matter daily. Cultivation came to be densely concentrated in the valleys of these great rivers, and most Indian soils yielded an average of two crops a year.

The tropical climate allowed the peasant in most Indian regions to make do with a mud house and clothe himself with a brief piece of coarse cotton cloth wrapped around the loins. Peasant women would similarly attire themselves with a somewhat longer unstitched wraparound. The contrast between the high agricultural yield and the dismal level of consumption by the bulk of the population made large surpluses available, quite early in Indian history, maintaining a substantial number of towns at an impressive level of civilisation.

The beginnings: The earliest known civilisation in India, the starting point of Indian history, was a highly developed one, dating back to about 2500 BC. Discovered in the 1920s, it was initially thought to have been confined to the valley of the Indus, hence its early identification as the Indus Valley Civilisation. Of its towns, two earned great renown, for they represented the high-water mark of that civilisation. These were Mohenjodaro and Harappa, both now in Pakistan.

Later archaeological excavations, however, established the contours of this civilisation to an area in northwestern and western India, far beyond the valley of the Indus; hence "Harappa culture" is the more recent label put on these discoveries. Among the Indian sites are the ones at Ropar in Punjab, and Lothal and Kalibangan in Gujarat and Rajasthan.

The towns at Mohenjodaro and Harappa were well planned, with streets criss-crossing one another at right angles, a system of sewage and a fairly clear division of localities and types of houses earmarked for the upper and the lower strata of society. There were also public buildings, the most famous being the Great Bath at Mohenjodaro, meant perhaps for ritual bathing, and the granaries.

Production of metals such as copper, bronze, lead and tin was undertaken and some remnants of furnaces have survived to bear evidence. There were two kilns to make the burnt bricks, used extensively in domestic as well as public buildings. The Harappa culture had developed its own pictographic script; unfortunately, the script still hasn't been definitively deciphered.

Among the discoveries at Harappa sites are a couple of thousand seals in various quadrangular shapes and sizes, each with a human or an animal figure carved on it. It is likely that these seals served as the trademarks of merchants, for Harappa culture had extensive trade relations with the neighbouring regions within India and with distant lands in the Persian Gulf and Sumer (in Iraq).

That the Harappa society was divided between rich and poor, traders, artisans and peasants is clear from the evidence pointing to different professions as well as from the standardised sizes of residential buildings characteristic of different localities. That such an advanced social and economic organisation should have had an organised government can be safely assumed, even if we know little about its form or actual working.

We know, however, that the Harappans worshipped gods and goddesses represented in male and female forms; they might also have held some individual trees sacred. They had perhaps evolved some ritual ceremonies. But we know little else for certain about their religious life.

By about 1700 BC the Harappa culture was

Preceding pages: mural depicting a royal hunt, Jodhpur. Left, the Lion Capital of an Ashokan pillar, the emblem of the Indian Government.

on the decline, partly due to repeated flooding of towns located on river banks and partly because of ecological changes which forced agriculture to yield to the spreading desert. When the initial migrations of the Aryan people into India, probably from northeastern Iran and the region around the Caspian Sea, began in the period around 1500 BC, the developed Harappa culture had already been practically wiped out.

Deriving its name from the four *Vedas*, the earliest Hindu scriptures comprising hymns in chaste Sanskrit, the Vedic Age was spread over several centuries; it was consequently not of one piece.

The Aryan immigrants were a pastoral

were barley, sesamum, cucumber, bittergourd and sugarcane.

The Harappa culture too had used the plough and was known to have grown rice, wheat and cotton besides sesamum and peas, but the early Vedic literature makes no reference to the first three of these crops. Cattle were highly valued, and beef-eating was reserved for very honoured guests.

The Aryans were organised into tribes which had settled down in separate regions in northwestern India. Tribal chiefship gradually became hereditary, though the chief operated with advice from either a committee or the entire tribe and, in time, the giving or taking of advice was institutionalised. With work

people who gradually familiarised themselves with agriculture. Cattle-breeding and agriculture perfectly complemented each other. The notion of individual landholdings and perhaps individual cultivation was slow to grow; indeed, in early Vedic literature, cattle and enslaved women are the only movable forms of property mentioned.

The local inhabitants whom the Aryans had defeated and enslaved might have been employed in the fields. The plough drawn by oxen was the primary agricultural implement; the Indian bull had mercifully been provided with a hump by nature, making the yoking of the plough so much easier. The crops cultivated

specialisation, the internal division of Aryan society developed along caste lines. The early division was between the fair-skinned Aryans and the dark-skinned slaves; hence caste was formerly known as the *varna* (colour) division. The Aryans themselves came to be grouped into the Brahmana (priests), Kshatriya (warriors), Vaishya (agriculturalists) and Shudra (menial workers)

It was, at the outset, a division of occupations; as such it was open and flexible. Much later, caste-status and occupation came to depend on birth, and change from one to another became far more difficult.

The Aryans were rather fond of intoxicating

drinks, gambling and horse-chariot racing. They worshipped many gods, most of them nature's elements such as the sun, the wind, water and fire.

Culture and leisure: The prosperity generated by agriculture and cattle breeding and the employment of enslaved labour gave the Aryans adequate leisure to meditate and seek answers to fundamental questions about the origin of the universe. Their language, Sanskrit, spoken with a musical intonation, was conducive to speculative thinking.

The relationship of one's life with the universe too was a subject of speculation and the notion of a cycle of lives in various forms through which the soul had to pass was hinted

Even though the Aryans had developed a sophisticated language, they were slow to evolve a script. Imparting of knowledge was therefore done orally and through repetitive memorising.

Iron and development: Around 1000 BC iron was discovered in India, a discovery that was to lead to several changes in society. Since iron axes made clearing of forests much easier, a considerable extent of forest land gave way to the plough; agricultural expansion was also facilitated by an iron ploughshare, sickle and hoe. One could perhaps assume that extension of the cultivated area led to growth of population, a greater degree of specialisation of functions and more trade; it certainly led to a second

at, if not yet fully developed. This was later to grow into the doctrine of *Karma* (one's deeds), according to which, one's next status in, or even form of, life depended on one's deeds in the present life. This doctrine served as a major deterrent to protest against oppression, for a person's current misery would be easily attributed to his or her past misdeeds, for which the person must undergo appropriate punishment in order to ensure a better life next time.

Left, a prehistoric cave painting from Central India. **Above**, Lothal, Gujarat, where a proto-historic city (2000 BC) has been excavated.

urbanisation. With land gaining prominence as a form of individual property and with the demand for it growing faster than could be met through primitive techniques of forest clearing, society came to be divided into the rich and the poor.

Poverty and misery in contrast with gross luxuries in the 6th century BC led two sensitive persons, Mahavira and Buddha, both of them *Kshatriyas*, to seek answers to the question: Why is there so much suffering in life? In the end both Mahavira and Buddha came upon simple truths as answers: a moderate, balanced life based upon non violence, abstinence, truthfulness and meditation would free one of greed and therefore of suffering. These teachings won immediate popular acceptance owing to their simplicity and practicality; the sermons of both were preached in commonly spoken languages. Both sects, Jainism and Buddhism, were essentially atheistic and therefore a challenge to Brahmanical orthodoxy.

With land becoming property and society being divided, conflicts and disorders were bound to arise. Organised power to resolve those conflicts and suppress disorders therefore emerged, giving rise to full-fledged state systems, including vast empires. The vastest and also the best known of these was the Magadha Empire, with its capital near modern-day Patna in Bihar, ruled by the Maurya

ian. Huge state-owned and private farms were cultivated by various forms of labour. While the state mobilised slaves, labourers and prisoners to work its lands, private fields were tilled by bonded or wage labourers and perhaps sharecroppers. The mighty Mauryan state also had amongst its sources of income gambling houses and brothels; but the chief source was taxes collected on land, trade and manufacture of handicrafts.

Pre-Mauryan and Mauryan India had become familiar with the Hellenistic civilisation. The Greeks came in contact with India in the 6th and 5th centuries BC, through their conflict with the Persian Empire, which bordered northwestern India.

dynasty. Emperor Ashoka was its most famous ruler; he ruled from 269 BC to 232 BC.

Ashoka inherited from his father an empire that covered practically the entire subcontinent, save Kalinga, modern-day Orissa. This Ashoka conquered; but the sight of the battlefield, with thousands of dead and wounded bodies strewn all over it, shook the emperor. He too asked the question: What is the end result of worldly ambition? And the answer that satisfied him was the one that the Buddha had given. From then onwards he turned to the Buddhist way of life, and his son and daughter became missionaries.

The Mauryan economy was essentially agrar-

In 327 BC Alexander of Macedon crossed into northwest India. When his armies seemed to have lost heart on the banks of the fifth river of Punjab and forced their chief to turn homewards, Alexander left behind Greek governors to rule over the territories conquered by him. Over time, these territories lost out to Indian states through conflict as well as through slow absorption.

But there was another sphere where contact between the two cultures left a far more lasting impact: art. Sculpture, especially of this region, bears a marked Greek influence.

The Mauryan empire did not long survive Ashoka. Its disintegration was an open invitation to invaders, mainly from Central Asia, to seek their fortunes in India. Among them were the Bactrian Greeks, survivors of Alexander's men who had settled in Iran and Afghanistan, the Parthians, the Shakas and the Kushanas. They established kingdoms in the northwestern and northern regions that lasted for varying lengths of time. Over the decades they were submerged in the mainstream of Indian life, just as happened with several earlier and later groups of invaders.

South India at this time was divided into several states, all of them continually at war among themselves. But a more durable aspect of South Indian society was then evolving: its culture, particularly a collective literature, was

establishment of trade relations between the Chola kingdom of the Tamil Nadu region and the distant Roman empire as well as with the Southeast-Asian regions of Java, Sumatra and Bali. The Romans imported spices, textiles, precious stones and birds like the peacock from India and paid for them in gold. It was in Malabar, in present-day Kerala, that India first came into contact with Christianity and later on, Islam.

The Gupta Age: The second great empire in Indian history emerged in the 4th century AD. It too covered a large part of the subcontinent, though not as large as the Mauryan empire; its administration was not as highly centralised. This was the Gupta Empire which lasted over

emerging in the form of poems composed in assemblies of wandering minstrels and bards. Three such assemblies were held at Madurai, then capital of Tamil Nadu (the country of the Tamils). At the third of these assemblies, over 2,000 poems were collectively composed: these are known as the Sangam literature, an invaluable source of information about early Tamil society, culture and polity.

The control over the eastern and western coasts of the subcontinent also facilitated the

Left, found at Mohenjodaro: representations of the Mother Goddess (far end) and a dancer. **Above**, series of enlightened beings at Gwalior.

two centuries. As this empire alternately waged war and entered into matrimonial alliances with the smaller kingdoms in its neighbourhood, its boundaries kept fluctuating with each succeeding ruler.

In the Gupta Age, orthodox Hinduism reasserted itself against the heretical sects that had sprung up. This was facilitated by the patronage the rulers extended to the Hindu religious tradition. However, there is little evidence of the use of violence to re-establish the supremacy of Hinduism; indeed, we have the evidence of the Chinese traveller, Fa Hsien, who came to India in the beginning of the 5th century, that the Buddhists and the Brahmins lived in peaceful coexistence. The Buddhist monastery at Ajanta, cut into the hillocks and decorated with breathtaking murals, was a creation of this period. The caste system, however, became far more rigid, and a group of people, the untouchables, below the rank of even the lowest caste, came to be treated at subhuman levels; even the sight of them was sufficient to pollute the upper castes.

Yet this age registered considerable progress in literature and science, particularly in the areas of astronomy and mathematics. The most outstanding literary figure of the Gupta period was the writer Kalidasa whose choice of words and imagery brought Sanskrit drama to new heights.

Aryabhatta, the astronomer, had argued that it was the earth that moved round the sun but he was completely ignored, though fortunately not persecuted. An iron pillar erected at Delhi during the reign of one Gupta ruler still stands there in the open, upright and without a trace of rust, evidence of advanced knowledge of metallurgy.

Post-Gupta India witnessed many significant changes. Indian economy had always been agrarian, though supplemented by trade and handicraft production. But with the end of the Gupta Age, both external and internal trade declined dramatically and this led to a greater ruralisation of the economy. The amount of money in circulation also contracted; this led to a localisation of economic and administrative units. Land became the primary, almost the exclusive source of state as well as private income.

Nevertheless, in many ways the centuries following the decline of the Gupta Empire witnessed a great deal of economic progress, especially in agricultural production.

New crops and new society: The high fertility of Indian soils has already been mentioned. For the realisation of this fertility water was the prime need. The early medieval centuries, the 8th to the 12th of the Christian era, witnessed impressive progress in irrigation. In northwestern and northern India various kinds of wheels were developed to draw water from ponds or wells. These were initially manually operated; later on, from about the 13th century, a geared wheel was drawn by a pair of oxen – this was the Persian wheel, which still caters to the irrigation needs of some of the region today, although electrical and diesel operated pumps are fast replacing it.

In South India, water tanks provided the chief source of irrigation. Small tanks were constructed by the individual farmer, the bigger ones by the village as a whole, or by the state. Canals and water channels also marked the rural landscape.

In this way, new lands were brought under cultivation and new crops began to be experimented with.

But this economic advance was creating a society far more complex than the earlier one, for it was creating greater social and economic disparities. While the Persian wheel could ensure water supply and thereby agricultural improvement, its installation was a costly affair. Only the upper stratum of peasants could make the investment and reap the benefit. The same applies to other agricultural implements and superior cash crops. Thus, the agricultural advance benefited farmers with different levels of resources differentially.

As noted earlier, one of the developments of this period was the development of a greater degree of rigidity in the caste system. One's caste status and profession came to be determined by one's birth, and it was not easy, though not impossible, to overcome it. It is possible that the demand for labour for agricultural production bore some relationship to this development. As the scope of agriculture widened, labour became scarce.

The operation of caste laws therefore excluded some of the lower castes from holding land of their own; it was their labour that came to be used by the entire community of cultivators, irrespective of its own stratification. This also introduced a paradox; a class of landless agricultural labourers was created in the context of an abundance of land. This was a peculiarly Indian solution to the problem of labour scarcity; medieval Europe had solved the same problem through the system of serfdom.

Greater agricultural production also meant greater resources for the rulers, who began to appropriate a large part of the produce, at times as much as a half of it, in the form of land revenue. This in turn necessitated a greater centralised control over the system of revenue collection. On a small scale, such developments had already taken place in the regional kingdoms of the 11th and 12th centuries all over the subcontinent.

Right, **Yakshi (tree spirit) sculpture from Barhut, Madhya Pradesh, 2nd century BC.**

At the outset of the 13th century, a new wave of invaders, again from Central Asia, made its way to north India. This time they had come to stay. They professed a different religion, Islam. A new state was established in 1206 which came to be known as the Delhi Sultanate. By the first quarter of the 13th century it had brought under its direct or indirect control the greater part of the subcontinent, although the territorial boundaries of the Sultanate kept fluctuating. During the 320 years of its existence, the throne of the Delhi Sultanate changed hands among six dynasties.

The process of centralisation of administrative control over revenue collection reached its climax under the sultans of Delhi. Land revenue was legally fixed at half the produce; soldiers and officers were assigned territories to collect revenue that equalled their annual salary. Other high officials were given charge of large territories from which they were to collect the revenue, maintain an army and, of course, themselves, and look after law and order. About 6 percent of the state revenue was given away in charity to religious institutions and pious individuals.

While this picture might suggest a considerable resemblance to feudal Europe, it is important to keep in mind some crucial differences. The assignees had no right over the land, which belonged to the peasants; they had the right merely to collect the revenue due to the state. Secondly, the officials (or assignees) were actually transferred from one territory to another every three or four years. This was to preempt their sinking local roots and gaining personal control over the administrative apparatus.

It is thus that the growth of a permanent landed aristocracy, with its power based on control over land, was cleverly prevented right down to the 19th century. It is only under the aegis of colonial rule that such a class took root in India.

The revenue system: Although a large majority of the administrative officials of the Sultanate were Muslims, the bulk of the revenue collection machinery was still run by Hindus. Often the tensions generated by conflicts of interests between the two sections were portrayed as being religious in nature. Inevitably, the establishment of the new state created manifold tensions, at times inter-regional, at times religious, and at times sectarian.

The increased produce from the land was beginning to find its way into an expanding network of markets. This process was accelerated when the Sultanate began to show its preference for the collection of revenue in cash. With a large number of officials, who were fairly mobile, and who were attuned to urban rather than rural life, cash collections certainly made more sense than collecting foodgrains and carting them around. Once liquid cash

came into their hands, they could spend it at the centres of their residence, which were also their administrative centres, in urban or semi-urban locales. This necessarily gave a spurt to the growth of urban centres, as well as to markets.

The Sultanate also introduced several new crafts and promoted or changed old ones. The spinning wheel, though of uncertain origin, is first encountered in India in the 14th century; its productivity compared to that of the distaff was five to six times higher. This led to a greater production of coarse cotton textiles, worn by the poor. Paper also came to India at this time, as did gunpowder, both perhaps from China. In the building industry, new styles were introduced; the Qutb Minar has no predecessor in India, though minarets were common in Central Asia; similarly, the perfect round dome sitting on top of a square or rectangular base, which marks all monuments of this and the subsequent Mughal period, surely required new construction techniques. The building industry also witnessed the introduction of the true (arcuate) arch.

However, in some regions, in periods when they had not yet been subjugated to the authority of the Delhi Sultanate, altogether different styles of architecture were creating some of the most exquisite pieces, especially in temple architecture. The temples at Konarak in Orissa and Khajuraho in Madhya Pradesh are expres-

sions of architectural grandeur and sculptural finesse that is hard to excel. Magnificent temples and sculptures were also created in South India – at Madurai, Rameshwaram and Thanjavur.

The break-up of the Delhi Sultanate began in the second quarter of the 14th century, during the reign of Mohammad bin Tughlaq. Tughlaq was an intellectual *par excellence*, enamoured of the force of reason, possessing a powerful imagination, impatient with those who failed to

Left, Mughal Emperor Jahangir at Fatehpur Sikri, the town built by his father Akbar. **Above**, Sher Singh, a Sikh chieftain.

keep pace with his ideas, and completely out of touch with the realities of life. His reign of 26 years was marked by 15 rebellions of his nobles. Among the parts of the Sultanate that broke away were two southern regions, each harbouring an independent dynasty, one Hindu, the other Muslim. Both these, the Vijayanagar Empire and the Bahmani Kingdom waged constant war with each other; both have left behind some of the most magnificent architectural monuments, though in ruins.

The much-contracted empire of the Sultans of Delhi lingered on as several of its regions went on detaching themselves and establishing independent kingdoms; the remainder of the "empire", much weakened, provided an irresistible temptation to any Central Asian adventurer with a strong army to reach out here for plunder. The most devastating of these plundering raids was led by Timur in 1398; among the prized loot that Timur carried home were numerous Indian artisans.

The Mughal Empire: A descendant of Timur as well as Changez Khan, an Uzbek prince who had failed to protect his kingdom against his cousins' intrigues and battles, was to follow the old invaders route of northwestern mountain passes into India in 1526. This was Zahiruddin Mohammad Babur, founder of the Mughal Empire in India. It was during the reign of his grandson Akbar, who ruled over practically the whole of north India and parts of the south from 1556 to 1605, that the basic institutions and policies of the empire were framed.

Ascending the throne at the age of 13, Akbar began to take interest in the affairs of state only after spending another four years in adolescent playfulness. However, at the age of 17 he took full charge of the situation and never looked back. Akbar realised that if the empire was to attain stability, it must grow local roots and seek support from the local ruling groups. He thus began altering the predominantly alien character of the nobility by recruiting groups of indigenous rulers from various regions.

The most powerful amongst these were the Rajputs of Rajasthan. He took the daughters of several Rajput houses as his wives, gave respect to their customs, bestowed upon them some of the highest imperial offices, but dealt ruthlessly with those who refused to surrender. Gradually he reduced every group in the higher nobility to a small minority, including his own Mughal brethren. Each group had to tolerate the others.

The administrative institutions of the Delhi

Sultanate were modified and a new bureaucratic framework was evolved. Under this, every official of state was placed on the army rolls, irrespective of his duties, and every official, from the lowest to the highest, was recruited and paid by the imperial department of the army. This greatly tightened central control. The system of transfer of officials was rigorously implemented. Payment of salaries was first made in cash; gradually, however, the old system of revenue assignment came back into vogue. But then a person might be posted in Gujarat and yet his revenue assignment might be located in Bengal. This necessitated revenue collection in cash.

Land was classified into four categories according to productivity and a graduated land tax was imposed on peasants, going by the period for which their land had remained fallow. The ideal was, of course, two regular crops each year from every field. Revenue was fixed on the basis of the previous 10 years and was converted into cash according to prices prevailing in the neighbouring market over the past decade; this revenue demand was valid until later revision which would take into account any rise in productivity or prices. Peasants were accordingly given documents stating their liabilities.

Akbar the Great: Himself illiterate, Akbar took great interest in intellectual discussions on matters of religion and metaphysics; he called assemblies of theologians professing various religions, including Christians, and engaged in an exchange of ideas with them, refusing to accept the absolute primacy of Islam. He also patronised the writing of history and a monumental historical work was compiled during his reign: the *Akbar Nama* (the "Book of Akbar").

In his numerous and massive buildings at Fatehpur Sikri and Agra, where he had established his capital, there is an exquisite assimilation of Islamic and Hindu architectural styles.

The structure of the Mughal Empire was strong enough to sustain utter mediocrities as rulers and an almost unbroken tradition of princes revolting against their fathers and fighting it out among themselves. Akbar's son and grandson, Jahangir and Shah Jahan, had little of the grandeur of their ancestors. There were, however, diverse cultural activities during their regimes.

Predilection towards cultural sophistication was a characteristic of the Mughal Empire. Both its founder and his last descendant were eminent poets; several of the emperors and princes were deeply concerned with problems of metaphysics, some others were writers of superb memoirs. Jahangir, besides leaving behind one such book, was a connoisseur and patron of the art of painting; Shah Jahan's fame rests on the creation of the Taj Mahal in memory of his queen who had died giving birth to his 14th child.

The austere emperor: There were, too, prosaic puritans in the line of Babur's descendants. Aurangzeb, the third of Shah Jahan's four surviving sons, was one such. Cold to freezing point, ambitious like other princes, and zealous on behalf of pristine Islamic purity, Aurangzeb fought a bloody war of succession with his brothers while their father was still alive. He killed his brothers one by one without mercy, and kept his father in prison for seven years in an octagonal room in the Agra Fort where he died watching the reflection of the distant Taj Mahal in a small piece of glass.

Keen on establishing an "Islamic" state in India, much in opposition to the Mughal tradition, Aurangzeb had no time for the finer things of life. In a desperate bid to make an appeal to the emperor's heart about their plight, some musicians of the capital (now Delhi) took out a funeral procession of music with loud wails that could not miss imperial ears. Aurangzeb looked out of the window of his palace and inquired about the goings-on. "Your Majesty," replied the mourners, "we are musicians, going out to bury our music for lack of appreciation." "Bury it so deep," said Aurangzeb, "that it never surfaces again."

The only time Aurangzeb betrayed some emotion was on his death-bed when he confessed to his failure in doing almost everything he had set out to do, particularly in ameliorating the conditions of life of the grossly exploited peasants. He died in 1707 after a reign of 50 years.

Europe comes to India: During the 17th century, India had also been host to a very large number of West European travellers; among them were Italians, Englishmen, Frenchmen and Dutchmen. Some had come to India for reasons of commerce, others in pursuit of knowledge, and still others bitten by the travel bug. Some, like the French doctor François Bernier, rose high in the confidence of princes; others went around on their own, noting down impressions to be published later.

Beside individual travellers, organised European intervention in India's commerce took place during the 17th century as several countries floated East India Companies: England, France, the Netherlands and Denmark. Chartered as trading companies by their respective governments, they sought chiefly Indian textiles, both silk and cotton, indigo and, at times, sundry other things. The spices of Malabar (in Kerala) had attracted the Portuguese as early as the end of the 15th century when, in 1498, Vasco da Gama had landed at Calicut, sailing via the Cape of Good Hope. Early in the 16th century, the Portuguese had already established their colony in Goa; but their territorial and commercial hold in India remained rather limited. During the late 16th and the 17th century

transported and sold on a scale to balance the purchase of textiles and indigo, and clocks did not make for a great success because the measurement of time was done altogether differently. They therefore had to make their purchases by paying mostly in gold and silver.

Valuable as the European trade was, it still formed a very small fraction even of commerce, leaving aside agriculture. Trade carried on by Indian merchants was far higher in value. One great Indian merchant of the 17th century in Surat, Abdul Ghaffoor, had greater assets at his disposal than the Indian assets of all the East India Companies together. There were many other merchants scattered in Surat and elsewhere in the country, not as great as Ghaffoor,

they remained unrivalled as pirates on the high seas; but inland the other European companies were making their presence felt, though entirely in commercial terms.

The companies were trading in a sellers market, competing with one another to purchase finished Indian goods. They had brought with them woollen cloths and garments, but these commanded a rather limited market, given India's temperate climate. At any rate, woollens were produced in India too. They also brought knives and clocks, but knives could hardly be

Above, Shah Jahan's Mughal masterpiece, the Taj Mahal in Agra.

but nonetheless important. Indeed the companies had often to depend upon individual merchants for loans to pay for their transactions.

India in the 17th century thus presented a picture of prosperity and dynamism. The fertile lands of the river valleys had not been fully brought under cultivation. The economy was essentially agrarian; yet trade and money had penetrated to almost every village. The currency was trimetallic, with gold, silver and bronze being molded into coins in a large number of imperial mints. Besides, anyone who had gold or silver in his possession could walk into a mint and have his metals coined for a nominal commission. There was considerable standardisation of coins in the empire, though, in the regions, both inside and outside the empire, local currencies continued to remain in circulation. All these monetary transactions had given rise to a highly skilled professional class of money-changers and moneylenders. Insurance and bills of exchange had also reached a high degree of sophistication.

If Indian economy was predominantly agrarian, there was yet a strong urban streak in it. One writer at the end of the 16th century enumerated 3,200 cities and towns in the Mughal empire. There were also plenty of them outside the empire, especially in the south; and about 15 percent of the population dwelled in urban centres, a percentage that was a shade higher than in contemporary Europe. It was commonly observed by 17th-century travellers that several Indian cities compared favourably with London or Paris in terms of physical dimensions and the size of the population.

The degree of centralisation of control over the administration of the vast empire was unparalleled in the contemporary world; this was combined with a high degree of centralised control over the empire's resources. It has been estimated that only 73 individuals (0.9 percent of the nobles) had under their command 37.6 percent of the revenues of the empire in mid-17th century and they did not include the emperor himself. The magnitude of such control can explain the grandeur which has almost become synonymous with the word "Mughal". But then the collapse of such authority usually occurs in comparable enormity; as it certainly did in this case.

Religion and literature: If impressive progress in the sphere of music, painting and, above all, architecture occurred under the aegis of the emperor or his nobles or under their indirect patronage, literature developed outside the imperial precincts. Sanskrit and Tamil were classical languages with highly sophisticated poetry antedating all empires by several centuries; but many regional languages, such as Hindi, Urdu, Gujarati, Marathi, Bengali etc., had begun to take shape from around the 15th century. By the 17th century, each had acquired a distinct identity with its own developed literature. The languages spoken today in most parts of India evolved and grew to maturity in this medieval period.

By the 17th century India had also learnt to live with a number of religious communities. Hindus still constituted the preponderant part of the population. Amongst Muslims the Sunnis predominated, though the Shias too had pockets of large population and two small but very powerful states in the northern part of South India. In Kerala, Indian Christians were a familiar sight. Among the older sects, the Jains continued to dominate trade in western India. Buddhism had, however, practically ceased to exist in any significant magnitude.

The medieval period, especially from the late 15th to the 17th century also witnessed the evolution of a new sect in Punjab, then stretching across the current border between India and Pakistan: the Sikhs. This sect, commanding the support of hardy peasants, cultivating the most fertile of Indian plains, denounced the caste system and emphasised social equality and devotion to God and the word of their Guru (teacher). Founded by a gentle and compassionate Guru, Nanak by name, the sect came into violent clash with the Mughals who executed two of its 10 Gurus. In self-defence, it transformed itself into a truly militant religion. Hospitable and generous to a fault, the Sikhs have adhered to a tradition of militancy whenever their religious institutions or symbols have been tampered with.

Even as clashes occurred between the Mughal state and various groups that were to form regional kingdoms in the 17th and 18th centuries – and these groups comprised Hindus in Maharashtra, Sikhs in Punjab and Muslims in several other regions – medieval Indian society was almost completely devoid of tensions between the many religious communities. Indeed, through the five-and-a-half centuries when most regions in India were under the rule of Muslim dynasties, there was just one single incident of communal rioting where Hindus and Muslims clashed over the slaughter of a cow, held sacred by the Hindus since the later Vedic period.

This was equally true of territories under the rule of Hindu dynasties but with substantial populations of other religious denominations. If we compare this single incident with the 400-odd incidents of communal clashes involving common members of different religious groups that have become an annual feature of Indian life today, we should be able to appreciate the absence of communal tensions at the social level in medieval India. The numerous European travellers in the 17th century were able to appreciate the harmonious relationship in which various religious communities lived in India.

This struck them as remarkable in the context of the history of massive clashes between the various sects of Christians in Europe.

An empire crumbles: The 18th century was to witness a sea change in the overall scene in India. After 1707, the mighty Mughal Empire began to crumble and give way to smaller regional kingdoms. Such of the empire as survived was riven with more friction and intrigue than could be matched by the flight of a playwright's wildest imagination. The ever-expanding class of officials was beginning to find the resources at its disposal utterly unequal to the demand; this led to intense struggles amongst officials at every level to grab whatever they could and strive to hold on to whatever others were seeking to wrest from them. The consequent loss of control over the delicate system of checks and balances within the administrative set-up gave free rein to officials to fleece the peasants; the peasants in turn resisted this by taking to arms. Individual and factional ambitions further intensified the prevailing conflict and chaos; it became a no-holds-barred situation for everyone.

The regional states which inherited the Mughal Empire were not of uniform character. Some of them had been established by eminent Mughal nobles who had broken away from the empire: among these were Bengal, Awadh and the newly founded state of Hyderabad; others had come into existence following popular rebellions against the imperial authority – these included the Maratha kingdom in Maharashtra and the state of an Afghan tribe called Rohillas who had settled in Uttar Pradesh. Inevitably, the Mughal model continued to exercise overwhelming influence on the evolution of regional polities in these states, although some of them stuck to the model more closely than others. However, the fact that the regions to be administered were much smaller units than the empire introduced a degree of efficiency and cohesion.

Of the states that had been erected on the debris of the Mughal Empire, Hyderabad maintained its existence down to 1952; the others went through several metamorphoses before freedom came to India.

The Maratha Empire: The power that came closest to imperial pretensions was that of the Marathas. Starting from scratch, the non-Brahmin castes in the Maharashtra region had been organised into a fighting force by their legendary leader, Shivaji. Diminutive in height, clever beyond his enemy's imagination, Shivaji led every day of his life like a drama in which he was always a step ahead of his adversaries. In the 18th century the Marathas moved like light-

Above, an Indian artist's impression of local government at the beginning of British rule.

ning and suddenly appeared in areas where least expected, at times hundreds of miles away from their home. They always went back with their hands full of plunder, looting both Muslims and their Hindu co-religionists. Gradually, states began to pay them vast amounts in "protection money", insurance against their plundering raids.

By the third quarter of the 18th century, the Marathas had under their direct administration or indirect subjection enough Indian territory to justify the use of the term "the Maratha Empire," though it never came near the dimensions of the Mughal Empire. The Marathas also never sought to formally substitute themselves for the Mughals; they often kept the emperor

under their thumb but still paid him formal obeisance.

The disintegration of the Mughal Empire was also an invitation to foreign invasions – a scenario so common in Indian history. Nadir Shah, an Iranian ruler, led an attack in 1739, massacred several hundred thousand inhabitants of Delhi, his whole army plundering the capital at will; in the loot he carried home were the Koh-i-Noor diamond and the Peacock Throne. This throne had been crafted in the shape of a peacock, studded with gems and diamonds, for Shah Jahan. It continued to be Iran's imperial throne until the establishment of the Islamic Republic there.

The second invasion in the 18th century, under the command of the ruler of Afghanistan, led to more permanent consequences. In 1761, the Afghan armies met the Marathas in battle near Delhi; the decisive defeat of the Marathas put an end to their imperial ambitions for all time and eliminated any chance of an indigenous power filling the vacuum created by the decline of the Mughal Empire. The road was now wide open for the British to move in and colonise India. Several Maratha houses continued to rule over small or large territories after 1761; but none of them had the capacity to rise to imperial stature.

Some of the intrigues that had characterised the imperial polity at Delhi had also found imitators in the successor states in the 18th century. In pursuit of factional or personal ambitions, overtures were at times made to the Europeans present there.

The European companies had organised their trade around the "factories" (their overseas agents were called factors) they had established in several towns; these "factories" were in reality mere warehouses for the commodities they had purchased. As the power of the Mughal Empire to protect them declined, they began to fend for themselves, recruiting their own miniature armies and using European weapons which were often superior to the Indian weapons. This provided an irresistible temptation to the groups engaged in ousting each other from positions of power in the states. The Europeans too were eager to sell their services to the highest bidder. Bit by bit they acquired a foothold in the political and administrative set-up in several of these states. Inevitably, different European groups often stood in opposite Indian camps; their own rivalries, operating through their Indian patrons, contributed greatly to the prevailing friction.

Of the European East India Companies which had come to trade in India, the Dutch had shifted their focus to Indonesia for spices in the 18th century; the Portuguese held on to Goa and two other small territories, but were no contenders for imperial status; the Danes were never a significant factor anyway. The real contest was therefore between the English and the French. The English ultimately outwitted the French to become masters of India for nearly two centuries.

Left, 18th-century depiction of the monsoon. **Right**, the Observatory at Jaipur.

It was in Bengal that the English made the first successful bid for rule in India. In 1757 and again in 1765 they defeated the Bengal ruler and, during the intervening years, engaged in the most unscrupulous intrigues at the court. The battle of 1765 was followed by an atrocious division of authority: while the local ruler was responsible for the administration, the British took charge of the revenues. The chaos that resulted is not difficult to imagine; the battle led, in the words of a Bengali poet, to "a night of eternal gloom for India".

landed aristocracy akin to the feudal aristocracy of Europe.

In Mughal India, while officials and other intermediate groups were entitled to a part or whole of the revenue due to the state, the land belonged to the peasants. The British devised "Permanent Settlement", which altered this situation and created a class that held its vast lands permanently so long as it paid revenues to the state. The peasants were placed entirely at the mercy of this class. Grateful that they had been granted unfettered rights, members of this class

The English East India Company continued its commercial activities, of course; but it no longer needed to import gold and silver into Bengal to purchase textiles for export to Britain and thence to Europe; it could make the purchases with the fabulous Bengal revenues. There was, besides, private trade carried on by private British citizens as well as the Company's servants. Nor was there any lack of financial corruption on the part of British officials, including governors.

Towards the end of the 18th century, the East India Company started planning for a long stay. For this purpose it required a degree of local support. This was obtained by creating a class of

were to remain loyal to the British cause for a long time to come. The increasing demand for revenue by the British was passed on to the peasants.

In the first half of the 19th century the British extended their hold. A large part of the subcontinent was brought under direct administration; some local rulers were retained as subsidiaries of the Company, militarily and administratively completely at its mercy. By 1857, "the British empire in India had become the British empire of India."

Vested interests: Although the activities of the Company were regularly and closely supervised by the British Parliament, there was little possibility of placing any real restraints on the Company's functioning, for the revenues drained from India in money and in trade brought prosperity on a large enough scale in Britain to create a widespread vested interest in the colonisation of India. This was apart from the personal benefit that many Members of Parliament derived from direct involvement in the Company's enterprises; indeed, not infrequently the Company or its retired employees invested money to purchase seats in the House of Commons for its agents. Among its patrons the Company could count even the sovereign.

The British hold over the Indian economy and society too underwent a substantial change in the first half of the 19th century. If the peasant

duties and fines were imposed. In 1760, one English lady had to pay £200 as a fine for using an Indian handkerchief.

Yet the demand for textiles did not decline. The decisive shift came with the industrialisation of cloth manufacture in Britain. The very scale of its production and low price brought it into distant markets and began to drive out the handloom-manufactured textiles. In 1794 the value of British cotton manufactures sold in India amounted to £156; in 1813 it had risen to £110,000. Under pressure of the manufacturers, Parliament in 1833 abolished the Company's monopoly over the Indian trade and opened the floodgates to British goods, the custom duties for which were fixed at nominal levels. By 1856

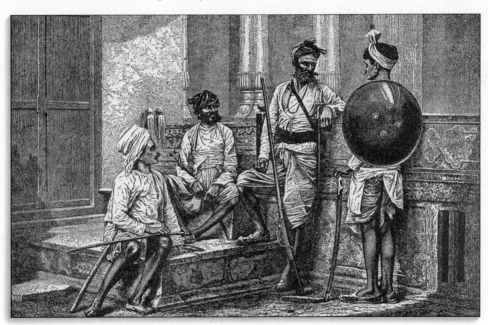

was carrying the ever-rising burden of supporting the government and the indigenous landed aristocracy, the artisan could still sell his goods to the Company, for which the demand had not contracted. This was particularly true of silk and cotton textiles, though the market for indigo was shrinking, for a better quality indigo was being manufactured in the West Indies. The superior quality of Indian textiles, however, posed a threat to the development of the English textile industry throughout the 18th century and heavy

British imports into India were valued at £6.3 million.

Inevitably, the Indian textile industry was ruined. Instead, Indian raw cotton was exported to Britain to be turned into finished goods and then sent back to the Indian market.

Another commodity exported from India by the British was opium, but this was taken to China and forced into the Chinese market in spite of the Chinese government's ban. Meanwhile the British meticulously observed their own government's ban on the import of opium into their own country.

For capturing the vast Indian market, it was necessary to develop the means of transport

Left, Indian troops under British officers pose for a picture, *circa* 1878. **Above**, the Rajputs are what the British used to call a martial race.

and communication. Steamships started navigating the network of Indian rivers; old roads were repaired and improved; but, above all, railways were introduced in India in 1853. In that year, the telegraph was also introduced.

Along with these modern means of transport and communications came certain modern concepts of social organisation. A separation of civil administrative functions from those of the army and the police, and the notion of the rule of law and equality before the law were all major departures from the then existing forms of social functioning. So also was the attempt at rooting out some of the social customs such as a widow burning herself at the funeral pyre of her husband, or the infanticide of female chil-

princely houses which had been deprived of their territories and power could hardly relish the goings-on; the Company's high civil and military officials seldom adhered to their own declared principles, for it was after all not easy to sacrifice the prospect of territorial expansion for the sake of a scruple. Impoverishment of ruling houses brought in its train misery on vast numbers of those directly or indirectly dependent on court patronage for their livelihood – courtiers, soldiers, servants, merchants, artisans. Artisans, especially textile weavers, suffered directly too when the Company, newly ensconced in levers of political and administrative power, first sought to depress the wages of labour and prices of goods and later flooded

dren. Western sciences and philosophy taught through the medium of English were also first experimented with in 1835, in Bengal. There was considerable support for these measures amongst many Indian intellectuals and social reformers who had had the opportunity to compare traditional Indian with modern European educational and social systems. Clearly, these changes were only the first step towards a transformation of Indian society; the overwhelming part of it still remained steeped in tradition, not all of which was admirable.

The progress of British rule in India had understandably generated varied kinds of resentment in different locales. Such of the

Indian markets with British goods. Several towns, centres of textile production, were ruined. In the countryside, peasants were being subjected to an ever-rising demand for revenue either by the Company's government directly or on its behalf by the indigenous landed aristocracy. Even the government's benign measures, such as the ban on widow burning, were viewed in some sections as unwarranted interference with age-old Indian customs.

The Rebellion of 1857: The British hold on India and the unfolding of its political and economic policies were marked by sporadic and local-level uprisings in some regions. What happened in 1857, however, was a concerted effort on a grand scale in large parts of India to be rid of alien rule. This was an endeavour in which the Mughal "emperor," a number of princely states in the regions, artisans and peasants and Indian sepoys of the Company's army joined hands. "Mughal" was still a hallowed name, although the "emperor" was an aged and decrepit man, whose "empire" did not extend beyond the walls of the Red Fort in Delhi which housed his palace and whose "revenue" was a pension settled on him by the Company. Yet this old man became the centre and the symbol of the massive rebellion.

The immediate cause of the rebellion was an order issued by the Company's army commanders to the Indian sepoys to bite the car-

by them. Thus, irrespective of the truth of the rumour, both Hindu and Muslim sepoys were alienated at one go; but then the fact that the rumour was easily believed pointed to the general level of alienation of the government from the people. The rumour clearly served as a spark to set the forest of discontent on fire.

On 10 May 1857, many sepoys stationed at Meerut, near Delhi, mutinied. This was the beginning of the rebellion. From Meerut the sepoys marched to Delhi where they were joined by the local infantry who killed their British officers and carried off the "emperor" to "lead" them. From Delhi the revolt spread to the whole of northern and central India; it also spread downwards into the ranks of townsmen

tridges before putting them into their rifles. A rumour began to spread that the cartridges were greased with the fat of cows and pigs. Since cows were held sacred by the Hindus and there were few sins greater than eating beef, this order greatly hurt their sentiment. The Muslims were on the other hand hurt by the utter indifference to their religious sentiment which forbade them even to touch pork, held unclean

Left, rajas of the period. Some resisted British domination and were destroyed; these others became British vassals and their states survived until after Indian independence. **Above**, Western India Turf Club, Poona, *circa* 1900.

and peasants. However, the class of landed aristocracy that the British had created through the Permanent Settlement stood by its master in that moment of trial. It was a fight to the end on both sides with all the accompanying bloodshed, violence and hatred; but the end did not favour India. While vast numbers of Indians rose in revolt, many groups and regions stood by silently; there were others who joined hands with the British. The latter were also better armed and had more efficient and quicker means of communication, the railways and telegraph among them. The "emperor" at any rate did not possess the capacity of leadership in a situation in which leadership was of critical importance.

The Rebellion lasted a year and a half; by the end of 1859 the "emperor" had been deported to Burma where he died a lonely death, bringing to a formal end the grand era of Mughal rule in India. Many of his sons were executed in Delhi and their bodies were left hanging for several days to drive the point home.

The Rebellion even in its failure, produced many heroes and heroines of epic character and the folklore around this event has produced some masterpieces of popular literature. Above all, it produced a sense of unity between the Hindus and the Muslims.

For one of the chief lessons the government was to draw from 1857 was that such unity must be preempted. Immediately following the Re-

could compete for high civil service jobs, the number of those successful remained too meagre to be of any significance. The higher posts in most administrative departments were reserved for the British subjects of the Crown.

The new government also sought to accommodate some of the princely states which had stood by the British in 1857; they were to be the bulwark of Britain's Indian Empire. But of course this accommodation was to be allowed within the overall framework of complete subordination to imperial authority. Given this subordination, their territories were declared proof against any further annexation.

Gone, too, was the zeal for social reform; the government began carefully to refrain from in-

bellion, the government pursued discriminatory policies against the Muslims: they were denied opportunities of employment in the government as well as modern education to ensure that they remained backward compared to the Hindus and thus for ever in contention with them.

The Rebellion saw the end of the Company's rule in India. Power was transferred to the British Crown in 1858 by an Act of British Parliament. The Crown's viceroy in India was to be the chief executive. The army was reorganised with a far greater number of British officers than had been the case hitherto. No Indian was allowed to rise to an officer's position until the second decade of the 20th century. Although Indians

terfering with any of the social customs of Indians, however backward-looking. Enthusiasm for imparting modern education to Indians too began to wane and university education remained confined for a long time to three cities – Calcutta, Bombay and Madras – where universities had been established in 1857. A most dramatic expansion took place in the army, on which 52 percent of the Indian revenues were spent in 1904. This army was used not only to suppress any form of popular protest either against the British government or the princely states, but also in fierce campaigns in India's neighbours: thus were Burma and Afghanistan subordinated to the British rulers of India.

Industrialisation: The Indian contact with Britain's growing industrialisation had initially undermined the market for the products of India's artisans. The effect on the weavers had been particularly disastrous, as already mentioned. Gradually, however, this contact also brought modern industry to India. The first textile mill began operating in Bombay in 1853 and the first jute mill in Bengal two years later. By 1905, more than 200 cotton textile mills and 36 jute mills were functioning. A large iron and steel plant was established in Bihar which continues to operate to this day. Some of these mills and factories were established by Indians, among them the iron and steel plant just mentioned. But most were under the control of

second half of the 19th century; apparent were the growth of modern ideas and realisation of the need for removing social evils. At times it took on a religious garb so that religious reform movements were often covers for protest against evils like the stigma on widow remarriage, or the practice of child marriage. Complicated religious rituals also came under attack, as they had several times earlier.

Above all, there was a growing political consciousness that encompassed all other spheres of activity. The violent uprising of 1857 had ended in failure; new methods of protest against alien rule had to be adopted if protest were to be effective. The crucial new method was to be based on organised strength, challenging the govern-

British capital, which saw enormous profits in the cheap raw materials and labour and a vast market in India and abroad. The introduction of modern industry brought with it incipient conflict between British and Indian entrepreneurs. Expectedly, the government extended all patronage to British-owned industries (and plantations such as tea, indigo and coffee) and discriminated against Indian capital.

There was too a remarkable degree of social awakening in various regions of India in the

ment on its own ground, within the framework of the British government's laws and policies. This clearly required a class of highly educated Indians, especially lawyers. British-trained Indian lawyers were indeed to play the crucial leadership role in the movement for India's liberation, the Indian National Movement.

Experiments had already been made at forming local and regional level organisations of educated Indians here and there. In 1885, a national-level organisation was formed which was to play a decisive role in the country's subsequent history until and after independence: this was the Indian National Congress. The initial thrust for its creation came from a retired

Left, an early 18th-century Sahib in a palanquin. **Above**, young Queen Victoria, from a painting at Fort St George Museum.

English civil servant, A. O. Hume, who collected eminent educated Indians in Bombay and held the organisation's first session. He had conceived of it as a "safety valve" against the spread of popular discontent. In his own words, "A safety valve for the escape of great and growing forces generated by our own action was urgently needed."

To begin with, the Congress sought to air reservations against the government's laws and political and administrative measures. Gradually, various strands began to appear within the organisation, not all of which were committed to mild expressions of views. The "moderate" and the "extremist" wings began to make their appearance by the beginning of the 20th century. While the Moderates sought gradual reform within the structure of law and government and expressed their aspirations through speeches and petitions, the Extremists were basically hostile to the very notion of an alien government and were prepared to use violence to achieve their objective. However, in either case, political activity remained confined to the highly educated Indians.

The perils of partition: A major departure in the growth of Indian nationalism occurred in 1905. In that year an order was issued for the partition of the province of Bengal into two units. The public justification for this order was that this would make the two provinces administratively more viable; privately, officials at various levels admitted that the objective was to stem the tide of nationalism then on the rise among Bengalis, by separating east and west Bengal and isolating them from the people of other linguistic regions (Assam, Bihar and Orissa) which together constituted a single province. Leaders of the National Movement understood the purpose of this move and prepared to oppose it tooth and nail.

If nothing else mobilised the masses of Indian people into opposition of the government, the proposed partition of Bengal did. There were hunger strikes, general strikes, marches, demonstrations, public meetings, in all of which milling crowds participated. Above all, a brand new weapon, likely to touch the British where it hurt most, was adopted: boycott of British goods and use of India-made commodities. This gave an enormous spurt to Indian industry in various sectors. The movement, with its nerve centre in Calcutta, began to spread all over the country in diverse forms, from peaceful strikes and protest marches to acts of terrorism.

The government countered with unprecedented repression, of which imprisonment was the mildest form. But a political manoeuvre on government's part at this moment was to have a far more lasting impact on India's future: calculated steps were taken to create dissensions between the predominantly Muslim east Bengal (now Bangladesh) and predominantly Hindu west Bengal, who proved easy to provoke. This was to become a central issue in

the National Movement and to lead to serious consequences. Several vain attempts were made to find a solution to this problem.

The British policy of weakening the National Movement by creating dissensions within it bore its first fruit in 1906 when the All India Muslim League was founded. It stood up in support of the partition of Bengal and demanded special concessions from the government for the Muslims, such as proportionate reservation of government jobs for them. However, the League's claim to be the representative of all the Muslims of India was challenged by a large number of Muslim leaders who had pledged their support to the Congress. Even so, two political entities, one representing

Left, Bahadur Shah Zafar, the last Mughal, who was deported to Burma on the fall of Delhi; **right**, Bhagat Singh, leading member of one of a number of revolutionary groups active in the 1930s, was hanged by the British.

the Muslims exclusively, the other the Hindus predominantly, began to operate on the Indian scene. At times they entered into agreements with one another, at others they adopted mutually antagonistic postures. In either case their separate identities persisted.

While the government responded to the growing Movement by resorting to repression as well as divisive tactics, it also sought to appease public opinion by amending its legal structure. It began to visualise legislatures with elected as well as nominated members and with some control over a few of the departments of administration. Voting rights were, however, severely restricted. Such measures were wide of the mark that the National Movement had set for itself.

Africa to practise as a lawyer after his training as barrister-at-law in England. In South Africa he witnessed and experienced humiliation because of the colour of his skin. In protest he began to organise the Indian victims of apartheid to wage a completely non-violent protest. The victims were to violate the unjust law publicly and take the punishment willingly, without even an expression of pain. The strategy was to appeal to the conscience of the oppressors; it also aroused the latent moral protest among the victims, and unleashed the energy and power of the multitudes without incurring any expense on arms.

The story of Gandhi's experiments had reached India, his homeland. When, therefore, he returned in 1915 he was already a well-

Most of the leaders of the Movement were lawyers who had had their legal training in England and had familiarised themselves with the working of the parliamentary system there. These leaders, while participating in these legislatures were forever dissatisfied with the severe limitations placed on them. Consequently they were ever willing to resign collectively and thereby paralyse the functioning of the legislatures.

The Gandhi era: In 1917 a new phase began in the developing struggle for India's freedom. In 1915, Mohandas Karamchand Gandhi had returned to India from South Africa where he had experimented with new forms of resistance to the apartheid regime. He had gone to South

known figure. Before launching himself into the struggle Gandhi sought to familiarise himself with conditions in India, from where he had been gone for a long time. He undertook extensive tours of various regions of India and saw for himself the immense poverty and degradation suffered by the masses of Indian people at the hands of both their Indian and foreign masters. The misery of the lower castes, perpetrated by the upper castes, the inhuman treatment of bonded farm labourers, the deprivation from which Indian women suffered everywhere – all these facets of inhuman existence came alive to him as he travelled in crowded trains, bullock-carts and on foot. Gandhi also realised that most of India still lived in villages; that it was there that India's real strength lay. But this resource could be tapped only if relief was brought to Indian peasants from exploitation both at the hands of Indian landlords and the British government and planters.

Gandhi reached a similar conclusion about the industrial workers; their living conditions must improve and Indian mill owners must sacrifice a part of their profit for this purpose.

From the beginning, Gandhi waged a moral protest against oppression by defying unjust laws and willingly taking punishment. He would often undertake fasts lasting several weeks until his demands had been conceded. Defying laws frequently led him into prison. Following him,

was altogether a new form of protest which it did not know how to handle. Consequently, it reacted clumsily. If it imprisoned the leaders, as it often did, multitudes of Indians would line up to fill the jails; they had to be released because prisons could no longer hold them. If it opened fire on unarmed and peaceful protestors, as it did in 1919 in Punjab, its own pretensions to civilised behaviour would be exposed and its legitimacy questioned. It was willing to give some concessions, but these fell far short of the demand.

Late in 1920 a "Non-Cooperation Movement" was launched. The government was asked to atone for the unwarranted killings in Punjab and for going back on the British government's word given to Turkey during World War I. The

other leaders went to jail for the same offence; then masses of people, moved by his inspiring leadership, followed suit. Gandhi, however, always imposed one inviolable condition: defiance of law, or "civil disobedience" as it came to be called, must always be completely peaceful.

The government had been familiar with the passing of resolutions at annual Congress sessions; it was familiar too with demonstrations, public meetings and terrorist activity; but this

Left, Gandhi and Nehru at a Congress meeting. **Above**, the closing negotiations of independence, where Mountbatten, Nehru, Jinnah and other leaders discuss the details.

British prime minister, David Lloyd George, had declared that Turkey would not be deprived of "the rich and renowned lands of Asia Minor and Thrace which are predominantly Turkish in race" once the war was over; yet Thrace was detached from Turkey just as the war ended. The British treatment of the Turkish Caliph also hurt Muslims who treated him as the head of the Muslim world. In India, the Muslims had launched a movement in protest; the Congress joined this movement to win the Muslims over for joint struggles against the British Indian government.

In 1921 and 1922 unprecedented scenes of mass participation in the Non-Cooperation

Movement were witnessed throughout India. People of all communities, regions and ages responded to the call by giving up their studies, jobs, everything. Women joined the movement in massive numbers. Boycott of European cloth became a public cry and bonfires of such cloths were made. Hindus and Muslims forgot all about their differences. A surge of human bonds, breaking all barriers, united the diverse people in this hour of magnificent struggle.

The government reacted as usual with imprisonment and use of gunfire, which only helped to bring ever more people into the movement. But the government was saved by Gandhi himself at a time when the movement was attaining ever higher peaks: he suddenly withdrew the struggle

was beginning to emerge both within the Congress and outside. This strand comprised a younger group of men and women inspired by the socialist ideas of Marx and Lenin and moved by the experiment of socialist revolution in the USSR.

In 1925 the Communist Party of India had been formed; its membership remained rather small, but its influence, particularly among workers, peasants and the intelligentsia, was quite disproportionate to its numerical strength. Within the Congress, leadership was beginning to pass into the hands of younger men, who also carried distinctly socialist sympathies: men like Subhash Chandra Bose and Jawaharlal Nehru, among others.

because in an obscure village in eastern Uttar Pradesh some policemen had fired upon a procession of 3,000 peasants and the peasants had, in a moment of rage, burnt the police station and caused the death of 22 policemen. Gandhi's basic condition of non-violence had been violated; he would have nothing to do with any protest which carried even a suggestion of violence.

This was an anticlimax which was not appreciated by most of the leaders of the National Movement, both old and young. Among the latter was Jawaharlal Nehru. The Movement began to drift without much force and without a clear aim. But this mood was not to last long. Late in the 1920s a new strand of leadership

There were, besides, young men and women who together constituted a stream of revolutionary terrorists. They were moved by a commitment to the vision of remoulding Indian society as much as by anti-imperialist sentiment. The most outstanding of these was Bhagat Singh who courted death by throwing a bomb into the central legislative assembly hall during a session. He was still studying the writings of socialist thinkers when he was sent to the gallows.

The influence of socialist ideas brought the concern with economic issues to the centre of the Movement's thinking. The shape of things after British rule was terminated began to emerge in the minds of leaders; it also found expression in their writings and speeches. This concern in turn brought even larger numbers of India's poor masses into the struggle; the struggle itself became more fervent.

The demand for independence: It was this mood that was reflected in the resolution of the Congress passed at its annual session in 1929: the resolution demanded complete independence for India. Jawaharlal Nehru was the young president of the session, succeeding his father. 26 January 1930, the day the resolution was adopted, was designated Independence Day, the anniversary of which was to be observed by all Indians every year by unfurling a new tricoloured flag and taking the independence pledge which declared that it was "a crime against man

and God" to submit to British rule.

A second movement of civil disobedience was launched early in 1930; this was to defy laws that were considered unjust. Gandhi chose to dramatise this defiance by taking up an item that touched the poorest of Indian households. The government had a monopoly on the manufacture of salt from which it derived a large revenue. Gandhi decided symbolically to "manufacture" salt on the Gujarat coast without paying any tax. After declaring his intention of doing so,

Left, Nehru's address at Delhi's Red Fort on 15 August 1947. **Above**, a December 1946 report in the *Ilustrated London News*.

he set out on foot to march to the coast about 150 miles (250km) away, accompanied by a handful of supporters. He was then 60 years old. As he walked people joined him in the thousands, a substantial number of them women.

Once again, mass participation in this movement eliminated differences of community, region, language and sex and brought out the noblest in the humblest of men and women.

The government's response was predictable: imprisonment and firing on unarmed people. It also called a Round Table Conference in London where representatives of various groups would confer on the future of India. The Congress demanded preparatory steps towards complete independence, but that was unthinkable for the British. The negotiations broke down; the Civil Disobedience Movement was resumed, but it had to give way in the face of the intense terror and repression unleashed by the government.

In 1935, the Government of India Act was passed by the British Parliament. This proposed a bicameral legislature at the centre in which the princes would nominate their representatives and about 14 percent of the people of India, who had been given the right to vote, would elect the others. Even with this balance between people's representatives and the government's allies, the legislature had very limited powers. In the provinces, however, the elected assemblies had much greater, though not full control over the administrative departments. The Congress opposed the Act but nonetheless decided to contest elections under it and form governments. Except in Bengal and Punjab, the Congress swept the polls.

Between 1935 when the Act was passed and implemented and World War II, the whole world was in a ferment. The growth of Nazism in Germany and Fascism in Italy and Japan was threatening the very existence of humanity; on the other hand the colonial people's struggles for liberation were getting more determined. India's sympathy clearly lay with these struggles all over the world, even as she was willing to side with her own imperialist master and its allies in the fight against Nazism. More than ever before, this brief period placed India's National Movement in the context of the developing global situation and established linkages between local and international issues.

However, India's support to Britain in the war was not unconditional. If India were to help Britain retain its freedom against possible enslavement by Hitler, surely this could not be done by India herself remaining enslaved. A free India, in fact if not in form, would be able to render much more effective assistance in resisting the Nazi onslaught than an India in bondage. The government would not even consider such a proposition; it was appalled by the fact that the Indian leaders should attach any conditions to their offer of support in fighting such an unmixed evil as Nazism.

Things came to a head in 1942. The Congress gave a call to Indians to ensure that the British "Quit India"; Indians were called upon to "do or die" in this endeavour. Once again, a massive movement was underway to achieve freedom; once again it was matched by massive

favour of seeing India a free nation. Indeed, there was growing support for India's demand for independence even in Britain; many sections of the Labour Party were in sympathy with the demand. As a result, things moved fast in that direction when the Labour Party came to power in Britain after the war. If Churchill's government had been adamant in retaining India – which had once been described as "brightest jewel in the British Crown" – and if the Prime Minister had declared that he had not been elected to that office "to preside over the liquidation of the empire", the new government headed by Attlee was less moved by considerations of past imperial glory than by the visible writing on the wall.

repression. In several regions the rebels were able briefly to establish their own administration; but all these victories were shortlived. Subhash Chandra Bose, who had quit the Congress earlier, organised Indians in southeast Asia into a powerful armed force called the Indian National Army. He sought Japanese help to lead this Army into India and free it from British control. The defeat of Japan in the war, however, put an end to this dream.

The Allies had won the war but the effort had left several of them with much depleted strength. Britain certainly was no longer a great power, economically and militarily. The new great powers, the USA and the USSR, were both in

It was becoming quite clear that the spirit of rebellion against the alien government was spreading and that the government could not long depend on this spirit keeping within the bounds of non-violence. There had been a strong tradition of terrorism in the Indian National Movement at the best of times and terrorists commanded as much respect with the people of India as the non-violent agitators; now, with the government's unbending attitude on the basic question of India's independence, non-violent methods would be increasingly discredited. Also, the government's grip over

Above, the Mountbattens bid farewell.

the mainstay of its authority, the army and the bureaucracy, was beginning to loosen. Sympathy for Bose's Indian National Army was often visible in the ranks of the Indian armed forces. In 1946, the ratings of the Indian Navy burst into a revolt in Bombay and waged a pitched battle with British forces; they were prepared to go on, if they had not been persuaded by the nationalist leaders to surrender. There were widespread strikes too in the Indian Air Force, the Signals Corps and the police in some cities. All this was in tandem with widespread strikes by the common people everywhere. Industrial workers, by now a sizeable force, were waging particularly militant strikes; the peasants too were getting ready for a last-ditch action. Attlee's government was sensitive to these developments as also to the weakness of Britain's position and, for the first time, independence for India came negotiable.

The Muslim League: There was, however, one major development that was to embitter the taste of independence for millions of Indians. The Muslim League, which always enjoyed the government's patronage, sought guarantees from the government as well as the Congress that the rights of the Muslim minority (about 10 percent of the population) would be safeguarded. The Congress was willing to give them oral assurances, but it was argued that the fact that the Congress itself had a strong wing of leaders who were staunch Hindu communalists justified a degree of scepticism concerning these assurances.

Since the Congress commanded the support of the majority community, the Hindus, it could always camouflage its own communalism under the slogan of nationalism as well as democracy, it was said. No one doubted the personal integrity of leaders like Gandhi and Nehru when they spoke of Muslims as their brothers: but much more was at stake than the promise of honest persons. How could the Muslims be certain that the future too would produce leaders of the same calibre and integrity?

A solution that the British government had worked out was to establish separate electorates for the Hindus and the Muslims, each community electing its representatives. This was tantamount to validating the theory that the League had begun to propound, namely that the Hindus and the Muslims were two separate nations, thus equating religion with nation. The Congress had never accepted this theory, for it implied that the Congress could not enrol Muslims as members, nor represent them. Some of the most illustrious presidents of the Congress had been Muslims and not all Muslims sympathised with the League anyway. Yet, the Congress contested elections on the basis of separate electorates while never giving up its reservations concerning them.

Separate electorates could only have reinforced the communal division. The paths of the Congress and the League began to diverge more sharply than ever. In 1940 the League raised the demand for a separate independent state for the Muslims, and frequently reiterated it subsequently. The state was to be called Pakistan.

The new state of Pakistan: The tension that this demand created led to widespread communal rioting of the most inhuman kind, as the prospect of independence began to take shape. Both Hindus and Muslims participated in the mass butchery in 1946, each blaming the other community for the first killing. There were, too, heroic people on both sides who laid down their lives in defence of brethren of the other community; but in a situation of such large-scale turbulence their effort was too feeble to bridge the wide chasm of hatred.

By early 1947 the decision to grant freedom to India had been taken; but this freedom would be accompanied by the partition of the country to create the new state of Pakistan. Not all the effort on the part of leaders of the Congress and the Muslim League could resolve the communal problem. Pakistan was to comprise two regions, one in the west and the other, separated by nearly 1,300 miles (2,000 km) of Indian territory, far out in East Bengal, now Bangladesh. Large numbers of Hindus from the regions that were to constitute Pakistan, and Muslims from India began to emigrate. Millions, often with no more than the clothes they were wearing, moved in opposite directions. Not all of them reached their destinations.

Thus it was that freedom came to India on 15 August 1947, in the midst of stupendous tragedy, a most senseless shedding of human blood. As the dividing hour between 14 and 15 August approached and people burst into the joy of breathing free air after two centuries of slavery, Gandhi lay forlorn on a thin jute mattress spread out on the floor of an unlit house in Calcutta, silently weeping over the loss of all that he had held closest to his heart: nonviolence, humanity, compassion and love for fellow human beings, irrespective of colour of skin, religion or creed.

THE STRUGGLES OF DEMOCRACY

Many argued in 1947 that it was premature to give the vote to the illiterate masses of newly independent India and unwise to adopt Britain's political system, designed for such different circumstances. But Jawaharlal Pandit Nehru, the country's first prime minister, believed that British-style democracy, a freely elected parliament consisting of an upper and lower house representing secular and federal interests, was what India needed. It would, he thought, keep under control the centrifugal forces of cultural, ethnic and religious values that might otherwise tear the country apart.

To achieve unity, more than 500 nominally independent princely states had to be integrated into the Indian Union. This tricky diplomatic task was, on the whole, successfully accomplished in 1950 by Nehru's deputy, Sadar Vallabhai Patel. But the decision to demarcate the new state boundaries on the basis of the regional language led to problems. Inevitably, a multitude of dialects and idioms had to be ignored. This meant that the ethnic and language divisions of the states were never really satisfactorily settled, with the result that violent disputes still flare up periodically all over the country.

Initially, the communal violence was traumatic, confirming the pessimists' worst fears. Hindus and Muslims, the main rivals, clashed bitterly over the partition of the subcontinent, slaughtering thousands and forcing countless others to flee their homes. Although Nehru tried to separate political and public life, confining religion to the private sphere, the distinction was never really understood by most of the population, who regarded their spiritual and secular lives as indivisible.

Nehru aimed to transform a caste-ridden, feudal society into one of liberal equal opportunity. He placed his faith in Democratic Socialism, a middle way between a capitalistic welfare state and a Soviet-styled centrally controlled economy. Encouraging self-reliance, he hoped, would stimulate profit-oriented free enterprise but would avoid polarising wealth. Imports were restricted, business excesses were checked by state institutions and key industries were kept under state control.

His ambitions for a dynamic economy were unlikely to be furthered by his own Congress party, a discordant group united only by their goal of forcing the British to quit India. Nehru hoped instead that his Silent Revolution might be advanced by the Indian Civil Service, an intricate bureaucracy inherited from the Raj. But the result was a labyrinth of laws and regulations controlled by bureaucrats who decided to whom concessions, permits and licences should be granted. The new system was not only stultifying; almost inevitably, it bred corruption and nepotism. But it did save India from falling into the trap of post-colonial economic dependence.

In the 1950s the emphasis was placed on heavy industries such as steel and mining, a decision some economists later blamed for India's initially slow economic growth. Industrial expansion was initially accomplished at the expense of agricultural development, still the main means of subsistence for more than two-thirds of India's population of 850 million. Subsequent land reforms brought relief to the mass of tenant farmers and redistribution effected considerable social change in the countryside. Cultivation suffered and it was left up to Indira Gandhi to correct this imbalance with her Green Revolution of the 1960s.

On the foreign front, India helped establish the Non-Aligned Movement and advocated in the 1950s that China be given international status. But Nehru's admiration of China blinded him to its territorial ambitions which led to war in 1962 over claims on the remote Aksai Chin area. India suffered a disastrous defeat, which badly dented Nehru's confidence and, some said, his health.

The defeat also harmed India's relations, hitherto good, with Western powers. Nehru determined to build up India's arms capability, but was opposed by the United States and Great Britain. He turned instead to the Soviet Union, furthering alienating the West.

Nehru dynasty: Nehru died in 1964, but a dynasty had been born. Two years later, his daughter, Indira Gandhi, took over the reins of power and vociferously championed her father's principles of Democratic Socialism. Her style of governing was very different from his: she tolerated no opposition and, allowing only soothsayers and sycophants as advisors, relied on her own political intuitions to make decisions.

Left, palace guards at Mysore.

Her authoritarian manner helped establish her as undisputed leader of a divided Congress, as did India's 1971 victory over East Pakistan (now Bangladesh). She nationalised banks and stripped Indian princes of their privileges and privy purses, in spite of her father's guarantees. Her Green Revolution turned tenant farmers into landowners, guaranteeing her a solid agrarian power base that lasted into the 1980s. The Peasant Movement forced politicians to waive loans, brought electricity to villages and installed irrigation systems.

It was a turbulent time. When, in June 1975, the Allahabad High Court found Mrs Gandhi guilty of corrupt political practices, she reacted by imposing a State of Emergency that was to

his ruthlessness had scarcely won him popularity, Sanjay was being groomed by Mrs Gandhi as her heir-apparent. On his death, she persuaded her second son, Rajiv, a pilot with Indian Airlines perceived to have little interest in politics, to make his first appearance on the political stage.

Punjab problems: Also making headlines in 1980 was Sant Jarnail Singh Bhindranwale, a charismatic, turbaned militant leader based in the Golden Temple in Amritsar, the holiest of Sikh shrines. Surrounded by a group of young, educated and fanatical Sikhs, he demanded greater rights for the Sikh community and separation of the state of Punjab from the rest of India. Indira Gandhi's tactic of pitting Sikh

last two years. The press was censored, more than 100,000 political opponents and activists were imprisoned, slums were forcibly cleared and enforced sterilisation was carried out.

Inevitably, there was a backlash. Her Congress (Indira) party decisively lost the 1977 election, which brought to power the Janata Dal party, led by the octogenarian Moraji Desai. In a political drama unusual even by Indian standards, Mrs Gandhi was put briefly behind bars just six years after being the heroine of the Bangladesh war. Against all odds, however, she was back in office in 1980.

Her joy was short-lived, for later that year her son Sanjay died in an air crash. Although

groups against each other only aggravated the crisis and the Sant's followers were able to terrorise, rob and murder Hindus unhindered.

By 1984, however, the threat had reached the capital and Mrs Gandhi was forced to act. She sent the army into the Golden Temple, large parts of which were destroyed. Much blood was shed and the Sant was killed.

Revenge was not long in coming: on 31 October, Mrs Gandhi was assassinated by her Sikh bodyguards. A shocked Congress party elected Rajiv Gandhi prime minister. It seemed to some a rash decision, given his inexperience, but the electorate overwhelmingly endorsed Congress's decision by sweeping Rajiv to power in the subsequent elections. His manifesto was ambitious, promising to modernise the economy and revive industry with 20th-century technology and management techniques. It was an appealing mix in a year which had seen a shattering accident at Bhopal, when gas leaked from a Union Carbide pesticide plant, killing at least 3,500 and affecting hundreds of thousands.

Rajiv's political honeymoon was heartening – even relationships with Pakistan improved for a while – but it was short-lived. The endemic corruption and mind-numbing bureaucracy made the problems of the disintegrating Soviet Union – whose restrictive economic policies India had emulated – look simple by comparison. In addition, the Machiavellian

jostling for power continued. The secessionist war in the Punjab, with its explosive population mix of 57 percent Sikh and 43 percent Hindu, was claiming thousands of lives a year. Like his mother before him, Rajiv sent in troops to remove Sikhs from the Golden Temple. He also sent in the Indian army to support the Tamil minority in their separatist struggle against the Sinhalese majority in neighbouring Sri Lanka – an enterprise that turned into a messy misadventure, eventually resulting in his assassination.

Left, graffiti depicting the assassination of Indira Gandhi. **Above**, rural political meeting.

Five years later, amid allegations of economic mismanagement and political corruption, Congress (I) lost catastrophically in the polls. A key issue was the Bofors scandal, in which suspect commissions had been paid by the Swedish arms manufacturer to secure a contract to supply guns to the Indian army. His defense minster, V.P. Singh, resigned in 1987 alleging Congress corruption in the affair and formed a new party, the National Front. In the 1989 election he won enough votes to form a minority government.

The Ayodhya issue: The new prime minister took over at a critical phase in Indian politics. Law and order in the Punjab had continued to deteriorate. Muslim extremists in Kashmir were agitating for an independent state. There were political tensions in Assam. Tribal groups in Bihar, West Bengal and Orissa were pressing for more autonomy.

With emotions already strained between Hindus and Muslims, a serious challenge came from an unexpected quarter. The VHP, the universal Hindu organisation, declared its intention to build a temple for Lord Rama in Ayodhya, Uttar Pradesh, the god's birthplace. The new Hindu temple was to be built exactly on the spot where a mosque stood, resulting in immediate clashes between the Hindu and Muslim communities. On 30 October 1990, thousands of Hindu volunteers stormed the 16th-century mosque, forcing the police to open fire. The Bharatiya Janata Party (BJP), a Hindu nationalist party until then providing crucial support for V.P. Singh's minority government, withdrew its backing over the issue and the government fell.

Rajiv Gandhi felt he could not stand aloof from such a crisis. When he had lost power in the 1989 general election, many felt that he would retire quietly to Europe with his Italian wife, Sonia. Instead, he had fought back, displaying considerable political cunning in an acrimonious environment still dominated by religious and caste rivalries. By the time the general election was forced in 1991, he was concerned not only by the alarming tensions between Hindus and Muslims but also by the fact that the country was running out of foreign exchange. Inflation was rising, and fuel rationing was threatened.

To make matters worse, no effective two-party system had been established, which meant that votes tended to be cast for the Congress (I) party or against it.

Inevitably, therefore, politicians in general

lacked a positive image. A leading astrologer, Jitendra Nath Sharma, expressed a general view. "They take the advice of their wives first, their astrologers second," he said. "Most of them are a pathetic lot."

Rajiv, believing that he had lost the 1989 election by being too aloof, plunged into a populist campaign, driving himself in an open Jeep through swarming crowds. His security men despaired, with good reason: as he was campaigning in the southern state of Tamil Nadu, a 25-year-old Sri Lankan Tamil woman approached him with a jasmine garland, bent to kiss his feet and detonated her bomb, decapitating him and killing about 20 others including herself. Rajiv was 46.

scams surfaced in the press. Innovative economic reforms were criticised for not reaching down to the underclass, and chronic indecision was lampooned.

But the old demons would not easily disappear. The fight for independence in Kashmir rumbled on, with stories of appalling atrocities. In 1992 tens of thousands of Hindu zealots used their bare hands to tear down the mosque in Ayodhya. The bloodletting, which spread to Delhi and Bombay, quickly claimed more than 1,000 victims and turned into India's worst crisis since independence. The crisis strengthened the support of the right-wing Bharatiya Janata Party, whose rallies were said to resemble scenes from *Mahabharata*, the Hindu epic.

Such had been the grip of the Nehru succession over the Congress (I) party that no obvious successor existed. Desperate attempts were made to draft Rajiv's widow Sonia as his successor, but she resisted – though rumours persisted that her daughter Priyanka, an Indira look-alike, could eventually maintain the family succession. In the end, power devolved to P.V. Narasimha Rao, a 69-year-old former minister recovering from a heart bypass. It was a classic compromise – but Rao's staying power was underestimated.

Under Rao, Congress lost considerable support. Reports of a cash-crammed suitcase left as a blatant bribe and profiteering from import

Bombay was rocked by a dozen bombs in a single day the following March, and terrified Muslims fled the city. Gangsters appropriated downtown land, now the world's priciest office real estate, and the BJP triumphed in the next state elections. The radical Bal Thackeray, leader of the Hindu chauvinist Shiv Sena (Shiva's army), called for state borders to be closed to all non-residents. As a sop to Muslims, the BJP ordered a translation of the Koran into Sanskrit.

Endless contradictions: India was not immune from the various ills of the modern world.

<u>Above</u>, a family from the emerging middle class.

Pollution was inflicting clear damage on the environment, with even the Taj Mahal said to be suffering from "marble cancer" caused by acid rain. Officials denied it, saying that the mausoleum was a monument of moods whose colour depended on the light and time of day.

Sexual taboos were breaking down, with magazines and advertising becoming more prurient. Faced with a major Aids epidemic, the government even tolerated sexually explicit billboards for Kama Sutra condoms.

Satellite television enabled better-off urbanites to evade the restrictions of the censor, and less wealthy viewers tried beating trashcan lids into satellite dishes, using one to serve 50 or 100 homes. Suddenly the inhabitants of mud-huts were able to see Australian soap operas; more worrying to the government, Pakistani programmes were beamed down to those who could understand Urdu. Five new government-controlled channels were launched in response, and efforts were made to bring cable channels under the censors' control.

But it wasn't easy to be a censor in the India of the 1990s. When the authorities moved to ban a slightly risqué film song entitled "What's beneath the blouse?", they were derided because the answer, contained in the second line of the lyric, was nothing less innocent than: "There is a heart beneath my blouse."

As ever, India continued to mesmerise the world with its contradictions. Middle-class protests about traffic-jams in Delhi caused by cows ambling across busy junctions or sleeping in the middle or roads led to the appointment of a few discreet cow-catchers; but Hindus regarded this as an affront to the holy cow. To fight elitism in the tourist trade, state-run hotels were ordered to give 50 percent discounts on Thursdays and Fridays to peasants wearing *dhotis*; but women (who wear saris, not *dhotis*) cried discrimination.

It was a country in which scores of *harijans* (untouchables) could be tortured and dismembered because one of them let his foot touch a brahmin. Hindu girls were still burnt to death for not bringing enough dowry to their husband, and an Arab could buy an 11-year-old child bride for a couple of hundred dollars.

It is hard to keep India's contradictions in perspective. The country was undeniably backward when the British left. A high percentage of the population lived below the poverty line and were vulnerable to drought, flood and other natural and man-made calamities. Illiteracy was high, especially amongst women, and the caste system allowed little social mobility.

The new nation has therefore made enormous progress. It ranks as the world's tenth largest industrial power and produces everything from satellites and heavy machinery to nuclear energy. Huge dams, a network of irrigation canals, and widespread distribution of fertilizers reduce the threat of starvation, even when a drought lasts for several years.

The policy of self-reliance may have led to stagnation in technology but it has given India a broad industrial base that has allowed some economic independence. It also helped to keep the country out of the foreign debt trap. A large new middle-class has emerged, demanding and consumerist, to forge the shape of the future economy.

India, once universally hailed for its doctrine of non-violence as preached by Mahatma Gandhi, today has the largest standing army in the world. Effectively the strongest power in the region, it is feared by its neighbours for its hegemonic vigour. Increased social movement has had its impact on the old caste system, clearing the way for many of the previously underprivileged to enter universities and take up positions in the administration.

Chaos and paradox: Yet many problems seem almost insuperable. The population is expected to exceed a billion well before the year 2000, challenging China as the world's most populous country. Birth control, though practised by the urban well-to-do, is scorned by the villagers who make up 80 percent of the population; they see sons as a pension fund to be drawn on in their old age. If India is to avert ecological disaster, huge sums have to be invested in ambitious afforestation programmes.

But problems have never been easy to solve in India. History shows that the country has an extraordinary ability to cope with chaos and paradox. It has a talent to turn into a positive force situations that would bring others to the brink of disintegration. It has staunchly defended the right to democratic rule and succeeded in keeping the army out of politics.

India is still, as Mark Twain described it in 1897, "the one sole country under the sun that is endowed with an imperishable interest for alien prince and alien peasant, for lettered and ignorant, wise and fool, rich and poor, bond and free, the one land that *all* men desire to see, and having seen once, by even a glimpse, would not give that glimpse for all the shows of all the rest of the globe combined."

INDIA TODAY

Every morning at dawn, an ancient ritual takes place in the city of Varanasi. Thousands gather on the banks of the Ganga and strip to their underwear. Then, uttering holy mantras, they wade into the muddy waters, scoop up handfuls and drink. The Ganga is dangerously polluted but Hindus believe it to be sacred: able to cure disease, absolve sins and confer immortality.

A plane ride away is Bangalore, India's fastest growing metropolis. Atop a four-storey building, a giant satellite dish points towards the sky, connected to computers in climate-controlled rooms below. These are the offices of Texas Instruments, where software engineers labour in hushed cubicles adorned with Bon Jovi posters. Every morning they receive assignments from Texas via the dish. In the evening, they beam the completed work back.

India has both the incredibly old and the startlingly new, but the old predominates. The Greek historian Herodotus said it lay in "the furthest region of the inhabited world"—a metaphor that, until recently, remained true. India has existed at the edge of the modern world, not just poor or backward but cut off and stagnant.

But as those engineers in Bangalore prove, change is coming. The India of the postwar years – ruled by the Nehru-Gandhi dynasty, allied with the Soviet Union, and socialistic in policy – is certifiably dead. No one quite knows what the new India will be like. As with the Soviet Union, it has been pushed on a conveyor belt to the future by the failure of its past.

New direction: If anything, India can be likened to Japan, which opened to the outside world in the 1850s and decided to change its destiny. A century and a half later, India has made a similar decision. It ended its voluntary seclusion, allowing in foreign television broadcasts, radio, fast food joints. It recognised that its restrictive school of socialistic economics was a bust and invited Indians to start getting rich – with foreign partners. It accepted that it had to develop and modernise and, in the process, embarked on a course of major change.

For visitors, this makes India an unusually rich place: filled with the old but energised by the new. Visually India's cities are little changed from the time of the Raj, with crumbling fa-

Left, the modern look in an ancient setting.

cades, cows ambling on the boulevards and hump-backed, cartoon-like cars. In the countryside are plenty of the "heat and smells and oils and spices and puffs of temple incense" that Kipling described in the late 19th century. At the same time, India's youth wear jeans and trainers. Their evenings are dedicated to rock videos or logging on to local computer bulletin boards. India is getting plugged in – and what that means to a society of 900 million people unused to change is anybody's guess.

Politics, religion, economics, society: all will change radically in the coming decades. The only real certainty is that change will come much more rapidly now, in an era of jumbo jets and the information superhighway, than it came to Japan in the time of clipper ships.

Will economic growth bring unprecedented social mobility – striking at the heart of the rigid caste system that dominates society? Will the political system bequeathed by the British in 1947, already looking somewhat shaky, hold up? There are no easy answers. Opening up an almost totally isolated land of 900 million people is like opening all the sluice-gates of a dam into a parched desert: instead of bringing the land the nourishing waters of change, the society might, instead, be flooded.

Economic change: The engine of change for India is economic liberalisation and, although India has a lot of catching up to do, the changes are already profound.

Jawaharlal Nehru, India's first prime minister, didn't believe in the economic power of the individual. He believed in the state and he gave India a planned economy, in which the government owned basic industries, such as steel and power generation, and had absolute control over what the private sector produced.

Manufacturers were licensed to produce goods in certain quantities, at certain prices and were issued raw materials. Competition was nil. And since an industrial licence was, in effect, a licence to make money, corporations were not allowed to increase production to meet demand. Increased production meant increased profits and wealth was a sin in independent India. Even those who had it, hid it.

By the 1980s, the inefficiencies of the system, as in the Soviet Union and China, were starting to smother the economy as a whole.

Rajiv Gandhi, Nehru's grandson, reduced income tax rates, allowed manufacturers to choose the size of their factories and delicensed some industries. After his assassination in 1991, successor P.V. Narasimha Rao went considerably further: he delicensed most industries, made the rupee convertible and allowed foreigners to control 51 percent of their joint ventures. Import tariffs were chopped and foreigners were allowed to buy and sell shares on India's 20 stock exchanges.

There is more economic ferment now than at any time in the past. The United States calls India one of the world's top ten BEMs or "Big Emerging Markets." Heavyweights like General Motors, General Electric, McDonald's,

NEC and Samsung are entering India with an eye towards its massive middle class market, estimated at upward of 150 million people. Meanwhile, Indian companies are doing their own expansion, raising money in Europe and the United States.

Political uncertainty: The big question is what kind of social changes the economic reforms will bring about. In politics, for example, India is often praised as the world's largest democracy. Most of its institutions need work – the British-based judicial system, for instance, is gridlocked – but the country has managed to sustain a working electoral system since 1947, with only a 19-month gap (when Indira Gandhi

declared emergency rule in the mid 1970s). That achievement is considered a near miracle in the Third World, where authoritarianism and dictatorships have prevailed for decades. India's democracy is highly popular: the average Indian cherishes his vote and the power it brings. Some analysts think elections have helped keep the poor, heterogeneous country together since independence.

But India's democracy, and the stability it has enjoyed, has been built on virtual single-party rule: that of the Congress, dominated for most of its post-war life by the Nehru-Gandhi family. The Congress's standing has been badly eroded by time, its mistakes, and since 1991, the death of Rajiv Gandhi.

For 30 years, Indians trusted only the Congress to lead India. The came a middle period when the electorate kicked it out of power to punish it for corruption or high-handedness – in 1977 and 1989 – only to call it back fairly soon. Today's Congress is a shadow of its previous self.

What this means is that politics is becoming a free-for-all. State governments are changing with dizzying rapidity and no one is sure what kind of government will lead India in the future. Most importantly, to gain power, political parties are pitching their campaigns to the country's various subgroups: the different religions, various castes and subcastes. They are playing on the disaffection of people in a period of social change – and the result might be serious divisions in a country with numerous fault lines, particularly religion and caste.

Religion is one of the most divisive areas of society. Hinduism is the religion of 82 percent of India's population. Islam is followed by 12 percent. When the country was partitioned in 1947, at least a half million people were killed in savage fighting between Hindus and Muslims. Other religions include Christianity, Sikhism, Buddhism and Jainism.

The Bharatiya Janata Party, or BJP, Congress's main rival, represents itself as the champion of the Hindus and accuses the Congress of being partial to the Muslims. The issue that raised the party to national popularity was a 16th-century mosque in the town of Ayodhya in central India. The BJP claimed it had been built on the birthsite of the Hindu god Rama, replacing a pre-existing Hindu temple. On 6 December 1992, BJP leaders led a group of militants to Ayodhya, who razed the mosque. The action stunned the nation: it was the first example of a national political party publicly participating in violence against the Muslims to gain votes. It prompted weeks of rioting that reminded many of partition. But it solidified the BJP as the party of choice for many Hindus.

Society: Caste is the other fault line. An ancient Hindu distinction between levels of society – derived from an individual's karma, or goodness in a previous life – caste is an essential component of Indian society and a major part of every Indian's self-identity. It is so pervasive that it is found even among Indian Muslims, Christians and Sikhs. Initially, India had four principal castes, which evolved into about 3,000 castes and over 25,000 subcastes.

Caste was outlawed by the constitution in

government went along with the job quotas.

The socialistic economic system was almost a caste system on its own: only certain people could set up businesses or factories; only the nod of the government above could make someone rich. The new India will be a country of economic growth, entrepreneurship and, inevitably, social mobility. This will loosen old social bonds and beliefs, posing enormous challenges to individuals and to a leadership trying to hold the country together.

Divide to rule: The danger is that politicians, as they are wont to do everywhere, will stir this bubbling pot in search of votes from various groups. Communalism and separatism have been threats to India since 1947 and the country

1950, but it continues to determine the function and status of a very large majority of the population. Increasingly, it plays a role in politics. The Janata Dal party, the third-most important in the country, started using the issue to gain votes from the numerous "backward castes" in 1990. It declared itself in favour of quotas for these backwards castes in government jobs and collages. In response, young middle-class Indians rioted and about a dozen burnt themselves in protest suicides. Nonetheless, the lower caste vote is so vitally important that the Congress

<u>Left</u>, computer control in a nuclear power station. <u>Above</u>, turning the wheels of industry.

has absorbed major challenges, such as the Dravidian independence movement of the 1960s. But that was when India was a young nation with strong prime ministers like Nehru and Mrs Gandhi, and there was strong belief in the ideals of socialism, secularism and democracy. These are less certain days, and many foresee a new phase of chronic instability.

Of course, change also brings hope, as those software engineers in Bangalore demonstrate. The dangers of such change are great – but so is the potential in 900 million people integrating with the rest of the world, bettering their lives and no longer looking on the modern world with contempt.

PEOPLE

To reflect upon the Indian people is to try to make sense of a variegated multitude. Brown, black or yellow, sinewy and lean, square and stocky, or softly rounded with a good lifestyle and lineage, nothing could bind such a variety together except the fact that they are all true Indians.

Flux is the essence of India, flux unfolding against a background of invasions and migrations which brought to the country people of varied looks and habits. Bounded by mountain and ocean, the subcontinent was a cul-de-sac, enticing streams of people through passes in its northern mountains but deterring major southward movement through uncharted waters.

Four major racial groups met and merged in India, producing men of different hue and stature. The pale-skinned Europoid entered from the western mountain passes, encountering settled populations of Dasyu, the dark-skinned ones of Rig Vedic description. Proof of initial fusion is evident in lingam (phallus) worship, which is a symbol of fertility in Aryan rites and traceable to Dravidian culture. The presence of people with Caucasoid features but dark skins in southern India where the Dasyu were eventually pushed is further evidence of the intermingling.

The Aryans dominated the northwest and the Gangetic plain, but the Himalayan region and the highlands of the northeast were the home of populations of Mongoloid descent. Their affinity with the Southeast Asian world was strongly marked and emerges today in their small-statured, slant-eyed offspring.

Though the Mongoloid people influenced the racial pattern of tribes in Orissa and Bihar, they stayed within central India. Splay-nosed southerners in peninsular India might have had a link with Negroid racial elements, as deduced from contemporary populations with dark skins and tightly curled hair. But the only true Negrito are isolated in the Andaman Islands, who have few links with the mainland.

The dovetailing and mingling of races did as much to looks as it did to the way of life. One must move then, from observing the physically

different people to understanding the traditions each race brought. Language encompassed diverse culture and identity, but geography and environment encouraged coexistence; the result was an ethnic and linguistic pattern of unparalleled complexity.

The folk regions of Madhyadesh, Chattisgarh and Bundelkhand in north and central India developed distinct literary traditions. The territory of Madhyadesh is today associated with the languages of eastern and western Hindi, Punjabi, Pahari and Rajasthani. Language welded together what is today a political region, the Hindi-speaking heartland whose uniform voting pattern can influence the political ambitions of vote-seeking politicians.

Political regions sometimes overlook internal differences of speech which mark off groups from each other. In the Hindi zone, speech separates upper castes and untouchables, signalling social separation. In South India, omnipresent caste divorces Brahmin dialect from non-Brahmin and both from untouchables.

For all the confusion, the 225 dialects identified by the expert, Grierson, in 1928, trace their origin to four major language families.

The Indo-European group concentrated as dialects of northwest India and the Gangetic plains, share a linguistic pool with modern French, English, Greek and Iranian, indicative of migrations of Europoid people.

The Dravidian language family consists of 23 languages, but only the four major ones form the basis of the southern states of India. Tamil is spoken in Tamil Nadu, Telugu in Andhra Pradesh, Kannada in Karnataka and Malayalam in Kerala. All four possess independent scripts and literary histories dating from the pre-Christian era, a lineage which is jealously guarded against intrusions from the Hindi-speaking north.

Scattered through the highlands of eastern and central India are the languages of the Austro-Asiatic family, spoken largely by tribal groups of Ho, Oraon, Munda and Santhal. However, many of the dialects with only oral traditions were lost to the more dominant intruders. In Orissa some tribes now address all "superior" beings, whether gods or administrators, not in their own tongue but in Oriya, the mainstream language. The presence of these languages in

Preceding pages: heavy goods vehicles, Indian style; Kashmiri bride and Rajasthani gent. Left, Muslim hawker in Bombay.

isolated mountain and jungle havens reflects a long history of retreat in the face of intruders. Rare tribespeople like the Birhor of Bihar might still steal away into their diminished forest refuge at the first sign of a motorcar.

Less than 1 percent of modern India's population speak languages of the Tibeto-Burman family. But the protection that geography and, later, political policy, afforded to the Mizo, Nagal, Lushia and Khasi, to name a few tribes, strengthened their sense of identity and sustained their ethnological and linguistic links with Tibet and Southeast Asia. Even Christian missionaries contributed. The lexicography, grammar and spelling of Khasi was standardised when the missionaries translated and published the Bible. Standardisation gave an impetus to the growth of a written literary tradition which culminated in Khasi being officially recognised at the university level, complete with the beneficence of state grants.

Conquests and conversions, migrations and resettlements, generated divergences within the same language family. Twenty-three major and minor dialects evolved from the Dravidian pool. But other processes reduced structural dissonance between languages of different families, in phonology, syntax and grammar, creating a situation where modern north-Indian languages are more similar to Dravidian languages than to Indo-Aryan languages outside the subcontinent. Marathi (Indo Aryan) and Kannada (Dravidian) switch codes with an ease born of long practice and intimate contact.

The modern-day Dravidian languages have adapted; all of them are used for basic courses in science and the arts. The new technological terminology is based either on indigenous linguistic material in Tamil or coined from Sanskrit models.

The caste system: Sanskrit not only provided a literary model but also a pan-Indian cultural one. The early Sanskrit text, the Rig Veda, expounded the Hierarchical division of socity into four *varna* (castes). The *varna* scheme conceived society as originating from a single source, the living body of a gigantic primordial "Code Man" who was possessed of the most powerful of coded substances, the words of the Veda. After producing a set of male and female genera by dividing himself in half, the Code Man generated four named and ranked classes or *varna*, each ascribed with a particular occupation and code of conduct. Brahmins (the priestly caste) were generated from his mouth, Kshatriyas (the warrior caste) from his arms, Vaishyas from his loins and Shudras from his feet.

Implicitly, the legend conceives of the four as interdependent; the well-being of the whole rests on the occupational exchanges made among the *varna*. The Vaishyas' code enjoins him to produce and accumulate wealth by trade, cultivation and rearing livestock. Unlike the three higher *varna,* the Shudra was not encoded with distinct occupational substances. His code, born of his lowly origin, was to render bodily service to the higher castes in exchange for maintenance.

While the *varna* scheme is the formal model of reference, and of legend, the social units of everyday life are the *jati,* defined as collectivities which reproduce their own kind. The *jati* scheme encompassed diversities of culture and religion, race and language, allowing their coexistence, and encouraging their interdependence. It affords a dynamic and mobile society of proliferating social groups which formed in response to a variety of circumstances. Each group had an occupation and a social milieu; and each found a niche within the order. But the order was not the static structure of *varna;* it is the living flux of *jati,* where power and wealth jostle with myth and text. The legitimacy of regarding a barber and sweeper as inferior rests upon the cultural notions of *dharma,* the prescribed code of conduct that ranks the groups along a scale of polluted to pure.

Powerful notions of pure and impure underlie interactions between *jati,* carefully governing exchanges of food, restricting marriages to within the group and regulating occupations of individuals, lest they affect the *dharma* of the *jati.*

The selection of a marriage partner is of immense concern for it is an event when two lineage groups merge. The alliance enhances the status of each or, conversely, degrades it. In village and city the caste of a possible partner is the first to be ascertained; only subsequently do astrology and gifts, temperament and looks, play a role in making the perfect union.

An individual, then, can be a real threat to the group, for the *jati* will share the shame of incorrect behaviour or improper sexual alliance by the individual. Thus the most important moments of an individual's life cycle are birth and marriage, events which incorporate people into groups, and these are stictly regulated by rite and prescription. The most urbanised of people will forbid their daughters to be wed in anything other than a red sari, an age-old attire mentioned in 7th-century Tamil texts.

Assimilation: The stress at every level is upon inclusion and incorporation of individuals into groups identified by *jati*, language or, crucially, by religion. India has for centuries given shelter to most of the major religions of the world, accommodating their proliferating sects through its ever-elastic caste system.

Hindus were quite willing to overlook the alien origins of people who might have wanted to graft themselves on Hindu society so long as such grafting took place over a sufficiently long period of time and was enmeshed with caste. Converts to different religions often

the "outside" and those which grew as movements within the overall order of Hinduism.

Buddhism and Jainism were early religious and social movements which revolted against a rigid caste structure and against Brahminical predominance within it. Buddhism was perceived as an assertion of Kshatriya power against Brahmin supremacy. Pali, the widely spoken language of the masses became a vehicle of protest against elitist, Brahminic Sanskrit. Jainism found support among the trading caste. Neither movement severed their links with Hinduism; rather they espoused some of its central principles.

More modern movements such as the Brahmo Samaj and Arya Samaj were cast in similar

continue to maintain their caste links and sometimes never entirely relinquish their Hindu beliefs. Modern-day Mazbhis of Punjab, who are adherents of the Sikh faith, recognise the primacy of their caste origin (sweeper) in intermarriages with sweepers who converted to Christianity. Though the bride wears white, a vermilion spot on her forehead symbolises her married status in a traditionally Hindu way.

Schisms and sects combined with caste to complicate matters. But it is necessary to distinguish between religions which came from

reform-seeking moulds. The rationalist philosophy of the Brahmo Samaj and the evangelical fervour of the Arya Samaj's *shuddi* conversions were western, Christian accretions; but explanation was sought from within Hindu philosophy as well. The bile of revolt was absorbed as reform, not expelled as rivalry.

In sharp contrast came the proselytising religions of the outside, particularly Islam and Christianity. Both were backed by highly articulate traditions and rich and varied civilisations which rivalled Hindu society and culture. More crucially, both were associated with ruling powers of long tenure.

In Punjab, the entrance hall of invasions, the

Left, Parsi (Zoroastrian) in stained glass, Bombay. **Right**, venerable Sikh.

impact of Islam was strong and deep. Here, Hindu dress disappeared even among women, who are thought to be the repositories of tradition. The sari was dropped in favour of the Islamic salwar-kameez. The rivalry between the stitched clothing of the Muslim and the unstitched draped garments of the Hindu was an expression in daily life of competing notions of civilised propriety. For years Hindu tailors were rare and even today some of the most skilful in north India are Muslims.

A mingling of cultures: With the rivalry, however, there were also strong undercurrents of interaction. Two cultures mingled to evolve a new identity epitomised in the emergence of Hindustani, a language based on Hindi and

Punjabi Jat employer does not speak the same tongue. They both understand the intricacies of soil, seed and weather and the urgency of crop cycles; the rest is not for them.

The rhythms of the agricultural cycle sustain the community of peasants both materially and morally. Because food is thought to make up the physical and moral fibre of an individual, its production and consumption are classified and ritualised. The physical processes of sowing, nurturing and harvesting which occur through the agricultural year are inextricably linked with the calendar of social and ceremonial activity of the community.

The act of harvesting is imbued with notions of prosperity and growth; marriages, which

Urdu, which is spoken in much of north India.

The principle of accommodation, of finding common ground, is most evident in rural society in which 80 percent of India's population lives. Agriculture and the growing of food provide a set of common experiences for a majority of rural folk. Overloaded trains with people clinging to roofs and doorways moving from Bihar in the east to Punjab and Haryana in the west bear testimony to the fact that Indians still find major outlets for employment in agriculture. The maintenance of separate identities receives a jolt in the face of an overwhelming demand for labour. It matters naught to a man of Ahir *jati* from eastern Uttar Pradesh that his

augment the household, are arranged in this monetarily lush and ritually auspicious period.

Inter-caste cooperation: The other face of caste which rests not only on hierarchy and separation but also on cooperation reveals itself in village society. Because occupations are specific to groups and prohibited for others, the exchange of services is the fulcrum of society. The *jajmani* of rural India is such a system. It links households of artisans with households of patrons in relations which are hereditary but alienable and which extend beyond the merely economic. The barber cuts his patron's hair, and acts as a marriage go-between for the patron's daughter. The sobbing wail of the barber's wife is the first public announcement of death in the patron's household. In return the patron is obligated to pay the barber in money and in a share of grain and fodder at each harvest, assist the barber in marriage and death rituals in his household, and share food with him on ritual occasions in acknowledgement of the barber's inclusion in the ongoing cycle of the patron's life.

The power of the patron to command the services and loyalties of his clients accrues as much from his ritual status as member of a higher caste as from his control over secular sources of dominance. In agrarian society, control of land supports dominance and can even be a lever up the ritual ladder. Hierarchies are

propagated on an interplay between ritual status and secular power. Merely a higher caste status is insufficient for heading the hierarchy. In Punjabi, the Bhaman (Brahmin) is a figure of ridicule; deference is displayed to the real power-holders, the landholding Jats.

For decades, the Brahmins of South India, the Iyers and Iyengars of Tamil Nadu, Nambudris of Kerala, and the Madhawas of Mysore, deftly manipulated the bureaucracy, politics and education to reinforce their ritual status, achieving a virtual stranglehold on society.

Far left, gipsy from Western India; **left**, tribal from the northeast. **Above**, a Brahmin.

People of lower *jati* adopted Brahminical ways in a bid to climb the ladder, for it was Brahmins who set the mores by which rank was judged. *Jati* beginning the arduous climb upwards shun meat, prohibit widowed daughters from remarrying and try to gain entrance into temples. The nearer they are allowed to approach the *sanctum sanctorum*, the purer they are considered to be. An enormous movement among non-Brahmin castes, protesting against Brahmin dominance in Tamil Nadu, focused upon the issue of temple entry, arousing passions on both sides to fever pitch.

The Kammas and the Reddis, peasant castes of Andhra, could more easily claim ritual purity, for few could resist their power. But the very low caste of Adi Dravidas in Tamil Nadu, with virtually no resources, faced a brutal backlash when they tried to adopt high-caste practices.

The attempts to prove status are of great concern for an individual's circle of interaction and the doors that readily open for him depend upon the group to which he belongs. The British census officials opened a virtual Pandora's box by trying to record the caste status of each group; claims and counter-claims clogged the courts of local magistrates, caste myths and genealogies were speedily requisitioned and Brahmins bribed to preside over life-cycle rites as proof of purity.

Placing the stranger: Over the years the concern has not vanished. It is difficult for a newcomer to be accepted until he has been "placed" and identified with a group. The perennial question, "From where you are, please?", "What is your native place?", and so on through a gamut of extraordinary constructions is not a mere gambit to keep a conversation from flagging. They are of intense interest, for the name of a man's village, town or locality reveals a great deal to the knowledgeable. Wonderfully elaborate names such as Thirumalai Kunnavakam Annantanpillai are an encyclopedia of information on a man's region, village, *jati*, lineage, father's name and of course his own identity.

Placing the newcomer will elicit the proper response because people's behaviour towards each other depends upon their respective positions in the social hierarchy. Less than proper conduct towards a guest signals a deliberate insult towards his group, and the onus is upon the insulted to fathom the reason for their fall.

Towns and cities stir up men's lives, accelerating the pace of change, and do a great deal to break down barriers. Who knows the caste of co-passengers in overcrowded Bombay buses? Distances are maintained when people are known quantities; amorphous urban contact undermines strictly defined relations.

But custom does not easily dissipate. A Keralite's mania for cleanliness travels with him. A Tamil will not only wash himself but douse his home and shop with meticulous thoroughness every evening. Nor do identities disappear. India's minority religious groups tend to be highly urbanised, reflecting tradition with its roots in history. The pattern of Muslim rule was to control the countryside from cities and forts. The present-day urban Muslim reflects a political tradition as well as the fact that many urban Muslims were, and are, craftsmen concentrated in old political centres.

Since they have for centuries lived an urban life the city Muslims, especially the literati, adhere to traditional form-bound lives rather than tension-filled ones. Jains and Parsis, enriched through commerce, are extremely important communities in the cities of Gujarat and Maharashtra. The pale-skinned Parsis, who sought sanctuary in India from the 10th century onwards, though distinct in looks and speech, found parallels at various levels with Hindu ideology. The cult of fire worship, beliefs in the protective powers of spirits (*Pitarah*, the Parsi guardian spirit, and *Pitr*, the benevolent ancestor of Hindu thought) were the source of tolerant acceptance of each other.

Acceptance and tolerance do not dissolve the need to belong. Urban space reflects the need in its clustered ghettos; in Delhi, the Muslim Jama Masjid lies cheek by jowl with Hindu Chandni Chowk. Refugees displaced from Sind or East Bengal settled together in suburban colonies.

The knots of tradition are loosened but do not slip away. Newspaper columns replace aunts and barbers as marriage go-betweens; the medium is new, the form as old as memory. Only a handful of matrimonial advertisements carry the magic phrases "Caste no bar", "No dowry required". The children of mixed marriage cull looks and habits from both groups but formally acknowledge one.

Norms and traditions are more consciously attacked by modern politics. The patron-client link is challenged by institutions of secret ballots and "reserved constituencies", where, by constitutional decree, candidates must belong to lower castes. They encourage attempts to

overthrow or displace the right of patrons to bank upon the unquestioned support of dependent castes. But the challenge is Janus-faced. While in the political arena, vertical caste links have lost some vitality, the horizontal links have gained in strength and significance with *biradari* (brotherhood) confronting *jajmani* (the traditional hierarchical interdependence between castes).

Demographic pressure encourages movement and migration, and the incoming stranger is quite distinct from the "native." Political issues of space and jobs simmer beneath aggressively couched cultural movements of "sons of the soil" or vernacular chauvinism. Traditional authority patterns which equate

age with wisdom confront a demographic expansion of under 25-year-olds, reflected in the changing face of votes and their wrinkle-free political leaders.

Women and untouchables: These two groups symbolise both the stability of tradition and the processes of change within Indian society. Traditionally, both groups were ranked below men of the three "pure" *varna*. Neither could directly approach God but worshipped their *swami* (lord), the "twice-born" male who mediated their access to God. But for all their impurities, or perhaps because of them, women and untouchables can act as bridges between two well-defined states of being.

In the early days after death, the funeral rites are presided over by lower caste men who assist in the incorporation of the lonely, wandering ghost in the realm of benevolent ancestors, meanwhile staving off the harm that ghosts can unleash upon the living. All over India, women transplant rice, when the plant is neither in its clearly defined state of seed nor in the fully matured plant.

Yet neither group is untouched by change. The caste of leatherworkers reviewed their low status when prosperity encompassed their ranks. The fervour for reform ignited the *Ad dharmi* (true religion) movement, transforming a diffuse group into a demanding, cohesive entity which was not easily ignored.

face the fact of its own intrinsic brutality.

The influence of women is largely ignored, for it is scarcely conscious. But the child's first world-view is imparted to him by the females of his home, and encompasses a dynamic tradition. Amazement is often expressed at the simultaneous participation of Indians in highly technological society and their involvement with traditional values and forms of living. A man educated in the United States will still seek an Indian bride through traditional channels. But in the Indian environment one's whole socialisation makes one adept at switching between contexts without any apparent disjunction.

The modern Indian is not a rootless person;

Mahila Mandals, the women's wings of political parties, are no longer token gestures toward the second sex. Urban activists agitating against confining notions of womanhood gather support in tenements and suburbs, among housewives and tellers in banks, washerwomen and weavers. A social order which still, from time to time, witnesses the smothering of newborn girls and the burning of young brides unable to satisfy the illegal dowry demands of their in-laws, is forced, by sari-clad agitators burning with their own passion for justice, to

Left, a Gharwali; above, woman from Tamil Nadu; and right, Jain nuns.

he is firmly anchored in the culture of his daily life. Coping with endless levels and unending divisions is hard. But there is also the power of Tirupati, a pilgrim centre in South India, and Vaishno Devi, in the far north, to excite and energise pilgrims from all over India; or Punjabi farmers throwing their political weight behind a leader from Maharashtra. The whole notion of *sangam*, confluence, merging, meeting, reverberates through Indian cultural perception.

A delightful legend points the way for such pilgrimages; every year the Ganga, in the guise of a black cow, takes a dip in the Kaveri, the holy river of South India, and, thus renewed, wends her way back to her proper place.

Religion is an integral part of the total Indian tradition. Four of the world's major faiths have met on Indian soil: Hinduism, Buddhism, Christianity and Islam. The first two of these were born in India. In addition, India gave birth to Jainism, Sikhism and countless minor cults and regional sects. India has also played host to Jews and Zoroastrians. A survey of Indian religions provides fascinating glimpses of the colourful, variegated pattern of Indian life and culture.

In prehistoric times: There was a time when historians looked upon the Aryans, who came to India in the second millennium BC, as the founders of the Indian cultural tradition. But recent archeological studies have changed the picture. It is now realized that pre-Aryan elements have played an important part in shaping religious attitudes and practices. The term "pre-Aryan" denotes the indigenous inhabitants of India, usually referred to as Dravidians, and the people of the Indus Valley, to whom the Dravidians were probably related.

Little is known about the religion of the Dravidians who lived mostly in central and southern India. They worshipped images of the Mother or Goddess, and of several animal deities. Their fertility and funerary rites seem to have been similar to those performed in other Middle Eastern civilisations.

We are on surer ground when we turn to the Indus Valley culture which flourished between 3500 and 2500 BC. This was a predominantly urban civilisation, the two main cities being Harappa and Mohenjodaro. As many of the important archeological finds came from Harappa, the Indus Valley culture is also known as Harappan culture.

Excavations have yielded a large number of terracotta figurines and clay seals bearing inscriptions. A few steatite (soapstone) and metal statuettes have also been found. The inscriptions have not yet been deciphered, but enough evidence has been gathered to suggest that many features of later Hinduism were anticipated by the Harappans. One of the statuettes shows a man meditating in a typically yogic posture. Figures of ascetics, standing rigidly, point to a world-negating attitude. The worship

Left, the Rath (chariot) Festival at Puri, Orissa.

of images, probably in temples, seems to have been popular. One of the images, which appears on many clay seals, is that of a god carrying a three-pronged weapon, surrounded by an elephant, a tiger and other animals. This figure has been described as "proto-Shiva" because it anticipates many features of Pashupati (Lord of the Beasts), a form of Shiva still worshipped several centuries later in many Hindu temples. The extreme conservatism of the Indus Valley culture suggests a theocratic state in which the temple dominated the court.

Historians differ regarding the causes which led to the decline of the Indus civilisation, but it can hardly be doubted that the final blow was delivered by invaders belonging to the Aryan tribes whose migrations from their original home, perhaps somewhere in southern Russia, were destined to alter the face of the civilised world. The arrival of the Aryans or rather the Indo-Aryans, as distinct from other branches of the Aryan family, marks the beginning of the religious tradition known historically as Hinduism.

Hinduism: "A museum of religions": that seems to be the only way to describe Hinduism. No other religious tradition is so eclectic, so diversified in its theoretical premises, as well as its practical expressions. It is the only major religion which has not been traced to a specific founder, and the only one which does not have a "holy book" as the one and only scriptural authority. One may regard the *Rig Veda* as one's personal "Bible," or one may turn to the *Upanishads*, or the *Bhagavad Gita*; or one may dispense with all sacred texts and still claim to be a good Hindu. One may worship Vishnu or Shiva or some other gods or goddesses; or one may not worship any deity and meditate on the Supreme Spirit dwelling within one's own heart. Some Hindus visit temples for prayer, worship or devotional music; others prefer sacrificial ritual, or bathe in holy rivers, or go on pilgrimages; still others regard all rituals as redundant. The same flexibility can be seen in Hindu theories of creation or the nature of God.

Hinduism thrives on contrasts. At one end is the most abstruse metaphysical speculation about Ultimate Reality; at the other there are popular cults based on the propitiation of tree-spirits and animal deities. Absolute monism goes hand in hand with extreme pluralism. On the one hand, Hinduism accepts the validity of many paths leading to the same goal, and is willing to recognise the divinity of the prophets of other religions. But along with this tolerance one sees rigid adherence to caste distinctions and custom-ridden practices.

This pluralistic approach, while hampering precision and homogeneity, gives Hinduism its amazing popular appeal and makes the Hindu tradition rich and colourful. The Hindu temple, which became increasingly elaborate with the passage of centuries, serves as the nucleus of the social and aesthetic, no less than the religious life of the community. Temple walls are adorned with sculptures, often painted. In the

A feature of Indian religious life is the presence of numbers of *sadhus* (wandering hermits). They are ubiquitous and can be seen in cities and villages, in the forests, on the banks of rivers and, of course, in the Himalaya. Usually dressed in yellow or ochre robes, with their bodies smeared with ash and foreheads anointed with sandal-paste, the *sadhus* carry all their worldly possessions with them: a bowl, a staff, a blanket. Some move alone, others in small groups. Some have taken vows of silence, others preach or chant hymns, sometimes bursting suddenly into songs of religious ecstasy. One is not supposed to ask questions about their homes or destinations. They are simply eternal wanderers.

courtyards, sacred poems are recited, hymns are chanted, dances are performed. All these show infinite variety of style, mood, theme and atmosphere.

Hindu festivals and ceremonies: There are 360 Hindu festivals, an average of one a day. (The Hindu calendar is lunar, with 30 days in each month.) There are festivals and ceremonies associated not only with gods, goddesses and heroes but also with the sun and the moon, stars and planets, rivers, lakes, oceans, animals, trees and flowers. Bazaars spring up, street-shows are put on by itinerant entertainers, ancient ballads are sung, leaders of different Hindu sects are taken out in procession.

The continuity and variety of Hinduism can be best appreciated by tracing its development.

The Vedic Age: The Indus Civilisation was on its last legs when the Aryans came into India. They brought with them a new language, Sanskrit, which they moulded into a remarkably versatile medium for the expression of sublime thoughts and rich images. Thrilled by the grandeur of the Himalaya and by the luxuriance of Indian forests and river valleys, the Aryans poured out their joy, their sense of mystery, their reverence for the Divine, in beautiful hymns and prayers. These have been collected in the four *Vedas* (Sanskrit root *vid*, "to know"). The most important is the *Rig Veda*.

The Vedic hymns, composed between 1600 and 1000 BC, were addressed to gods and goddesses who were regarded as personifications of the powers of nature: Indra, god of rain and thunder; Prajapati, "Lord of the Creatures"; Agni, god of the sacred fire; the Maruts, gods of winds and storms; Savitr, the sun god; Ushas, goddess of dawn; and Varuna, god of the sea and upholder of the moral law. The hymns are believed to have been composed by *rishis* (sages) who were divinely inspired. Hence they are known as *shruti* ("heard"), as distinguished from *smriti* ("remembered").

The Vedas are regarded as the fountainhead of Hinduism. they contain ideas and suggestions that have shaped the entire Hindu tradi-

perfection, the concept that the man of wisdom must combine the intellectual clarity of the philosopher with the faith of the sage and the aestheticism of the artist.

Lighting the sacred flame: On its practical side, Vedic religion consisted mainly of sacrificial ritual. The sacred flame was kindled in the center of a raised platform. The sacrificer offered oblations to the flame while the priest chanted hymns and invocations. In the centuries that followed, the mystical and symbolic meaning of the *yajna* (sacrifice) receded into the background. The ritual became all-important and increasingly conventional. Every detail had to be meticulously followed: the kindling of the fuel, the shape of

tion and show a tendency to move from pluralism to monism. Although different gods were worshipped, they were increasingly seen as manifestations of a single Divine Principle. The Vedic concept of *rita* (cosmic law) points to a single rhythmic force animating the entire universe. This led to deep feeling for the close kinship between man and nature which has always characterised Indian life. Also, by combining religion with philosophy and poetry, the Vedas initiated a typical Hindu concept of

Left, images of Hindu deities on rocks in the River Ganga at Hardwar. **Above**, Hindu ascetic at peace – coins and flowers presented in homage.

the vessel containing the holy water, the exact intonation of the words. The Brahmins, who had the expertise for performing this complicated ritual, became the dominant class of society.

The *Upanishads* (800 to 400 BC) represent a reaction against this decline in values. They are dialogues between teachers and disciples and are regarded as a continuation of the *Vedas* and hence a part of *shruti*. The monistic trend in the Vedas is developed to the point where Reality, in its essential nature, is declared to be absolutely one. By implication, multiplicity is illusory. The human soul is identical with the Absolute. Viewed objectively, as pure, all-pervasive Being, Reality is described as *Brahman*. Viewed subjectively, as the essence of our own existence, it is called *Atman*. The Absolute (Brahman-Atman) cannot be known through reason. It can only be experienced through intuition, though reason can prepare us for the supreme vision.

The most popular text in the Vedic tradition is the *Bhagavad Gita* ("Song of God"). Although it is a part of the *Mahabharata*, an epic poem which belongs to a much later period, the *Bhagavad Gita* (usually shortened to the *Gita*) is strongly influenced by the *Upanishads*. "The *Upanishads* are the cows," says a famous Sanskrit couplet, "and the *Gita* is the sweet, nourishing milk which the cows yield." Mahatma Gandhi once described the *Gita* as his "spiritual dictionary".

The *Mahabharata* revolves around the conflict between the five Pandava brothers and their cousins, the Kauravas, who had wrongly usurped the kingdom. Krishna, an incarnation of God, became the advisor of Arjuna, the commander of the Pandava army. On the eve of battle Arjuna was beset with doubt and refused to fight against his kith and kin. In this dramatic setting, Krishna gave him a discourse on the immortality of the soul and his obligation to fulfil his *dharma* (sacred duty).

Krishna's discourse, with occasional questions from Arjuna, covers almost every aspect of human life. The *Gita's* tremendous appeal derives from its earnestness, optimism and tolerance. There is something in it for everyone. The *Gita* accepts the validity of three different paths leading to the common goal of self-realisation: the path of *Jnana* (Knowledge), the path of *Bhakti* (Devotion and Love), and the path of *Karma* (Work). These correspond to the intellectual, the emotional and the practical sides of human nature. In addition, the "special path," the path of *Yoga*, is also recognised. For 2,000 years, millions of people have derived hope and consolation from the *Gita's* simple message: Work without attachment, dedicating the fruit of your work to the Divine. Krishna says to Arjuna: "Whichever path you tread, you can reach me. Offer me but a flower, a fruit, even a leaf, or a little water. I will accept it if you come to me with a pure and loving heart."

Hindu mythology: In India, mythology has always been very close to the actual life of the people. It has performed the important function of transforming abstract philosophical concepts and ethical ideals into concrete realities, strengthened by the sanction of religion. There are hundreds of myths about gods, goddesses, heroes, sages, demons, and natural phenomena like the sun and the moon, lakes, rivers, mountains, trees, flowers and animals. These myths are picked up and remembered even by people who have had no formal education. They are kept alive through fairs and festivals, and the daily round of religious ritual, during which myths are celebrated in folk songs, folk plays and dances. In classical Indian music and dance, too, mythology provides the main motifs.

Hindu mythology begins with the Vedas, but Vedic deities gradually lost some of their

importance – not that the Vedic gods like Indra and Varuna were forgotten, but other gods, Rama and Krishna in particular, became more popular. Vishnu and Shiva, who were minor deities in the Vedas, became predominant in the later Hindu pantheon.

The two great epic poems, *Ramayana* and *Mahabharata*, are a treasure-house of mythology. Stories from these epics, and other myths derived from various sources, were later elaborated in a literature known as the *Puranas*. Of these, the *Shiva Purana*, the *Vishnu Purana* and the *Bhagavata* are especially important since they contain myths of Shiva, Vishnu and Krishna respectively.

discard this illusion. He did not, however, reject the Universal Spirit of Self *(Atman)* of the *Upanishads*.

The Buddha's first sermon contains an excellent summary of his teaching. It is called the Sermon of the Middle Way, in which he offers a balanced, harmonious view of life, steering between two sets of extremes: on the ethical plane, the extremes of self-indulgence and asceticism; and on the philosophical plane, the extremes of naive acceptance of everything as real and the total denial of everything as unreal.

The Buddhist religion rests upon the Four Noble Truths enunciated in the first sermon. These truths are: (i) suffering is universal, (ii) suffering is caused and sustained by *trishna*

("thirst", craving), (iii) suffering *can* be prevented and overcome, (iv) there is a *way* leading to the removal of suffering. The fourth "noble truth" spells out the practical side of the Buddha's teaching. The Middle Way now becomes the "Eightfold Path of the good life", consisting of right conduct, right motive, right resolve, right speech, right livelihood, right attention, right effort and right meditation.

By following this path of many-sided restraint and self-perfection, one can conquer craving. Then one is within sight of Nirvana,

Above, a Sikh priest reading the *Guru Granth*, the Sikh scripture.

the transcendental state of complete emancipation. Being by its very nature beyond the sphere of phenomenal experience, Nirvana cannot be defined or described. Asked what Nirvana was like, the Buddha merely smiled – suggesting, perhaps, that it was blissful. And when pressed hard for an answer, he only said, "*Shantam Nirvanam:* Nirvana is peace, silence."

Buddhism is thus not the gloomy, pessimistic creed that its critics make it out to be. The Buddha begins with suffering but proceeds to the conquest of suffering. Nirvana is not an "afterthought" introduced to mitigate a sorrow-centered world-view. It is basic to Buddhism. "Just as, O Ananda," the Buddha once said, "every drop in the ocean has the taste of salt, so does every word that I have uttered carry the flavour of Nirvana."

Buddhism after the Buddha: Shortly after the Buddha's death, his oldest disciple, Kashyapa, convened a Council at Rajagriha. The Master's teachings were classified into three main sections, known as *Tripitaka* (Three Baskets). These, along with later commentaries, became the scriptures of Buddhism. A century later, another council was convened at Vaishali to sort out the differences that had arisen. In the 3rd century BC the great Mauryan emperor, Ashoka, saddened by the bloodshed of war, became a Buddhist. Ashoka's conversion marked the beginning of the expansion of Buddhism. Ashoka set up inscriptions throughout the vast Indian subcontinent exhorting his subjects to follow the Buddha's message of compassion and tolerance.

Differences between the two main trends in Buddhist thought, later resulting in a schism between Hinayana and Mahayana, first surfaced at the third Council convened by Ashoka at Pataliputra (modern Patna). In Hinayana ("Little Vehicle") the psychological and ethical aspects of the Buddha's teachings are emphasised. Hinayana is also known as Theravada ("Doctrine of the Elders") because its followers claimed that their views had the support of the Buddha's immediate followers. The Mahayana ("Large Vehicle") was more philosophical in its approach. To the Hinayana, the Buddha was the supreme teacher, the man who unravelled the cause of suffering, the man of absolute self-control, the *Arhat* (Conqueror). The followers of Mahayana looked upon the Buddha not merely as a teacher but as a saviour, a Bodhisattva ("Wisdom-Essence") who, not content with attaining enlightenment through insight and self-mastery, dedicated himself to the service of all living beings.

The difference between Hinayana and Mahayana is largely a matter of emphasis. They both claim conformity to the Buddha's teachings. Both accept the basic principles of Impermanence and Causation. They also accept Nirvana as the ultimate goal, and craving as the main obstacle. They derive their inspiration from two different sides of the Buddha's personality. While the Hinayanist glorifies the Buddha's insight and moral perfection, the Mahayanist is stirred by his compassion, love, joy, tranquility and sensitivity to beauty. The profound influence of Buddhism on India's religious consciousness arose from a combination of the two approaches.

Buddhism and Hinduism compared: Buddhism has played a decisive role in moulding India's values and ideas. Yet at one time it was seen as being opposed to Hinduism and as signifying a break in the Indian religious tradition. Actually, the two faiths supplemented each other. The Buddha rejected the infallibility of the Vedas, the supremacy of the Brahmins and some of the external features of Hinduism. But he accepted the basic structure of Hindu thought as expressed in the Law of Karma and Rebirth. Buddhism, like Hinduism, gives priority to experience over thought, and sees a universal rhythmic principle uniting man with nature.

In the first phase of the development of Buddhism, these similarities were overshadowed by the differences in emphasis. But a few centuries after the Buddha's death, the two faiths came close to each other. The Mahayana evolved a concept of Absolute Reality very similar to that in the Upanishads. The Buddha was venerated as a god. Buddhism produced its own mythology. Buddhists adopted Sanskrit in preference to Pali, the dialect in which the Buddha himself had delivered his discourses. It is significant that the great epoch of Brahmanical revival, such as the golden age of the Gupta dynasty (4th and 5th centuries AD), coincided with a splendid blossoming of Buddhist philosophy, art and poetry.

Even in its heyday, Buddhism was not the religion of the majority of Indian people. In the Middle Ages, Buddhism remained dormant in India while it became the dominant religion of Thailand, Cambodia and some other Asian countries. In modern India, there has been a revival of interest in Buddhism.

Yet, Buddhists constitute a very small proportion of the Indian population. This has led some people to assert that India "repudiated" and "banished" Buddhism. But something which has been assimilated until it flows through the very bloodstream of Indian culture cannot be said to have been rejected simply because we cannot see it on the surface. Even when there was an ideological conflict between Hinduism and Buddhism, the Buddha's personality and character attracted the admiration of Hindus and Buddhists alike. The Buddha's emphasis on compassion, love and non-violence has become a permanent part of India's spiritual heritage.

Buddhism has inspired some of the finest architecture, sculpture and painting. The stupas of Sanchi and Amaravati, the frescos of Ajanta, the remains of the university of Nalanda, the monasteries of Buddha-gaya and Rajagriha and, above all, the Buddha images of the Mathura and Sarnath schools – all these bear witness to the fact that the influence of Buddhism has been much more enduring than its numerical strength might lead one to expect.

Jainism: About the same time as the Buddha was preaching his *dharma* and in the same region, another religious tradition was being established. Vardhamana, better known by his title Mahavira ("Great Hero") was an elder contemporary of the Buddha. The two teachers had much in common: both were *Kshatriyas* of royal descent and went through prolonged and rigorous discipline after renouncing the worldly life; both rejected caste barriers and questioned the sacredness of the Vedas. Mahavira's fame has been eclipsed by the Buddha's; Jainism, the religion preached by Mahavira, counts more than 3 million adherents in India today, whereas the Buddha's faith has almost twice as many. Together, they account for barely one percent of religious Indians.

The theme of self-conquest, common to all religions, is supremely important to the Jainas. The very word Jaina is derived from *jina*, conqueror. Carrying the idea of self-conquest to its extreme, Jainism has become the world's most rigourously ascetic faith. God has no place in this system. The popular gods of Hinduism are accepted, but they are placed lower than the *jinas*, who are regarded as the true recipients of worship. Mahavira, though usually accepted as the founder of the faith in the context of history, is said to be the last of a line of 24 *jinas*. All of them are said to have attained perfect wisdom *(Kaivalya)* by vanquishing their desires and breaking their bonds with the material world. The *jinas* are also known as Tirthankaras ("crossing-makers"). The "crossing" refers to the passage from the material to the spiritual realm, from bondage to freedom.

Jainism not only rejects the notion of a Personal God which is assumed by most religions, but also the ideas of a single impersonal Absolute Reality. It regards each living being as an independent *jiva* (soul). In its mundane condition, the soul is permeated by material particles through the working of *karma*. To attain liberation, a double process is necessary: the incursion of new karma-particles must be stopped;

and those that have already tainted the soul must be expelled. This is possible only through right faith, right knowledge and right conduct: the *tri-ratna* (three jewels) of Jainism.

Right conduct is spelled out negatively as the rejection of falsehood, theft, lust, greed and violence. Of these five sins violence is the most heinous. The highest virtue is the total abjuration of any thought or action which can hurt a living being. *Ahimsa paramo dharmah:* "Non violence is the supreme religion" – this Jain motto was adopted by Mahatma Gandhi in the modern age. Sometimes, however, the

Above, *Navjote*, **initiation ceremony for Parsis.**

Jains carry their non violence, like their asceticism, to extreme limits. For instance, Jaina monks are often seen with their nose and mouth covered by a fine cloth mask to ensure that they do not involuntarily "kill" germs while breathing.

Jains have made valuable contributions in many areas of Indian culture: philosophy, literature, painting, sculpture and architecture. Their poetry is often excessively didactic. Their sculpture is of a very high quality, and some of the images of Tirthankaras are technically perfect. Their faces are, however, devoid of any expression, as they are supposed to have transcended all human emotions. The greatest glory of Jaina religious art lies in temple architecture, particularly at Girnar, Palitana and Mount Abu. These temples reveal a breadth of aesthetic sensitivity and a feeling for ornamentation reminiscent of the finest specimens of classical Hindu and Buddhist architecture. It is fortunate that, while building their temples, the Jainas forgot to be solemn!

Opposites together: No two religions in the world appear on the surface to be as dissimilar as Hinduism and Islam. Unlike Hinduism, Islam was founded by a historical person and has a specific scripture, the Quran. Hinduism is eclectic and pluralistic; Islam is homogeneous and has a definite concept of God. Hinduism has the luxuriance of the tropical forests and river valleys; Islam has the simplicity and austerity of the desert. The Hindu temple is enclosed on three sides, and there is an air of mystery in the dark inner sanctum; the Muslim mosque is open on all sides, exposed to light and air. The Hindu worships sculptured images of deities; to the Muslim, idol-worship is the most grievous sin. Hinduism shuns proselytisation; Islam regards conversion of non-Muslims as a meritorious deed.

Yet these two faiths met in India, influenced each other and, after an initial period of confrontation and conflict, accommodated and enriched each other. Within a few decades of their arrival in India, Muslims began to consider India as their home. Between the 13th and the 18th centuries, northern India witnessed a fruitful synthesis of Hindu and Islamic elements in almost every sphere of life and culture.

Muhammad and his creed: Muhammad was born at Makka (Mecca) in 570 AD, a fatherless child. His mother died when he was four. Muhammad's childhood was not a happy one. As a boy, he earned a paltry living doing odd jobs for traders in caravans. He was 25 when he married Khadijah, a wealthy widow who had employed him. Arabia was at that time a battleground for warring tribes. Religion was ridden with superstitions. People worshipped stone images of gods. Muhammad, introspective and sensitive by nature, was distressed by this and often sought solitude in the desert.

He had his first mystical experience at the age of 40. The archangel Gabriel appeared before him in a vision, hailed him as the *Rasul* (Messenger) of God and called upon him to proclaim the glory of Allah, the one true God. Gabriel repeated his message in several dreams. Muhammad was disturbed by the visions. A period of depression followed. Khadijah, the first to believe in the genuineness of the revelations, urged him to proclaim his message publicly. Meanwhile, Gabriel had again appeared in a vision and shown Muhammad a written text which later became a part of the Quran.

As the number of his followers increased, Muhammad became bolder in his denunciation of idolatry. The tribesmen harassed and threatened him. In 622 AD Muhammad left Makka and went to Medina, a town 200 miles to the north, at the invitation of some merchants. The Islamic calendar is dated from this migration *(hijrah)*. In Medina, he consolidated his new religion, Islam ("Submission to God"). His followers, the Muslims "Those Who Have Submitted") now numbered thousands. Eight years later he returned to Makka and defeated his opponents in battle. He died in 632 AD.

Within two decades the Muslims had conquered Iraq, Syria, Egypt and Turkey. By 670 the Arabs were masters of Iran and the whole of northern Africa. In 710 they invaded Spain and penetrated into the south of France. Their success was the result of their faith in the Prophet and the holy book, their strong sense of brotherhood and equality of all Muslims, and the precision and simplicity of their creed. Its success cannot be attributed to force alone. Muhammad himself was a man of deep generosity and wisdom. The God of Islam is Compassionate and Merciful *(Rahman* and *Rahim)*. He is not the God of Vengeance.

The basic injunctions of Islam are summed up in the "Five Pillars": a good Muslim is to assert that "There is no God but Allah, and Muhammad is his Prophet"; to pray, preferably five times a day; to perform acts of charity; to observe a fast from dawn to dusk throughout the month of Ramadan (this is a holy month for Muslims because the Prophet received his divine revelation in this month); and to go on a pilgrimage to Makka at least once during one's lifetime.

Islam in India: Arab traders came to India as early as the 7th century. After that, Muslim invaders made sporadic raids into India from time to time until, at the end of the 12th century, the first Muslim kingdom was established at Delhi. The Muslims gradually extended their rule eastwards and southwards. In the reign of Alauddin Khilji only the southern tip of India remained outside the sphere of Muslim power. The Mughal Empire was founded by Babur in 1506. The greatest among the Mughal emperors was Akbar (1556–1605) whose policy of religious tolerance brought Hindus and Muslims together.

In its first phase, Islamic rule in India was aggressive. But the mystics of Islam, known as Sufis, played an important part in spreading the message of universal love and toning down the aggressive trends in Islam. This message was conveyed most effectively by the classical Persian poets, particularly by Rumi who expressed the spirit of Sufism through beautiful symbols and images. Persian, not Arabic, was the court language during Muslim rule. The Sufi poets were very popular in India throughout the Middle Ages.

Renowned Sufi saints came and settled in India. Among these, Moinuddin Chishti of Ajmer and Nizamuddin Aulia of Delhi were the most influential. Even today festivals in their honour are celebrated annually. Amir Khusrau, poet, musician and historian, was a disciple of Nizamuddin. Khusrau was famous as a poet in the classical Persian tradition, but he also wrote religious poetry in language. The prevalent spirit of Hindu-Muslim integration was reflected admirably in Khusrau's work.

This process of bringing Hinduism and Islam close to each other was continued by two remarkable men: Kabir and Nanak. Born in a Brahmin family, Kabir was brought up by Muslim foster-parents. He was a disciple of Ramananda, a famous Hindu saint, but he was also deeply influenced by Sufism and used Sufi terminology in many of his poems. Inspired by Kabir, Guru Nanak founded the Sikh religion with the avowed purpose of synthesising Hinduism and Islam.

Islam's spirit of brotherhood helped in loosening the rigidity of the caste system. The simplicity and directness of Islam led many Hindus to question the value of conventional rituals. The interaction of the two faiths found aesthetic expression in poetry, music and architecture.

Sikhism: Nanak (1469–1539), the founder of the Sikh faith, belonged to the Punjab, a region where Hindus and Muslims had come in closer contact than in any other part of India. Nanak was attracted, from his childhood, towards Hindu as well as Muslim saints and poets. He visited the sacred places of Hinduism and also made the pilgrimage to Makka. A Hindu by birth and training, his closest companion was a Muslim musician. Inspired by his discovery that the essential

started building the temple at Amritsar which later became the holiest of Sikh shrines. Arjun also systematised the collection of sacred hymns and poems by Nanak, Kabir and other saints. This collection became the scripture of the Sikhs. It is known as *Adi Granth* ("The First Book") or *Granth Sahib* ("Book of the Lord").

The spread of the Sikh faith alarmed orthodox Muslims. The Sikhs were persecuted. Guru Arjun was put to death on a charge of sedition in 1606. Arjun's martyrdom convinced his successors that Sikhs must have military training to defend themselves. The 10th Guru, Govind Singh, transformed the pacifist Sikh sect into a martial community. He introduced rites of initiation into a well-organised Sikh

teaching of both religions was the same, Nanak began to preach his message of unity. He attracted many followers and soon came to be known as Guru Nanak. His disciples came together, and a new religious tradition was born. The term *Sikh* is derived from the Sanskrit work *shishya* (disciple).

Angad, who succeeded Nanak as the Guru of the Sikhs, started compiling the master's writings. He also introduced a script which was already being used by some Punjabis. He called it *Gurmukhi* and made it the official script of the Sikhs. Guru Arjun, the fifth in succession,

Above, Roman Catholic procession in Kerala.

army known as the *Khalsa*. Govind Singh also decided to terminate the succession of gurus. He asked his followers to look upon the *Granth Sahib* as the sole object of veneration. The Holy Book became the symbol of God.

Sikhism is strongly monotheistic. It is opposed to the caste system, and all Sikh men carry the last name "Singh", Idol worship is also rejected. These features show the influence of Islam. But the ideas of *karma* and rebirth are accepted. In their religious life and ritual, Sikhs are very close to the Hindus.

It is not uncommon for a Hindu householder to bring up one of his sons as a Sikh. There are frequent intermarriages between Hindus and

Sikhs. In spite of these similarities, the Sikh community at just 2 percent of the population has evolved its own unmistakable identity. They are tall and well-built; the men all grow beards and wear turbans over their long hair which is never cut. Every Sikh considers it an obligation to wear a *kara* (steel bangle). There are other religious injunctions, like abstaining from tobacco, which are obeyed rigourously.

Christianity: According to a strong tradition prevalent in South India, Christianity in India is as old as Saint Thomas, one of the Apostles of Jesus Christ. The saint is said to have spent a few years near Madras and to have died there. Other legends describe Saint Bartholomew as the first Christian missionary in India. Latin

conquest naturally gave the Anglican Church an advantage over others.

Two remarkable men, William Carey and Alexander Duff, played key roles in establishing Christianity. Carey founded the Seminary at Serampore and was closely associated with the Fort William College at Calcutta. He established the first printing press and the first newspaper in Bengali. Alexander Duff came to India in 1830 and continued Carey's work. Throughout the 19th century, Catholic as well as Protestant missionaries, besides preaching Christian doctrines, made contributions to education and scholarship.

Indian social reformers, like Keshab Chandra Sen of the Brahma Samaj, realised that Chris-

historians in the Middle Ages have made frequent references to Christian settlements in India. Historically, however, Christian missionary activity can be said to have begun with the arrival of Saint Francis Xavier in 1542. His tomb in Goa is still visited by thousands of Catholics every year.

Saint Francis Xavier was succeeded by Portuguese missionaries. Some of them visited Akbar's court, and even entertained the hope of converting the emperor. Other Catholic countries soon began to send missionaries to India. In the 18th century, Protestant missionaries, especially from Denmark, Holland and Germany, started their work in India. The British

tianity had enriched India's religious life in many ways. Ramakrishna lived as a Christian for several months. A Christian poet, Michael Madhusudan-Dutt, is regarded as one of the pioneers of modern Bengali poetry. Significantly, he selected a theme from the Ramayana for his most important poem. Later, Tagore paid homage to Jesus Christ in several poems. Mahatma Gandhi was deeply influenced by Christianity, particularly the New Testament.

Indian Christians, who now number nearly 25 million, are almost every denomination:

Above, interior of a 16th-century synagogue at Cochin, the oldest in India.

Catholic, Methodist, Baptist, Presbyterian, Maronite, Seventh-Day Adventist, and others.

The Parsis: Parsis are the descendants of Persians, who emigrated to India in the 8th century after the Arab conquest of Iran. They brought with them the ancient Persian religion founded by Zoroaster in the 6th century BC. This religion is based on the worship of Ahura Mazda ("Wise Lord") who is eternally in conflict with Ahriman, the Evil Force. The Avesta, which is the scripture of the Parsis, includes the Gathas (songs) composed by Zoroaster.

The Parsis settled down on the western coast of India and adopted the Gujarati language. They have always adhered strictly to their ancient faith. In their agiaries (fire temples) the sacred flame is always kept burning. The Parsis still retain their Iranian physical features: a light olive complexion, an aquiline nose, bright black eyes. They are a rather exclusive community and do not allow non-Parsi inside their temples.

The office of *dastur* (priest) is hereditary. The dasturs are dressed entirely in white, and they are held in great esteem. Although the Parsis are conservative in their religion, they have identified themselves with their fellow-countrymen in other areas. They have contributed to the educational, scientific and industrial progress of India; and in the early phase of Indian nationalism, the Parsi community produced great leaders like Dadabhai Naoroji.

Though their number never exceeded 30,000 in the vast ocean of India's hundreds of millions, India has two ancient indigenous Jewish communities – the Malayalam-speaking Cochinis and the Marathi-speaking Bene Israel (children of Israel). While, obviously, these miniscule groups could hardly influence Indian religious thought even on a local scale, they merit mention as a living illustration of the spirit of accommodation of the Hindus and Muslims among whom these groups have lived for more than a thousand years. Today, migration to Israel, England, the United States and Canada, has reduced the Indian Jewish population to 5,000, who continue to live in security and peace.

Religion in contemporary India: Religion has always had a tremendous hold on the Indian mind. Even today, in spite of the impact of science, technology and materialistic ideologies, religion is a powerful force in Indian life. Mahatma Gandhi, who led India to national independence, was a deeply religious man. In the 20th century, many famous religious leaders established spiritual centers which continue to attract thousands of people. Prominent among them were Sri Aurobindo of Pondicherry, Ramana Maharshi of Tiruvannamalai, Swami Shivananda of Hardwar and Sai Baba of Shirdi. Satya Sai Baba of Puttapuriti in Andhra is perhaps the most popular among living Hindu religious leaders.

In the West, India is often wrongly regarded as the land of the Hindus. We have seen that India has been a meeting ground for all the major religions of the world. Even today, Muslim Sufi saints are venerated all over India. Meher Baba, the "silent sage" of Maharashtra, was a Parsi.

There has been a great revival of interest in Buddhism. Themes from the Buddha's life have inspired modern poets and artists. Yoga has transcended credal affiliations. Every town has a yoga centre and Hindus are not the only ones who come to learn yoga. Religious movements of Indian origin have gained thousands of followers outside India – Iskon Krishna-Consciousness Movement, Transcendental Meditation, Center for Self-Realization and many others.

India is a secular republic. The state has no connection with any particular religion. But the protection of religious minorities is recognised as one of the obligations of the state. The constitution of India guarantees the right of religious freedom to all citizens. By and large, barring incidents of religious conflicts when fanatical elements temporarily gained the upper hand, adherents of different religions have been living together peacefully.

Important festivals of all religions have been recognised as national holidays: Diwali and Holi; Christmas and Easter; Id and Muharram; and the birthdays of the Buddha, Mahavira and Nanak. The three colours of the Indian national flag have religious significance. Orange represents Hinduism, green the colour of Islam, and white represents all the other faiths. And in the beautiful national anthem, composed by Rabindranath Tagore, a tribute is paid to the different religions of India.

Addressing the Divine Power as Bharata-bhagya-vidhata (the "dispenser of India's destiny"), the poet says: "Your call goes out to the Hindus, the Buddhists, the Sikhs, the Jains, the Parsis, the Muslims and the Christians. They all come, gather around your throne, and weave a garland of love for your worship."

On almost every day of the year, there is a festival in some part of India – inevitable perhaps, given the thousands of deities, saints, prophets and gurus named by six major religions who must be worshipped, propitiated, offered thanks or simply remembered.

No dichotomy exists between the sacred and the secular. The vitality of deep religious belief is enhanced by an exuberant celebration of life. Colour and pageant merge with ritual, spontaneous enjoyment with worship. And festivals become important social events: occasions to meet and exchange news, to contract marriages and shop for little luxuries, to feast on traditional delicacies, and to share in the exhilaration of a community gathering.

Naturally, a large number of Indian festivals stem from Hinduism. A myriad cults and subcults, an enormous body of legend and historical events, bring an extensive range of significance and association to most major Hindu religious occasions.

Dussera commemorates both the victory of the warrior-goddess Durga (consort of Shiva) over the buffalo-demon, Mahishasura, and that of Rama, a god king (an incarnation of Vishnu), over Ravana, the ten-headed king of Lanka, who had abducted Rama's wife, Sita. Worship of the goddess is the older tradition, significant in this case as it represents the female deity's supremacy over the male gods who were unable to destroy the demon.

Navratri is a nine-day festival, when the goddess is venerated as the supreme mother. Images installed in homes are worshipped every day and *kathas* (stories) are told. In Gujarat, women dance the *garba* with swaying steps and rhythmic clapping around an earthen lamp. In the south, girls sing and dance around a pitcher crowned with a coconut symbolising the goddess during Pongal in January.

In Bengal, the main festivals are Kali Puja and Durga Puja. During these festivals, rituals at the Mahakali Temple in Calcutta and other temples dedicated to the goddesses attract large crowds.

In Durga Puja praises to the *devi* are sung and

much cultural activity is initiated. On the 10th day, buffaloes representing Mahishasura are ritually slaughtered and offered to the goddess. Household and communal images of Durga are then taken out in procession and immersed.

Durga worship also has social implications. As goddess of war, she is a particular favourite of the Kshatriyas, the warrior caste, once constituting the ruling elite and aristocracy. After the sacrifice on the 10th day, it was customary to embark on the season's military campaigns. Today this is symbolically re-enacted in the magnificent Dussera processions of Mysore and Jaipur. The erstwhile ruler, seated in state on an elephant, rides in glittering procession from the centre of the city to a point just outside its gate. Trumpets blare and war drums boom. Richly caparisoned elephants, soldiers in ceremonial uniforms and nobles in traditional attire are in attendance.

Meanwhile, preparations are being completed for the evening's spectacle commemorating Rama's victory symbolising the triumph of good over evil in his ten-day battle against Ravana. Over nine evenings the epic story (the *Ramalila*) has been narrated or presented in dramatic form. On the 10th night comes the climax: colourful effigies of Ravana, complete with curling moustaches and princely ornaments, his son and his brother, are burnt, setting off a fusillade of crackers – and good is established for another year.

Continuing the story of Rama, Diwali or Dipawali (literally a row of lights) is celebrated 20 days after Dussera. It commemorates the hero-king's return from voluntary exile undertaken to fulfil a father's rash vow. Twinkling oil lamps (*divas*), replaced latterly by candles or even electric bulbs, light up every home, symbolising the lifting of spiritual darkness. Fireworks explode in a riot of noise and colour. Ritual devolves on the worship of Laxmi (consort of Vishnu), goddess of wealth and prosperity, of whom Sita was an incarnation. The beginning of a new financial year, Diwali is particularly significant for traders and businessmen. Old books are closed, new accounts opened and there is a general emphasis on a fresh beginning.

Laxmi is a fastidious goddess, averse to dirt and squalor. Houses are spring-cleaned to en-

Preceding pages: Krishna plays Holi (Kangra School, *circa* 1780). Left, child dressed to play the part of Rama during the Dussera festival.

sure her favour. City homes are whitewashed, while in villages walls are plastered with insulating and antiseptic cowdung paste. Decorative designs are painted on floors and walls. Families gather and sweets are distributed.

Festival of Holi: On the day after the full moon in early March, the whole country goes wild in a celebration of the festival of Holi. People throng the streets, smearing each other with brightly hued powder (*gulal*) or squirting coloured water on all within reach. Marijuana-based *bhang* or *thandai*, traditionally eaten or drunk during Holi, adds to the relaxation of the usual restraints of propriety and a general atmosphere of hilarity prevails.

Originally a fertility festival, later legends

with gulal and coloured water, there are colourful processions, with much music, song and uninhibited dance, and boisterous scenes in and around the temples.

Kama, god of love, and his consort, Rati (passion), are also worshipped on Holi in commemoration of Kama's destruction and resurrection by Shiva. To rouse in the ascetic god a passion for the maiden Uma, Kama loosened his flowery shaft at him. Enraged at this disturbance of his meditation, Shiva reduced Kama to ashes, but later succumbed to Uma's charms. On Rati's pleading, he relented and restored Kama to his beloved. Holi songs of the south dwell on Rati's distress.

The day after Holi, the sleepy town of

have ascribed varied origins to Holi. One speaks of a king so arrogant that he demanded that his people worship him. Only his young son, Praladh, dared refuse. Attempts to kill the prince failed. Finally his father's sister, Holika, said to be immune to burning, sat with the boy in a huge fire. So potent was Praladh's devotion, that he emerged unscathed while Holika burnt to death. Huge bonfires are lit on the eve of Holi in commemoration, and the grain of the harvest is thrown into the flames.

The playing of Holi is closely associated with the Radha-Krishna story. In Vraj, legendary homeland of the pastoral god, the festival is spread over 16 days. Apart from the usual fun

Anandpur in Punjab comes to life with boisterous Sikh war games. Mock battles, tent-pegging, archery and fencing, organised by the blue-and-saffron-clad Nihangs are the major attractions of the day.

Vishnu is invoked in his human incarnations as Rama and Krishna on their birth anniversaries in the festivals of Ramanaumi and Janamasthami respectively. Thousands of pilgrims converge on the temples of Ayodhya and Pondicherry, which are closely connected with the events of the *Ramayana*, to participate in Ramanaumi festivities. Colourful processions are held carrying images of Rama, Sita (the epitome of self-sacrificing Indian womanhood), his loyal brother Laxman and Hanuman, Rama's monkey general.

Janamasthami is particularly extravagantly recalled in the temples around Vrindavan. The Rasalila is performed to recreate incidents in Krishna's life. Midnight birth ceremonials centre on the ritual bathing of the image of the divine infant. It is placed in a silver cradle and toys are offered for its diversion and songs of intense personal devotion and love are sung. Similar ceremonies take place at all Krishna temples, especially those of Rajasthan and Gujarat.

The anniversary of Krishna's birth is known as Gokulashtami in Maharashtra. Devotion is expressed in exuberant enactments of the god's honour reaches its peak in Bombay. Preparations begin months in advance. Domestic figurines are installed and so are spectacular community images. Different areas vie with one another to produce the biggest, most impressive idols. Elaborate arrangements for lighting, decoration, devotional singing and cultural activity are organised for the two to 10 days during which Ganesh is fervently worshipped. In the days of the freedom movement, when British laws often prohibited political gatherings, the nationalist leader, Tilak, used this and other festivals to arouse feelings of nationalism. On Ganesh Chaturthi, the last of the days dedicated to Ganesh, thousands of processions converge on Chowpatti beach, bringing their

childhood endeavours to reach pots of curds and butter placed out of his reach. Matkas (earthen pots) containing his favourite foods are suspended between buildings high above the street. Groups of young men form multi-tier human pyramids till one is able to reach and break the matka. As the contents include coins there is an added incentive.

The God of Wisdom: Ganesh, elephant-headed son of Parvati and leader of Shiva's attendants, is widely venerated as the vivacious and munificent god of wisdom. The festival in his images with them for immersion. Drums beat and devotees dance and sing nostalgically, calling upon the god to return early next year.

The night of Shiva, Shivaratri, occurs on a moonless night in February or March. This is the night on which the great god of destruction performed the *tandav*, the dance of primordial creation, preservation and destruction. A fast and a night-long vigil are considered particularly meritorious on Shivaratri. Temple bells ring, sacred texts are chanted, traditional offerings of *bilwa* leaves and milk are offered to the *lingam*, the phallic symbol of the god. Major Shiva temples are inundated with devotees. Large *melas* (fairs) spring up near the temple

Left, festival participants at Madurai. **Above**, Durga image immersion at Calcutta.

sites to cater to the needs of worshippers.

Secular asides to major festivals, *melas* or fairs are also organised during more localised religious occasions. People come from miles around to buy and to sell. One of the best-known festival fairs is held at Pushkar in Rajasthan on the eighth day after Diwali. Religious activity centres on bathing in the lake, one of the most sacred places of the Hindus. On the secular side, the fair has become the annual market for livestock from all over Rajasthan. Horses, camels, cows, bullocks, even sheep and goats, all decorated with elaborate halters, exchange hands. Bullock-cart and camel races add to the excitement. Wandering minstrels, puppeteers and entertainers mingle with crowds

of immortal nectar from the *asuras* (demons), a god in the form of a rook flew with it to paradise. Prayag was one of the places where he rested. The journey took 12 days. Since each divine day is equivalent to 12 earth years the cycle was established. One *ardh* (half) *kumbha* occurs every six years.

The extensive riverbed draws crowds unparalleled anywhere else in the world. Heads and representatives of all Hindu sects participate. The prospect of their *darshan,* of the benedictory act of *seeing* them, is an added attraction. *Kumbha Melas* also occur at Hardwar, Ujjain and Nasik.

Celebrating the seasons: Some Hindu festivals are connected with the annual cycle of the

decked in traditional rural finery. And little shops sell handcrafted rural wares.

Similar fairs are held at other hallowed sites. There is the Bhakteshwar fair near Agra, where the Yamuna flows from south to north; the Garh Mukteshwar *mela* 37 miles (60 km) from Delhi and dozens of others. At Sonpur in Bihar there's a brisk buying and selling of elephants.

The greatest and most important of Hindu fairs, the Kumbha Mela, is held every sixth and 12th year at Prayag (Allahabad). The city's supreme sanctity as the confluence *(sangam)* of the Ganga, Yamuna and the mythical Saraswati, is accentuated by the story behind the gathering. After wrestling the jar *(kumbha)*

seasons. Nationwide festivities mark the beginning of the northward journey of the sun. *Pongal* or *Sankranti* in the south marks the withdrawal of the southeast monsoon as well as the reaping of the harvest. Festivities are spread over several days. A general spring cleaning and the burning of accumulated junk on household bonfires before the festival symbolises the destruction of evil. Beautiful *kilars* (decorative designs) are traced on floors with moistened rice flour. On Pongal day, the new rice of the harvest is ritualistically cooked until it boils

<u>Above</u>, Sikhs celebrate Baishaki by doing the *bhangra* dance.

over to joyous cries acclaiming the bounty of the gods.

The next day, *Mattu Pongal* or *Jellikattu* is dedicated to the cattle. Bathed, decorated and sumptuously fed, they are paraded through the village. Bulls are stampeded down narrow lanes and are faced by daring young men who leap at their horns to wrest the money tied in bundles around them and for the garlands of rupee notes often strung around their necks.

Meanwhile the people of Ahmedabad have their eyes fixed to the sky. It is Makar Sankranti, the kite festival. The entire city participates actively or vicariously in the skills of kite fighting. From dawn to dusk the sky glitters with fluttering colour. As night falls, little oil lamps attached to kites multiply the stars.

Other harvest festivals include the Assamese Ranguli Bihu. Rituals are performed for the welfare of the herds and for a good harvest and young men collect orchids for the maidens of their choice. In the evening Bihu drums throb, love songs are sung, and graceful folk dances are frankly sensual.

Temple festivals: Each Hindu temple has an annual festival in honour of the particular deity it enshrines. These are especially elaborate and colorful in the southern and eastern parts of the country, where more ancient shrines have survived the iconoclastic destruction that occurred elsewhere. Spread over several days, these festivals are important regional events. People from neighbouring towns and villages gather to pay homage to the god or goddess, with whom they have had close cultural, racial and religious ties for centuries.

The marriage of the local goddess Meenakshi to Lord Sundareswara (Shiva) is celebrated for several days every year at the magnificent Meenakshi Temple in Madurai. Appropriate rituals leading to the nuptials culminate in a spectacular procession. The goddess and her divine husband riding a golden bull (Shiva's mount) are carried through the city in elaborately carved temple chariots.

Another spectacular Madurai festival is the Floating Festival, commemorating the birth of Tirumala Nayak, a 17th-century king. Elaborately decked images are taken in procession to a tank outside the city and installed there in an ornamented barge illuminated by thousands of lamps.

The Pooram festival at Trichur in Kerala honours Lord Vatakunnathan (Shiva) in the temple dedicated to the god. Friendly rivalry between two groups culminates in a parasol display. Richly caparisoned elephants carry the ceremonial umbrellas with much rhythmic fanning with yak-tail and peacock-feather whisks. They flank the elephant carrying the temple.

Farther east, at Puri in Orissa, a major temple festival celebrates Lord Jagannath. Considered a living manifestation of Krishna, the unfinished and crude image is invested with tremendous sanctity and attracts huge crowds. The high point is the drawing of the temple deities through the city to their country residence. Temple images of the god and his brother and sister are placed on giant chariots *(raths)* which are then pulled by pilgrims. An atmosphere of almost hysterical devotion prevails. In earlier years devotees were known to have thrown themselves under the wheels of the *rath* in the hope of obtaining instant salvation.

Onam, an unusual and important Kerala festival, reveres the memory of a local demon king, Mahabali, who was ousted from his kingdom by Vishnu. So attached was the king to his country and subjects, that he was granted permission to return once a year. Houses are cleaned, floral decorations constructed to welcome the beloved ruler. Songs are sung of the happy days of his reign, sports are arranged for his amusement. Snake boats manned by around a hundred oarsmen rowing to the rhythm of cymbals and drums race at Aranmula, Champakulam and Kottayam. Competitions of *thallu,* a local martial art, are also organised. In Trichur there is a colourful procession with resplendently caparisoned elephants.

Associated with Shiva as well as Vishnu, snakes are considered immortal by orthodox Hindus and are worshipped on Naga Panchami. Milk and flowers are offered to live cobras and at snake shrines, while snake charmers demand their tithe. Hundreds of snakes are released by trappers at Shiva temples in Varanasi and Ujjain. Worshippers pour milk over themselves to ensure lifelong immunity to snake-bite.

Tribal festivals: Celebrating the sun god and local deities, most tribal festivals retain much of the ancient racial traditions. The harvest, hunting expeditions, marriage and other social events are welcome opportunities for an unsophisticated expression of joy. Quantities of local brew are imbibed and feasting is followed by dancing, some of which is quite intricate and highly skilled. The focus in most festivals is on a medium, who, possessed by the spirits of the dead, enthralls the people with pronouncements both spiritual and material.

Non-Hindu festivals: Islamic festal events occurring throughout the year range from major festivals to localised *urs* held at tombs of various Muslim saints. Visits to mosques, much feasting, visiting, and the donning of new clothes, mark all Muslim festivals. But there is little to actually see except at Muharram, which is not a festival in the celebratory sense as it mourns the murder at Karbala of Imam Hussain, grandson of the prophet.

Despite their connotation of grief, the memorial processions are colourful and dramatic. Profusely decorated and vividly hued *taziahs*, bamboo and paper replicas of the martyr's

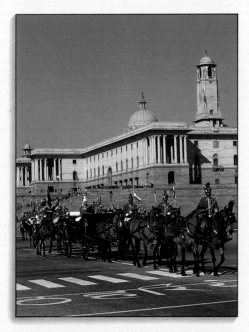

tomb embellished with gilt and mica and with domes that revolve in the breeze, are carried through city streets. A frenzied beating of drums and the wail of wind instruments mingle with songs of praise and lamentation. Wrestlers and dancers enact scenes depicting the battle of Karbala and at each step young men beat their breasts crying "Hussain! Hussain!" in collective sorrow.

Processions are particularly splendid in Agra, Lucknow, Delhi and Hyderabad, while at Baragaon, near Jaunpur, commemorative ceremonial is extravagant.

Buddha Jayanti, the birth anniversary of the Buddha, is widely celebrated. But this and other Buddhist festivals have less visual interest than the lamaistic festivals of the Himalayan states. Celebrations commemorating the birth of Padmasambhava at the Hemis Gompa in Ladakh and in Towang in Arunachal Pradesh are alive with folk vitality. Ritual dances represent the ancient shamanistic evil spirits in conflict with the powerful deities that developed in Mahayana Buddhism to subdue them. Grotesque masks worn by the dancers symbolise the power and fearsome ability of the deities as well as the malignancy of the demons. Bright robes and swirling emphatic movements create a great impact.

Jainism, with its preoccupation with the sad reality of life and emphasis on salvation, does not lend itself to outward spectacle and gaiety. Religious events such as the birth of Mahavira, its founder, are largely observed in quiet prayer. Deep Diwali, however, marking Mahavira's liberation from the cycle of life, is celebrated 10 days after Diwali. Illuminations are said to be an endeavour to mitigate the darkness caused by the passing of the "light of the world" and are particularly splendid at Mount Girnar near Junagadh.

Celebrated every 15 years at Shravana Belgola in Karnataka, the ceremonial anointing of the colossal image of Gomateshwara, a prince turned ascetic, is also a major Jain communal event. Scaffolding is erected for the ceremony and the image is "bathed" in 16 traditional precious substances which include gems, gold and silver.

The festivals of the Parsis too are not outwardly demonstrative. Pateti, their New Year, and Jamshedji Navroz, two major festivals, occasion visits to the fire temple and prayer. Secular manifestations involve socialising, feasting and the wearing of new clothes.

Christian festivals in India follow the same basic patterns as elsewhere, with a few interesting differences, among the Syrian Christians. Obviously influenced by local Hindu tradition, elephants, umbrellas and traditional music are important accessories.

Catholic Goa comes to life with the Carnival preceding the Lent period of penance. Similar to Mardi Gras, it is a boisterous event. A colourful carnival parade, presided over by Momo, king of the underworld, is accompanied by much drinking, song and dance.

Left, Independence Day parade in Delhi. **Right**, typical village god all dressed up for festival day.

धोज़त धोज़

मामला परीग

RAJKUMAR KOHLI
DIRECTS

SUNEEL DARSHAN'S

INTAQAAM

MUSIC
LAXMIKANT PYARELAL
LYRICS
ANAND BAKSHI

SURAJ ENTERPRISES
RELEASE

A
STAR IS
BORN

SANJNA
KAPOOR

PLA PRODUCTIONS

HERO
HIRALAL

DIRECTOR KETAN MEHTA PRODUCER GUL ANAND MUSIC BABLA PRUDENT FILMS

FEROZ KHAN'S

DAYAVAN

(TRUTH IS POWER)

MUSIC
LAXMIKANT PYARELAL

HINDUSTAN AUTO CORPORATION

हिन्दुस्थान ऑटो कॉर्पोरेशन

AUTOFLEX (IN

MRO

"LML," says girl to boy. "GTH," says boy to girl. Capiche?

No? Try again.

"Let's make love," says girl to boy. "Go to hell," says boy to girl.

Oh *baby!* Romance just isn't what it used to be in the Hindi movies. No more covert glances, no quickening heartbeats, no moonlit duets, no agonising suspense. Today's screen lovers get down to the nitty-gritty in an instant and to hell with the consequences.

The aggressor, increasingly, is the woman. The contemporary miniskirted virago is no simpering doormat. She winks. She leers. She threatens. And if her brawny, woolly-headed male counterpart is too busy contemplating his biceps, she's off with a shrug of her delicate shoulder singing "Sexy sexy sexy, *mujhe log bolein*" (Sexy sexy sexy, people call me). In modern India love has become a three-letter word: sex.

The evidence is all too visible. Until recently, *Debonair*, a *Playboy*-like mix of off-beat writing and erotica, was the only English-language magazine to carry pictures of semi-nude women. Today the newsstands display a choice of lascivious publications and even film magazines (or fanzines, as they call themselves) compete to provide bold pictures. *Stardust*, the leader of the pack, provoked demonstrations from women's organisations for putting topless starlets on its cover: its competitor, *Movie*, replicated the celebrated Demi Moore nude body-paint job in *Vanity Fair* with the local teen idol, Pooja Bhatt.

The contents are equally salacious. Advertisements for products as diverse as condoms and coffee use lust to attract customers while *Stardust* illustrated its 1994 annual cover feature on "The New Morality" with photographs of bare-chested hunks.

The bestsellers of popular novelist Shobha De, are scattered with expletives and fornicating couples. Scantily clad models peek alluringly from magazine covers and the TV screen. A new show on FM radio discusses sexual queries sent in by listeners and a slew of television chat shows are blowing the lid off previously taboo subjects such as adultery and pre-marital sex.

Puritan India is shedding its inhibitions. And the call for revolution is widely perceived to have emanated from a single source; the television set.

For decades following inception, the mass media – radio and television – had been firmly controlled by government. Television, in particular, specialised in a heavy-handed mix of education and government propaganda though its reach was restricted to 13 percent of the country's area.

In the early 1980s, however, an ideological shift rightwards resulted in a dramatic transformation for the media. Indian television went from black and white to colour. A special expansion plan was put into motion to broaden its reach. The focus shifted from social development to entertainment and advertisers were allowed, for the first time, to sponsor programmes made by private producers. The government also liberalised the import of colour TV sets and video cassette recorders.

Consequently, along with television, video has proliferated all over the country. Among the cassettes in circulation were pirated copies of Hindi and Hollywood films, video magazines and pornography. The chief mode of dissemination was cable TV; a rudimentary arrangement of wires connecting several households to a single VCR, operated by sharp but inexperienced entrepreneurs in return for a monthly fee from subscribers.

In April 1980, another event occurred which has had a significant impact on the Indian media. A Chinese Long March rocket put a refurbished Hughes HS 376 satellite into orbit over Southeast Asia, and Star TV was born. Star, the brainchild of the Hong Kong-based businessman Richard Li, was conceived as an advertising-driven network with primarily American programming – its four channels consisted of an entertainment channel, Star Plus, Prime Sports, MTV and the BBC World Service – to beam across Asia and the Middle East.

While newspaper articles bemoaned the "invasion of Western culture" from the skies, cable TV operators began to install the huge dishes that would enable them to receive the

Left, the Indian viewing public has more choice than ever before.

satellite signals. In 1992, a Hindi channel was added to the Star service. Zee, with its talk shows, games, sitcoms and soaps turned out to be a huge hit with the young and burgeoning middle classes and has spearheaded Star's growth in India.

Stung by this competition, Doordarshan, the Indian state-owned television network, launched an entertainment channel, Metro. Independent entrepreneurs also jumped into the fray by hiring transponders on various satellites and floating channels in Hindi and other Indian languages. A substantial segment of this new programming was film-based, but controversial social issues were tackled; one channel even took to telecasting a late night "adult" film

had limited success in India. The more popular fare consists of indigenously produced films, soaps, music programmes and talk shows modelled on American TV formats and hosted by lively local presenters. In the South, regional languages predominate, while in other parts of the country the emerging lingua franca of TV seems to be Hinglish: an arbitrary mix of English and Hindi.

Most of the initiatives so far have been in the area of entertainment. But the government monopoly over news is soon to be challenged by local producers. Business India, one of the country's leading publishing groups, is launching a network with one channel devoted exclusively to current affairs. Other publishing groups

on Saturdays.

Currently, more than 40 million households have access to Doordarshan's main channel DD1: 12 million of these are connected to cable operators and can tune into anything between three and 20 channels.

Star's success in India has attracted established foreign networks and software producers. Pending the availability of satellites, a host of new entrants – including Warner Brothers, Home Box Office, the wildlife channels, Discovery and others – are expected to enter the market. CNN, in India since 1990, also plans to introduce an entertainment channel.

Truly foreign programming, however, has

are already producing news-based programmes for Doordarshan.

The trend is bound to affect the print media, which in India has a significant presence with over 20,000 publications in various languages. So far, thanks to the government stranglehold over television and radio, the printed press has had a rather colourful evolution. The 1970s witnessed the birth of the glossies – magazines on films, politics and celebrities – followed by the war for the "upmarket readers" in the 1980s. Now journalists have begun to cross over to television and new publications coming out tend to be television-based.

The medium worst hit by television, however, has been the cinema. In the late 1980s, the Indian film industry – which produces a stupendous 800 films a year – saw its fortunes begin to plummet. Video piracy and the spread of cable TV took away a large chunk of the audience. Films grew increasingly vulgar in order to cater to the front benchers but profits continued to drop nevertheless. The industry survived by agreeing to sell video rights and from the money poured in by glamour-struck suckers and the underworld.

But now, after almost a decade of resistance, the film industry appears to have come to terms with the changes ushered in by television. Directors from the mainstream and the dormant art cinema are making soaps and telefilms

the importance of chastity and faith in God. These are values associated with temple, church or mosque and therefore close to the heart of a religious, poor and not highly literate audience.

These "virtues," however, are not what one might call the stuff of entertainment. Indian cinema solves this problem by concentrating on the *antithesis* of these values. Thus films will generally feature characters whose wealth is displayed with ostentatious garishness, who frequent cabaret shows of startling vulgarity and whose attempts at violating feminine purity are shown in graphic detail. These are the bad guys. They get their comeuppance at the hands of the good guys who overcome picturesque poverty with impossible standards of

for the small screen. The trend is likely to snowball with the launch of pay movie channels: at present three are imminent. Rupert Murdoch, who bought Star for US$525 million in 1993, has also announced plans to set up studios to produce programmes for the local market.

Analysing Indian cinema: Indian films are totally unrealistic morality tales which uphold traditional virtues: the intrinsic goodness of poverty, the preeminence of familial loyalty,

goodness.

There is, of course, catharsis involved in all this and that's why critics of Indian cinema often accuse it of pandering to the establishment: the disadvantaged who make up the bulk of the audience get their wish-fulfilment at the movies and accept the inequalities of real life with greater equanimity. Supporters of Indian cinema, on the other hand, see virtue in this: movies help to keep the lid closed tight and prevent a blow-up in Indian society.

The supporters also say that almost all Indian films drum in the message of religious harmony, of vital importance in India's frequently strife-torn multi-religious society. *Amar, Akbar,*

Anthony, directed by successful filmmaker Manmohan Desai, is the story of three brothers, separated by accident in their childhood from their parents and each other. Each child drifts away to be adopted by a family belonging to one of India's three dominant religious groups, Hindu, Muslim and Christian (hence the title of the film). The long arm of coincidence – often stretched beyond yogic proportions by Indian scriptwriters – brings the three brothers together as adults. "We are like brothers," they proclaim in many a song, unaware how near the truth they are.

The end of the film sees them defeat the villains in a long-drawn-out fight which leaves them "drained". Urgent blood transfusion is needed;

farcical comedy to wrenching tragedy. The sub-plots make a film's seemingly excessive length (about 150 minutes) an absolute necessity: each film isn't dealing with one story, but three or four.

Only 25 percent of films recover their investment, but it's the 5 percent that are big box-office successes – plus cinema's glamorous image – which act as siren songs. They are in many of India's languages and dialects but mostly in Hindi (generally made in Bombay), Telugu (Hyderabad), Tamil (Madras) and Malayalam (Trivandrum).

Actors' fees not only use up 40 percent of a film's budget but producers' excessive reliance on a few bankable names means that a few

their blood is of the same type (they are like *blood* brothers!); the type is rare. But a donor is found. It's an old lady, and as she lies in a hospital bed, connected by rubber tubes to the three men into whose veins her blood flows directly, we discover that she is one of the lost parents. The film fades on that image of Mother India.

The biology may be weak, but the symbolism is strong and it pervades through Indian cinema. Also coursing through its veins is an adherence to traditional theatrical forms which lay strong emphasis on the *nav ras* (nine emotions), plots and sub-plots plus song and dance.

The *nav ras* theory means that a single film runs through the entire gamut of feelings, from

stars are so much in demand that they work in a number of films simultaneously to a system of dates and shifts. "Dates" are the days of a month when the star will act in your film; "shift" indicates the hours in that day (a day consists of three shifts) in which he or she will be available to you. At the peak of his career Shashi Kapoor was signed on for 140 films at one time and called himself good-humoredly the Taxi Star of India: you could take him anywhere as long as you paid the fare. No wonder films take such a long time to make. Two years is considered zipping along; four years is not uncommon.

It was not just disenchantment with this

system gone haywire but also with the industry's values and its essential vulgarity that led to a breakaway group of filmmakers, often referred to as the New Wave. Unlike the French *Nouvelle Vogue,* this was not a cohesive group united by a single ideology; the New Wave's members often did not speak the same language. The one language they did share was cinema and through it they were determined to portray the *reality* of India.

Almost all of these filmmakers also wanted to get away from the star system (although ironically, many New Wave actors and actresses have now become stars of the larger film industry).

The initial inspiration came from Satyajit

New Wave directors shattered a well-nurtured myth of the Indian film industry: Hindi is the national language, crossing regional boundaries not only of language but culture. So, the myth had held, to draw audiences from disparate centres, the Hindi film must appeal to their lowest common denominator. The statement is still occasionally heard, but it is now made with less conviction.

Initially, the focus of the New Wave was almost entirely on rural India, where 70 percent of India still lives and where development takes time to catch up, but the emphasis has now moved to contemporary problems in the cities, areas spiritually and physically much closer to the film-makers themselves. How-

Ray, who brought India into the international film scene with *Pather Panchali* (The Song of the Road, 1955). Later, aided by the government-funded Film Finance Corporation (now the National Film Development Corporation) other directors began to emulate his example. Mrinal Sen, also from Ray's Calcutta, was notably successful – both critically and commercially – with *Bhuvan Shome,* financed by the FFC. This success was the spur the movement needed and soon outstanding movies were being made in regional languages.

Left, audiences are widening. **Above**, scene from a pot-boiler being shot on Madras beach.

ever disparate their subjects, these films are distinguished by their passionate intensity.

The world – or at least that part of it which is India – is not so easily changed. Like the two Indias – the rich and the poor – which live together in uneasy co-existence, the Indian box-office cinema and the New Wave live warily with each other, one envious of the other's popularity, the other resentful of the critical acclaim and prizes denied to it. More and more of the 3½ million people who go into Indian cinema houses every day, now go to see New Wave films, but their number is still minuscule.

The majority of viewers go to see films like Ramesh Sippy's movie, *Sholay*, which became one of the biggest box-office successes in Indian history. A name was coined for it, "Curry Western", a tribute to its inspiration, the Italian Spaghetti Western, which was itself a derivative of the Hollywood Western. *Sholay* invented a country of kind desperados fighting a gang of vicious bandits. Critics aimed their intellectual six-shooters at its appalling violence and its make-believe world but even as they pulledd the trigger they couldn't but admit that the film was entertaining. For an audience which wants to forget the tribulations and indignities of life in India, films like *Sholay* are the perfect answer.

Marketing and music: In cinema, as in television, competition has arrived from the West.

For years Hollywood served as an inspiration for Indian directors ("inspiration" implying the plagiarisation of technique, car chases and sometimes entire plots). Yet Hollywood itself could make little headway in India, mainly due to the language barrier. The dubbing of blockbusters into Indian languages has vastly expanded the market. *Jurassic Park,* the first dubbed experiment, collected half a million dollars in a fortnight from Indian viewers compared to the US $160,000 earned by *Indecent Proposal* in English over a whole year.

Many film industry hot shots are also moving into allied businesses of setting up studios, celebrity marketing and so on. Recently top film stars Amitabh Bachchan and Sridevi and directors such as Subhash Ghai and Mukul Anand have launched public issues to raise funds for their new companies.

But succour for the ailing film industry has also come from a new factor, or rather the expanded potential of an old factor: music. Music has always been an integral part of Indian cinema. In fact, the film song, performed by a variety of characters in myriad situations and locations, can be said to be the precursor of the contemporary music video.

Despite their undeniable significance, songs were considered appendages to the film. But over the last couple of years, a spate of Top Twenty-style television programmes based on film songs, combined with the proliferation of tape recorders and cheap audio cassettes has created a massive demand for film music.

Sales of popular scores run into millions. The busiest people in the film world today are music directors and choreographers. According to the prominent fortnightly, *India Today,* the amount spent on a single song in a film has increased tenfold in five years. The recent *1942 – Love Story,* an epic romance, actually had a special director just for the songs.

The surging attraction of film songs has also blurred age-old boundaries. One of the most sought after musicians in Bollywood (the common term for Bombay's Hindi film industry) is A. R. Rahman who made his mark with South Indian films, and the top-rated dancer is Prabhu Deva, the Michael Jackson of the South.

The strict division between film and non-film music is also fast disappearing, In the old days the only popular indigenous music was Hindi film music. The emergence of MTV Asia provided exposure to other, non-film musicians such as the wannabe rock band Indus Creed, and Apache Indian rappers, Baba Sehgal. Channel V, the music channel that has replaced MTV on the Star network, devotes almost 50 percent of its time to both film and non film Indian music. In fact, Channel V, with its irreverence, wacky humour, fizzy mix of old and new, east and west, north and south is a pretty accurate reflection of the chaotic, unpredictable nature of the Indian media today.

But no one's complaining. As Quick Gun Murugan, a flamboyant South Indian cowboy hero of a Channel V filler would say: "Mind it. We are like this only."

Left, modern business, traditional game.

HINGLISH AS SHE IS SPOKEN

In big block letters, English assaults the eye in India. Billboards, handpainted by gangs of boys on scaffolding, unleash all the colours of the Bombay screen onto each hoarding. Subtlety is not the name of the advertising game here, and words are apt to get hopelessly scrambled in an alphabetical masala.

"Keep your Maruti a cutie," chimes one rhyming automobile advert. "A smart motorist dares/ to avoid spurious spares."

"Lane driving is sane driving," reminds a road safety poster. "Hundred buck fine if you cross the white line."

Painted messages on the back bumpers of tremendous smoke-belching trucks urge drivers to "Horn Please", and then, in their jolly post-Raj way, say "Bye-bye, Ta-ta!" to all overtaking cars.

An Aids awareness campaign, based on the most common handscrawled highway reminders, was aimed recently at truck drivers who unwittingly bring the HIV virus from urban prostitutes back to their villages. "Use dipper at night," they are advised coyly, the "dipper" being a condom. What's more, no extra funds were needed to get the message out, since the majority of trucks already had the safety slogans daubed on their fenders.

Many of the turns of phrase read or overheard in India seem like dated hangovers from the Raj era. Anachronisms abound: a colleague assured us that the press conference we'd missed was a bore: "At the fag end of the day, chaps, it was just a damp squib."

Lists of bureaucratic regulations are a constant source of bemusement. Frequently they are done by signpainters who are clueless about spelling or even the formation of letters and more accustomed to curvilinear swirls of Hindi which cling to a top line like leaves to a stalk. The signboards bark out the rules like an angry ex-colonel: "Keep your dickey locked"; "Commit to no nuisance"; "Plucking of flowers prohibited".

The crossover of vocabulary is two-way. Without India, the English would not have a word to describe a movie mogul lounging on the verandah of his bungalow in his calico pyjamas after a pukka polo game. The colour khaki, so redolent of heat and dust, would not exist. Nor would chintz, madras checks, muslin, bandanas, dungarees or even the bazaar, where all these textiles are bargained for.

Hybrid words, which grow in abundance, are newly linked up within the Latinate connector "cum". As in "Kindly ring the office-cum-residence

Right, learning a new language in Calcutta.

of the filmstar-cum-politician on your telephone-cum-fax machine." Sometimes a string of extraordinary adjectives is put together like a magic mantra for business, as in a shopfront in New Delhi which reads "Exclusive Commercial Lucrative Private Ltd".

It is because English is the language of business that it has persisted so long past its original sell-by date of the end of the Empire. The educated elite still speak it at home, and some regions still balk at speaking Hindi, unwilling to be heard kowtowing to central government.

The political arena generates its own words. Politicians "airdash to votebanks" (fly by jet to their constituencies) to prevent "goondahs from boothcapturing" (heavies tampering with poll booths). Inventive Indians even coined a new word, "to prepone", which means to advance an

appointment, the opposite of postpone.

In modern India, "miscreants" (criminals) abscond until they are "nabbed". "Eveteasers" (sexual harassers) should be given "two tight slaps" for bad behaviour, or be locked away if they "outrage a woman's modesty" (rape).

In a country of so many dialects and tongues, you must pepper your talk with Hinglish to make sure the right message gets across. Off for a wild weekend? Say, vaguely, "Sahib is out of station for some time". Red tape to be cut? A small bribe will do the trick only if the right code is spoken. With cash folded, look the official in the eye and say, completely straight-faced, "This matter must be expedited by the proper authorities. Kindly do the needful." ∎

In India, dance and music are all-pervading, bringing colour to numerous festivals and ceremonies, and reaffirming the faith of the people in their heritage. The tradition of the performing arts in India has its roots in age-old texts, the *Vedas,* in which ritual manifested itself through music, dance and drama.

The *Natyashastra,* an ancient treatise on dramaturgy, explains that when written texts became the sole prerogative of an educated few, the gods appealed to Brahma, the Creator, to promulgate a fifth Veda, in the form of audiovisual art, that would be accessible to all, irrespective of caste or formal education. Thus the *Natya Veda* was conceived, drawing for content and teaching from the other four and presenting the quintessence of all the arts, whether literature, sculpture, music, painting or dance.

In India, religion, philosophy and myth cannot be divorced from their art forms. Dance and music are tied inextricably to ceremony. Weddings, births, coronations, entering a new house or town, welcoming a guest, religious processions, harvest time – any or all of these are occasions for song and dance.

Indian music and dance demand a spirit of devotion and of total surrender. For the physical is transitory and easily transmuted, while a sincere practice of the arts can achieve the highest spiritual experience.

Classical dance forms: Spontaneity, intuition and the joy of life are the soul of dance and music and the quest of every artist. The endeavour is to search for the ultimate in perfection of body and mind through these art forms. Rukmini Devi, a pioneer and one of the most renowned figures in the world of performing art in India, has said: "The keynote of good art is when its message does not merely appeal to the senses and through them to a purely external enjoyment, but to the soul of the artiste and of the perceiver."

India offers not one, but several well-defined classical dance forms. Each of these has been nurtured in a different part of the country and has taken on the hue and texture of its region. Each represents an entire culture, the ethos of a people and a personalised artistic signature. Chief among them and at present the most popular classical styles of dance seen on the stage are Bharata Natyam of Tamil Nadu, Odissi of Orissa, Kathakali of Kerala, Kuchipudi of Andhra Pradesh, Kathak of Lucknow and Jaipur and Manipuri of Manipur. But these are not all. Several other forms of traditional dance that fall into the categories of semi-classical, folk, drama, and martial arts, contribute to the panorama of dance in India. Today the major styles are performed all over the country and not exclusively by people from the regions of their origin. Together, these styles offer a large variety in costume, in richness of literary content, in beauty of musical mode and instrumental accompaniment, and in variation of theme and creative scope.

The fundamentals: Indian dance is based upon the concepts of *nritta* and *nrittya,* of *raga* and *tala,* of *hastas* and *nayaka-nayika bhav,* and of the *guru-shishya parampara* (guru-disciple tradition) – the common foundation of all its major forms resting on the authority of ancient and revered texts, numerous temple sculptures and frescoes, and in the myth and legend of the land.

Nritta is pure dance. It is abstract movement that signifies beauty. It is performed in union with rhythm and expresses human ecstasy very simply. *Nrittya* on the other hand is expressional, the enactment of a theme. Here, the dancer is aided by *sahitya* or verse; by *hastas* which are gestures of the hands, each representing a word, a phrase or an idea; and by *abhinaya,* or facial expression. In combining these with music, a "language" is established, so that the viewer sees words fly off the tips of the dancer's fingers, each moment reflected in her eyes and in her smile. This capacity for expression is a unique feature of Indian dance.

Raga is the musical mode of an item, a melodic base with rules governing its elaboration and yet allowing for improvisation. The *raga* decides the mood of a situation and governs its emotional impact. *Tala,* on the other hand, is the heartbeat of a song, a time cycle that weaves itself through the music, reining it in, conserving its strength yet lending it mood and character.

For generations, all this, and more, has been invested in the hands of *gurus,* the traditional preceptors. They were the receptacles of knowledge and transferred it orally, demanding, in return, a high degree of faith and loyalty from the student. Ideally, the guru represents for the *shishya* (student) the personification of his art form. This one-to-one relationship, of God and devotee, of parent and child, of master and disciple, derives from the *guru-shishya parampara* and is a central concept of Indian culture.

Themes: Indian dance forms take their themes from the Hindu pantheon and from a variety of folk legends. Vishnu, the Protector, in his 10 incarnations, is perhaps the most popular deity depicted in classical Indian dance. His consort is Lakshmi, goddess of

tions that provides an endless variety of moral themes, characters and incidents for expositions in dance form.

Each style draws liberally on stories that depict the life, folklore, ethics, and beliefs of the people of India. Like Hindu philosophy, they explore life and nature and man's interaction with them. Much of the thematic content of Indian dance thus reflects, on the spiritual level, man's interaction with God, and on the human level, his relationship with other men or women.

Nayaka-nayika bhav, the "hero-heroine" concept in Indian dance provides inexhaustible scope for the representation of the man-woman theme.

beauty and wealth. She reappears as Sita and Radha, consorts to two of his later incarnations. Rama, Vishnu's seventh incarnation, is celebrated, along with his consort Sita, in the epic *Ramayana,* a rich source of themes and anecdotes for presentation in Indian dance. Another popular incarnation is the colourful Krishna, beloved of Radha, and charioteer and counsellor to Arjuna on the battlefield of Kurukshetra. Krishna's childhood is described in the *Puranas* and he figures also in the *Mahabharata,* an epic of enormous propor-

Above, Flautist accompanied by *tablas* and *tanpura.*

Bharata Natyam and Kathakali: Bharata Natyam is Tamil Nadu's most celebrated art form, a tradition that demands of the dancer a detachment from wordly ties, a sublimation of the self to the deity and her art. Such *devadasis*, "servants of God", carried a temple tradition forward, till patronage shifted to the hands of the landed aristocracy who marked them with the stigma of courtesanship.

Bharata Natyam is a dynamic, earthy and extremely precise dance style. It is built upon a balanced distribution of body weight and firm positions of the lower limbs, allowing the hands to cut into a line, to flow around the body, or to take positions that enhance the basic form. *Padams,* poems on the hero-heroine theme, are a special feature of expressional dance that allow the dancer great scope for the enactment of a theme. The tempo of these love songs is slow and each phrase is crystallised into a specific mood and aspect of love.

Kathakali is the most developed dance drama art of India. In Kerala, the drums roll, beckoning an audience to a spectacle most magnificent. Here, the actors depict characters from the *Puranas* and from the *Mahabharata* – superhuman beings, demons and ordinary men and women.

The dancers, who are all male, adorn themselves in huge skirts and headdresses, wearing

the iconography of a whole culture is echoed in its structure. The *tribhanga,* a three-bend posture, interlinking a people's philosophy with the physical, is a series of triangles which are not only physically difficult to execute, but which also call for immense restraint and finesse on the part of the artist. The numerous postures of the style reflect specific moods and adorn the carved panels of the Konarak Sun Temple.

Popular devotion to Sri Krishna is embodied in Jayadeva's unique Sanskrit love poem, *Geet Govind,* and its verses are interpreted by every representative of Orissa's culture, whether he be a singer, dancer or devotee.

Waves of influence of various cultures have

what must surely be the most intricate make-up known to any dance style anywhere in the world. Dialogue is combined with dance to bring myth and legend vividly to life in the temple courtyards of Kerala. So strong is the identification of the dancers with the characters they play, so absolute is their conviction, that they display an incredible level of histrionic skill.

Odissi and Kathak: The ambience of Orissa, the philosophy of Lord Jagannath and the sculpture of the 13th-century Sun Temple of Konarak, are reflected in its dance form – Odissi. Perhaps the most lyrical style of dance in India, Odissi follows unique body norms;

traversed India's northern plains, giving Kathak its Hindu-Muslim texture, and its exciting and entertaining quality. The *kathak* or storyteller of yore was a versatile actor-musician-dancer who addressed himself directly to his audience, throwing a web of verse and verve over them. Involved and complicated footwork and rapid pirouettes are the dominant and most endearing features of this style. Long strings of bells are tied around the ankles of the dancer and a whole gamut of rhythmic patterns are woven into a chosen time cycle. Balance, poise and control are strong requisites for this exacting art. Traditionally the dance of the courts, Kathak reflects a simplicity and vigour that is visually most attractive.

Manipuri: Protected for years in a valley of exceeding beauty, Manipuri is the art expression of every man, woman and child of Manipur. The musical forms of that culture reflect the worship of Vishnu. It is around episodes from his life that the faith of the people is entwined. The *sankirtan* and the *raas* are revered musical traditions enacted appropriately at different times of the year by the community as a whole. Manipuri is not aggressive. It is tender and almost reticent on the one hand, and extremely vigorous on the other. A continuity of movement and a restraint of power are underlying features of the style.

to this ancient exposition of their principles.

Indian classical music is broadly divided into two systems, commonly described as the Hindustani and Karnatak systems. Hindustani music is practised in North India and Karnatak music in South India. As in the case of the dance styles, their heritage and philosophy is a common one; their base and general structure is the same. Their *ragas* however, are usually different, and they have unique methods of articulation and treatment, even when they present the same *raga.*

While Karnatak music remains untouched by foreign influences, the same cannot be said of Hindustani music, which felt the influence of Persian and Central Asian music after inva-

Music, the soul of dance: All these dance styles depend upon music for their sustenance. *Nada* (sound) is believed to be the very process of creation and ancient verses from the holy scriptures were chanted in a special manner, peculiar to India. This tradition continues and is a form of meditation, of concentration and of worship.

Indian music has its traditional origins in the *Sama Veda,* an age-old text. It is believed that a musical scale, aesthetics in music, basic rhythm, and a system of notation, all go back

sions and migrations from those areas.

Essential ingredients: Indian music, as mentioned earlier, is built on a subtle combination of *raga* and *tala. Raga* is an aesthetic and emotional rendering of a scale of notes. It is a melodic mode having rigid conditions that govern its elaboration; yet it is capable of infinite improvisation. *Ragas* have specific moods and flavours and a given *raga* may be sung only during a particular season of the year, or at a specific time of the day .

Ragas have an inbuilt harmony and are, in fact, not a rendering of mere notes, but a rendering of *swaras,* which are notes that have the frequency of the human voice. This

Left, *garba ras*, folk dance from Gujarat. **Above left,** Kuchipudi dancer; and **right,** Bharata Natyam.

is why pride of place was often given to vocalists rather than to instrumentalists.

However this attitude is no longer as common as it used to be, thanks to the amazing skill of great contemporary instrumentalists. An instrumentalist's constant endeavour is nevertheless to match the inflexions of the human voice with his instrument and in this achievement lies his greatness. The instrument he uses thus becomes an extension of himself. A *raga* leaves one unmoved if the spirit of the artist does not come through in the mood being attempted.

Tala, on the other hand, binds music together. It is a time cycle that remains fixed throughout a particular rendering. Romanti-

North Indian music: North India offers a variety of forms of music like the *dhruvapada, khyal, thumari, tappa* and *ghazal.* Each of these has a specific history of development and the listener may not be able to identify the particular form. Such identification requires some familiarity with the school from which the particular vocalist or instrumentalist hails, or at least an understanding of the structure of these forms.

The *dhruvapada* is a strictly classical and slow form. The *khyal* incorporates into this rigidity the romanticism of yet another form, the *thumari.* This is why, for a casual listener, it is perhaps simpler to appreciate a *khyal* than a *dhruvapala,* without exactly

cally, it is believed to be the divine fusion of the masculine and feminine forms of dance. The *tala* repeats itself in cyclic regularity, offering amazing dimensions for improvisation between beats. Virtuoso percussionists render extremely complex variations within these cycles. *Tala* is the pulse of Indian music. To listen to the interplay of *tala* with musical phrases is a fascinating experience. The division of time into minute pulses, the crisscross patterns, the regular and off-beat emphasis of time, the running together of two contrary cycles meeting creatively at a point, offer a regularity that calms the mind and an excitement that heightens mood.

knowing why, since all these forms follow the same basic tenets of the *raga-tala* system. The *khyal* is perhaps the most widely performed form of classical music in all North India.

The *thumari* is used quite extensively to accompany Kathak. This is because it incorporates a high degree of emotional and aesthetic content – speaking, as it were, from the heart. The *tappa* is a lighter form of classical music that is brisk and replete with a variety of phrases, which makes it particularly difficult

Left, Kathakali dancer depicting Hanuman, the monkey god.

to render without a good degree of virtuosity.

North Indian music has a wide range of ancient and beautiful instruments, each having a tonal quality quite unique. Some of the more well-known are the *sitar,* the *sarod,* the *rudravina,* the *santoor,* the flute, the *shehnai* and the *saarangi.* Among the percussion instruments are the *tabla* and *pakhawaj.* The *tabla* is used in accompaniment of most music recitals. The *pakhawaj* has a deeper tone than the *tabla.*

A word often heard in relation to North Indian music is *gharana,* literally meaning "house". This word is used to denote the house of a specific school of music. The nomenclature arose in the days when artists were retained in the courts of particular princes, thereby confining the area of their performances and their training of disciples. Some of the better known among these *gharanas* are those of Gwalior, Agra, Delhi and Jaipur.

South Indian sounds: South Indian music, Karnatak music as it is called, differs from the Hindustani in its stricter adherence to structure, thereby shifting the emphasis away from improvisation within that structure. The musician of the South adheres very firmly to his composition and even more firmly to the *tala* cycle. *Ragas* in the South mostly have Sanskrit names, unlike in the North, where their names often come from specific regions or from the dialects of regions.

A certain rigidity marks recitals of Karnatak music, and *bhakti* or devotion, is its mainstay. Karnatak music is therefore deeply spiritual. It was blessed with a plethora of greatly devoted composers and musicians. The literary content of the *kritis,* or songs, are in the form of offerings. The immortal Trinity of Karnatak music are Thyagaraja, Shyama Sastry, and Dikshitar, whose compositions are widely sung. Every great musician maintains the purity of the original structure of these compositions, but embellishes them with ornamentation peculiar to his skill or his instrument.

The flute, the violin, the *veena,* the *nadaswaram* and the *gottuvadyam* are among the most well-known South Indian instruments. The *mridangam, ghatam* and *ganjira* are the most loved and widely heard percussion instruments.

Appreciating performance: Watching an Indian music concert heightens the pleasure of listening to it. This is because the Indian musician tries to "speak" to his audience. Perhaps unconsciously, he uses his hands and fingers to express himself. These actions help to spell out his thoughts, and bring into focus the intricate pattern of his creative process. A small venue, with a restricted gathering of interested people, is the ideal setting for an Indian dance or music recital. Informality tends to a deeper appreciation of the artist's endeavour. At close proximity, one is able to share some of the emotional involvement of the artist in the presentation. A closer rapport enhances mood and intensifies the *rasa,* the flavour, experienced both by the artist and the audience.

It is wrong to believe that the classical arts of India are rigidly bound by rules, regulations and ancient traditions. The *Shastras,* the holy texts, merely laid down the framework and the boundaries of these art forms. Practice, research, experience and intuition make for a continuity in the arts, giving them a living tradition.

Truly gifted artists soar into this world of creativity where no conflict exists between the past and the present, and where the pursuit of happiness is a subordination of the self. Technique and talent do not lift one from the temporal. The god of dance, Nataraja, brought body and soul together, thereby unifying the heavens and the earth.

No account of what India has to offer by way of music and dance can be complete without a mention of at least some of the other classical, semi-classical, folk, martial art, and drama traditions. Kuchipudi of Andhra Pradesh and the Bhagavata Mela Nataka of Tamil Nadu are solo and group dance drama forms performed originally by men only. Mohini Attam, a sensuous female dance form; Theyyam, a ritualistic art-form; and Kalaripayatu, a superb martial art form, are the treasures of Kerala. Manipur's martial art and wrestling techniques; the strong Chhaw traditions from Seraikella, Mayurbhanj and Purulia; and a host of folk and tribal forms are performed seasonally in the villages scattered over the country.

These spontaneous expressions of rural culture vary in costume, language, instruments, style and zest from one another. Every village has its own festive days, its own peculiar customs, its own favoured lyrics, and its own sense of music and dance. To witness and listen to these art forms in their own environment is a special pleasure.

Classical Indian sculpture does not seem as though it were cut and chiselled as much as growing from the rock, organically, like a ripe fruit to be plucked. There does seem to be, too, a remarkable affinity between the figures of tree goddesses (*yakshis*) and the branches of trees which they embrace – as though the vital sap of energy of life flowed from vegetation into their veins. The *yakshis* embody the trees, as much as the celestial goddesses, embody the flow of rivers Ganga and Yamuna. Divinity exists. It is expressed through the elements, the rivers, the mountains, the trees.

Divinity exists as much in a stone. The most obvious instances of this belief are to be seen in the elemental shapes of stones that are enshrined, daubed red and orange and silver, and worshipped with flowers, under the shade of a tree or beside a river. Offerings are made to the *salagrama,* the stone that represents the god Vishnu, to the *tulsi* plant in the garden by the housewife, to the *lingam* which represents Lord Shiva, to the *peepul* tree outside almost every village that represents the local guardian deity.

The inherent continuity of beliefs is remarkable and observed even in the earlier archeological excavations from the Indus Valley of the 2nd and 3rd millennia BC. Tiny terracotta seals introduce *peepul* leaves surrounded with a railing, as though marked sacred. In another seal a horned deity in the yogic posture is enthroned, surrounded by four animals which have earned him the name of *Pashupati,* the Lord of animals. This archaic deity is an early form of the god Shiva, in aspects that are worshipped to the present day.

The mother goddess is moulded in clay with pellets building up to an elaborate headdress, necklaces and girdle, to accentuate her breasts and hips – in her role as the earth mother. Through the centuries to the 3rd century BC, when other material evidence is mostly lacking, the earth mother continued to be moulded and worshipped in terracotta – as much as she is today in every village *mata,* in the forms of Durga or Lakshmi being ritually immersed each year in the river, so that earth returns to earth.

Two outstanding objects from the first cities of India depict its cosmopolitan culture. The superb head of a priest in limestone, with its accentuated mongoloid cheekbones and slit eyes is in sharp contrast to the sensuous tribal features

of a bronze dancing girl. Although worked on a miniature scale, the latter figure shows tremendous sophistication in rendering a young poised tribal girl with slender angular limbs and a pouting face.

Official and popular Buddhist art: Much of Indian art is religious in purpose; but we would be mistaken to believe that it is all religious in content. The next chapter of great Indian sculpture opens in the 3rd century BC, with the Emperor Ashoka adopting Buddhism as the official religion of the Mauryan Empire. The legend goes that in his zeal to embrace the new religion, he constructed 84,000 *stupas* (dome-shaped monuments). His edicts were inscribed upon rock and pillar, from Girnar in Gujarat to Tiruchirapalli in Tamil Nadu.

The lion capital at Sarnath, now the official emblem of the Indian Republic, gleams in polished sandstone, representing the hieratic art and the political aspirations of the empire. Originally surmounted by the *dharmachakra,* the sacred wheel of the law that refers to the Buddha's sermon, these pillars were actually worshipped, as we witness in later reliefs at Sanchi. Thus, homage was paid by the populace both to the Buddha and to the empire.

A more persuasive, natural art was that in terracotta – not only of the mother goddess, but of urban ladies from Tamluk in Bengal or Pataliputra in Bihar, replete with elaborate headgear and jewellery. There are also terracotta plaques depicting *mithunas* or couples, seated in a love seat with the group strewn with flowers; or of a young boy writing the alphabet with his chalk on a board. These are evidence of the urban sophistication of the times.

Buddhism did not remain the preserve of the orthodox. To acquire new members of the laity, it had to yield and accept more popular cults and legends. The goddess Sri is beckoned, rising from lotus petals and watered by elephants, as the auspicious omens of wealth and fertility. *Yakshas, yakshis* and *nagas,* the familiar true spirits and water spirits, are now established as the guardian deities on railposts which encircle the *stupas.* The names are inscribed, and although divine, they appear occasionally in the form of local tribal men and women. From Barhut, we encounter the unexpectedly sensuous face of a Koli girl, with tattoo marks on her face and with flowers braided through her hair.

The foundations of the Great Stupa at Sanchi were first built by the Emperor Ashoka, along with his edict and pillar that now lies in the site museum. Monasteries were set up here as a retreat from the hectic city life of Vaishali, 7 miles (11km) away. Here, on an open hill rising above the city sounds, in touch with the sun and sky and the elements, there is tranquillity. Even today the visitor senses that he is on a pilgrimage, as he takes the ritual path of circumnambulation around the *stupa* – following the course of the sun through the heavens, with the four gateways *(toranas)* to the east, west, north and south marking out the four directions.

These gateways were carved in the 1st century

Originally, at Sanchi, there was a certain reluctance to represent him except through symbols: the *Bodhi-tree* with which he so closely associated himself, the *dharmachakra* which he used by way of analogy in explaining the righteous path, the *stupa* which enshrined his mortal remains. Later, interest shifts to the story of his life. In sculptures of northwest India and Gandhara (now in Afghanistan), these scenes acquired a heightened degree of pathos and realism, believed to have been borrowed from Roman reliefs.

A cult image of the Buddha became essential for acts of ritual worship. How else was he to be represented but in the form of man? And if he was to be rendered in human form, and he was

AD with reliefs depicting the Buddha as a prince, his moment of enlightenment at Bodhgaya, his sermon at the deer park, miracles, and conversion of the serpent king, the gods in paradise and the acolytes at the *ashram*. These reliefs shimmer with light as the sun moves around the *stupa,* expressing a tremendous joy in nature and an affinity with all creatures of the earth.

In the 1st century AD, the position changed radically in art – to focus almost entirely on the human figure. The Buddha, meaning "the Enlightened One", came to represent one of the highest aspirations of human thought and art.

Above, miniature of the Basholi school.

divine, how was his divinity to be expressed? These were basic questions that seem to have obsessed the sculptors at Mathura and Gandhara, when they evolved the anthropomorphic image of Shakyamuni, the royal prince of the Sakya clan who became the saviour of mankind.

To emphasise the Buddha's divinity, certain *lakshanas* or signs were described upon his person: the *urna* between the eyes, the *ushnisha* rising from the head, the *dharmachakra* incised upon the palms of his hands and the soles of his feet, the halo that spelt illumination, the lion throne that implied his royal ancestry. When he sat, it was in the yogic pose of meditation, when he spoke it was with a gesture of the hand that said "do-not-fear". These early images of the Buddha are awe-inspiring in terms of sheer size and physical presence. It has been shown by the scholar Coomaraswamy that they were inspired by the colossal cult images of the 1st and 2nd centuries BC such as the Parkham Yaksha near Mathura, and the Besnagar Yaksha, towering to a height of 14 ft (4.5 metres).

By the 5th century, a different sensibility is evident. The Buddha is yielding, meditative, with a body so subtle in modelling that it seems insubstantial, with a face that glows with illumination. In the seated Buddha, the body seems to melt away and our eyes are focused upon the exquisite hands unfolding, the gesture of teaching, and on the eyes that are half-closed in retrospection. This then becomes the ultimate definition of the divine.

Saviours of mankind: Buddhism was not the only religion to conceive icons of the deity (*pratima*) for worship. At Mathura, said to be the birthplace of Lord Krishna and the centre of the Vaishnava sect, there are powerful images of Balarama, the brother of Krishna; of Surya, the haloed sun god wearing a tunic and boots (as did the Kushan invaders and kings); of Kartikeya designated the lord of war; and of the goddess Mahisha Mardini in her magnificent moment of triumph as, with remarkable composure, she slays the demon buffalo and thus redeems all mankind.

The early centuries AD witnessed a tremendous resurgence of Hinduism; more especially when it became the official religion of the Gupta Empire in the 4th, 5th and 6th centuries. The images were then militant. At this point the gods were designated as the great heroes, the saviours of mankind. How else was Hinduism to compete with the reformed sects and win over the faithful?

The most singular monument to this victory is heralded in the colossal image of Lord Vishnu, at the Udaigiri caves just a few miles from the Buddhist monasteries at Sanchi. Here we witness the gods and the sages rejoicing as Vishnu, in his incarnation of the bear Varaha, rescues the tiny, exquisite image of mother earth from the depths of the ocean. An inscription refers to the Gupta emperor, Chandragupta, whose empire extends "from sea to sea" – thus creating a political allegory, to present his ambitions materialised in the image of Lord Vishnu as the great saviour.

At the National Museum in Delhi a superb bust of Lord Vishnu from the 5th century AD counterposes a sense of poise that could rival any image of the meditating Buddha. Another bust in the same museum depicts Lord Shiva in his terrifying aspect, his third eye burst open on the forehead, two arms flung wide open holding the *damaru* or drum of destruction as he dances. Yet a profoundly different dimension of the same deity is revealed in the *mukhalingam* from Khoh (Uttar Pradesh) where he is conceived as the supreme *maha-yogi*. The head of Shiva in his ascetic form is superimposed upon his symbol of the phallus to render an image of ineffable calm, of serenity.

Fusion of the arts: The link between literature and the visual arts is crucial to our understanding of these images. An aesthetic sensibility had evolved that was shared between dance, drama, literature and art.

The celebrated beginning to the ancient text of the *Vishnudharmottaram* describes the predicament of the king who wished to learn the art of painting (*chitrar kala*). He was informed that to paint, to render figures in plastic volume, he must first learn to sculpt. To attempt sculpture, to understand gesture and movement, he must apply himself first to the principles of dance. And to dance he must have recourse to the appreciation of rhythm, of *tala* of instrumental and then vocal music. And music, of course, seeks its inspiration from poetry. Thus the king learnt that to be skilled in one of the arts, he must be informed about all of them.

Nowhere is this fusion of the arts better illustrated than at the caves at Ajanta. Instances of such cave "temples" have survived from the 3rd and 2nd centuries BC as retreats for Buddhist and Jain monks, especially during the monsoon months. At Ajanta itself the earliest *chaitya* hall for a congregation dates back to the 2nd century BC with a simple unadorned stupa set into the apse, to serve as the symbolic image; but with fragments of surviving paintings that illustrate the *Saddhanta Jataka*. Gradually, the entire surface of walls in the interior came to be decorated with sculpted and painted figures.

The experience of entering these caves is dramatic. Usually, light enters them from only one source at the entrance, through the giant rose window above the door. As the eyes get used to the darkness, the figures loom larger than life-size, they become palpable and infused with life, "As though breathing" to quote from the *Vishnudharmottaram*. Add to this the sensation of colour, defining the figures that are now suffused with a kind of languid flow of movement. Add to this the acoustics of a closed hall, with the sound resonating around the *stupa* and up to the high ceilings, and the flicker of oil lamps offered in prayer, the viewer is transported into another state of consciousness where sound and light and colour and palpable form are fused into one inseparable reality. Even the ceilings are painted, in magical circles that seem to float upwards and are adorned with a thousand flowers. The experience, then, is one of a total wrap-around mystery that transports the pilgrims into another world.

These images are not representations of a clinical reality – not any more than are the figures of the Dark Princess or of the Bodhisattva Padmapani, looming out of the darkness as a water-lily blooms out of the water. Not any more than the deer and geese and flowers and creepers, the pavilions and processions through gateways are part of the everyday experience of the

monks who painted them. They grow out of the imagination; and yet, occasionally, there is a sudden, unexpected thrill of a portrait of an old monk, that pulls us back to observations from life. Evidently monasticism in India, although enjoined to celibacy, did not resemble the Christian monasticism of medieval Europe. The monks were free to paint whatever they willed, dreamed or experienced.

Emboldened by drama and poetry, the visual metaphor becomes even more explicit. At the National Museum, Delhi, a life-size image of

Above, Chola bronze showing Nataraja, Shiva performing the cosmic dance.

Ganga, the divine river goddess, depicts her swaying on the aquatic animal, the *makara*, the wet folds of her garment flowing as a river in spate. Profiled, both the river goddesses, Ganga and Yamuna, flank the doorway to the terracotta temple at Ahichchatra (Uttar Pradesh), and lead the pilgrim into the shrine.

The location of the sculptures of the gods in the temple corresponded with their position in the hierarchy. *Dwarapalas* or door guardians flank the entrance, as do the river goddesses. The *dikpalas* or guardians are stationed at the different directions. The front lintel above the doorway carries the *navagrahas* or nine planets, and often a small relief of the deity who is enshrined in the sanctum within. The projecting walls on the south, west and north sides of the temple may carry an epic relief of the major deity performing a miracle, slaying the demon Gajasura, or grandly recumbent on the serpent Ananda on the ocean bed. The temple is in essence the cosmic mountain. As the Greek gods lived on Mount Olympus, so the gods in India live on Mount Kailash, in the Himalaya. The greatest temples, such as the Kailashanath at Khajuraho, and the Kailash of Ellora testify to this belief.

Both at the caves of Ellora and Elephanta in the Deccan, we see an attempt to "reconstruct" the image of Shiva's home in the Himalaya that is a thousand miles away. Giant reliefs enact the legend of his marriage to Parvati, the "daughter of the mountain", of their conjugal bliss as they play chess on Mount Kailash, undisturbed by Ravana shaking the mountain, of the descent to earth of the river Ganga through the locks of Shiva's flowing hair, of his vanquishing demons and dancing the fearful *tandava* dance, and finally of his being stilled into deep meditation. These are some manifestations of the same deity, who is both destroyer and saviour, the lord of dance (Nataraja) and the lord of meditation (Mahayogi).

The most profound aspect of this deity, and one of the greatest aspirations of Indian art is found at the Shiva Temple at Elephanta. Set deep into the recesses, looming up from the darkness to fill the full height of the cave is the three-headed Maheshamurti. In this image the seemingly irreconcilable aspect of Shiva as Aghora, the malevolent being with terrifying eyes and tusked teeth, is fused with his feminine aspect of man-woman, Ardhanarisvara. These two faces being profiled, meet in a frontal image which is composed, calm and beatific, unmoving as the Mahayogi. This is also an image which transcends the material and the scope of the human imagination, to achieve a grandeur that remains with us.

The most spectacular case of "mountain building" is surely the great temple of Kailash at Ellora. At the insistence of a Rashtrakuta king, the temple was excavated a hundred feet downwards into the mountain rock, scooping out 3 million cubic feet of stone before it was completed a century later. An inscription declares the delight of the final architect who exclaims, "Wonderful! O how could I have ever done it!"

It must have taken infinite patience and manpower to carry out the detailed plan, on two storeys. In addition, there are free-standing pillars of victory *(kirti-stambha)* in the spacious courtyard, ancillary shrines surrounding the

daily service of the pilgrims. At Nathdwara in Rajasthan, the mural painters and *pechwai* painters (who paint on cloth) also produce the paintings which serve as popular mementos and souvenirs. At the classic 10th-century temple of Thanjavur known as the Brihadesvara, mural paintings have recently been discovered in the inner sanctum. At the Virupaksha Temple in Vijayanagar, magnificent 16th-century wall hangings have been preserved.

Although these murals are in a fragmentary condition today, it is possible to suggest that they inspired the narrative style of manuscript paintings. Here, our earliest records are to be found in religious institutions – the Jain and Buddhist libraries *(bhandars)* where such manuscripts have

courtyard that are dedicated to the mother goddesses *(matrikas)* and other deities, long galleries filled with images, and a stupendous relief, at the entrance porch, of the goddess of fertility, Gajalakshmi, seated upon beds of lotuses in full bloom. These militant sculptures are carved from living rock – asserting the triumph of the Brahmanical faith in India.

In medieval India the temple grew in importance and power, in its cohesive role as the centre of religious, political and social activity. To this day, many temples maintain their own craftsmen: chariot-makers, lamp-makers, sculptors, painters, weavers and bronze-imagemakers – as well as the cooks and scribes who were in the

been carefully "bound" in wooden covers wrapped in cloth and preserved since the 10th and 11th centuries. Since paper was not introduced into India until the 14th century, these writings were inscribed on palm leaf or on parchment, with illustrations that related specifically to the texts of the Jain *Kalpa Sutra* or the stories of the *Balagopala Stuti*. Curiously, no manuscripts of that time have survived of the Hindu epics such as the *Ramayana* and the *Mahabharata*. They appear only with the tremendous surge of vernacular literature in the 16th century.

As opposed to images in stone and in bronze

Above, salacious sculpture from Khajuraho.

that were installed for worship, paintings were commissioned for both religious and secular reasons. Manuscripts were often commissioned as an act of piety by merchants. Remarkable attention was given to details of the interiors of homes, to door hangings, to fine jewellery and patterns of cloth.

Much of the art was inspired by the dance dramas (*natakas*) that formed part of the entertainment of medieval India. In paintings from Malwa, passages from the epics of the *Mahabharata* and the *Ramayana* are dramatised against a red ground with the figures of the heroes profiled, with Hanuman leaping across the great blue divide of the ocean, and his army of monkeys poised to attack the kingdom of Lanka. The narrative element of the pictures is all-important.

A great religious fervour was awakened in medieval India. The *Ramayana* was rewritten in the vernacular by Tulsidasa. Ecstatic poems on Lord Krishna were composed by the blind singer Surdas, the princess Meerabai and a host of other mystics. Most of all, it is the *Geet Govinda* of Jayadeva which transports us into romance, immortalising the passion of Krishna and his beloved Radha. Their secret meetings beside the river Yamuna, Krishna's dalliance, Radha alone pining with blossoming trees that wound her like arrows, and their ultimate reunion became favourite themes in painting. Here the lotus, the peacock and the sky thundering with clouds, all contribute to the essential mood of the text.

Another set of mood paintings are the Ragamalas, where modes of music are personified in pictorial situations. The colours here are inflamed with passion, undiluted. In Raga Bhairavi, for example, a brilliant red serves as the background to a captivating woman seated before the Shiva *lingam*, performing a *puja*. A remarkable affinity is shared between her and the dark peacock on the roof, set off by the white flower garlands draped on the *lingam*.

In Rajput paintings from the state of Bundi, lovers are shown in different seasons watching the lightning and clouds gathering in the monsoon skies, or bathing in the river in the hot months of the summer. These are the Baramasa paintings, depicting the activities of the 12 months of the year, and they are imbued with the natural beauty of the landscape.

Krishna becomes the archetypal love, so much so that every prince or lover is portrayed as Shyama, the blue god, with lotus eyes and a skin as dark as the clouds.

Book illustration: In Islam, the proscription against idolatry and the making of images resulted in the refinement of the decorative arts. Yet it was the art of the book that was held to be the noblest form of expression, combining as it does the talents of the calligraphist, the illuminator in gold, the illustrator and the book-binder. Calligraphy acquired a semi-mystical place in the arts, being reproduced on paper and vellum, on leather, metal and canvas, on tile and ceramic, and on the walls and arches of the monuments.

In the three sultanate courts of India, book production was encouraged. The Mughals also were a very literary dynasty, with Babur, the founder, having written his memoirs as the first guidebook to Hindustan, in which, with the eye of the naturalist, he describes the different species of fruits and trees and animals of Hind. Almost 100 years later, his great grandson Jahangir also wrote his memoirs of the Tuzuk, where he boasts of the fact that he can improve on the passages of Babur. He can summon his master painter of animals, Mansur, titled the Wonder of the Age, to paint with great accuracy and remarkable detail and so illustrate his descriptions of exotic animals such as the zebra and the turkey cock.

Curiously, it was the Emperor Akbar, reputed to have remained illiterate all his life, who became the greatest patron of painting, perhaps because he couldn't read the text, which he would have read aloud to him. To commemorate the Mughal dynasty, histories of the reign were commissioned – the *Babur Nama*, the *Timur Nama* and the *Akbar Nama* – as official chronicles. Each of these was illustrated, not once, but several times. To develop an understanding of other religions, Akbar had the Hindu epics translated into Persian, and illustrated.

Thus a new studio of artists had to be recruited from all over India. The fusion of the Islamic and the Hindu elements resulted in a new style that was bold and dynamic, bursting with energy. There is tremendous curiosity for the anecdotal in these works, as well as an inbred realism in depicting people from the court and the village. Singers, sufis, dervishes, horse-trainers, falconers, musketeers, carpenters, and stone masons appear to be rendered with as much interest as are the courtiers, the ambassadors and the princes. This becomes then, the ultimate contribution of Mughal painting: in rendering the details of life and in introducing a quality of portraiture that remains unsurpassed even today.

"The natives there show very much ingenuity in their curious manufactures, as in their silk stuffs, which they most artificially weave, some very neatly mingled either with silver or gold or both… They make likewise excellent carpets of their cotton wool, in mingled colours, some of them three yards broad and of great length. Some other richer carpets they make all of silk, so artificially mixed as that they lively represent those flowers and figures made in them. Their skill is likewise exquisite in making of cabinets, boxes, trunks and standishes, curiously wrought within and without, inlaid with elephants' teeth or mother of pearl, ebony, tortoise-shell or wire, and curious they are in cutting of all manner of stones, diamonds as well as others."

What the English explorer Terry saw in his *Voyage to the East Indies* in 1655 holds equally for India today. A feast of colours, textures, techniques and motifs awaits the traveller. Every village in each state of India has its own unique skills and exquisite objects, made often by the same families in a continuing tradition.

Indian crafts can be broadly divided into two streams, those created for personal use and adornment by men and women whose primary livelihood is agriculture or animal husbandry, which only incidentally find markets elsewhere; and those made by professional craftsmen on commission for a particular market or buyer.

Some states and regions predominate in one kind of craft and others in another. In the hill states and Gujarat, every village surface, utensil and garment is vibrantly alive with colour and ornamentation spontaneously created for their own pleasure, while the equally skilled and varied hands of Uttar Pradesh and Kashmir make almost entirely market-oriented shawls, silverware, carpets, ivories and brocades. Is it history, geography, economics or the weather that impels the directions creativity takes? If it is the dry, brown parched landscape of the Bani desert that causes the contrasting exuberance of Kutchi craft, and the green fertility of Kerala that evokes the austere simplicity of its architecture, bronze *varpus* and white cotton weaves, how does one explain the flowering lushness of Kashmiri craft motif?

Left, applique artist, Orissa.

Craftsman traditionally have had the status of artists, tracing their descent from Vishwakarma, "Lord of the Many Arts, Master of a Thousand Handicrafts, Carpenter to the Gods, Architect of Their Celestial Mansion, Designer of All Ornaments, the First of All Craftsmen." Products of their skill can be traced back 5,000 years and the same skills endure today. The fine muslins used as shrouds for royal Egyptian mummies draped Mughal emperors 3,000 years later, and were given poetic names like "running water" *(abrawan)*, "evening dew" *(shabnam)*, and "woven air" *(bafthava)*, by court poets. Now they are commissioned as scarves by Yves St Laurent and Zandra Rhodes.

Weavers in Bengal tell the story of the Emperor Aurangzeb rebuking his daughter, Princess Zebunissa, for appearing in public naked. She showed him that her muslin drapes were wound seven times round her body.

For the novice tourist, the first overwhelming impact is of Kashmiri crafts – papier mâché, crewel embroidery and carpets, all vibrant with the flowing imagery and colour of the foliage, flora and fauna of Kashmir's enchanted landscape. The glint of metal comes next. Brass, copper, silver and gold – hammered, beaten or cast; engraved, enamelled or repoussé – have been used through the centuries all over India in shapes consecrated by tradition to temple ritual or court ceremonial, or simply to bring water from the village well. Each metal has its ascribed attribute: according to an ancient text, the *Kalika Purana,* gold "removes the excesses of the three humours and promotes strength of vision", and silver is "favourable and inimicable to bile, but calculated to increase the secretion of wind and phlegm", bronze is "agreeable and intellectual," but brass is "windgenerating, irritating",and iron is "beneficial in overcoming dropsy, jaundice and anaemia".

Metals made to do wonders: Techniques and traditional craft forms worth looking out for are the engraved and enamelled *meenakari* brassware of Rajasthan and Uttar Pradesh, with its main centres in Jaipur and Moradabad, known as *siakalam, chikan* and *marori* work. The designs are chased on tinned brass, then filled in with black or coloured lacquer applied with a hot tool and finally polished. The coloured patterns, generally flowing arabesques of flowers and foliage, stand out on the glittering metal. In Jaipur and Udaipur, you will also find exquisitely enamelled silver and gold ornaments and *objets d'art,* with precious stones embedded amongst the brilliant blues, greens and deep reds, fired in furnaces sunk deep into the ground.

Less well-known but stunning in its dramatic black and white is *bidri,* the silver damascene or inlaid metal originating in the old Hyderabad state. The stylised floral motifs or geometric trellis designs from Mughal architecture are engraved and set in silver leaf on boxes, bowls and vases made of an alloy of copper, zinc and lead treated with a solution of copper sulphate and saltpeter which turns it jet black.

gold and silver, or copper and brass – either by inlaying or embossing, or welding them together, the resulting contrast of colour and texture is known as *Ganga-Yamuna* (the confluence of India's two rivers). This is a favourite technique all over India, from the Tanjore plates of the South, with mythological figures encrusted in high relief in white metal on copper, to the brass and copper utensils of the hill states in the northeast.

Cire-perdue, or the lost-wax technique of casting brass, bronze and bell metal objects, is also used all over India. Made in this way are the life-size bronzes of Hindu deities made at Swamimalai in Tamil Nadu; the austerely elegant ritual vessels of Kerala; and the delightful

The more common form of damascene wirework – the base of brass or bronze, with gold and silver wire ornamentation –which travelled to India via Iran and Afghanistan from its original home in Damascus, was patronised by the Emperor Akbar. His warriors went to war with Koranic verses inscribed in golden *koftagiri* calligraphic arabesques on their sword hilts. In Udaipur, Alwar and Jodhpur, you can still see beautiful daggers and shields made by descendants of the royal armourers who now occasionally turn their hands to more utilitarian objects such as nutcrackers, scissors, and betelnut cutters.

When two metals are used in conjunction –

dhokra toy animals of Madhya Pradesh and Bengal. Styles differ, but the technique remains the same; the object is moulded in clay, coated with wax, and then encased in more clay. The molten metal is poured in through a small hole in the outer layer, melting the wax which runs out, with the metal taking its place and hardening. The clay coating is then removed and the object polished, chased and finished on a lathe.

Stoneware and woodwork: Everyone's image of India is the Taj. Its exquisite marble mosaics

Far left, *Zari* (gold embroidery) on palanquin cover, Jodhpur. **Left**, potter at work, Gujarat.

and inlays and delicate trellises are still reproduced in Agra today in beautiful boxes, tabletops, plates and bowls, the translucent white marble or alabaster inlaid in Mughal flower designs in mother-of-pearl, lapiz and cornelian.

Other stoneware to look out for is the statuary of Mamallapuram (Mahabalipuram), which echoes the vibrant, powerful themes of South Indian temple art; the green serpentine or rust Gaya stone; rock crystal and alabaster boxes, bowls and animal figures of Jaipur, Varanasi and Bihar; the black chlorite utensils of Orissa; and the wonderful red and buff sandstone pillars, balconies and windows of domestic and temple architecture all over Rajasthan and Gujarat, whose stone lattice-work is often described as "frozen lace".

Similar themes and patterns are echoed in wood. India was once called "the land that has no furniture", but wood was always extensively used, not only in architecture and sculpture but also for ceremonial carriages and palanquins, dowry chests, screens and myriad smaller articles, ornamental or utilitarian. Sandalwood was considered the most auspicious and in both South and North India, finely carved statuettes, fans, frames and boxes are made of this delicate, aromatic wood. Walnut in Kashmir; black wood, mahogany, redwood and ebony in the south and east; teak everywhere, are carved and ornamented in a variety of ways, though the ancient *Shilpashastras* sagely prohibited the use of wood from trees struck by lightning or withered by disease; those in which birds had built nests; or those growing near burial or cremation grounds; or those trampled by elephants.

The *sadeli* marquetry work of Surat in Gujarat; the *tarkashi* brass wire inlay of Rajasthan and Uttar Pradesh; ivory and mother-of-pearl inlay in the south; the brass sheet inlay *pattara* dowry chests and doors of Saurashtra; the *kamangiri* figurative painted woodwork of Jodhpur and Jaipur; the brilliantly hued lacquer work of Sankheda, Nirmal and Sawantwadi; the lattice lace of *jali* screens from Saharanpur; the flowers and foliage carved into the satin finish of Kashmiri walnut; the gesso and goldleaf of Bikaner, are all worth looking for. (Bikaneri gold gessowork is also done on lampshades and scent bottles made of the translucent inner hide of camels.) Kondapalli in Andhra, Udaipur and Sankheda all make delightful, painted wooden toys.

Ceramics and terracotta are not the most durable of souvenirs for the tourist to take home but no visitor to India should miss the sight of the village potter turning his wheel with his big toe and producing, with a few flicks of his thumb, a shape identical to that which his forefather threw in Mohenjodaro 5,000 years ago.

Not turned on a wheel but moulded is the famous Blue Pottery of Jaipur. Made of ground felspar mixed with gum rather than clay and painted a pure, opaque white with turquoise and cobalt blue floral and figurative designs, it is reminiscent both of Persian tiles and Chinese porcelain and yet is richly, eclectically Indian in feel. Other lovely shapes and glazes are the blue and green cutwork pottery of Khurja, the black ware of Chinhat and Azamgarh in Uttar Pradesh, and the huge terracotta horses of Tamil Nadu and Bengal.

The language of colour: Colour in India is one's most enduring impression and, as Kamladevi Chattopadhya, one of the foremost names in the local art scene, has said, every colour has its tradition, emotional content and rich significance. "Red, the colour of marriage and love; orange, saffron the colour of the ochre earth and the *yogi* who renounces that earth; yellow, the colour of spring, young mango blossoms, of swarms of bees, of southern winds and the passionate cry of mating birds. Blue… the colour of indigo also the colour of Krishna, the cowherd child god… he that is of the colour that is in the newly formed cloud, dormant with that darkness that is rain. Even the great gods had their colour – Brahmin was red, Shiva was white and Vishnu was blue."

Textiles: The richness of colour and motif in Indian textiles is overwhelming. The *Vishnudharmottaram* speaks of five white tones – ivory, jasmine, the August moon, August clouds after rain, and mother-of-pearl. A *tanchoi* brocade from Varanasi will play on the contrast of one delicately differing shade against another in shadow and sun, while a South Indian temple sari might have a body of shocking Indian pink and a border of parrot green with stylised elephants, tigers and peacocks.

Woven, waxed, embroidered, appliquéd, brocaded, block-printed, painted, tie-dyed, tinselled: running the whole gamut from simple to splendid, a few rupees to a fortune, there is something for every season and ceremony.

Often seen abroad are block-printed cottons and Saurashtrian mirrorwork, Indian silks and brocades, Kashmiri carpets and shawls. (The celebrated "ring-shawl" is made from the fleece the wild Himalayan ibex sheds on rocks and bushes and is so fine that a metre-length passes through a man's signet ring.) Textiles have been among India's major exports since the Pharaohs.

Fascinating lesser known techniques are the tie-and-dye *bandhani* saris and scarves of Rajasthan and Gujarat, in which fine cotton or silk is knotted into minute patterns with waxed string and dyed in successive deepening shades of different colours. The knots are untied later to produce delicate spotted designs, each dot often no bigger than a matchhead, all over the body of the fabric. In *laheria bandhani* the

ated with marriage, and no bride's trousseau is complete without one or the other.

Kalamkari, literally "the art of the pen", a wax-resist technique taking its name from the bunch of steel wires attached to a wooden handle with which the melted beeswax is painted on to cloth before it is dyed, is another beautiful and subtle textile, similar in technique to Indonesian *batik,* but with very different colouring and designs. There are two main centres in coastal South India: Machlipatnam specialising in the delicate, all-over floral trellis designs that were the origin of chintz *(Chhint);* Kalahasti in bold, black-outlined, heavily stylised mythological panels where calligraphy and pageantry, goddesses and warriors, riot together in ba-

cloth is tied to make fine diagonal stripes of contrasting colour. When the Prince Regent's passion for snuff in the late 18th century made snuff-taking a European fashion and coloured handkerchiefs to hide the ensuing stains a painful necessity, it was the *bandhani* or bandanna spotted kerchief that came to the rescue.

Allied to the *bandhani* technique is *ikat.* In the case of the *patola, pochampalli, telia rumal* and *mashru* weaves of Gujarat, Andhra and Orissa, the warp and weft threads are separately tie-dyed before being woven into intricate, stylised designs of flowering shrubs, birds, elephants and fish set in geometric squares and stripes. Both *bandhani* and *patola* are associ-

roque curlicues. Both styles use indigo and myrobalam vegetable dyes on handspun fabric with deep blue, ochre and dun as the predominant colours.

Marco Polo said of India in the 13th century: "embroidery is here produced with more delicacy than anywhere in the world." Two differing but equally exciting techniques are the *phulkari* (flower-craft) of Punjab and the *chikan* work of Uttar Pradesh. In its bold surface satin stitch in vivid satin floss oranges, pinks and flames, the *phulkari* reflects the vigour and vibrant energy of the Punjabi peasant; while the *chikan's* typical delicate white on white floral net and shadow work shows the subtlety and refinement of the Mughal court, where, legend has it, Noorjehan, Queen Consort to the Emperor Jahangir, devised the craft.

Delightful too are the *kantha* quilts of West Bengal. *Kantha* literally means rag, and is done on old *saris* laid one on top of the other and quilted in white asymmetrical circles and swirls. Coloured threads are then extracted from the borders of the saris and used to embroider folk motifs of animals, humans and trees all over the quilt, either in a spiral formation, starting with a central lotus or in squared-off panels, each with a different design.

All over India, embroidery, unlike weaving, is a female occupation. Secluded by custom or religion from the public eye, women get to-

exporters and the tourist trade. The gold and silver sequin and *zardoshi* embroidery of Uttar Pradesh, and the crewel, *Kani* and *Kashida* of Kashmir are all done by men. Making the various coiled and twisted gold and silver wires, spangles, sequins and braid is a craft in itself.

Images of Indian crafts are inescapably accompanied by images of their makers. It may be an 80-year-old ivory carver in the shadow of the Jama Masjid, his white beard curved over an ivory that's already taken him seven years, calmly speculating whether he'd live the further two he'd need to finish it; or apple-cheeked Kashmiri boys in skullcaps weaving carpets to the singsong drone of the pattern-reader's chant; a Rajasthani cobbler embroidering gold pea-

gether and sew either for pin money or their daughters' dowry chests. Designs and stitches are handed down from generation to generation as are the wooden pattern blocks. In Kutch, villages less than a couple of miles apart will each have their own distinctive stitches, patterns and colours.

The exceptions in this female-dominated field are Uttar Pradesh and Kashmir, two states whose crafts have traditionally been practised by skilled professionals for patrons, originally the Imperial Court and local nobility, but are now for

Left, *Ikat* **sari being woven, Andhra Pradesh. Above, carving in soapstone.**

cocks on shoes whose turned up toes echo the ends of his moustache; or a papier-mâché painter chasing a squirrel for new hairs for his brush.

So many of these images are of old men. Despite the vitality and variety of Indian craft, some skill dies every year. Mill prints and plastic are elbowing out traditional crafts in the village and greedy middlemen, ignorant of tradition, with their eye on foreign markets, are debasing them in the town. Craftsmen, generally illiterate, keep no records of what their forefathers made. The skills are in their fingertips but if you paint Mickey Mouse to order on a papier-mâché box often enough instead of a Mughal rose, eventually the memory of the rose will fade away.

Food is a serious business to most Indians. A gift of the gods, it is treated with respect and is subject to innumerable prescriptions. Based on pragmatic medical precepts evolved over hundreds of years of experimentation and observation, most are aimed at nourishing the body and pleasing the mind and eye.

Governing the ingredients in each meal are the time of the year and minute classifications on heating or cooling foods, age, and even personality. Once there were also injunctions on the six *rasas* or flavours that

Characteristic of all Indian cooking is the inspired use of spices. Far from being used only for flavour, they are appetite stimulators and digestives. "Heating" condiments for the winter are also used. Immense care is taken to ensure that spices enhance rather than dominate the basic flavour, and that they do not diminish nutritive value. Thousands of different dishes have been developed using various combinations of the dozen-odd basic-condiments.

Other important ingredients are milk and

must be included in every meal – sweet, salty, bitter, astringent, sour and pungent. Each was believed to have its particular physical benefit and was prescribed in a specified ratio to the others. Since food was thought to influence behaviour as well as physical wellbeing, these canons were taken very seriously, becoming, through time, part of the "subcontinental subconsciousness".

Despite the universality of these attitudes, there can be no generalisations about Indian food. The cuisines of India are as diverse as the country's culture, its racial structure, and the varied geographic conditions that determine climate, crop patterns and occupations.

milk products, particularly, ghee and *dahi* (curd). To the orthodox, a meal is pure only if cooked in ghee – an emphasis that derives not just from its distinctive fullness and unique flavour but from its acclaimed preservative qualities. With rising prices, vegetable oils have replaced ghee in most homes and restaurants.

Dahi is part of almost any Indian menu. Served to mitigate the chili "hotness" of some dishes, it is often mixed with vegetable or fruit and is lightly spiced to create the *raitas* of the north and the *pachadis* of the south. An important ingredient in several recipes, *dahi* is also churned and salted or sweetened to taste and served in summer as a cooling drink called *lassi*.

Dals (split lentils) too, are common to most parts of the country. Regional preferences and availability dictate the type used. This, together with the wide range of ingredients, has resulted in a bewildering variety, ranging from the thick tamarind-flavoured *sambhars* of the south and the sweetish dals of Gujarat to the delicious *maaki dal* of North India topped with fresh cream or butter.

Vegetables naturally vary with region and season. The style of cooking is determined by the cereal or main dish with which they are served. Deep-fried vegetable crisps are perfect accessories to the *sambhar* and rice of Tamil

with ghee, it is served with *sambhar, rasam* (a thin peppery soup), vegetables, both dry and in a sauce, and *pachadi*. Coconut is lavishly used in cooked foods as well as chutneys. Made of fermented rice and dal batter, the *dosa, vada* and *idli* are inexpensive South Indian snacks popular all over the country.

The semolina-based *upma*, cooked with curry leaves and garnished with nuts and copra, is another favourite. Other in-between bites found everywhere are the *samosa*, a three-cornered flour patty with potatoes, and *pakoras* or *bhajiyas* – vegetables coated in a gram batter and deep-fried. All are inexpensive and safe, provided they are eaten hot.

In Gujarat, another region famous for its

Nadu. The thick *avial* stew of Kerala cooked in coconut oil, or the *kaottu* in a coconut and gram sauce, are perfect for rice-based meals. *Sarson ka sag*, mustard greens, eaten with *maki ki roti* (maize bread) is a particularly well-known favorite in the Punjab, while the delicately favoured *chorchori* of Bengal complements the Bengali's rice and fish.

Vegetarian variety: India presents a vast range of vegetarian cooking. The largely non-greasy, roasted and steamed food of the south is very light. Rice is the basis of every meal. Saturated

vegetarian food, gram flour, a rich source of protein, is used in the making of breads and as a component of various dishes. *Kadi*, made from *dahi* and gram with a subtle combination of spices, is delightful. An interesting difference is the use of *gur* or jaggery to add a hint of sweetness to piquant sauces. *Aam rasa*, the puréed pulp of mangoes eaten with *puris* is a summer treat.

Although Bengali food is never actually sweetened, it is customary to serve a sweet along with the other food as a foil to the hot chillis or for a change in flavour. In keeping with religious mandates, Gujarati (especially Jain) and Bengali vegetarian food is often

Left, raw materials. **Above**, the ever-popular pork *vindaloo* from Goa.

cooked without the garlic, ginger, onions, and the "heating" or stimulating spices.

Possibly the purest form of North Indian vegetarian food is the Banarsi. Lightly spiced, many specialties are based on *paneer* (cottage cheese). A perfect protein substitute, it is cooked in innumerable ways, with spinach (*palak paneer*), in a gravy with peas (*mutter paneer*) or lotus seeds (*paneer phulmakhana*).

Then there is a whole range of deep-fried or stuffed breads, made of combinations of refined and wholemeal flour; the golden puffs called *puris*, the *parathas*, *baturas* and so on. Most widely eaten and internationally known is the simple *chapatti*, baked on a griddle in homes all over India.

subtypes evolved: the rich *kormas* and *nargisi koftas* (meatballs shaped around a hard-boiled egg) of Lucknow; the *pasandas* or mutton steaks cooked in an almond sauce; the *biriyani*, a layered rice and meat concoction famous in Hyderabad; and a variety of *kababs* that literally melt in the mouth.

Laden with nuts, dried fruits and saffron, Kashmiri Muslim food is a gourmet's joy. *Haleem*, mutton pounded with wheat; *gaustaba*, incredibly light meatballs; and *rogan josh* are well-known Kashmiri specialties.

Although rice is not the staple cereal of the north, it is an important accessory to many meals. Indeed, a good *pilau* (rice cooked in stock, with meat, vegetable or nuts) is consid-

Muslim influence is most evident in the cooking of meats. The major contribution was the *tandoor*, the conical earthen oven from which emerged a delectable array of *kababs* and *rotis*. This was the origin of the famous *tandoori* cooking, brought from the Northwest Frontier, but available all over the country – the *tandoori* chicken, *seekh*, *boti* and *barra kababs*, and recently, *tandoori* fish. Among the *rotis* are the elongated *nan*, the *tandoori roti*, or its richer equivalent, the *tandoori paratha*.

The fastidious Mughals transformed local recipes, developing the superb Mughlai cuisine, with its luscious sauces of *dahi*, cream and crushed nuts. An amazing variety of types and

ered the supreme test of a good cook. Innumerable variations have been evolved, but the most commonly available is the plain *muttar* or chicken *pilau* – rich, heavy and sustaining.

Vinegar lends a different taste to the meat dishes of Goa. The pork *sorpotel, vindaloo*, the Goan sausages and the chicken *shakuti* or *cafreal* are inimitable.

Fish too is prepared in dozens of different ways: the mustard-flavoured *macher jhol* and malai or cream prawns of Bengal, the chilli-hot curries of Andhra, and the coconut and curry-leaf flavoured specialties of the south, as well as the west coast and, of course, the memorable fish and shellfish curries of Goa.

Dried fish, misleadingly known as Bombay duck, is cooked with vegetables or *dals* and adds interest to the simpler fare of Maharashtra.

The Parsis also contributed interesting dishes. *Dhansak,* meat cooked with five different *dals* and an unusual blend of spices, and *patrani machi,* lightly spiced fish steamed in banana leaves, are just two examples.

Chutneys and pickles, sweet, sour or hot, or all three, whip the appetite and add relish to a meal. Many ingredients can be used: mint, coriander, mango, ginger, lime and different kinds of vegetables. Some are extravagantly spiced, while others may contain only salt.

Papads (or *papadums),* roasted or fried savoury crisps, are also popular meal adjuncts.

nuts. Crisp golden *jelabis,* dripping with syrup, made even in the tiniest bazaars all over the country, are breakfast and tea-time favourites.

Kheer, the Indian equivalent of rice pudding; *shahi tukra,* an exotic variation on bread pudding; *phirni,* made of powdered rice and served in earthenware bowls; and *kulfi,* a rich nutty ice cream; are common northern desserts.

Sweets from the south include Mysore *pak* and the creamy *payasum* while the Gujaratis are partial to *shrikhand* made of drained, sweetened and spiced *dahi. Halvas,* another genre of traditional desserts, are created from ingredients as diverse as carrots, semolina, *dals,* eggs, or even wholemeal flour.

And finally, there is the satisfying ritual of

Made of previously rolled and dried lentil or rice dough, or of vegetable tubers, they provide the crunchiness essential to every repast.

Often too sweet for the non-Indian palate, the huge array of Indian confections and desserts is largely milk-based. Bengal is particularly well-known for its confections. These include the *rasagulla, sandesh, rasamalai* and the steaming hot *gulab-jamuns.* Typical of the north are the *barfis* (milk cakes), some of pure milk, others of coconut or various types of

the after-dinner *pan,* a must for any true connoisseur of Indian food. Lauded for its digestive and medicinal properties, it is a fragrant combination of betel leaf, areca nut, catechu, cardamom, cloves and a choice of a whole host of other exotic ingredients of varying flavours, effects and strengths; an acquired taste perhaps, but quite an addiction thereafter.

Rising costs and time pressures inherent in urbanisation have led to a decline of the traditional Indian meal, now to be enjoyed only on very special occasions. In compensation, food from all over the country is now available in larger restaurants, everywhere, which are less authentic perhaps, but certainly most welcome.

Left, *samosas,* **one of India's favourite savoury snacks. Above left,** **the ubiquitous** *pan-walla;* **and right, essential ingredients.**

In India, animals are never far away. Even common house pests could include such exotics as a red-rumped monkey or a mongoose, besides the geckoes flexing on the wall or a scorpion hiding inside a shoe. Mynah birds and an occasional cobra in the garden come as no surprise. Camels and elephants wander in the street traffic and enormous humped cattle sometimes outnumber the vehicles on the road. Water buffalo loll beside the dhobi-ghats, where laundry is done. Huge birds of prey – vultures or pariah kites – spiral high overhead. These animals seem pretty wild, but wilder ones await.

Lions, tigers, and bears – savage and shy – inhabit the varied terrain of the sub-continent from Himalayan cloud forests to desert scrub. Landclearing had encroached on much of the former hunting grounds, and without the hundreds of game reserves and sanctuaries that have been established in India, many more might disappear. There's no chance of spotting a cheetah now, since the last of these swift cats died in 1994. The government of India continues to permit the destruction of big cats which are proven man-eaters, and so-called "cattle lifters" are often gunned down for revenge as well. These can be leopards, panthers, or tigers, though snow leopards and the daintier clouded leopard often are spared. Small jungle cats and fishing cats of Bengal still can be counted among India's feral felines.

Hundreds of stocky Asiatic lions prowl the Gir Forest Reserve in Gujarat, the only place in the world where they thrive. Unlike African lions, these cats don't have much mane, but carry most of their shaggy hair on the tip of their tails and elbows. Recently some young males strayed outside the park and were neutered by rangers, who were anxious that local cattleherders shouldn't start shooting randy lions if they dared put a paw outside their sanctuary. Striped hyenas feed on the lions' leftovers and there are more panthers visible in the Gir – pronounced "gear", not "Grrrr" – than at any other Indian park.

Bears are more aloof. Himalayan brown bears are heavy-set and larger than their black cousins, who live below the tree line on Himalayan slopes. Sloth bears, found over much of India, are mostly nocturnal. All three varieties can climb trees and swim if put to the test. The sloth bear grunts with pleasure or anger, and digs for termites and other grubs. It gobbles bees, but prefers honeycomb or sweet fruits and berries. The bears are hunted down for their gall bladders, sold for Chinese fertility medicine. Sloth bears can be seen in cities, shuffling along in chains and a muzzle, and earning a few rupees for their captors. In the northeast, small pandas are found and red pandas, which resemble slim, auburn racoons, hide in the trees.

Big beasts: The weird one-horned rhinoceros, which looks riveted into armour plates, keeps mainly to the northeastern woods around Kaziranga in Assam, though a number have been re-introduced to Dudhwa park in Uttar Pradesh, nudging India's total of rhinos over 2,000. Their horns, used as an aphrodisiac, fetch princely sums on the black market and are also prized as handles for ritual daggers used in Yemen, and hence a status symbol in the Middle East.

The rhino is usually viewed from elephant back. These mounts would be domestic elephants, huge yet capable of retrieving a lost lens cap in thigh-high brush. Wild tuskers found in the jungles are feared, with good reason. Some roam too close to villages, develop a taste for liquor and go on the rampage after guzzling the contents of a still. Others stampede through a cluster of thatched huts, mowing down everything in their path. Yet spying a herd of wild elephant, tearing calmly through the shrubbery, is a definite thrill. Such enormous beasts can move with surprising silence. An awe-struck villager will sometimes prostrate himself before "Lord Ganesh" who, puzzled, proceeds to crush his head with one mighty step.

There are an estimated 9,000 wild elephants in India, with thousands more working at temples, logging camps, game parks, or hired out for weddings. Periyar, in Kerala, is the best place to view elephants in the wild. Parks in West Bengal and Assam are also good bets. Elephants' memories are legendary and ailing beasts know just where to seek out curative

Preceding pages: egrets in flight at Bharatpur. Left, in India, wildlife walks the streets and takes part in the parties.

plants in the forest. Veterinarians tend to turn them loose to find their own cures.

Game tourism: Indian game viewing began on a grand scale in the 1950s, and even today the arrangements sometimes resemble gentlemen's shooting parties of that era. Creature comforts are not ignored in the wild, and some tents are quite luxurious, though many forest houses are rustic; basic ones are run by the government. Safari suits are worn mostly by chauffeurs for the middle class, not by would-be hunters with zoom lenses.

Unlike Africa, where great herds of beasts romp across the savannah giving photo opportunities galore to tourists in zebra-striped buses, wild animal watching in India takes patience.

Yet with almost 350 species of mammal, a couple of thousand types of bird, and at least 30,000 kinds of insect (more than you want to know personally), India provides an unmatched range and diversity that justifies several trips.

Tiger tales: Toothless tigers are not a sentimental myth out of Kipling's *Jungle Book*. The bodies of old, arthritic tigers – solitary hunters who obviously failed to kill enough prey once their vision got fuzzy – are sometimes found in Indian forests after they have starved to death. Some die of hunger in spite of an ability to hunt because their aged and wobbly fangs can no longer manage to tear raw flesh. Their only real enemy is man.

Tiger sightings are very rare these days. The

Many of the best beasts hide in the shadows, lone predators waiting for their opportunity. Game reserves are not easily accessible (except for Ranthambore in Rajasthan, near a railway connection), and many are downright remote. A few parks require special permits in advance, usually for a minimum group of four. In the northeast, where shy pandas and macaques hide in shadows, militants and tribes often do, too. The government limits visits near strategic borders or guerilla areas. It is always wise to check shortly before setting out, since situations change without much warning. At any sanctuary, dress in sensible camouflage and keep quiet; the creatures are easily spooked.

latest census by Project Tiger tallies only about 7,000 beasts in the world, more than half in India. A typical day's kill on a hunt in the days of the British Raj would be close to a hundred. Now, dead tigers are pegged out in clandestine markets while exporters barter ghoulishly over the bits to be sold to Chinese pharmacists. The brain makes an effective acne treatment; the kidney fat is rubbed onto a man's ailing organ to cure impotence. Assorted meat is chopped up and used to ward off snakes; the penis is preserved in an extravagantly exotic wine. In China, haemorrhoids are treated with tiger spore, and the animal's bile, its eyeballs, even its whiskers go into jars of medicine. A cruel assassination technique practised for centuries was to add ground tiger whiskers to food, supposedly causing the victim's digestive tract to be destroyed from the inside.

Because of the tiger's multitude of medicinal or magical properties, the tiger trade is extremely profitable. Stealth is essential. The majestic striped hide is unmistakable, and those caught with it are criminally charged or pay a phenomenal bribe. Genuine tiger skin is not fashionable among the politically correct and smuggling fur coats and rugs is difficult, though not impossible, for impoverished hunters. But tiger bone fetches a high price per kilo, and the amount for sale is easily stretched out with other powdery materials. Some buyers insist

itself by the mid-1990s. After more than 20 years overseeing a comeback of the big cats in India from a lowpoint of just 1,800 head, by promoting national parks and keeping a careful census each year in 300 reserves, their work may soon prove useless. The organisation was warned that the future of the Bengal tiger is bleak, unless the the Chinese population can be convinced to stop buying it. Seven thousand cats can't satisfy 1½ billion people.

People still stalk tigers through many terrains in India, from the high Himalayas, to the mangrove swamps of the Sunderbans or the thorny scrub of Rajasthan. At the turn of the century, there were over 40,000 big cats in the sub-continent. The tiger hunt, the Shirkar, be-

that tiger bones be ground before their eyes.

Imagine the temptation for forest dwellers, who are banned even from gathering wood in former hunting grounds, to poach a tiger. With one lucky shot, they can earn the equivalent of years spent labouring. Poorly paid game wardens are no match for organised poachers working in the remote game parks.

Project Tiger, a conservation organisation launched in 1972 with the support of Indira Gandhi, had become a bit of a toothless beast

came a cult among royal sharpshooters. Blasting away from high on elephant back, hunters would later pose beside a stack of striped pelts. During the British Raj, men in pith helmets and khaki shorts decimated the wild population. Even Britain's Prince Philip, now president of the World Fund for Nature, couldn't resist an invitation to a tiger shoot on any early royal visit to India. Today, with the jungle cover disappearing at a quick clip, the tigers are more at risk than ever.

Modern slaughter gives the tiger no dignity in death. Greedy poachers rarely use guns, especially since there is no longer a premium on intact pelts. Instead a carcass is wired to a

Left, a sambar hind on alert at Bandavgarh, Madya Pradesh. **Above**, a tiger in Ranthambore, Rajasthan.

few sticks of dynamite, and a curious tiger comes along and triggers an explosion. Roadworkers, who have blasting equipment and typically fish the rivers with dynamite, are often to blame. Others simply poison the tiger's own kill, usually a deer or goat, or lay snares for the beasts.

Throughout India, wildlife conservation laws are openly scorned. Game wardens fudge the statistics of sightings to keep the subsidies and the tourists coming. Meanwhile parcels of tiger bone are intercepted almost daily at airports and in the post.

Once worshipped as a symbol of strength, power and fertility throughout the east, the tiger is on its last legs. Recently, the Indians

ers penetrate. Even during the dry season, when thirsty animals slow down and are visible against the parched leaves, luck is still a key ingredient. Dusk or dawn is a likely hour. Jeeps, elephants, even dugout canoes carry visitors deep into the bush, and few will be disappointed by the experience, even if they only see the pug marks of big predators.

Other exotics: Such expeditions readily produce other specimens. Look out for the pangolin, a scaly anteater which resembles an armadillo but lives high in the treetops, using a prehensile tail help it to climb. This nocturnal creature, found mainly in dense eastern rainforest, hisses and rolls up into a bullet-proof ball when agitated.

refused the offer of tigers raised in captivity in Taiwan and earmarked to return to the wild. Officials felt they couldn't guarantee the tigers' survival in the diminishing Indian jungles. They feared the big cats would wind up back in China, on the shelf.

And yet the best bet for glimpsing a tiger in the wild is still to visit an Indian sanctuary before it is too late. Tiger reserves are especially rich in prey, so opportunities to see most animals increase accordingly.

At Kaziranga (Assam), Bandhavgarh or Kanha (Madhya Pradesh), Dudhwa or Corbett (Uttar Pradesh) or Bandipur (Karnataka) odds are more favourable than at parks where poach-

The rare slow loris curls into a fuzzy ball by day, then moves hand-over-hand through the trees, hunting in slow motion.

One tourist asked about the motorbike tracks in the back reaches of Corbett Park, only to be told that they were actually the trail of a great python, at least five inches wide. The python was later spotted snoozing under a rohini tree, belly bloated with a spotted fawn it had gobbled down whole. In comparison, the monitor lizards and iguanas seemed puny.

Crocodiles rarely look small. Although on the official list of endangered reptiles, hefty

Left, fine specimen of gaur, the Indian bison.

mugger crocodiles have been replenished by Romulus Whitaker, an American-born herpetologist who breeds them outside Madras. He sustains 10,000 by feeding them live rats like vitamin pills, and officials say that India's riverbanks and coastlines are now so well stocked that they have banned the release of any more. Narrow-nosed Gharial live well on fish, growing up to 16ft (5 metres) long in Indian rivers. In winter, they emerge to sun themselves and are more easily spotted. The huge saltwater crocodiles that sometimes will eat a child or a cow as an hors d'oeuvres are confined to the Andaman Islands, the Sunderbans in West Bengal, and Bhitar Kanika in Orissa.

Elsewhere on the plains, groups of black buck cluster together and look set to drill holes in the sky with their magnificent corkscrew horns. Antelope (some confusingly known as blue bulls) survive where religious sentiment outweighs hunger. Hangul stags, found only in Kashmir, are even bigger than sambar deer, and on the higher slopes ibex clamber. Brow-antlered deer, the country's rarest creature, hide in the northeastern forests.

Himalayan flowers seem to hover above the meadows, until closer inspection reveals that they are exotic butterflies evaporating dew from their iridescent wings. Gazelles or wild boar, leatherback turtles or blind river dolphins, porcupines or flying squirrels – all sorts of animals take sanctuary in game reserves around the country.

Bird life: Many rare birds stop over in India, joining the beauties that reside year round. Heavy-headed hornbills wing in pairs over northeastern and southern jungles. Raucous flocks of parakeets wheel over the trees in city parks. Near water, look for kingfishers, herons, spoonbills, flamingoes, egrets, or teal ducks. Birdwatchers in game parks should not ignore dangers: one eager ornithologist, binoculars trained on a nesting pair of minivets, was killed from behind by a tiger in Corbett Park.

Keoladeo Ghana sanctuary at Bharatpur near Agra is renowned for the number and variety of its feathered visitors, but in recent years, the Siberian cranes which usually winter at the park have failed to show up. Scientists blame trigger-happy militants in Afghanistan, which lies beneath their flight path, for the disruption.

Meanwhile volunteers, dressed up in odd beaked costumes to prevent the nestlings from bonding with humans, are hand-rearing Siberian crane chicks here in the hope that they might learn the migratory routes from ordinary cranes and eventually attract more birds from the cold wasteland of Russia.

Luckily, most travellers need not go to such lengths to enjoy the wildlife of India.

The top 15 wildlife parks: Following is a brief listing of the major parks and the wildlife that visitors can hope to see there. More details can be found in the Travel Tips section at the back of this book.

Kanha (Madya Pradesh): Tiger, deer, most species. Best months: from February to June (closed July to November).

Corbett (Uttar Pradesh): Tiger, mugger, gharial, deer, most species. Best months: from February to May.

Namdapha (Arunachal Pradesh): Tiger, clouded leopard, snow leopard, panther, red panther, gibbon, loris. Best months: from October to March.

Jawahar National Park (borders of Karnataka, Kerala, Tamil Nadu): Elephant, gaur, leopard. Best months: March to July, September and October. Includes the Bandipur, Mudumalai, Nagarhole and Wayanda reserves.

Kaziranga (Assam): Rhino, swamp deer, wild buffalo, tiger. Best months: from November to March.

Bhandavgarh (Madhya Pradesh): Big cats, deer, bear. Best months: November to June.

Periyar (Kerala): Elephant, monkey, some tiger. Best months: September to May.

Gir (Gujarat): Asiatic lion, wild ass, deer. Best months: from December to April.

Dudhwa (Uttar Pradesh): Tiger, rhino, sloth bear. Best months: from December to June.

Nanda Devi (Himachal Pradesh): Mountain goat, snow leopard. Best months: from April to October.

Ranthambore (Rajasthan): Tiger, jackal, deer, monkey. Best months: October to April.

Kumbulgarh (Rajasthan): Wolf, leopard, flying squirrel. Best months: from September to November.

Sunderbans (West Bengal): Tiger, turtle, crocodile. Best months: from December to February.

For the birds:

Keoladeo Ghana (Bharatpur, Uttar Pradesh): Cranes, migratory fowl. Best months: from August to February.

Chilka Lake (Orissa): Wading birds, flamingo, dolphin. Best months: from December to March.

Indian Railways is a huge state-run conglomerate that employs a massive one and a half million people (the world's largest employer) and moves 10 million passengers a day yet still remains remarkably efficient and uniquely poetic. There is no better way to get the pulse of the subcontinent than to view the changing scene from a carriage window. Incidentally, a "window" comprises several layers to keep out the sun, dust and ticketless travellers.

Though the British laid most of the 38,525 miles (62,000 km) of track, it was assumed at independence that the end of colonial rule marked the beginning of travel as you please. Your train may be held up while a "travelling magistrate" disillusions these believers in the socialist millennium who've tried to enter by the windows.

Because it is run by the government, the logic of transport is often ignored in favour of political mileage. Thus the fast trunk inter-city services known as *Rajdhani* (to various state capitals from Delhi) are apt to be slowed down by demands for intermediate halts to suit local members of Parliament. Recently, the overnight switch of political power from North India to the constituencies of the South resulted in the conversion of metre gauge to broad gauge, a decision that had been considered unrealistic under North Indian prime ministers.

And yet in spite of political interference the working of the railways is impressive. Serving under the Rail Minister is the Railway Board whose chairman is invariably a railway engineer. The system is divided into nine zones which derive in part from the reach of the imperial private companies. For example, today's Central Railway has inherited the extent and style of the Great Indian Peninsular lines. Zonal profiles vary considerably with the southern states profitably in command of their assets (borne out by the smart livery of both rolling stock and railwaymen) while those in the north and east wilt under the burden of saturation (evident in the scruffy turn-out of the rolling stock and the surly mood of staff).

Reservation is now computerised at most of the big stations and the overseas traveller will find various special quotas available to him if pressed for time. Indrail Rover Tickets, bookable abroad, provide a good bargain for the dedicated traveller just as the Palace on Wheels trains (being extended from the desert forts of Rajasthan to cultural destinations in other parts of India) give an intensive introduction to a specific area.

Certainly for the luxury of service if not for speed and fittings the first class air-conditioned compartments of Indian Railways are as good as any in the world. When you compare what the railways give you for about the comparable price of a plane ticket with all the delays and charmlessness of airports, then body and soul travels more meaningfully by train. After a relaxed journey you arrive in the middle of town. Budget travellers can also go by second class air-conditioned or three-tier air-conditioned sleeper coach so that the heat and dust of yesteryear are filtered out.

On board, there are rules and there are rules. Officially, no drinking is allowed, but those most likely to benefit from abstention from alcohol are least troubled by warnings. Just as first class passengers are free to indulge, so are they allowed to take their pets aboard with them, an instance where revenue potential has outgunned ideology.

Diesel fumes account for most of India's civic pollution so don't be too hard on the cinder-spewing steam locomotive, condemned officially to the scrap heap. (Rumour had it that the constant pilfering of coal was a major factor in the fate of steam.) Luckily, two famous tourist lines will continue steam-running for as long as their vintage fleets are able to take on the challenge of the Himalayas (to Darjeeling) and the Nilgiris (to Ootacamund).

India boasts two of the oldest locos still at work in the world. *Tweed* and *Mersey* get up steam (1873 vintage) each winter on private industrial lines to cart sugar cane on the metre gauge east of Gorakhpur in Uttar Pradesh.

Steam traction, although officially abolished, can still be glimpsed up forgotten branch lines, usually in areas where respectable citizens rarely tread. For example, in the North East zone paralleling the Uttar Pradesh and Bihar border with Nepal, you may find the standard workhorses of the metre gauge, the UP and YG class of engines hauling local passenger trains.

Left, all clear down the line.

Do not make the mistake of enquiring at Indian Railways headquarters at Rail Bhavan in New Delhi about the existence of these overlooked steamers. Nostalgia has no place here and steam is frowned upon as a sign of backwardness.

To photograph Indian Railway assets, it is necessary to get permission from New Delhi and entry to the immaculate portals of Rail Bhavan will be an eye-opener to anyone who believes all Indian government offices to be run-down and stained by betel-nut juice. Photography restrictions usually apply to prohibited areas, military installations and other sensitive subjects. Make sure your permit states a time-frame, otherwise nit-picking under-

Assam you can still tool along parallel to the entire length of the Himalayas to Jhaj in Gujarat, a 2,490-mile (4,000-km) journey that takes anything up to five days. The contrast in scenery is sensational, with the lush rhino tracks of the Brahmaputra giving way to the rice paddies of West Bengal and then to the wheat fields of Uttar Pradesh. Rajasthan brings the desert sands that stretch to the bare but beautiful Rann of Kutch – home to the galloping wild ass.

The coasts on both sides of the subcontinent offer some fine scenery but the Coromandel leading to Madras is more impressive. With the new length of Konham Railway from Bombay to Mangalore, a fabulous stretch of coastal scenery is soon to open up. Probably the most

strappers at loco sheds are sure to argue it is valid only for the day of issue.

The most serious defect in Indian Railways is that the combined forces of feudalism and bureaucratic palsy can conspire to erase the very real poetry of the railroad – if you let them. The art is to escape from your zone of despair and try another. Generally, anything south of Delhi tends to get better.

Prime lines: Not all progress is forwards. Up till 1994 the traveller could cover the entire subcontinent by one gauge, but since then the metric has been sacrificed to a broader option that does not (nor probably ever will) have such extensive coverage. However, from Ledo in

sensational coastal run of all is to Rameshwaram, on the isle of Pamban. Formerly this line ran another 12 miles (20 km) along a narrow spit of sand to Danushkodi, but the entire line was obliterated by a storm in 1965.

Inland the hill railways of India are famous for their character and quaintness. Not far from Bombay is the climb to Matheran by tiny narrow gauge stock. Darjeeling's toy railway is well known. Ooty's also is widely loved but contrary to popular notions about its "rack" (which only runs as far as Coonoor) this is not a narrow gauge railway but metric. Whereas the Darjeeling engines are of Scottish extraction, the tankers that push up the Ooty train (from the rear) are Swiss with an extra set of pistons to work the rack mechanism.

While the hill line to Simla is famous for its 103 tunnels, a better view of the Himalayan peaks can be had from its sister narrow gauge line that runs through the Kangra Valley.

For the mechanically-minded the world's highest broad gauge track is notable for the triple-headed trains that carry down iron ore from Kirinul to the port of Visakhapatnam for export, a modern engineering triumph for Indian expertise. A daily mixed train from Fizag runs up this line and over the Eastern Ghats to the tribal capital of Bastar.

Other impressive crossings, this time of the Western Ghats, are from Tenkasi to Quilon and

most common bookseller in the North and Higginbottom's in the South. Similarly the cries of vendors announce regional tastes. *Chai* (tea) is the popular drink to the North, whereas coffee is the choice of the southerners.

An Indian *Bradshaw* is published monthly by Newmans of Calcutta. One advantage of consulting this timetable will be to prove wrong those who say you can't find steam outside Ooty and Darjeeling. It mentions a stretch of narrow gauge that takes off from the Indian border to comprise the total length of Nepal's 34-mile (54-km) railway system.

Timetables have their own language. Express trains are numbered according to a code that lists their point of origination. Locomotives

the newer and more dramatic alignment from Mangalore to Hassan. Yet another memorable ghat line is over the Aravalli range from Jodhpur to Udaipur in Rajasthan, past craggy forests and the highest point on the Western Railway.

On the platform: A lot of old railway fittings are of British inspiration. Look out for platform furniture, ticket issuing machines, weighing machines and the Neale token dispenser in the station-master's office. At some rural halts, wall clocks dating back to Queen Victoria can be seen. Platform bookstalls are a giveaway of your geographical locations. Wheeler's is the

are classified according to gauge and duty. Broad gauge locos are prefixed by W, metre gauge by Y and the diminutive narrow gauge by Z. P or G is affixed to indicate passenger or goods train. For diesel engines the letter D has been introduced and for electric traction A (the current used).

As well as "passenger" and "goods" classification, you can find "mixed" duty locos that boast the letter M. For example, WDM4 will refer to a broad gauge diesel loco designed for mixed duties. The number following it refers to development from prototypes, meaning that three earlier models had led to this improved

Left, Toy Train at Ooty. **Above**, wheels on rails.

mark 4.

PLACES

No one feels neutral about India. It slams you in the face with heat, spice and dirt, then seduces you with colour and sensual pleasure. Time distorts, and assumes surreal yogic contortions: distance takes longer to travel, minutes crawl during interminable waits, then vanish into a blur of hours, even days. The constant chaos can charm or repulse, as everything jostles for attention at once.

And there are so many different facets of India: 25 states and seven Union Territories offer a bewildering number of travel options.

Trekking to tribal villages in the Western Ghats is a physical challenge. Chugging across the Deccan Plain in a three-tiered sleeper car while the other passengers snore away is a mental one. The pride of an artisan working at his potter's wheel or loom is obvious; the appeal of rural villages trimmed with whimsical murals is unforgettable.

Visit an old Portuguese fort or an ancient Jewish synagogue. Take refuge in a remote pleasure palace a full day's camel ride away from the rest of the world. Barter in a bazaar for old silver, new rugs, inlaid daggers, or go for the miniature paintings brushed with a squirrel's whisker, the antique opium boxes, or new jewellery made with crushed gemstones: it's all spread out before your eyes in a former caravanserai.

Many visitors come to India seeking something within themselves, some spiritual calm beyond the cacophony. Volunteering to work in Mother Teresa's orphanage or undergoing an ascetic course at a retreat beside a holy river can be life-changing experiences.

Indian's travel experiences can be similarly uplifting. Take a hot air balloon over a river where elephants bathe. They'll glance skyward and puzzle over the spectacle of a Mughal dome in free flight. White water rafting down the Ganga, practising yoga on a sunrise beach, tracking wildlife in game sanctuaries, climbing a Himalayan peak, sketching wildflowers in a hill station meadow, or examining erotic sculpture at tantric temples: it would need immense stamina to undertake all the travel possibilities in India. The following pages will help readers awaken their wanderlust and give a rounded view of the people and places that might otherwise be omitted from a journey because of shortage of time.

Some run away from India; others keep returning.

Preceding pages: ghats on the Ganga, Varanasi; dry valley in Ladakh; dusk in Pushkar, Rajasthan; Dilwara Temple, Mount Abu. **Left,** homeward bound after a day in the fields, Gujarat.

DELHI, A LIVING HISTORY

History lives in Delhi, the capital of India. The ancient and the modern, the old and the new are in constant juxtaposition here, not only in the remains of a succession of empires, but in contemporary social structure and lifestyles.

The name Delhi, Dehali or Dilli is derived from *Dhillika*, the name of the first medieval township of Delhi, located on the southwestern border of the present Union Territory of Delhi, in Mehrauli. This was the first in the series of seven medieval cities. It was also known as Yoginipura, that is, the fortress of the *yoginis* (female divinities).

There was, however, an ancient urban settlement in Delhi known as Indraprastha on the banks of the Yamuna which is traditionally believed to have been founded by the Pandava brothers, the mythical heroes of the *Mahabharata*, the national epic of India. Excavations at the site of the township inside Purana Qila suggest that the date of the oldest habitation in the Delhi area is around the 3rd and 4th century BC.

A more significant phase of development of Delhi, however, commenced around the 8th to 9th century AD with the foundation of Dhillika, the first of the seven medieval cities under the Tomars, a local line of Rajput chieftains. Dhillika, which was protected by a stone fortification, now known as **Lalkot**, had beautiful temples, tanks and other buildings. Around the middle of the 12th century, the Tomar kingdom of Delhi was conquered by the Chahamanas (Chauhans) of Central Rajasthan. Prithviraja Chauhan III extended the area of the town by constructing a second defence wall with gates, now called **Qila Rai Pithora**, on three sides of the Tomar fortification.

The authority of Prithviraja did not last long. In 1192–93, Muhammad-bin-Sam, the Turkish invader from Ghor (Central Asia), defeated and killed Prithviraja. With this, Hindu rule came to an end and a new epoch of Islamic ascendancy began.

Preceding pages: Gurkha troops at Republic Day Parade, Delhi.

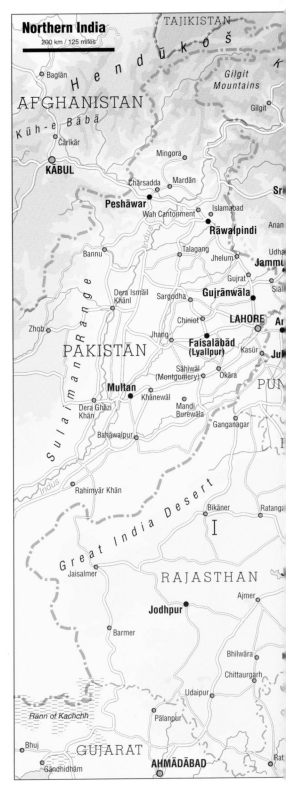

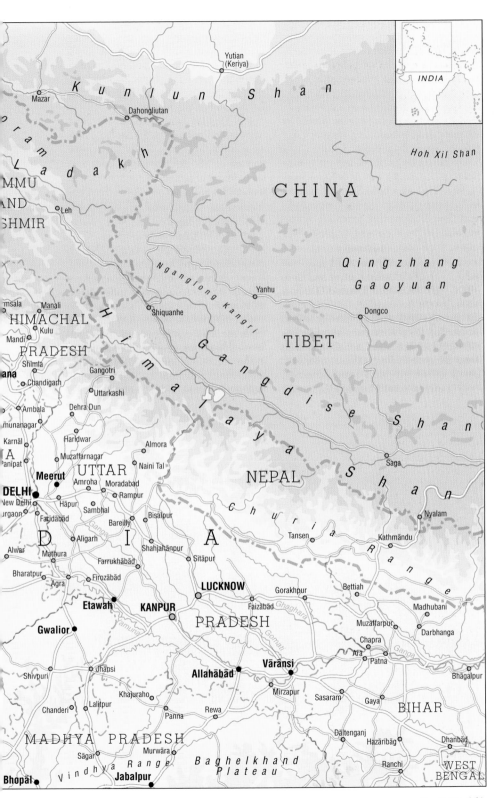

Gradually, the invaders got Indianised and developed a unique composite culture, the reflection of which can be observed in the Indian way of life even today. From this cultural fusion came a unique style of architecture termed Indo-Islamic, the poetic language of Urdu and forms and styles of music, dance, dress and cuisine. Delhi, as the main Indo-Islamic city, played a significant role in the process.

The Khalji Sultanate came to power in Delhi in 1290 and it was Alauddin Khalji (1296–1316) who built **Siri**, the second Delhi northeast of the original Tomar township. The Khaljis were followed by the Tughlaqs as the masters of the Delhi Sultanate. The founder of the new royal house, Ghiyasu'd-Din, within his short reign (1321–25), raised the third city of Delhi called **Tughlaqabad**, 5 miles (8km) to the south of Lalkot.

His successor, Muhammad Tughlaq (1325–51), transferred his capital to the south, but soon shifted it back to Delhi where he founded the fourth city, **Jahanpanah** between Siri Fort and Qila Rai Pithora (the first city).

The third Tughlaq, Feruz Shah (1351–88) constructed the fifth city of Delhi under his own name, **Feruzabad**, away from the hills on the banks of the Yamuna. The citadel area of Feruz's town and the remains there is still called **Feruz Shah Kotla** and is a city landmark.

The Tughlaq line continued till 1414 when it was replaced by the Saiyads, who were followed by the Lodis from 1451 onwards. Under the Saiyad and Lodi Sultans, the seal of construction was modest in the Delhi area. The last of the Lodis, Ibrahim, was defeated and killed by Babur, the Mughal conqueror from Kabul, in 1526.

Babur, during his short rule of about five years, introduced the formal Persian garden in India. He had his capital at Agra and did not enrich Delhi. In 1530, Humayun, the second Mughal emperor, laid the foundation of the sixth capital city of Delhi under the name **Din Panah** on the bank of the Yamuna to the south of Feruzabad, around the ancient site of Indraprastha. It comprised a citadel (Purana Qila) and city.

Akbar, son and successor to Humayun,

Tughlaqabad Fort, citadel of early Delhi.

162

spent his childhood in Delhi but later moved to Agra. It was his grandson, Shah Jahan (1628–58) who, finding Agra too congested, selected a site north of Feruzabad and constructed the seventh Delhi, a well planned township which he called **Shahjahanabad**. The famous Red Fort was its citadel on the river bank.

Shahjahanabad functioned as the Mughal capital till as late as 1857, although the Mughal rulers, after 1707, gradually lost their power and prestige. The British East India Company became the supreme controller of the affairs of most Indian states.

In 1857, the last attempt to restore the authority of the Mughal emperor failed and the old Mughal ruler was dethroned: for the next 50 years Delhi was just an ordinary provincial town.

The historic city once again became the capital of India under the British in December 1911, when the then British Government transferred the viceregal headquarters there from Calcutta, in view of Delhi's secure and central location, and its strong traditional association as a royal seat of power. Simultaneously, a decision to build a new Indian metropolis, befitting the glory of the British Crown, was also taken. After much thought and exploration, a site to the south of Shahjahanabad, covering a part of the Ridge on the west was selected.

Two architects, Edwin Lutyens and Herbert Baker, were assigned the task of designing and building the new capital, styled as New Delhi, which was formally inaugurated in January 1931.

Some of the landmarks of the Lutyens-Baker Delhi are **Rashtrapati Bhavan,** official residence of India's President (the former Viceregal Lodge), built in a commanding position on Raisina Hill with adjoining administrative North and South Blocks and the **Parliament House** on one side, beside the Memorial Arch of the First World War called **India Gate,** and a circular marketing centre with double-storeyed blocks around a park known as **Connaught Circus**.

The principal aim of the builders of New Delhi, which is often described as a city of gardens, was to serve the administration and to provide comfortable living

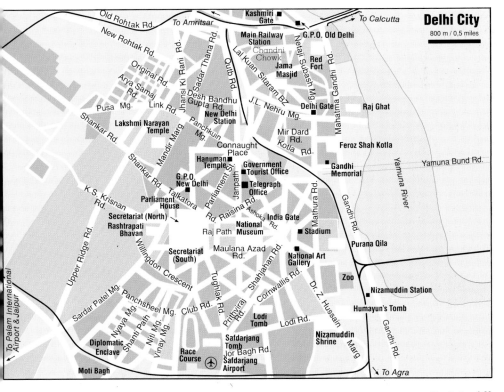

to the colonial rulers. Little provision for its future expansion was made.

Yet, with World War II and the change of the political situation, especially after independence in 1947, New Delhi had to grow. In the decades since independence, despite difficulties, Delhi has increased steadily, both horizontally and vertically, covering a much greater area than all its predecessor seven cities put together.

Monuments and ruins: This rapidly changing and growing city is also a city of monuments and historical ruins. Mostly, such remains are medieval in origin and Islamic in character. The tourists intending to see pre-Islamic ancient remains may visit the site of the Rock Edict of the Buddhist Emperor Ashoka (273–236 BC) near Srinivasapuri (south Delhi) which contains the appeal of the great humanitarian monarch to his people to follow the path of righteousness. Further elaboration of the same theme is also in his inscriptions on two pillars, one in Kotla Feruz Shah and the other on the Ridge in north Delhi.

The architecture of Delhi of the medieval period is Islamic in nature. Standard Indo-Islamic architecture with developed techniques and refined features, like the pointed true arch, low dome and geometric decoration, emerged during the Khalji period. Of the extant structural specimens of the Khalji period, Alai Darwaza in the Qutb complex is the finest.

Tughlaq architecture is characterised by battered (sloping) walls, plain exteriors, pointed arches and arcuate doorways with lintels. During the era of the Saiyads and Lodis, some of the structural features of Tughlaq monuments were modified; octagonal tombs with verandas around them and kiosks above were popular.

Edifices raised during the Mughal period, however, represent the best of Delhi's structural style. The Mughal monuments also possess traditional Hindu and the late sultanate traits. Shahjahanabad has some fine examples of architecture of the time of Shah Jahan and later kings.

The main attraction among the remains of the first four cities is of course the Quwwatu'l Islam (Might of Islam) Mosque complex located inside the Tomar Fortress. Built by Qutbu'd-Din during 1192–

Left, Purana Qila, the Old Fort. Right, Jantar Mantar.

98, out of ruined Hindu temples, as a congregational mosque, it consists of a courtyard, cloisters and a prayer hall. A lofty arched screen was erected facing the prayer hall. A fascinating aspect is the enclosing wall and corridor of reutilised Hindu carved pillars. In the courtyard stands a rust-free iron pillar, raised as a standard of Lord Vishnu, by Chandra Gupta, a ruler of the 4th century AD.

Qutbu'd Din started building the **Qutb Minar** in 1199 as a memorial of victory and also as an accessory to the adjoining mosque, to call the faithful to prayer. The Minar is a tapering tower of five tiers 240 ft (72.5 metres) high.

Alai Darwaza is the southern entrance to the enlarged enclosure of the Qutb complex, added by Alauddin in 1311. Its well-finished form and decorations in a mixture of red sandstone and marble illustrate a maturity in structural experience. Amongst other remains of the complex is the rather ornate tomb of Sultan Iltutamish.

A little west of Qutb Minar is the township of **Mehrauli,** conspicuous on account of its narrow labyrinthine bazaar. It has two notable shrines: the temple of goddess Jogmaya and the tomb of Muslim divine Khwaja Bakhtyar Kaki (1336) visited by local pilgrims.

Other interesting monuments in Mehrauli include **Adham Khan's tomb, Shamsi Tank, Jahaz-Mahal** and **Jamali's Tomb** with its coloured ceiling.

Built by the first Tughlaq ruler on rocky ground with high rubble walls, **Tughlaqabad** (perimeter 4 miles or 6.5 km) was a well-planned city with a citadel and a vast reservoir to its south. Here is the mausoleum of Ghiyasu'd-Din Tughlaq, a red-stone edifice with sloping walls and a marble dome enclosed within a mini-fortress, with bastions and battlements.

On the way back from Tughlaqabad within the ruined Jahanpanah (fourth Delhi) are some notable Tughlaq (14th-century) buildings like **Khirki Mosque** modelled like a tiny fortress, **Begampuri Mosque** with its extensive facade, and the damaged mansion called **Bijay-Mandal**.

Mosques and mausoleums: Leaving the Siri (second Delhi) fortifications on one side, past newly constructed localities in a northerly direction is the tomb of the Muslim saint Nizamuddin Aulia. This saint, who died in 1325, was well-known for his miracles and learning. His tomb is regarded as a holy shrine and many visit the place to pray for the fulfilment of their desires. Close by the shrine stand the **Jamaatkhana Mosque** (1315) and other historical ruins.

To the east of Nizamuddin, lies **Humayun's Mausoleum** raised by his spouse in 1565. Exemplifying early Mughal architecture, it is a garden-sepulchre with an irregular octagonal plan and double-domed elevation and was to serve as the model for the Taj Mahal.

Further north, on Mathura Road, are remains of Humayun's Dinpanah township. On the right are visible ruins of a market, a city gate and a mosque built by Akbar's wet-nurse (1561) and opposite are ramparts, a moat and portals of **Purana Qila** (Old Fort), Humayun's citadel. Inside stand a beautiful mosque and a double-storied octagonal pavilion (**Sher Mandal**) of the 16th century.

At a short distance from Purana Qila, to the north is the **Kotla** (fort of) **Feruzshah,** built of rubble. The inscribed Ashokan column is installed in one of its buildings.

Adjacent to the south wall of Purana Qila is the **Delhi Zoo,** famous for its white tigers and other varieties of animals and birds, many of them migratory.

A little westward from Purana Qila lie **India Gate**, the memorial of World War I, with spacious lawns and shallow tanks, and the **Presidential Palace,** with its 340 rooms and extensive grounds. The drive between the Memorial Arch and President's Palace serves as the arena for the colourful spectacle of India's Republic Day Celebrations on 26 January each year.

Just southeast of the India Gate lawns is the **Gallery of Modern Art,** housing work by artists of modern India. It also exhibits a number of paintings of the famous Indian poet Rabindranath Tagore, Amrita Shergil and Jamini Roy.

On the southern side of the lawns is the **National Museum of India,** which contains representative collections of Indian art and archaeology besides several Central Asian murals and antiquities.

Specimens of traditional crafts of India in different mediums are displayed at the

Crafts Museum, northeast of India Gate on Mathura Road.

Indo-Muslim sepulchres are to be seen at the **Lodi Gardens**. The structural harmony of the medium-sized tombs of Saiyad and Lodi rulers is set off by the beautifully laid-out garden which surrounds them.

Further west is another mausoleum of Safdarjung, a Mughal noble of the early 18th century, built in the characteristic Mughal garden-tomb style.

Central circle: A drive along Aurobindo Marg, past **Vijay Chowk** (Victory Square) and Parliament Street leads to **Connaught Place** with its shops, hotels and restaurants. Of special interest are the rows of small shops along Janpath, especially those of Tibetan refugees selling all kinds of curios and oriental objects. The official emporiums dealing in regional handicrafts are on Baba Kharak Singh Marg, which runs off Connaught Place.

A curious structure, not to be missed, near the junction of Parliament Street and Connaught Circus is Mughal grandee Jaisingh's (1699–1743) observatory, **Jantar Mantar** with huge astronomical "instru-ments" built in rubble masonry. Its main purpose was standardisation of almanacs.

However, more significant structurally is another shrine to the west on the Lower Ridge, the **Lakshmi-Narayana Temple** built some decades ago by the Birlas, a famous family of industrialists. It is a grandiose complex with a central shrine dedicated to Narayana or Vishnu and his spouse Lakshmi, the goddess of wealth.

Planned as a quadrant (of a circle), **Shahjahanabad**, the last historic city of Delhi, had several gates, some of which are still standing – the Delhi, Ajmeri, Turkman and Kashmiri Gates, for example. Its narrow lanes, flanked by houses with traditional central courtyards, are usually crowded, for Shahjahanabad still continues to be a major business centre.

The **Red Fort** stands along the eastern edge of the walled city, on the west bank of the Yamuna River. It was planned as an irregular oblong (1½ miles/2.4 km perimeter) and was built as the royal residential and official complex by Shah Jahan. Entry is through the **Lahori** and **Delhi Gates**, via the **Naubat Khana**, the middle portal. The

View of Old Delhi from Jama Masjid minaret.

fort has also a market known as the **Chhata Bazaar** (covered market) between Lahori Gate and the Naubat Khana. The palaces, mostly in marble, are along the river front. Notable amongst the edifices inside are the **Halls of Public and Private Audience**; the royal baths with inlaid floors; the **Moti Masjid** (Pearl Mosque); the private palace of the king, **Rang-Mahal**; and the ornamental canal, **Nahri-Bahisht**, beside the gardens. Some of the finest aspects of Mughal art can be seen in the *pietra dura* panels in the royal mansions.

Opposite Red Fort is the principal marketing street of Shahjahanabad, **Chandni Chowk** (Silver Square), which had, originally, a canal dividing the central thoroughfare. During the British period the canal was covered and a church, a fountain and a clock tower were added. The area is the commercial heart of Old Delhi, with many markets. It is noted for traditional silver jewellery, handicrafts and varied sweetmeats.

On the left of the road to Chandni Chowk from the Red Fort are three important religious buildings. These are the **Lal Mandir** of the Jains, **Gauri-Sankar Temple** dedicated to Lord Shiva and his family, and a Sikh Gurdwara built at the site of the martyrdom of the ninth Sikh preceptor, Guru Tegh Bahadur. He was killed under the orders of the Emperor Aurangzeb (1656–1707) because he refused to embrace Islam.

The **Jama Masjid** (Congregational Mosque) was constructed on a natural elevation by Shah Jahan about a mile west of Red Fort during 1651–56. It is one of the largest mosques in India and is most impressive structurally.

To the north of Red Fort, beyond Kashmiri Gate, are **St James's Church** (1824), with its artistic sculptures; **Metcalfe House** built as the home of the British Resident in 1835; an Ashokan pillar brought to Delhi by Feruz Tughlaq; and the **tomb of Princess Roshanara** placed in what was originally her pleasure garden. In fact, the area between Kashmiri Gate and the Ridge on the north was developed by the British before the construction of New Delhi and is still known as **Civil Lines**. **Delhi University** and its institutions are located in this area around the old Viceregal Residence.

Parliament House.

UTTAR PRADESH: A FUSION OF CULTURES

Uttar Pradesh, literally "northern province", one of India's most densely populated states, is popularly styled U.P. The state's population comprises diverse religious, cultural and ethnic elements. Through the centuries all have lived together in cordiality and have been accommodating to strangers. This is why U.P. is often spoken of as "everyone's home".

Uttar Pradesh occupies an area of 113,500 sq. miles (294,000 sq. km). It shares borders with Tibet (China) and Nepal on the north and northeast; and with five other Indian states (Himachal Pradesh, Haryana, Delhi, Rajasthan and Madhya Pradesh) on the west and south; and Bihar on the east. The whole territory can be divided into three distinct physiographical regions: the Himalayan region in the north, the Gangetic plain in the centre, and the Vindhya Range and plateau in the south.

The Himalayan region, with valleys and hills of varying altitudes and colder climate than the plains, is the area where most of the rivers of U.P. rise. The Himalayan forests with cedars, oaks, pines, rhododendrons and other varieties of trees and flowers, together with charming streams and high mountains make excellent scenic surroundings. The prominent Himalayan peaks within Uttar Pradesh are: Kamet (25,446ft/7,756m), Nandadevi (25,646ft/7,817m), Trisul (23,340ft/7,120m), Dunagiri (23,182ft/7,066m), Badrinath (23,418ft/7,138m), Kedarnath (22,778ft/6,943m), and Bandarpunchi (20,718ft/6,315m).

The central part of the state, the Gangetic plain, is alluvial and fertile. It is watered by mighty rivers like the Yamuna, Ganga, Ghagra, Gandak, Gomati, Ramganga and Chambal, and their tributaries. Almost all the important towns and trading centres of Central U.P. are located on these rivers. The confluence of the Ganga and the Yamuna, the two most sacred rivers of India, at Allahabad has been a popular place of pilgrimage through millennia.

The southern fringe of the Gangetic plain is marked by the low Vindhyan hills

The sun silhouettes the Taj Mahal.

and the adjoining plateau has a variety of soils, including black cotton soil. Two important rivers of the area are the Betwa and the Ken which flow into the Yamuna.

Uttar Pradesh is India's most populous state, with over 110 million people, a sixth of the total population of the country. Of diverse ethnic origins and varied socio-cultural complexion, distributed mostly on a regional basis, the people of the state consist of Hindus, Muslims, Christians and others, besides tribal and aboriginal communities in isolated pockets.

Archaeology and history: Hindu myths and legends claim a hoary antiquity for Uttar Pradesh but archaeological data reveal a different picture. The beginning of human cultures in the state, according to archaeologists, can be traced back to the stone age, as attested by the discovery of tools like hand-axes, choppers, scrapers and cleavers in the southeastern area around Mirzapur in the Vindhyan tracts.

By about the beginning of the first millennium BC, iron had begun to replace copper technology in north India, including Uttar Pradesh. In the ensuing centuries the new technology brought about remarkable socio-economic changes with greater colonisation of the forested Gangetic plain, increase of population and improvement of agriculture due to the growing use of iron implements like pickaxes, saws, axes, sickles and ploughshares. A surplus in agricultural production brought about trade, which was initially based on barter, but, by 600 or 500 BC, was transformed into money-based exchange, with the introduction of "punch-marked" coins issued by trade guilds. Increased commercial activity made for the emergence of urbanism and many important townships came into existence. In fact, the history of some of the well-known cities of modern Uttar Pradesh like Varanasi, Saket (Ayodhya) and Mathura can be traced back to this period.

Around the 6th century BC, the territory today covered by U.P. consisted of some eight semi-independent or independent principalities which were either monarchical or oligarchical.

A birthplace of new faiths: The early history of Uttar Pradesh during the 6th and 5th century BC is linked with Buddhism

Fatehpur
Sikri.

and Jainism, the two anti-orthodox religious movements professing *ahimsa*, non-injury to living beings. The site of the Buddha's native city, Kapilavastu, has been recently identified by some scholars with a village called Piparhawa (Basti District) in eastern U.P. (It has, so far, been traditionally located in Nepal.) The Buddha first preached his doctrines at Sarnath (near Varanasi) aged 35. He and his elder contemporary, Mahavira, the founder of historical Jainism, preached in several areas included in Uttar Pradesh, and each died in the Malla principality. Amongst politically notable personalities of the period associated with the Buddha were Prasenjit, ruler of Kosala, and Udayana, king of Vatsa and a hero of later Indian romances.

Gradually, the states of Uttar Pradesh were annexed into the growing empire of Magadha, now located in the neighbouring sate of Bihar, and, by about the 4th century BC, virtually the whole of U.P. became a part of the Magadhan kingdom under the Nanda dynasty. The Nandas were followed by the Mauryas who unified India into a strong and vast empire. U.P. still preserves several archeological vestiges of the Mauryan epoch, including pillars and epigraphs of Ashoka, the great Mauryan monarch (272–236 BC).

The Maurya dynasty was succeeded by that of the Sungas in a major part of north India. The founder of the dynasty, Pusyamitra Sunga, a former commander of the Mauryan army, successfully repulsed the invading armies of the Indo-Greeks then occupying the northwestern regions of the subcontinent. The post-Sunga period was marked by the rise of local kingdoms in U.P. which even issued their own coinage. It seems there was a general improvement in trade and artistic activity. This was also the time when Mathura and Kausambi emerged as important centres of art.

Towards the end of the 1st century BC, the Sakas, a foreign tribe, established themselves at Mathura. They were succeeded by another line of Central Asian adventurers, the Kushans. They extended their kingdom up to Varanasi and even beyond in the further east under one of their noted rulers, Kanishka I. Under the Saka-Kushan

monarchs, northern India enjoyed prosperity, and great achievements were made in the field of culture, literature and art, with the fusion of many new and even foreign ideas into the cultural fabric. The city of Mathura, one of the capitals of the extensive Kushana Empire, became the epicentre of growing cultural activity under its newly acquired cosmopolitanism.

After the downfall of the Kushanas, about the 3rd century AD, their north-Indian empire got divided into small states which were again unified in the 4th century AD into a strong kingdom under the Guptas who had their capital at Pataliputra (modern Patna in Bihar). Uttar Pradesh which formed a constituent of the Gupta empire was one of the main centres of cultural activity of the Gupta kings and played an important role in the growth of art and literature in the period. It still has many notable archeological remains of the Gupta period (4th to 6th centuries AD), including highly graceful sculptures like the Sarnath and Mathura images of the Buddha.

With the disintegration of the Gupta empire, the Maukharis captured political authority in Uttar Pradesh and a part of Bihar. Their capital was Kanauj (Farrukhabad District) which in the 7th century AD passed on to Harsha, originally a prince of Thaneshwar in Haryana. Harsha was a successful ruler known for his patronage of Buddhism and for holding quinquennial assemblies at the confluence of Ganga and Yamuna at Allahabad, now echoed in the Kumbh Mela celebrations.

Encounter with a new culture: In the post-Harsha period, the kingdom of Kanauj continued to play an important role in the political and cultural life of the Gangetic plain and neighbouring regions. The throne of Kanauj was occupied in almost a direct succession by Yasovarman, The Ayudhas, the Pratiharas and the Gahadwalas, till the beginning of the 13th century, when nearly the whole of U.P., except some border areas in the Himalayan and Vindhyan belts, was annexed into the Sultanate of Delhi, under its Mameluke rulers.

The Mamelukes were followed in succession by the other Delhi Sultanate rulers belonging to the houses of the Khaljis, Tughlaqs, Saiyads and Lodis who, generally, controlled U.P. till 1526 through their governors or fief-holders. On some occasions, the local chiefs or governors of U.P. revolted against the central authority at Delhi. Towards the end of the 14th century, Malik Sarwar, a Tughlaq noble, established an independent kingdom with Jaunpur (eastern U.P.) as its capital.

Sarwar's successors were known as Sharqis (easterners). The house came to an end with the defeat of Husain Shah Sharqi at the hands of Bahlul of the Lodi dynasty in 1458.

Under the Sharqi sultans, Jaunpur became a seat of learning and a centre of arts – the "Shiraz of the East". The Jaunpur rulers developed a unique variety of Indo-Islamic architecture with ornamental qualities and high and impressive facades which can be observed in their extant edifices.

Cultural synthesis: During the early Sultanate rule, the Hindu population of U.P., after initial resistance, adjusted to the changed situation and discarded their earlier hostile attitude towards the Islamic rulers. Consequently, some new cultural elements, with composite ideas and prac-

tices, related to both Hinduism and Islam, developed. The best products of this cultural synthesis were the Urdu language, which was essentially a variation on Hindi, written in Arabic script; the graceful styles of medieval Indian architecture; and the medieval Hindu reformation movements.

With the foundation of the Mughal rule by Babur in 1526, Agra, his capital, rose to prominence. Even earlier it had been the capital of Sikandar Lodi (1489–1517). Yet the real glory of Agra belongs to the periods of Akbar (1556–1605), Jahangir (1605–27) and Shah Jahan (1628–58). During the time of Akbar, both Agra and the nearby Fatehpur Sikri not only served as imperial capitals, but also turned into renowned centres of trade and commerce, culture and learning, with their celebrated architectural wealth and material riches. In fact, Agra achieved international fame for its grandeur during early Mughal rule. Other towns of the Ganga plain like Mathura, Allahabad and Varanasi also attained considerable importance during the Mughal epoch.

Throughout the early Mughal age, Uttar

Sacred rivers meet at Deoprayag in the Himalayan foothills.

Pradesh prospered with its urban centres, producing and selling a number of commodities, including textiles. These cities also witnessed the growth of literature, art, architecture, crafts, music and dance, all of which received generous patronage from the court and the nobility. They developed a composite city culture which was widely imitated in other regions of India.

During later Mughal rule, following the death of Aurangzeb in 1707, the sixth of the Great Mughals, the process of internal dissension and disintegration of the empire set in. The kingdom was raided by Afghans, Iranians, Jats and Marathas, and most provincial governors, including the Nawab of Lucknow, declared their independence. Gradually, the well-organised British East India Company captured the administrative power, which ultimately resulted in the overthrow of the Mughal authority and that of other local rulers like the Nawab of Lucknow and Rani of Jhansi in U.P., and elsewhere, by 1857, when the popular rising against the British East India Company was crushed. In 1858, the British crown took over from the Company.

Not just the Taj: Uttar Pradesh presents a variety of attractions for the traveller. The state is well-covered by a network of motorable roads, railway lines and airports. Delhi or any of the main U.P. cities is a convenient starting point for a tour of the state. Southwest U.P. is right next to Delhi, the usual point of entry to north India. Agra, Fatehpur Sikri and Mathura lie in this region.

The main part of **Agra** city, on the right bank of the Yamuna, continues to be medieval in structure, with narrow, crowded streets and lanes, full of colourful shops selling all kind of goods, especially local handicrafts, including gold and silver embroidery and imitation Mughal inlay on marble and fine leather goods. The place is also known for its petha (pumpkin sweet) and dalmoth (savoury fried chickpeas) and delicious non-vegetarian dishes of Mughal origin.

Agra Fort lies on the bend of the River Yamuna, almost in the heart of the town. It was built by Akbar as his citadel over the years 1565–73 in the finest architectural style. It has imposing gates and walls

Left, terraces in the Kumaun Hills. Below, the Imambara complex, Lucknow.

of red sandstone and a moat. The fort, approachable through its two lofty main portals on the west and south, besides a private gate on the east, was successively occupied by three great Mughals – Akbar, Jahangir and Shah Jahan, each of whom made significant structural contributions to this complex.

Of the conspicuous edifices inside the fort, mention must be made of Jahangiri Mahal; Khas Mahal (Private Palace) with its attached vineyard called Anguri Bagh, and the ornamental bath called Shish Mahal; the ornate Musamman Burj, where Shah Jahan died as a captive of his son, passing his last days gazing at the Taj Mahal (the tomb of his beloved wife), the Diwan-i-Khas (Hall of Private Audience) and Diwan-i-Am (Hall of Public Audience), Machchhi Bhawan (palace with fish-tanks), and Moti Masjid. Most of these were built during the reign of Shah Jahan. Shah Jahan's architectural creations are mostly in marble and display great refinement in contrast to the building style of his grandfather, Akbar, which is bold, original and virile.

The Diwan-i-Khas and Diwan-i-Am in royal Mughal complexes are halls intended for official meetings and public assemblies (durbars) respectively and state functions in which the emperor was seated on a throne placed under a raised canopy built into the back of the hall.

A dream in marble: Not far from the historic fort is the **Taj Mahal**, the mausoleum of Empress Mumtaz Mahal, the beloved spouse of Shah Jahan, who died in 1631. The Taj complex comprises a forecourt, a lofty entrance, a charming formal Mughal garden with canals and a central tank with a series of fountains, the tomb proper, and an attached mosque on the west, and its symmetrical counterpart on the east. The main mausoleum, where Shah Jahan also lies, is a domed two-storied octagonal building, with four tall minarets at the corners – all built of brick and encased in marble. The actual graves are in the crypt.

The Taj is remarkable for its perfect proportions and rich pietra dura, with minute details executed with great skill. The building, often styled "a dream in marble", is said to have taken 18 years

(1631–48) to build. It marks the most developed stage of Mughal architecture. The designer of this grand sepulchre is believed to be Ustad Ahmad Lahori, a master architect of the age. The calligraphic ornamentation on the Taj Mahal was authored by Amanat Khan Shirazi, a great writer of the 17th century.

According to popular belief, Shah Jahan wanted to build another mausoleum in black marble for himself opposite the Taj, but, for reasons unknown, could not do so.

Across the river from Agra Fort, lies the small but beautiful sepulchre of Mirza Ghayas Beg, called Itimadu'd–Daula, who was the father of Jahangir's most beloved consort, Nurjahan. Mirza was elevated, due to his daughter's influence, to the rank of high chamberlain and prime minister to the emperor.

The edifice also enshrines the mortal remains of the empress's mother. It was built between 1622 and 1628, and has an unusual structural character in relation to other Mughal tombs. It is a square building with four corner towers and a crowning pavilion with a canopy-shaped roof and floor inlaid with an arabesque pattern. It has a well-decorated marble exterior notable for its bold inlaid design in semi-precious stones. The interior is painted.

To the northwest of Agra proper, some 7½ miles (12 km) away, is **Sikandarabad**, the locality named after Sikandar Lodi. Here stands the tomb of Emperor Akbar, within a spacious garden enclosed by high walls on the Agra-Delhi road. It has on the southern side a high gate with four towering minars rising above its roof and the false gates placed, for the sake of symmetry, at each of the other three sides of the walled enclosure. The gate is further distinguished by bold ornamental mosaic patterns. The mausoleum, which is centrally located, was begun by Akbar himself, but was completed in 1613, in the reign of Jahangir. Jahangir modified its design and added the top terrace with marble cloisters containing a false grave of the emperor. The real grave lies in the crypt-like sepulchral chamber.

Close to Akbar's tomb, on the road to the southeast, is a realistic stone figure of Akbar's war horse, and a little to the southwest is the tomb of his Christian wife, Mariam Zamani, mother of Jahangir.

Other significant edifices in Agra include the unfinished marble memorial *(samadhi)* to the 19th century founder of the Hindu Radha Swami order; the remains of an old Roman Catholic cemetery belonging to the Mughal period; Raja Jaswant Singh's Chhatri (memorial canopy); and Chini-ka-Rauza, a ruined tomb of the period of Shah Jahan, known for its coloured-tile decoration.

Imperial ruins: About 20 miles (35 km) southwest of Agra lie the imperial ruins of the Mughal city of **Fatehpur Sikri**, Akbar's capital for a short 12 years. It occupies a sandstone ridge and the area around it, within a circumference of nearly 9 miles (11 km), enclosed within a wall. The royal residences and offices were located on the ridge itself and important markets on the slope. Emperor Akbar is said to have selected Sikri as the seat of his government believing it to be auspicious for himself as prophesied by the saint, Shaikh Salim Cheshti, who lived there. Actually, Fatehpur Sikri was raised by the great emperor as a city expressing his ideals and vision, where he carried out his experiments in art and architecture.

The red-sandstone mansions of Sikri exhibit a robust stability combined with originality. Their design combines several regional elements of Indian architectural styles with that of Central Asia and Iran. Each of the important edifices here represents a type by itself. The finest monuments are the cloistered **Diwan-i-Am**; the single-pillared **Diwan-i-Khas**; the astrologer's kiosk; the Turkish sultana's house with minute carvings; the storied pavilion called **Panch Mahal**; **Mariyam's house** with its interesting paintings; the ornate **house of Birbal**; **Jodhabai's grand palace**; and the **Jami Masjid** complex, with its pillared hall, monumental portal (**Buland Darwaza**) and charming **tomb of Saint Shaikh Salim Chishti** which is visited by many seeking fulfilment of their wishes.

Krishna country: About 30 miles (50 km) from Agra, on the highway to Delhi, is **Mathura** on the right bank of the Yamuna. It is a great centre of Hindu pilgrimage, being regarded as the birthplace of Lord Krishna. Mathura has several temples dedicated to this deity, of which the most outstanding are the **Dwarkadhish shrine** in the crowded marketplace, the temple at the birthplace of Krishna, and **Gita Mandir** on the way to Vrindavan, where Krishna grazed his cattle during his childhood. Mathura's bazaars are known for their sweets and ritualistic objects associated with the Hindu system of worship.

Mathura has an excellent museum, famous for its collection of ancient red sandstone sculptures of Buddhist, Brahmanical and Jain association, produced by the artists of Mathura between the 2nd century BC and the 6th century AD. During the early centuries AD, Mathura was a fortified town of international importance.

Vrindavan, 6 miles (10 km) north of Mathura, is also a pilgrim centre and home to many devout widows. It abounds in medieval and modern Hindu temples. Significant among them are the **Govind-deo Temple** (1590); the **Jugal Kishore, Radha-Vallabh** and **Madan-Mohan Temples** (17th-century); **Rangji's and Shahji's temples** (19th-century); the famous **Bihariji shrine; the temple of Pagal Baba** and the International Society for Hare Krishna temple. Mathura also has a large number of monasteries, with almost every Hindu sect and sub-sect being represented. Free meals are offered to the pilgrims at these monasteries. Lost in devotion to Krishna, pilgrims sometimes dance in ecstasy *(Ram Liala),* imploring the love of Lord Krishna.

Central Uttar: The main industrial centre of U. P., **Kanpur,** stands on the right bank of the Ganga. It produces mainly leather and textile goods of fine quality. It has amongst its historic remains the **Memorial Church**, built in 1875 in Romanesque style, which contains tablets bearing the names of British citizens who died during the great sepoy revolt of 1857 against the East India Company. There is also a fine brick temple (16th century AD) at **Bhitgargaon**, a village close to Ghatampur in the vicinity of Kanpur.

Lucknow, the capital of Uttar Pradesh, straddles both banks of the River Gomati, a tributary of the Ganga. It rose to importance during the Indo-Islamic (medieval) period, especially under the Mughals and, subsequently, under the Nawabs of Oudh and, still later, the British. The city is famous for its cultivated manners and refined urban culture. Fine *bidri* (silver-inlaid black metalware), jewellery, cotton embroidery (*chikan* work) and toys are produced in Lucknow by traditional craftsmen.

Lucknow developed its own style of architecture during the 18th and 19th centuries. It began as a rather ornate, modified form of Mughal prototypes, but built in brick and stucco. Later, it incorporated many European traits, like triangular pediments, Corinthian capitals and round arches. The buildings of the Nawabs of Oudh are very often embossed with a pair of fish, their royal emblem.

Imported historical sites in the city include **Nadan Mahal**, a Mughal tomb; **Bara Imambara** (1784), containing the tombs of the builder, Nawab Asifu'd-Daula, and his family; the ruins of the **British Residency**; the **Husanabad Imambara**; the **Chhatar Manzil;** the **Qaisarbagh** quadrangle; the **tombs of Saadt Ali** and his wife; **Dilkusha Palace**; and Constantania, now **La Martiniere School**, built by Claude Martin, a French-

man, in the 18th century. The Bara Imambara stands in a large enclosure, with an attached mosque and a great ornamental gate, the **Rumi Darwaza**. A point to be noted about this monument is its charming arcuate labyrinth, supporting the roof of the edifice, which is locally called the *bhul-bhulaiya*.

Other attractions of Lucknow are its picture gallery displaying portraits of the Oudh Nawabs, the state museum mainly displaying ancient sculptures from various parts of U.P., and the zoo with a variety of animals and birds. The city is the home of light classical Hindustani (North-Indian) music and Kathak, a traditional school of dance.

Sravasti and Kusinagara: Located respectively in Gonda-Bahraich and Deoria Districts of U.P., **Sravasti** and **Kusinagara** were ancient cities associated with the Buddha. The sites are visited by Buddhist pilgrims from all over the world. Sravasti is also sacred to the Jain community. As a result of archaeological operations in the 19th and 20th centuries, remains of ancient structures were exposed

The Bara Imambara, Lucknow.

in these sites and interesting antiquities were recovered. At Kusinagara, a sculpture showing the dying Buddha is of great value as it was here that he passed away.

Ayodhya is a popular place of Hindu pilgrimage considered the birthplace of Lord Rama, mythological hero and an incarnation of God Vishnu much earlier than the Krishna incarnation. At Ayodhya, the performance of orthodox Hindu rituals can be observed in the scores of old and new temples, and especially in **Kanak Bhavan** and **Hanumangarhi.**

A controversial Mughal mosque, the **Babri Masjid**, was torn down in 1992 by 250,000 Hindu zealots, triggering riots across India. Only rubble remains. Meanwhile the Muslims want the mosque restored while Hindus want a temple to mark Rama's birthplace.

At **Faizabad**, a town of medieval origin 5 miles (8 km) from Ayodhya, are the tombs of Nawab Shujau'd-Daula of Oudh (1754–75) and wife, and a small museum.

Allahabad, Varanasi and Jaunpur are the historically significant towns of Eastern U. P. **Allahabad**, also known as Prayag in Hindu tradition, is a peaceful city where life usually moves at a slow pace. But being regarded as one of the holiest places in the country, it springs to life during religious festivals and fairs. In particular the massive Kumbha Mela, meeting ground of various Hindu sects and their ascetic orders, is held every 12 years and attracts hundreds of thousands of pilgrims.

In Allahabad stands one of Ashoka's stone pillars carrying his own epigraph and those of the Gupta king Samadragupta (335–75 AD), and later rulers. Allahabad's Mughal legacy includes a historic **Akbar Fort and Palace** and **Khushrobagh**, garden containing the impressive tomb of Mughal Prince Khushro and his family. The town has a fine museum housing mainly ancient sculptures and paintings.

Mirzapur, a small district town between Allahabad and Varanasi, is famous for its woollen carpets with fast colours prepared by traditional Indian craftsmen.

On the left bank of the Ganga is **Varanasi** (Benares), also known as Kashi. Like Rome, it is traditionally regarded as "an eternal city", surviving through the

Bathing *ghats* on the Ganga at Varanasi.

ages. Lord Shiva, under his name Vishvanath or the Overlord of the World, is believed to be the presiding deity of the town. According to a common belief, those who die here will be close to God in the other world, and many orthodox Hindus come to Varanasi to pass their last days.

The antiquity of Varanasi can be traced back to at least the middle of the 1st millennium BC. Since time immemorial, it has served not merely as a holy centre of pilgrimage but also as a great seat of traditional Hindu learning and culture. Despite modernisation, it still preserves some of the carefree and colourful aspects of the traditional Hindu way of life.

Amongst the handicrafts of Varanasi are silks, shawls, brocades and embroideries, ornamental brassware, modern brass idols of Hindu deities, and toys.

A spectacle in the city is its long series of *ghats* (stepped landings) on the river front linked with crowded streets at the back, always full of travellers, devotees and pilgrims. A sampling of Varanasi's almost countless temples is provided by visits to the **Visvanath Temple**, **Durga Kund**, **Sankat-Mochan** (shrine of the monkey god, Hanuman), and the **Annapurna** and **Kal-Bhairava** temples.

Conspicuous in the Varanasi skyline is the historic **Mosque of Aurangzeb**. In the 18th century, Raja Jaisingh built one of his celebrated observatories in this town. A good museum in the Benares Hindu University called **Bharat Kala Bhawan** contains a rich collection of ancient and medieval sculptures, paintings, manuscripts and textiles. The old palace of the Raja of Varanasi, within the **Ramnagar Fort**, has a private museum housing objects of personal use, and other materials belonging to the erstwhile ruling family.

To the north of Varanasi, about 4 miles (6 km) away, are the Buddhist remains of **Sarnath** or the ancient **Mrigadava** (Deer Park) where the Buddha delivered his first sermon after attaining enlightenment. The remains include the **Dhamekh Stupa**, the main shrine, and an Ashokan pillar. The local museum has good specimens of sculpture. Outstanding are the superb seated Buddha (6th century AD) and the Lion Capital of Ashoka (3rd century BC), the Government of India's emblem.

Jaunpur has medieval historical associations. Akbar built a stone bridge over the Gomti here which is still standing. Surviving the Sharqi period are a **Tughlaq fort** and the **Atala** and **Jami Mosques**. Fine perfumed oils and scents are made by traditional methods in this town.

South and west: In south U.P. are the strong medieval fort at **Kalinjar** (Banda District), Chandella dynasty tanks at **Mahoba**, a fort at **Jhansi** and ancient temples at **Deogarh** (Lalitpur District). Jhansi also has a museum of regional antiquities. A well-known scenic spot in the area is **Chitrakuta**, which is also regarded as a holy place because of its association with the story of Lord Rama.

Western Uttar Pradesh has a number of commercial towns like **Bareilly, Muradabad, Meerut** and **Saharanpur** which manufacture mainly furniture, ornamental brassware, sports goods and carved woodwork, respectively.

Hardwar where the River Ganga descends to the plains, and **Rishikesh** and **Dehradun** nearby are rich in natural beauty. Hardwar is amongst the holiest places of pilgrimage in India.

The Himalayan belt runs along the whole northern border of U.P. It consists of several ranges, of which the outermost is the **Shivaliks**, with hill resorts **Mussorie, Landsdowne** and **Joshimath** in Garhwal, and **Nainital, Mukteshwar, Ranikhet, Almora** and **Kausani** in Kumaun.

The Himalaya are rich in scenery. The best spots are **Pindari** and **Milam glaciers** in Kumaun; the Hindu shrines of **Kedarnath** and **Badarinath**; **Ganogotri** and **Yamanotri**, sources of the Ganga and Yamuna; the enchanting **Valley of Flowers**, which is in full bloom during August and September; and the Sikh shrine of **Hemkund Sahib** in Garhwal.

Ancient temples are at **Baijnath, Jageshwar, Katarmal, Champavat** and **Dwarahat** in Kumaun and Lakhamandal, **Deoprayag, Ranihat** (Srinagar), **Adibadri, Gopeshwar, Joshimath** and **Pandukeshwar** in Garhwal.

Close to the foothills, near Ramnagar (Nainital District), is **Corbett National Park**, a wildlife sanctuary. Elephants, tigers, leopards, hyenas and varieties of deer are found here.

HIMACHAL PRADESH

Himachal Pradesh, nestling in the northwestern lap of the Himalaya, abounds in exotic valleys, glorious green hill-slopes, snowcapped mountains, and gushing streams. In this mountain wonderland, the pace of life is measured and tranquil.

Himachal Pradesh straddles the Himalaya from the foothills, over peaks, to the valleys of Lahaul and Spiti beyond. Its capital, Shimla (Simla), had the distinction of serving as the summer capital of India in the days of the British viceroys, a refuge for the sahibs from the heat of the plains. Not only the viceroy, but a substantial part of the secretariat of the Government of India, from members of the Viceroy's Executive Council down to clerks ("babus," the British called them) and "peons," with boxes of files and red tape, made the journey to the hills, mostly by toytrain. It is Shimla that is the scene of many of Rudyard Kipling's stories, in his book *Plain Tales from the Hills.*

In summer, the fragrance of fresh flowers pervades these enchanting hills and the coolness of the melting snow tempers the heat. The monsoon brings a spectacle of lush greenery and cascading waterfalls. Autumn is marked by pleasant sunny days ending in gorgeous sunsets. Winter brings snow. There are basic ski facilities at Narkanda and Solong, or Auli in U.P.

Himachal is accessible by road from Pathankot (Punjab) in the west, Chandigarh in the south, and Dehra Dun in the east. There is also a rail link between Kalka and Shimla, and one between Pathankot and Jogindernagar. An air service to Kulu is also available from Delhi and Chandigarh.

A large majority of Himachalis are Hindus, but Buddhism is also a major influence and is the religion of the Lahaul and Spiti valleys. The Buddhist existence has become particularly marked with the presence of the exiled Dalai Lama at Dharamsala and the large settlements of Tibetan refugees in the state.

As many as 6,000 temples are spread all over the area of this comparatively small **Himalayan panorama.**

state. Each year sees a cycle of rituals and ceremonies. Gay and colourful fairs and festivals are often associated with them, along with the folk dancing which is often a part of the celebrations.

Himachal Pradesh is essentially rural. Its towns are small. The traditional village house is of special interest. The lowest story is occupied by the household cattle; the middle provides space for storing grain and other things, but also for sleeping in winter; the top floor *(dafi)* provides living space.

Folk songs and dances: The folk songs of Himachal Pradesh are very melodious and rhythmic. *Naati* is the most popular folk dance performed in chain formation with hands linked by dancers wearing appropriate masks. In Kinnaur and Lahaul-Spiti, the dances depict the perpetual strife between gods and demons. In the lower regions, they are more sophisticated and similar to those of the plains.

Shimla (Simla) lies at a height of 6,900 ft (2,100 metres) and spread over 7 miles (12 km) along a ridge. Around Shimla are excellent walks through rustling woods. The green slopes are covered with fir, rhododendron, pine and the Himalayan oak. Nestling among the foliage are traditional homesteads. The level ground at the ridge is the favourite evening rendezvous, with Scandal Point at the end and the Mall for shopping.

Shimla's mood changes with the seasons, each with its own charm. Perhaps the best time of the year is autumn, when the days are warm and bright and the nights crisp and cool. The spring brings colourful flowers, and the monsoon some of the most magnificent sunsets in the world. Winter is known as the season of "long moon nights" in Shimla. The city glistens with frost.

In spite of changes and considerable growth since India became independent, Shimla, perhaps more than any other spot in India, is reminiscent of an attempt to build an English town in India. Relics of styles of building long forgotten in Britain are still evident here.

Narkanda, at a height of about 8,850 ft (2,700 metres) and 40 miles (64 km) from Shimla on the Hindustan-Tibet road, is

Himachal village.

famous for its apple orchards and its beautiful scenery, especially during summer. It is a convenient starting point for visits to many places in the heart of Himachal Pradesh: Bagi, Khandrala, Rampur and Kalpa on the Hundustan-Tibet Road (the last is not very far from the Skipki-La Pass to Tibet); the apple-growing Kotgarh area and Kulu. This area, along the valley of the River Sutlej, is called **Kinnaur**.

The Valley of the Gods: On the bank of the Sutlej, **Rampur Bushahr**, is 90 miles (140 km) from Shimla. It provides an overnight halt for visitors and trekkers to Kinnaur. It is one of the biggest commercial towns of Himachal Pradesh and is famous for its three-day market fair, Lavi, which is held in November. Traders from Kinnaur, Spiti and Lahaul participate. While the days are spent in making bargains, the evenings are given to song and dance.

Kulu Valley on the banks of the Beas is at an altitude of about 3,900 ft (1,200 metres). It is famous for apple orchards, beautiful women, old wooden temples and folk music and dances. It offers ample scope for trekking, climbing and angling, and big and small game are plentiful in its forests.

The best time to visit the Kulu Valley is October, when the Dussera festival is celebrated. The statue of Raghunathji, the presiding deity of the valley, is ceremonially brought down to the valley from the mountains. The god stays in state in the valley for a week, along with other gods who are also present in their festive palanquins. The highlight of the fair is the dance competition held every evening.

The most remarkable temple of the valley is that of **Bijli Mahadeva** which is located a few miles away from Kulu. The temple is built of large blocks of stone without the use of cement and its 65-ft (20-metre) tall flagstaff is reputed to attract lightning which, according to the local legend, is an expression of divine blessing. Every time the flagstaff is struck by lightning, the Shiva *lingam* (phallic symbol) inside the temple is shattered. It is put back together each time by the priest and covered with *sattoo* (a paste of roasted

Bus stop, Dharamsala.

gram and wheat powder) and butter. The image, thus restored, stands till another similar flash repeats "the miracle."

The well-known **hot springs of Manikaran** are just 30 miles (45 km) from Kulu town, in the heart of the valley.

The road from Kulu to Manali runs along the swift and rushing torrents of the Beas. It is flanked by lofty mountains and spreading forests. On this road is **Katrain**, famous for its fruit orchards and its trout hatchery. Near Katrain, across the river, is a small town **Naggar**, where the medieval world still survives, untouched by time. The town has been made famous by the late Russian painter, Nicholas Roerich, whose gallery can be seen there.

Manali, another major resort, is circled by beautiful glades of deodars and flowering horse chestnuts. It is an ideal place for walks, climbs, treks and picnics. It is also an important trade center. The **Dhoongri Temple** at Manali, dedicated to the goddess Hidimba, is believed to be over a thousand years old.

Two miles (3 km) from Manali are the **sulphur springs of Bashishta** and a little higher up is the small **Bhrigu Lake**, named after a sage. The Kulu Valley ends as the road winds up through rocky ranges to the Rohtang Pass, the gateway to the enchanting Lahaul and Spiti valleys.

Special valleys: In the northeast of Himachal Pradesh, across the 13,200-ft-high (4,020-metre) **Rohtang Pass** lie the two valleys of **Lahaul** and **Spiti** at a height of 9,800 to 15,700 ft (3,000 to 4,800 metres). Both valleys remain cut off from the rest of the world for much of the year. The Rohtang Pass remains open only from May to October, and it is only during this period that one may cross the still higher **Kunzam Pass** at an altitude of 14,800 ft (4,500 metres) to enter Spiti Valley. Otherwise, one has to reach Spiti by trekking up along the Sutlej and Spiti river valleys from Kinnaur.

Among the valleys, mountains, glaciers, rivers and pastures of Lahaul and Spiti are forts, *gompas* (monasteries) and ancient buildings with frescos on the walls and ceilings.

The people of these two valleys have a distinct culture of their own. Their songs and dances are as pure as the snow that glitters around them. Their *gompas* are repositories of Buddhist art treasures.

Milk and honey: The romantic valley of **Chamba,** a former princely state, has few rivals for scenic beauty. Its valleys, meadows, rivers, lakes, springs and streams have a unique charm. The altitude of this valley ranges from 2,000 to 20,600 ft (600 to 6,300 metres). **Chamba town** is situated on the right bank of the River Ravi at an altitude of 2,950 ft (900 metres). It can be reached from Pathankot (Punjab) by a 75-mile (120-km) road which passes through lush green forests. There is also a 100-mile-long (160-km) foot-track from Dalhousie to Chamba, through dense forests. The town is noted for its ancient Shiva and Vishnu temples, some of which date back to the 10th century.

The **Bhuri Singh Museum** in Chamba is a veritable treasurehouse of exquisite paintings of the famous Kangra and Basohli schools and a mass of epigraphical material relating to the history of the region.

Among the innumerable fairs and festivals celebrated in Himachal Pradesh, the most important is the **Minjar Fair** of Chamba, held around August to celebrate the coming of the rains and the flowering of maize. A procession of decorated horses and banners marks the beginning of the week-long fair.

Dalhousie, Bharmaur and **Nurpur** are other places of interest around Chamba town. Dalhousie is a quiet hill-station located on five little hills. Bharmaur, the ancient capital of Chamba, is famous for the Pahari architecture of its ancient temple, and Nurpur for its handmade textiles.

The Kangra District: Kangra is one of the most beautiful and charming valleys in the Himalaya. **Dharamsala**, the headquarters of the District, is located at the foot of the Dhauladhar Range. The town consists of a lower and an upper Dharamsala, its altitude varying from 3,280 to 6,560 ft (1,000 to 2,000 metres). Upper Dharamsala is where His Holiness, the Dalai Lama, now lives. The ancient town of Kangra is famous for its historic temples, the most popular being the one dedicated to the goddess Vajreshwari. The valley is also famous for the distinct school of painting which grew and flourished there.

Near Dharamsala, there are a number of picturesque picnic spots - the waterfalls of **Bhagsunath,** whose tank and spring are considered sacred; the beautiful **Dal Lake; Dharamkat,** nearly 6,900ft high (2,100m); **Triund** and the **Kareri Lakes** nearly 10,200ft (3,000m) above sea level.

Dharamsala is a convenient base for trips to other places worth seeing in the Kangra Valley, such as **Kangra city** (30 miles/48 km), **Palampur** (164 miles/263km), **Baijnath** (220 miles/352 km) and **Jawalamukhi** (180 miles/288 km).

Fair town: Offering varied climates as its height ranges from 1,970 to 13,120ft (600 to 4,000 m) above sea level, the town of **Mandi** is situated on the left bank of the River Beas at an altitude of 2,460ft (750 m). It is 130 miles (210 km) from Pathankot and 102 miles (165 km) from Shimla via Bilaspur.

The town has several striking stone temples with beautiful carvings, among which **Bhootnath, Triloknath, Panchvaktra** and **Tarna** are the more famous.

For the Shivaratri Fair, the town is tastefully decorated. Devotees put the *rathas* (carriages) of their village family gods and goddesses on their shoulders and go in procession to Mandi town on Shivaratri day. They present themselves at the **Raj Madhan Temple** and later pay homage to Lord Shiva at Bhootnath Temple. On this day, a week-long fair, a feast of fun, music and dance begins.

Bilaspur is 56 miles (90 km) from Shimla. Among the town's major attractions are **Vyas Gufa** (cave) and the **Lakshmi Narayan** and **Radheshyam Temples**. The **Shri Naina Devi Temple**, which attracts thousands of pilgrims during its many fairs, is situated at the top of a triangular hillock just 35 miles (57 km) from Bilaspur. This sacred place provides an unparalleled view of the holy **Anandpur Sahib**, the birthplace of a Sikh guru, on one side, and Govind Sagar (named after the guru) on the other.

Nahan is a small holiday resort tucked away on an isolated ridge in the Shiwaliks. Its proximity to the plains and its low altitude make most of the area specially attractive during autumn. Nahan has several famous temples and tanks. This town's special attraction is its lovely, lonely walks.

Poanta Sahib, 30 miles (45 km) from Nahan on the Nahan-Dehra-Dun Road, is an important pilgrimage centre for the Sikhs. Its impressive *gurdwara* (temple) on the bank of the River Yamuna is thronged by thousands of pilgrims during the Hola festival in the month of March.

Renuka is a picturesque lake town about 30 miles (45 km) from Nahan. The sacred **Parshuram Tal** (tank) is located near Renuka Lake which appears shaped in the profile of a goddess. It is said that Rishi Jamdagni, displeased with his wife Renuka, instructed his son Parshuram to chop off her head. The son promptly carried out the order. The *rishi,* pleased with his son, offered him a boon. Parshuram instantly asked for the restoration of his mother to life. Renuka was brought back to life and, thereafter, her reunion with the family has been commemorated by a large fair held in her honour every year. People from far and near pay their homage and pray to the goddess for her blessings for a happy and prosperous family life.

Winter sports: The little hamlet of **Kufri**, 10 miles (16 km) from Shimla, is the centre for winter sports. The ice skating rink is the only one of its kind in this part of the world. The skiing season starts in the last week of December and lasts up to about the end of February, depending on the weather. Skiing opportunities are also available at **Narkanda** (40 miles/64 km from Shimla) and **Solang** (6 miles/10 km from Manali).

Naldera, 14 miles (23 km) from Shimla, has one of the oldest golf courses in the country. The nine-hole course is very popular with enthusiasts since it is perhaps the most reliable one east of Suez.

Chail, a small town 39 miles (63 km) from Shimla, is at a height of 7,000 ft (2,150 m). It was once the summer capital of the Maharaja of Patiala and is now a lovely tourist resort. It boasts a cricket pitch reputed to be the highest in the world and certainly the most scenic. The town and its environs provide excellent facilities for fishing, tennis, squash and golf, in most beautiful surroundings. Bird-watchers and wildlife enthusiasts will find the forests around Chail alive with hundreds of species.

Trekking: There is no end to the trekking possibilities in Himachal Pradesh, but for those who prefer to keep on the beaten track, there are a number of established routes of great interest.

Manali-Chandrakhani-Malana is a seven-day trek. The stages en route are Ramsu, 6,760 ft (15 miles/24 km); Chandrakhani, 11,980 ft (4 miles/6 km); Malana, 6,890 ft (4 miles); Kasol, 5,180 ft (5 miles/8 km); Jari, 5,120 ft (9 miles/14 km); and Bhuntar, 2,950 ft (7 miles/11 km).

Manali-Chandratal involves 11 days' trekking. It covers Chikka, 9,700 ft (8 miles/13 km); Chhatru, 11,020 ft (10 miles/16 km); Chhota Dara 12,270 ft (10 miles); Batal 13,000 ft (10 miles); Chandratal, 14,010 ft (11 miles/18 km); Topko Yongma, 14,170 ft (7 miles/11 km); Topko Gongma, 15,520 ft (6 miles/10 km); Baralacha, 1,600 ft (6 miles); Patseo 12,530 ft (12 miles/19 km); Jispa, 10,890ft (9 miles/14 km); Keyong, 10,960 ft (13 miles/21 km).

Manali-Deo-Tibba, a seven-day trek, covers Khanul, 6,630 ft (6 miles); Chikka,

9,840ft (6 miles/10 km); Seri 14,990 ft (3 miles/5 km); Chandratal, 14,990 ft (6 miles) and back to Manali.

Manali-Solang Valley is again a seven-day trek and covers Solang, 8,140 ft (7 miles); Dhundi, 9,320 ft; Beas Kund, 11,610 ft and back (6 miles/10 km); Dhundhi-Shigara Dugh, (5 miles/8 km); Marrhi, 11,090 ft (6 miles).

Dharamsala-Chamba via Lakagot and Bharmaur is an eight-day trek. Lakagot is at the foot of Indrahar Pass at 18,600 ft (5,660 metres) on the majestic Dhauladhar range.

There are ample opportunities for trekking in the Chamba District. The Pangi Valley and the Manimahesh range of mountains are attractive areas.

A number of treks can be undertaken from Shimla: **Shimla to Kulu via Jalori Pass**; **Shimla to Mussoorie via Tuini**; and **Shimla to Churdhar via Fagu**.

Most of the peaks in Himachal Pradesh are still unscaled. However, some of the easily accessible mountains provide a good training ground for mountaineers with their sights set on the ultimate Himalayas.

Buddhists at prayer, Dharamsala.

JAMMU AND KASHMIR

The storybook scenery of the vale of Kashmir has been legendary throughout history, but few outside the Indian subcontinent are aware that the state of Jammu and Kashmir combines three distinct areas, each unique physically, culturally and aesthetically. Not only do people in Jammu, Kashmir and Ladakh live in radically different environments; they also speak different languages, worship different gods and think along separate cultural lines. This diversity enhances the mystery of remote mountain valleys and flavours the cultural complexities of busy urban centres.

However, in the predominantly Muslim valley and surrounding mountains, militants have been waging a fierce guerilla war against Indian security forces since 1989. Sometimes tourists have been swept up in the conflict, so be careful.

Jammu: Jammu is the home of the handsome Dogras, Hindus and Sikhs whose warlike forefathers rode north out of their foothill villages to conquer the disparate kingdoms of the high Himalaya. These were united under Maharaja Gulab Singh in the early 19th century. Most Dogras today are small farmers eking out an existence on the dry sandstone slopes of the Shiwalik range, the lowest and youngest mountains in the Himalaya. The countryside is rolling, broken here and there by sudden escarpments where visible layers of the earth's crust fold up at incongruous angles. At lower elevations, cattle and goats graze between large flowering cactuses, and spreading fig trees provide shade to village men wearing loose turbans and cotton pyjamas.

The city of **Jammu** is a big, sprawling entrepot town situated at the interface of the plains and the hills. It is difficult to enjoy Jammu in the heat of the summer, but the old part of the city has a number of unusual attractions.

There are two major temple complexes: the **Ranbireshwar Temple**, with a towering 246-ft (75-metre) tower, is dedi-

Houseboats in winter, Srinagar.

cated to Lord Shiva and is renowned for its large crystal *lingams* (the phallic symbols of Lord Shiva); and the **Raghunath Temple**, which is surrounded by one of the largest temple complexes in northern India. Its interiors covered with gold leaf, the temple is dedicated to Rama, the eighth incarnation of Lord Vishnu.

The **Dogra Art Gallery** contains over 500 paintings in the delicate miniature style which was sponsored by the royal families of neighbouring hill kingdoms like Basohli and Kangra. The rough stonecut **Bahu Fort** on the opposite bank of the Tawi River is undoubtedly the oldest monument in Jammu while the **Amar Mahal Palace** claims first prize as the oddest. Designed for an eccentric maharaja by a French architect, the Amar Mahal resembles a medieval chateau, complete with turrets. Converted into a museum, it now houses a library, portrait gallery and more beautiful miniature paintings.

A number of interesting excursions can be made from Jammu to small lakes and temples in the surrounding hills. The **Mansar Lake**, with its shrine to a local goddess, is a wonderful oasis in the dry hills. Bordering the southern edge of the sacred lake are a tourist bungalow and a small enclosure for deer.

By far the most important shrine to north India's Hindus, is the **cave temple of Vaishno Devi,** 37 miles (60 km) northwest of Jammu city. Thousands of devout Hindus make the pilgrimage to this temple every year, many of them fulfilling vows that they would cover the distance on foot or bicycle.

The Kashmir valley: For the visitor, the first view of Kashmir is unforgettable. In the verdant summer the valley is a sea of deepest green rice fields, intersected by rigid avenues of tall poplar, dotted with neatly planted orchards of apple, plum and almond trees. Interspersed are villages of tall, double-storey farmhouses made of wood and brick. The Mughal emperors who came here in the summer months coined a word for the valley: "Paradise." And no one would dispute that, no one who has seen the valley in its correct perspective – shaded by magnificent chinars (the oriental plane trees), surrounded on all sides by a ring of mountains and rushing streams, and blessed with the scent of wild briar roses.

This beautiful land has been settled since very early times. Excavations have unearthed circular residential pits and stone implements dating from 2500 BC. In 250 BC the Emperor Ashoka is credited with having introduced Buddhism into Kashmir. On gently terraced slopes above the village of **Harwan,** just north of Shalimar, the ruins of an ancient Buddhist settlement have been found. A marvellous circular patio of fitted and decorated terracotta tiles was found surrounding a building made of pebbles and boulders which may have housed a temple. Curiously, Buddhism faded out in the Kashmir Valley to be replaced by Hinduism, and later, largely, by Islam.

The glorious age of Hindu rule reached its apex under King Lalitaditya who lived in the beginning of the 8th century AD. His memory is immortalised in the remains of his massive temple of stone at **Martand**, near the modern village of Mattan on the road to Pahalgam, and in the ruins of his city of **Parihasapura**, 3 miles (5 km) off the road to Baramullah, beyond the Gulmarg turn-off.

The valley is sprinkled with hundreds of other ancient temples, including the famous **Avantiswami Temple** in Awantipura on the Pahalgam tourist route.

Srinagar and Dal: The lush greenery of the valley with its terraced rice fields, fruit orchards and swirling waterways spills into the city of **Srinagar** via the Dal Lake and great avenues of poplar and chinar trees. This fresh natural atmosphere combined with the clamour of the old city's twisting medieval streets gives Srinagar a distinctive, vital flavour.

The water world of the Dal and Nagin lakes in Srinagar can be explored in the almost decadent comfort of *shikaras,* hand-paddled water taxis. In the mountains, sturdy hill ponies are available for riding or as pack animals to carry trekking supplies on a number of beautiful trekking routes.

Srinagar is connected by air with Delhi, Chandigarh, Amritsar, Jammu, and Leh in Ladakh. The Srinagar-Leh flight is operated twice a week and is one of the most spectacular short plane-rides in the world. Buses and taxis ply between Jammu and Srinagar and between Srinagar and Leh, though the latter route closes between late October and early May because of snow.

Life on the Lake: Although local politics has inhibited tourism of late, most visitors begin their tour of Jammu and Kashmir in Srinagar, with a stay on a legendary houseboat. Houseboats have been a part of Kashmir's aquatic culture for centuries and a number of lake people continue to live off the bounty of their watery world on the small prototype *doonga* boats of the past. It was only with the advent of the British that houseboats began to develop as a form of lodging.

Houseboats of all sizes and costs range the banks of the busy Dal Lake and the quieter, cleaner Nagin. Itinerant waterborne merchants cruise the lakes and are often eccentric characters with names like Mr Crocodile or Mr Marvellous the Flowerman, occasionally as devious as they are colourful.

From houseboats the world of the water people can be observed first hand. A visit to the early morning vegetable market by *shikara* is well-worth the extra effort. Farmers emerge from the maze of floating gardens and canals with their little flat-bottom skiffs loaded with vegetables, to gather in an open waterway to trade from boat to boat. The first light of early morning tinges the wild gardens of lotus flowers with a delicate pink light; kingfishers dart about, flashing their azure wings, and day breaks over the lake.

Mughal Gardens: The famous Boulevard Road circles the Dal Lake and leads out towards the magnificent **Mughal Gardens**. The first two gardens – **Chashma Shahi** and **Pari Mahal** – are to the right of the Boulevard, set into the slope of the circling hills. Chashma Shahi, attributed to Shah Jahan, is named after a gushing mountain spring that feeds it, while Pari Mahal is set up within a series of enclosed terraces and buildings which were once a Sufi garden college. Both are small and command beautiful views.

The two larger gardens, **Nishat** and **Shalimar**, are located much farther down the boulevard. They are built on a symmetrical plan of a central waterway with fountains dividing a series of gardened terraces. Nishat is the larger of the two and has an impressive plantation of huge chinar trees on the highest terrace, planted perhaps by the great Mughals themselves. The Shalimar is the more famous garden because of the celebrated romance between its builder, Emperor Jahangir, and his queen, Nur Mahal. An audiovisual in English and Urdu retells this love story every evening. The centerpiece on the upper terrace is the *baradari* or summer house of Jehangir, where the emperor and his bride reclined on warm summer afternoons – surrounded by the heady bouquets of a million roses, strained through a fine spray of cool spring water.

Nagin Lake and Hari Parbat: A beautiful circular drive through apple orchards and rice fields connects Shalimar with the Nagin Lake and the old city of Srinagar. Visitors take this drive to visit the shimmering white marble mosque of **Hazratbal,** which possesses a hair of Prophet Mohammed. On the lake margin a short distance from the mosque is the tomb of Sheikh Mohammed Abdullah, the "Lion of Kashmir". Abdullah, who died in 1982, was the undisputed leader of Kashmir and its chief minister for the last years of his long political life.

Just beyond Hazratbal and separated from the Dal Lake by a causeway, is the **Nagin Lake**. Much cleaner than the Dal, the Nagin is popular with tourists searching for a quieter vacation. Four swimming boats anchored in the deepest part of the lake offer facilities for swimming, water skiing and surf-board riding. (Swimming is not recommended in the more polluted Dal Lake.)

Behind the Nagin Lake looms the **Hari Parbat** fortress, atop a small hill. The walls that surround the base of this 19th century fort were built 300 years earlier by the Mughal Emperor Akbar. Across the combined lakes from Hari Parbat, atop the Takht-e-Suleiman (throne of Solomon) hill is the temple of **Sankaracharya** which dominates the surrounding landscape. A motor road leads up the hill to this ancient Shiva temple. From the boulevard there are several nice foot trails to the top. The view is superb.

Kashmir mosques: Foremost among the mosques in the valley is the **Jami Masjid,** a massive congregational mosque. Originally built in 1402, the mosque has been completely reconstructed twice after severe fires destroyed it. The mosque is laid out on a square, symmetrical plan, and is remarkable for its colonnades of lofty deodar (cedar) columns.

The wonderful **Mosque of Shah Hamadan** is built on the banks of the muddy Jhelum River. Made entirely of wood, the mosque is named after a great saint who is credited with the peaceful conversion of millions of Hindus to Islam during the 14th century. Non-believers are not allowed into the mosque but many look through the door at its intricately painted papier-mâché ceiling and walls. As with many mosques in Kashmir, a screened verandah running around it is used by praying women, as they cannot enter the central hall.

Farther upstream, near the Zero Bridge is the **Bund**, a long promenade that runs along the river lined with a number of buildings dating from the turn of the century. This was the fashionable district for visitors in the days of the British Empire. The General Post Office, the Srinagar Club, the Residency building, which now houses the Government Arts Emporium, and some of the old shops like Suffering Moses's House of Handicrafts (run by the charming and eccentric Suffering Moses himself), are located along the Bund.

Famed craftsmen: Kashmir boasts an unrivalled tradition of craftsmanship which flourishes to this day in the villages and back alleys of the valley. Drives through the countryside reveal hundreds of carpet looms hidden in crumbling village homes, the hand knotted Persian rugs being washed amidst clucking chickens on open courtyards. Patient and delicate wool embroidery on shawls is often the work of village men stitching away under the apple boughs. The finest quality shawls are made of pashmina wool from small Ladakhi goats, and can cost thousands of rupees. The royal shawl (*shahtoosh*) can be passed through a ring; local sapphires are renowned; pounded

felt rugs or *namda* are often decorated with appliqué work in designs.

Finely painted papier-mâché boxes, ashtrays, writing sets and other articles have long been a specialty of Srinagar's artisans – the skills being passed from father to son over the generations.

Woodcarving, and in particular, the making of beautiful walnut furniture, is another craft in which the Kashmiris excel. The walnut and its incredible grain make each piece a unique work of art.

Kashmir's Islamic culture is a lively one, with something going on all of the time. Influenced by their Hindu forefathers, the Kashmiris have modified their customs and observances in noticeable ways. The worship at wayside shrines dedicated to *rishis* (holy men) can be observed throughout the valley. Important days of the Muslim calendar are celebrated with great festivity, and there is considerable variation in the observance of the month-long, sunrise to sunset fasts of Ramadan. Lively religious and folk music enjoys widespread popularity. During the wedding season, women link their arms and sing while the groom departs for the bride's home. *Shikara* drivers croon as they paddle along, and village women sing when they are transplanting rice. One of the most easily appreciated cultural forms is the distinctive Kashmiri cuisine, popularly served as part of a feast called a *wazwan*. Consisting of up to 36 different meat preparations eaten with rice, the wonders of the *waza* chef are incredible.

Hill resorts: Pahalgam, Gulmarg and Sonamarg, the three most popular hill resorts in Kashmir, each offers a different experience of wild alpine beauty. **Pahalgam**, at the confluence of two wooded valleys at 6,890ft (2,100metres), lies 60 miles (90 km) northeast of Srinagar. The town is little more than a single street running along the bank of the Liddar River, fronted by provision stores and a variety of hotels and guesthouses. Dotted around the town are clusters of government-owned tourist huts, tented camps, and private lodges nestled amongst stands of blue pine and fir.

Pahalgam is very popular with Indian

Gulmarg, Kashmir.

188

tourists as the staging point for the famous pilgrimage to the sacred ice *lingam* in the **Amarnath Cave**, four days, walk to the east. A growing number of foreign tourists go to Pahalgam to relax in surroundings that compare favourably with the Swiss Alps, to play golf on the rough little nine-hole course, or to start off on a number of treks into the high altitude meadows beyond. Tents and pack ponies can be hired in Pahalgam for treks to the 11,800-ft (3,600-metre) Kolahoi glacier, which can be done in three days, or for the arduous 10-day walk into Ladakh, across the main Himalayan range.

In the summer, trekking routes and camping sites may be shared with the nomadic Bakkarval shepherds who bring herds of sheep, goats and buffaloes to graze on high pastures. They are tall handsome people, the men bearded and turbaned, the women with their hair plaited into hundreds of tiny braids, their children tied on the backs of pack ponies along with pots, pans and puppies.

Gulmarg with its famous 18-hole golf course attracts sportsmen in the summer just as its ski runs make it India's premier skiing centre in the winter. The small market and a number of lodges and hotels are scattered around a broad bowl of sloping meadows at 8,860 ft (2,700 metres). Several short trekking routes and numerous day walks can be taken from Gulmarg which is only 32 miles (52 km) from Srinagar, to the southwest. Both Pahalgam and Gulmarg have a number of trout-stocked streams where fly fishing is allowed on the basis of a permit issued in Srinagar.

Sonamarg is the smallest of the hill resorts. It is located on the road to Ladakh and has grown in recent years to accommodate travellers breakfasting on their way to the Zoji La pass. At an altitude of 8,860 ft (2,700 metres), Sonamarg is 52 miles (84 km) from Srinagar. It has a Government tourist bungalow and is the staging area for the popular Gangabal Lake trek. Many local day visitors ride ponies to the nearby Thajiwas meadow.

Ladakh: Crossing the 11,480-ft (3,500-metre) Zoji La pass into Ladakh is like stepping into another planet. From the verdant, forested hillsides above Sona-marg, through the hair-raising twists and turns of the Zoji La climb, still carpeted with wild flowers, one passes into an immense landscape of jagged barren rock. It is as if the Himalaya were suddenly stripped of all its flesh, leaving a rare old skeleton of majestic barren bones. The mighty range forces its rain shadow on the lands to the north, isolating them from the influences of the south. This barrier, effective from the cultural as well as the geographical perspective, has ensured that the various people of Ladakh – the animist Dards, the Shia Baltis, and the Buddhist Ladakhis – have retained their traditions unchanged over the centuries.

In **Dras**, which is the first major town in this western side of Ladakh, the houses are single storeyed mud-brick structures. In front of them women of the Shia Muslim Balti population, dressed in heavy black woollen robes and red scarves, work in golden fields of buckwheat. Old, gnarled Balti men, with creased faces that look like topographical maps, pass driving donkeys loaded with dung and dried thistle. The Baltis have Central Asian features. The Dards, who also inhabit Dras and a number of secluded villages to the northeast, are distinctly Caucasian in their features. This extraordinary people speak a language quite unrelated to their neighbours in either direction. Dards are neither Muslim nor Buddhist, but seem to observe festivals and practices of either group in addition to their own customs.

District headquarters **Kargil**, at 8,700 ft (2,650 metres), is one of the lowest towns in Ladakh. It was once a trading town on the route between Central Asia and the Indian plains. Now buses and trucks crowd its one main street, their occupants packing into the little hotels and restaurants which have sprung up to cater to the town's new position as a night halt on the Leh road. Another road leads south from Kargil past the towering peaks of Nun, 23,300 ft (7,100 metres), and Kun, 23,200 ft (7,070 metres), to Padum, the capital of Zanskar. This road is negotiable by truck or jeep if the Pensi La pass is open. Some of Ladakh's finest and most rugged trekking routes branch off from this road to lead into the rock-hewn wilderness. Trekkers in Ladakh need to be better equipped and better organised than on the Kashmir side, because the environment is more extreme, and human habitations are sparse.

Wherever there is a good water supply in Ladakh, there is usually a small cluster of mud-brick homes; earth coloured if their owners are Muslims and white-washed if they are Buddhist dwellings. Carefully tended willows and poplars give each little oasis a brilliant dash of colour in a landscape dominated by the brown earth and the blue sky.

As one begins to pass from predominantly Muslim to Buddhist villages, other landmarks appear, replacing the small tin-covered domes of the Muslim mosques. Monasteries in all shapes and sizes, fluttering with prayer flags, dot the semi-desert countryside. *Chortens,* or whitewashed stupas, often line the road, as do long walls covered with *mani* (prayer) stones, carved with Buddhist prayers. Attire changes too; the bright maroon and saffron robes of monks and nuns mingle with the peculiar jaunty Ladakhi cap and the turquoise and coral jewellery of the women.

In the town of **Mulbekh**, a giant statue of the Maitreya, the Buddha to come, looks over the passing tourist buses from a rock pinnacle on which it was carved in ancient times. Over the 13,430-ft (4,094-metre) **Fatu La pass**, the road reaches the incredible **Monastery of Lamayuru**, looming like a Hollywood movie backdrop of Shangri La. Lamayuru is venerated as one of the oldest monasteries in Ladakh as it houses a cave where one of Tibet's great teachers, Naropa, is said to have meditated for several years in the 10th century. Like all monasteries in Ladakh, the complex includes a number of different buildings, each with shrines to different gods and incarnations of the Buddha.

A form of Tibetan Mahayana Buddhism is practised in Ladakh in which the pantheon incorporates a number of pre-Buddhist deities. In Ladakh, monasteries are traditional centres of religious as well as cultural activity. They are also the largest landowners and have, over the centuries, concentrated much of the wealth of the land in their coffers. Traditionally dependent on donations, the monasteries have started charging visitors admission fees.

Leh town: After Lamayuru the road finally joins the Indus River at Khaltsi and more or less follows this famous waterway to the wide valley of **Leh**.

The drive from Srinagar to Leh by bus or taxi takes two gruelling days, but it is an unforgettable experience. In marked contrast, the flight takes only 25 minutes. On a clear day, the route goes right over the peaks of Nun and Kun, while stretching across the horizon to the north is the mighty Karakoram range, which at 28,250 ft (8,611 metres), is the second highest mountain in the world. The view is so breathtaking that the flight seems to last only a few minutes.

Leh is a rapidly growing town, spreading in all directions from its original position beneath the long abandoned **Namgyal Palace**. While the town has come a long way from the days when polo was played on its main street, Leh still retains a pleasant, traditional quality and is a good place to acclimatise to the altitude while admiring the lovely vegetable sellers, dressed in their coral necklaces and turquoise-encrusted headgear and seated comfortably behind baskets of huge vegetables.

Busy monasteries: The most visited monasteries in the area are Shey, Thikse and Hemis, all spread along the Indus River. These can be visited in a half-day tour, but midday is not a good time to visit monasteries. It's better to go in the early morning and late evening, when the monks say their prayers, and when the mystical chanting, the ringing of bells, the clashing of cymbals, and the blowing of long brass horns lend magic to the visit.

Shey is the oldest of these three monasteries and is not in regular use, so it is open only until nine in the morning. It contains a two-storey high statue of the Buddha seated in meditation. Above and below are the crumbling walls of the old summer capital of Ladakh.

Thikse is a very large monastery built on a triangular spur of a mountain 11 miles (17km) from Leh. A series of out-buildings work up the side of this hill culminating in the main red-coloured monastery building at the top. Thikse is especially noteworthy for its new wing which houses a gigantic seated statue of the Maitreya. As in other monasteries, Thikse's prayer hall houses hundreds of rectangular prayer books – loose sheets of printed prayers stacked between wooden covers and bound in silk. *Thanka* paintings hang from the rafters and giant urns containing melted yak butter and water line the altars.

Hemis is the richest of the monasteries but the least hospitable. Unfortunately, some pilferages have occurred with the advent of tourism and many precious statues and relics which were once displayed openly have been hidden away. Hemis is famous for its great three-day festival which usually takes place in June.

There are dozens of other large and well endowed monasteries in Ladakh. Many can be approached in the local jeep taxis from Leh. Among these, **Alchi** on the Indus, 1½ hours' drive from Leh, is the oldest and contains the most remarkable wall paintings.

A happy people: The native greeting of the Ladakhis, *juley,* is spontaneous and friendly. They enjoy dancing, archery, polo, and their strong barley beer, known as *chang*. Most Ladakhis are farmers, and they can be seen ploughing their small dry plots with their hardy *dzos,* cattle crossbred from yaks and hill cows. People living in remote villages subsist on a simple staple diet of roasted barley or buckwheat flour, called **tsampa,** and green salt tea mixed with butter. A strong and vibrant culture survives in the harsh and imposing landscape of Ladakh, and unusual desert flowers bloom amongst barren rocks.

The state of Jammu and Kashmir is a wide open place full of untapped mountain torrents, densely wooded mountain slopes and rugged moonscapes. Its great variety of people and the depth of its varied history and culture reflect the natural bounty of the Himalaya mountains, which cradle the paradise state in their nurturing folds.

Monastery, Ladakh.

PUNJAB AND HARYANA

It is sunburnt land, flat as a pancake, sloping imperceptibly down from the Himalayan foothills towards the deserts of Rajasthan on the one side and the extensive plains of Hindustan on the other. At one time Punjab extended northwestward up to the River Indus and beyond. The entire terrain was known to the Greeks as Pentopotamia because of the five rivers that ran through it. The Persians named it *Panj* (five) *aab* (waters) – a name which has stuck. In 1947 when India was partitioned, the larger half of Punjab went to Pakistan. Nevertheless, both Pakistan and India retained the name "Punjab" since the Punjabi language is spoken on both sides of the border. In 1966 the Indian smaller half was further divided into three: Punjab, Haryana and Himachal Pradesh.

The people of Punjab (both Indian and Pakistani) and Haryana are of the same racial stock. The peasantry are largely Jatt (to rhyme with gut) or, in Haryana, Jaat (to rhyme with part). Tall, brawny and rugged, they are renowned for their pugnacity and fierce attachment to the soil. Townsmen are equally go-ahead as traders and entrepreneurs. While Pakistan Punjabis are Muslims, Indian Punjabis are Sikhs or Hindus. Haryana is predominantly Hindu and its language is a dialect of Hindi.

The climate ranges from bracing cold in winter to scorching heat in summer with winter and summer monsoons. The spring comes with Basant Panchmi, a festival in early February when "all is seemly; the woodlands are in flower and loud with humming of bumble bees" (founder of the Sikh faith Guru Nanak, 1469–1539). The countryside becomes an ocean of mustard yellow broken by green squares of sugarcane with its fluffy pampas plumes. As the mustard is harvested, wheat and barley take its place. Springtime sounds that pervade the countryside are brown partridges calling to each other and the monotonous *kooh kooh* of flourmills.

Birds and blossoms: The short spring gives way to a long summer, with fresh foliage. Silk cotton, coral, flame of the

Golden Temple, Amritsar.

forest and flamboyant trees are a scarlet red; laburnum which flowers in late May is like burnished gold. The partridges are silent; instead the incessant screaming of koels in mango groves and the metallic call of barbets are heard. By the time wheat is harvested the summer is full on. In the words of Guru Nanak, "the sun scorches, the earth burns like an oven. Waters give up their vapours, yet it burns and scorches relentlessly." The parched earth becomes a vast stretch of mud-coloured plain with dust devils spiralling like dancing dervishes. The blazing inferno lasts from April to the end of June. By mid-July, the summer monsoon comes and within a few days the heavy down-pour turns the land into a vast swamp. Life begins anew.

By the time the monsoon is over, it is cool again. A new crop of rice, maize, millet and pulses is sown. Peasants adorn themselves in brightly-colored starched turbans, embroidered waistcoats, and dance the *bhangra* to the beat of drums. Through October to the festival of lamps (Diwali), usually in November, there is a succession of fairs and festivals. Then once more it is wintertime, when nights are cold, the days full of blue skies and bright sunshine.

There are several Mughal monuments in Haryana of which the most popular is **Pinjore Gardens** at the base of the Shiwalik hills on the road to Simla. Inside the Mughal battlements is a beautifully laid out garden with fountains and cascades running below open balconies. It has for good reason become a favourite spot for lovers and honeymooners.

The state government has exploited its scenic spots to their best advantage. Close to Delhi is **Suraj Kund,** an 8th-century Hindu sun temple, and beyond it the **Badkhal Lake** with a resthouse over-looking its stretch of water. A few miles southwards is **Sultanpur bird sanctu-ary,** and beyond it the hot spring of **Sohna.**

Punjab and Haryana were the cradles of Indian civilisation. Archeologists have found implements made of quarzite fash-ioned over 300,000 years ago. Agricul-tural tools made of copper and bronze prove the existence of rural communities

The Temple interior.

around the 25th century BC. Later excavations have unearthed whole cities built around that period with market-places, marble baths and drainage systems and intricately carved seals with hieroglyphics. The Indus valley civilisation, as it came to be known, was among the oldest in the world. Relics of these olden times continue to be unearthed.

Both Punjab and Haryana have more history than historical monuments, more facilities for tourists than places of touristic interest. It is through these two states that invaders from the northwest – Greeks, Turks, Mongols, Persians and Afghans – entered India, and where many battles which decided the fate of India were fought. Their sites are still marked with commemorative stones and mausoleums of kings and commanders who fell in action. The most famous of these are at Panipat and Karnal in Haryana. There are innumerable forts, too many to be named, scattered all over the countryside.

Both states have developed wildlife sanctuaries along lakes, swamps and rivers with attractive tourist bungalows from where visitors can see a wide variety of wild fowl and herds of deer. Along all major highways are chains of milk-bars and cafes named after birds of the region: blue jay, dabchick, hoopoe, magpie, myna, parakeet, etc.

Le Corbusier's city: There are many things that Punjab and Haryana have in common; the most important of these is a common capital, **Chandigarh**. Since both states have laid claims to the city, it is administered by the Central Government as a Union Territory till a final decision regarding its future is made. However, in the same city reside governors of the two states; in the same office buildings but on different floors are their separate secretariats and their respective High Courts. For the visitor, more interesting than the wrangle over its future is the city itself, which is beautifully located below the Shiwalik range of hills.

Two hill torrents were canalised to form a large lake with a most attractive boulevard, along which the citizens take the morning and evening air and watch waterfowl which have made **Sukhna Lake** a halting place on their migrations from

Central Asia to India and vice versa.

The layout of the city was designed by the famous French architect, Le Corbusier assisted by his cousin, Jeanneret, and an English husband-and-wife team, Maxwell Fry and Jane Drew. Corbusier himself designed most of its important public buildings, including the Secretariat, the Legislative Assembly and the High Court. Many of these buildings are on stilts, an architectural style copied by many private institutions and homes.

Chandigarh is a very green city with a large variety of flowering trees specially chosen for their beauty by Dr M. S. Randhawa, a renowned civil servant and botanist. It has an extensive **Rose Garden** named after the first Muslim President of India, Dr Zakir Husain. There is also a park with statuary made out of broken pieces of cups and saucers of which the Chandigarhians are very proud.

Punjab: The Punjab's largest city is **Amritsar** with its **Golden Temple**, the holiest of holy Sikh shrines, and a flash-point for religious and political conflict. The temple was most recently stormed by government troops in 1984.

As Indian cities go, Amritsar is not very old; it was founded a little over 400 years ago by Guru Ram Das, the fourth of the 10 Sikh Gurus. His son and successor, the fifth guru, Arjun, raised a temple in the midst of a pool, sanctified its waters and installed the Sikhs' holy scripture, the *Granth Sahib,* in its inner sanctum. The city takes its name from the sacred pool – *amrit* (nectar) *sar* (pool)

In 1803, the Sikh ruler, Maharaja Ranjit Singh (1780–1839) rebuilt the temple in marble and gold (its domes took 880lbs/400kg of gold leaf to be covered). Ever since, it has been known as the Golden Temple. The Sikhs usually refer to it as the *Harimandir* (the temple of God) or *Darbar Sahib* (the court of the Lord).

It is well worthwhile spending an hour or two in the temple complex (be sure to have your head covered and feet bare), listening to the hymn-singing which goes on non-stop from the early hours of the morning till late into the night and watching the thousands of pilgrims at worship.

The complex has a number of shrines of historical importance, notably the Akal

Takht (throne of the timeless God) facing the temple where arms of the warrior gurus, their dresses and emblems can be seen, and the eight-storied Baba-Atal tower.

Besides the Golden Temple, there is its Hindu counterpart, the Durgiana Temple, built in recent times; and Jallianwala Bagh where, on 13 April 1919, General Dyer fired on an unarmed crowd and killed 300 people, shocking the nation. The garden has a monument commemorating the event and has become a place of pilgrimage.

There are many other Sikh temples in Punjab which are both historic and beautiful. On the foothills of the Himalaya is Anandpur where, in 1699, the last of the Sikh gurus, Govind Singh, baptised the first five Sikhs into the militant fraternity he called the Khalsa or the pure. Here are several temples as well as a fortress, Kesgarh. Every spring at the Holi festival (Sikhs celebrate it a day later as *hola mohalla*), thousands of Sikhs, notably the Nihangs, descendants of two orders of warriors, gather to indulge in displays of mock combat on horseback and on foot.

An equally large complex of temples, palaces and forts is to be seen at Sirhind near Patiala. Besides these there are also remains of a Mughal and pre-Mughal city and the mausoleum of a famous divine, Hazrat Mujaddad-ud-din Altaf Sheikh Ahmed (died 1624 AD), popularly known as Sirhindi.

Haryana: This state could rightly claim to be the birthplace of the most sacred religious scripture of Hinduism. At Kurukshetra (not far from Panipat) was fought the famous battle between two Aryan tribes, the Kurus and the Pandavas. On the eve of the battle, Sri Krishna, a reincarnation of God Vishnu, persuaded Arjuna, the reluctant commander of the Pandava army, to wage the battle for righteousness. This sermon known as the *Bhagavad Gita* emphasises the moral principle of doing one's duty without consideration of reward, victory or defeat and is regarded as the essence of the teachings of the *Vedas* and the *Upanishads*.

Kurukshetra is full of temples and tanks where pilgrims come to bathe on auspicious days.

Le Corbusier's Chandigarh.

RAJASTHAN, DESERT STATE

The concept "desert state" doesn't conjure up images of palaces shimmering on idyllic lakes; blazing heat doesn't seem the right context for temples and forts of stunning artistry carved from stone that is honey or rose, marble-white or sandstone-red; nor would anyone expect painted streets where pageantry and colour walk out of life-size frescos, producing crowds of brightly turbaned men with proud moustaches and women whose beauty is lethal, though, alas, veiled.

But this is the desert state of Rajasthan. The past lingers on. Visitors can still ride caparisoned elephants that recall the royal courts or stay in fantasy palace hotels built by descendants of the sun and the moon.

More than half of Rajasthan is desert or semi-arid, a continuation of the sand belt that girdles the world. This desert belt is separated from the Indian peninsula by the Aravalli Ranges, geologically the oldest mountains in India.

Both the Thar Desert and the Aravalli Ranges lend their distinct personalities to the landscape of Rajasthan. It is interesting that this picture of a rocky, rugged skyline over the soft-staired dunes where camels plod, is only one of the two clichés which depict Rajasthan. The other, diametrically opposed, is a refreshing contrast: placid blue lakes with island palaces, gardens with pavilions and kiosks – always with a few dancing peacocks.

The first dwellers: Few places in the world can boast an ancestry dating beyond 2500 BC. It has now been proven that the very ancient civilisation of the Indus Valley had its precursors in north Rajasthan. It seems that the Bhil and Mina tribes inhabited this area. Around 1400 BC the Aryans wheeled their fast equestrian chariots into Rajasthan. The local people were overawed and dispersed eastwards and south. The Aryans had come to stay and to father the future generations of Rajasthan.

It is not possible to trace back the mingling of blood in the prehistory of the 2nd millennium BC with any precision, but history has continued unabated in this land which first featured in the active campaign to spread the message of Buddhism (around the 2nd and 3rd centuries BC). The rest is a story of blood and battle, battle and blood.

Afghans, Turks, Persians, Mughals followed, mixing their blood, first in war then in peace. Such a past is what gave a martial ancestry to the Rajputs. From the reign of Harsha (7th century AD) to the time when the Delhi Sultanate was founded by the Muslims (1206 AD), Rajasthan was fragmented in competing kingdoms. Perhaps it was during this time that, by their wealth and power, the Rajputs, "sons of rajas," were able to persuade the Brahmins to provide them with genealogies that invented links with the sun, the moon, and the fire god. The mixed bunch of warriors who called themselves Rajputs were born fighters. They fitted the Aryan martial Kshatriya caste slot only naturally. In time, they were divided into 36 royal clans.

After the 14th century, prosperity declined in the area. In the 16th century the Mughals made North India their home. Winning over Rajasthan was the achievement of Akbar, the Great Mughal, who mixed military might with the soft touch of religious tolerance. His trump card was matrimonial alliances with the Hindu Rajputs which turned them from dangerous enemies into faithful allies.

Jaipur and Jodhpur provided many princesses to the Mughals. By the 17th century, the Mughal emperors had posted an agent or writer (*nawis*) to the major Rajput courts who informed them of any princely decisions or events affecting imperial interests. But when the Mughals weakened, the Rajputs were quick to reassert their sovereignty. In 1757 the British captured Bengal in the east but Rajasthan resisted. By the beginning of the 19th century, all the Maharajas surrendered most of their powers to the British, retaining only a limited internal administrative autonomy.

Rajputana was Rajasthan's old name, land of the Rajputs, brave and proud. The Maharana of Mewar (Udaipur) was the acknowledged head of their 36 clans.

When India became independent, 23 princely states were consolidated to form the State of Rajasthan, "abode of rajas".

This is an essential destination in India. Two days are sufficient to get a feel of Jaipur (which is only 140 miles/230 km from the Taj Mahal), but two weeks are needed to do justice to Rajasthan.

Capital: The "pink city" of **Jaipur** (the city of *jai* or victory), the capital of Rajasthan, was built in 1728 by Maharaja Sawai Jai Singh II. This royal house had ruled from Amber, 7 miles (11km) away, since the early 10th century. Jaipur was not always pink. The original city was light grey, edged with white borders and motifs. In honour of the visit in 1883 of Prince Albert, consort to Queen Victoria, it was ordered to be painted the traditional colour of welcome, which has been retained since.

The city was designed by Vidyadhar Chakravarty, a young Bengali architect, who succeeded in making a marvellous synthesis of many influences – Hindu, Jain, Mughal (with Persian overtones), besides his own ideas from eastern India. Jaipur's nine rectangular sectors symbolise the nine divisions of the universe.

The **City Palace,** a part of which remains the residence of the Jaipur family, is definitely worth a visit. Several gateways lead from the crowded streets into the palace, but the Museum entrance is recommended, through the courts of justice to the **Jantar Mantar,** the observatory of Maharaja Jai Singh II. The construction and precision of the observatory were a unique achievement for the year 1716. Jai Singh's Delhi observatory had preceded this and three others followed: in Mathura, Ujjain and Varanasi, when the Maharaja travelled over north India as the Governor of Agra.

The **City Palace Museum,** named after Raja Man Singh, is a treat, no matter what the interests of the visitor are – textiles, arms, carpets, paintings, manuscripts. It houses two large urns, possibly the largest silver vessels in India, which were used by Maharaja Madho Singh to carry a six-month supply of holy Ganga water to the coronation of King Edward VII in London.

One of the best known sights in Jaipur is the **Hawa Mahal** or Palace of Winds,

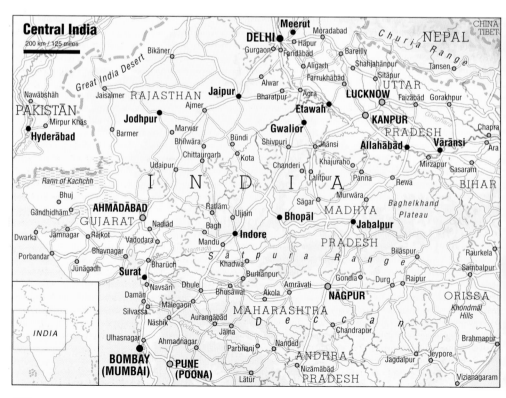

which is, in fact, no palace, but an extraordinary facade of 953 airy windows used by the ladies of the palace to watch the outside world without being watched.

Forts on rugged hills: Surrounding Jaipur stand wondrous forts. **Amber** was once the capital of the Mina tribes believed to be the original inhabitants of this area. Now, painted elephants take visitors up the hill to admire the massive gateways, courts, stairways and pillared pavilions and palaces, that recall the glory and wealth of Amber's association with the Mughals. Raja Man Singh was the Commander-in-Chief of Akbar's army and Mirza Raja Jai Singh was a powerful ally of Jahangir. Of special interest is the **Sheesh Mahal**, the palace of mirrors, where the walls are inlaid with exquisite mirrored motifs that dance to the flame of even a single candle.

Jaigarh Fort was recently opened to the public after being sealed for seven years, following a rumour that an enormous treasure in gold was buried in vaults under deep reservoirs. The vast purity of its austere spaces is admirable. The high-

light of the fort is the Jaya Vana – the largest antique cannon in India.

Nahargarh Fort provides a marvellous view of Jaipur city and, en route, of the **Jal Mahal**, the lake palace of Jaipur. The cenotaphs of the Jaipur maharajas at Amber and Gaitor as well as the *chhatris* (memorials) of the maharanis are well worth a visit.

Five miles (8 km) down the Jaipur-Agra road is the charming garden of the Sisodia queen, and a mile (2 km) further are the holy springs of **Galta**, with temples that have a large daily attendance. The **Hanuman Temple**, in particular, is worth a visit on Tuesdays.

Northwest to Alwar: Five major roads lead out of Jaipur. National Highway No. 8 leads north to Delhi. One can branch off right, about 35 miles (60 km) from Jaipur, turning northwest to **Alwar**, picturesque and dotted with historical sites. At **Bairath** or **Viratnagar** are ancient Buddhist rock edicts of Emperor Ashoka, a Buddhist *chaitya* (temple) dating back to the 3rd century BC, and a painted garden pavilion which was built around 1600 AD.

Founded in 1771, Alwar is one of the most recent of the princely states of Rajasthan. Beginning as distant cousins of Jaipur, they manoeuvred their way through the chaos of the 18th century, changing sides for quick gains, till the British finally acknowledged and rewarded them for their help against the Marathas. But the affairs of Alwar remained troubled, with only a few scattered years of peace, which, however, must have been very prolific, for Alwar has some very fine palaces, built by milking the people dry and using one half of the state exchequer – an extremely high proportion even by feudal standards – for the purpose.

Twenty-three miles (37 km) from Alwar is the **Sariska Palace**, once a hunting lodge, now a private hotel set on the outskirts of a wildlife sanctuary where tiger, panther, blue bull, wild boar and deer roam the scrubby thicket and bush. Closer by, 5 miles (8 km) from Alwar, the charming **Siliserh Palace** commands a wonderful view of a lake full of water fowl. This is a Rajasthan state hotel.

Hawa Mahal, Palace of the Winds, Jaipur.

The **Alwar Museum**, housed in the City Palace, has a fine collection of miniature paintings, manuscripts, arms and the famous solid-silver dining table that aroused the curiosity of royal visitors. Adjacent to the museum is a remarkable reservoir with delicate temples, kiosks and symmetrical stairs considered masterpieces of Indo-Islamic architecture.

Shekhavati and Churu: The second northern road (National Highway No. 11) leads to the painted towns of Shekhavati and Churu and to Bikaner.

En route, the first stop 20 miles (31 km) from Jaipur is **Samode**, a palace hotel set among steep hills. It doubled for Afghanistan in the shooting for *The Far Pavilions*. Its durbar hall is painted with frescos, among the most delicate in Rajasthan. One can stop at this charming spot or drive on through Sikar to Nawalgarh – the first stop in Shekhavati.

Shekhavati was once subordinate to Jaipur. In 1471, Rao Shekhav asserted his independence, giving Shekhavati his name. His successors maintained their independence for nearly 300 years. Shekhavati was fortunately located on the caravan route from the Gujarat ports and from Central India to Delhi. Trade in opium, cotton and spices flourished. The wealthy merchants built palatial *havelis* (mansions) for themselves, cenotaphs in memory of their ancestors, and reservoirs, temples and caravanserais for the people. Most of these buildings are covered with frescos painted between 1760 and 1920. The havelis were fortified houses which walled in the secluded life of the women who spent most of their days in the *zenana* (ladies' apartments) built around an inner courtyard. The men conducted their business on the white cotton mattresses of their sitting rooms.

Nawalgarh's streets are lined with the richly painted facades of *havelis* and the market bustles with activity. A garden palace on the outskirts provides a cool stopover. From Nawalgarh the road leads on to **Dundlod** and **Mandawa**, the rugged forts of which are now well-stocked hotels of a rare medieval charm.

Fatehpur too offers a wealth of painted *havelis*. A road to Bikaner starts from there, but one can detour to roam in the fascinating towns of **Ramgarh** and **Churu**, where the architecture and the art of the region are at their best, before linking up again with the Bikaner road.

Bikaner was founded in 1488, 29 years after Jodhpur. A younger but more intelligent son, Rao Bika, was given an army and asked to seek his own fortune to avoid a war of succession. Thus Bikaner was founded in heart of the wilderness called Jangaldesh. Perhaps the very bareness of the landscape spurred the human hand to create beauty. The red sandstone carvings at the **Lalbagh Palace** and those in marble are among the finest in delicacy and profusion; the fortress, built in the 15th century, contains palaces and temples of great refinement; Bikaner's art of miniature painting is rated high; the **Hall of Audience** has breathtaking frescos, gilded stucco mouldings, floral patterns, and incredibly delicate carpets.

Outside, the countryside is still rugged, dotted here and there with intricately carved Jain temples of the 16th century. The men of Bikaner are wiry and handsome and the Bikaner Camel Corps is still a showpiece of the Indian Army's display parade in Delhi on Republic Day.

On the outskirts of Bikaner, the camel farm makes an interesting visit, particularly at sunset when herds of camels return from the dunes.

The temple of **Karni Mata** at Deshnoke (17 miles/28 km from Bikaner) is inhabited by hordes of rats which are revered. They roam around the temple with total freedom. It is a unique sight for those who can overcome their queasiness.

Devi Kund (5 miles/8 km from Bikaner) is where the cenotaphs of the rulers of Bikaner were built and **Gajner** (20 miles/31 km) has beautiful palaces set around a lake.

Sixty miles (100 km) from Jaipur, on the road to Ajmer, is **Kishangarh**, an interesting city of palaces and lakes. The **City Palace**, the **Phool Mahal** and the **Kalyan Raiji Temple** are beautifully located by the side of a lake. From there one can walk the narrow streets of the old walled city. The largest collection of paintings of the renowned Kishangarh School is at the **Majhela Palace** and can be viewed there by prior appointment.

Kishangarh is a convenient starting point for visits to the marble cenotaph at **Karkeri**, the **Krishna Temple** of the Nimbarkachari sect at Salemabad, and the fort and palace of **Rupangarh**. A little further away, the salt lake of **Sambhar** is a unique sight along with the marble quarries at Makrana, source for the Taj Mahal. It continues to be exploited today. Nearby, Kuchaman has one of the most beautiful lived-in fortresses of Rajasthan.

Sacred site: About 80 miles (135 km) southwest of Jaipur lies **Ajmer**, the most sacred of all Muslim places of pilgrimage in India. Supposedly founded by Aijpal in 1100 AD, Ajmer later became a twin Chauhan capital with Delhi. In 1193, its Muslim history began, when Prithviraj Chauhan lost Ajmer to Sultan Mohammad of Ghori. The Persian saint, Khwaja Moinuddin Chisti, who had come with Ghori, settled and preached here.

When Akbar captured Ajmer in 1556 he made it his military headquarters and visited the tomb on foot to pray for a son. The boon was granted and the fame of Ajmer was enhanced. Large cauldrons were presented by Akbar that, till today, are filled with a rice and milk preparation weighing 6.7 tons (6,720kg) and distributed to the pilgrims and hangers-on at the shrine. Important monuments here are the large gateway built in the 13th century by Sultan Iltutmish of Delhi, the tomb of the water-carrier who saved Emperor Humayun's life, and the delicate white marble mosque of Shah Jahan.

Ajmer is well-known for a mosque that was hurriedly assembled from building material taken from a Hindu temple and possibly a Sanskrit university dismantled by Muhammad of Ghori. Not far from here is the pleasant sight of Ana Sagar, a lake constructed in the early 12th century. There are cool marble pavilions built by Shah Jahan and a circuit house constructed by the British.

Nine miles (14 km) from Ajmer is **Pushkar**, considered high up in the hierarchy of Hindu places of pilgrimage. It is the site of a temple to Brahma, the Creator, of which there are very few. Here

Palace, Jaipur.

every year, on the full moon of November, hundreds of thousands of pilgrims gather to bathe in the sacred lake. This is the occasion for one of the largest cattle and camel markets in Rajasthan where the abundance of colour, jewellery, turbans and moustaches is unmatched.

The road to Tonk: About 7 miles (12 km) south of Jaipur, the airport road leads to **Sanganer**, a name synonymous with fine block-printing on fabric. It is said that the water of Sanganer makes the colours fast. Traditionally, only coarse cotton was printed for the ankle-lengh, flared skirts of Rajasthani women. A 15th-century Jain temple and a Krishna temple are among spots worth visiting in Sanganer.

Continuing south, the same road winds past **Chaksu** where large numbers gather at the temple every year to pay reverence to Shitala Mata, the Goddess of Smallpox. Although this disease has now been eradicated from India, the goddess continues to have her following.

Some 50 miles (80 km) from Jaipur lies **Tonk,** once ruled by Muslim Nawabs, descendants of Pathan tribesmen from Afghanistan, who had come to India in search of *Zan, Zar, Zamin* – women, gold and land – possibly in that order. Tonk has charming painted mosques and a host of colonial buildings that housed the British resident and his entourage. Of particular interest is the **Sunehri Kothi** or golden mansion. A fairly small and simple structure from the outside, its interior is studded like a jewel box. An inlay of coloured glass, mirrors, gilded stucco and strappings, painted and polished lime floors, stained window panes, all add up to an extraordinary opulence.

From Tonk, the road continues south to Bundi and Kota. But wildlife fans can turn left and continue eastward to **Sawai Madhopur** where the royal Jaipur household used to come for big hunts accompanied by their VIP guests. Queen Elizabeth stayed here in 1962.

Overlooking the wildlife sanctuary of Sawai Madhopur (8 miles/13 km from the town) is the formidable fortress of Rao Hamir – **Ranthambore**, which was conquered by Alauddin Khalji in the 14th century and then again by Akbar in 1569.

City Palace and Lake Palace Hotel, Udaipur.

Even though in ruins, its palaces, temples and cenotaphs are well worth a visit. Spend the night at the Maharajah's former hunting lodge.

Jatt states: The Jaipur-Agra road leads to Bharatpur and on to Dholpur – both Jatt states in the predominantly Rajput stronghold of Rajasthan.

The **Bharatpur Palace** houses a museum with exhibits of mixed antiquity, but what makes Bharatpur famous is its 11 sq-mile (29 sq-km) **Keoladeo Ghana sanctuary**, with the largest concentration and variety of birdlife in Asia. Migratory cranes arrive every November. Prior to 1940, this was the favourite shooting ground of the British viceroys, with a record kill of 4,273 birds in a single day. Sunrise or sunset from October to February is the best time to see the birds.

Eighteen miles (30 km) from Bharatpur are the wondrous palaces of **Deeg**, set at the water's edge, with cool channels, fountains and water alleys below, where giant iron balls were made to roll and rumble like monsoon thunder. The rooms have an exquisite beauty.

Dholpur, a small Jatt state, is only 34 miles (55 km) from Bharatpur. Founded in 1805, it is famous for its stone of which the president's palace in New Delhi and the facades of many buildings are made. In the wilderness is the first **Garden of Babur**, the founder of the Mughal dynasty. Nearby, the artificial lake of **Mach Kund**, surrounded by dilapidated temples, is a place for meditation.

Bundi, Kota, Jhalawar: Founded in 1342, the ancient kingdom of **Bundi** lies well protected within the ranges of the rugged Aravalli Hills that drop into rocky ravines traversed by four narrow passes. The highlight of Bundi is its stunning palace-fort, the **Chattar Mahal**, which reflects the changing colours of the greenish serpentine of its walls in the **Naval Sagar** lake. These are ribbed with the tracks worn into them by rainwater that has poured over the crenellations through the centuries, giving the structure a stature and dignity that prompted the widely travelled Lt. Col. James Tod to grant it the first rank in Rajasthani architecture. Incredible ramps and stairs zig-zag between the ramparts as overhanging balconies frame perfect views.

Besides its architecture, the palace is famous for the **Chitra Shala**, a gallery of very refined frescos painted in the 17th and 18th centuries, unmatched in their harmony of blues, greens and terracotta colours.

The Bundi territory was first claimed by Udaipur and later by Jaipur. It shrank in size when a part of it was given in 1579 as patrimony for a favoured younger son. This tract, set in the open plains, grew to be **Kota**, larger than its parent state, bustling with the youth of a commercial city, while Bundi gracefully mellowed into old gold. Its secluded position saved it, so to say, from the hybridisation of the 19th century, even though the British virtually controlled its affairs from 1818 when Lt. Col. Tod concluded a treaty between "Boondee" and the East India Company. "Bundi is deliciously behind the times," writes the Maharaja of Baroda.

A rather curious feature of the main Bundi market street is the height at which the shops are built. The reason for their height is not obvious unless the visitor

Mosaic at City Palace, Udaipur.

stays over for one monsoon to see how the overflow of the town's reservoir, which is atop the hill in the **Taragarh Fort**, is emptied when the sluice gates open. Water gushes out like a cloudburst, flooding the streets. But everyone is forewarned and there has never been damage to life or property.

Kota has had to stay awake and alert all through its history because its strategic location on the plains along the Chambal River drew the envy of Udaipur, Jaipur, the Marathas and also the British – to whom it was the first to accede, due to the foresight of Zalim Singh the Regent. Spasmodic spells of peace led to spurts of architecture and a mélange of pillared halls, kiosks, commemorative gateways, carving and painting. Some of the finer frescos and miniature paintings of India belong to the Bundi-Kota school. The **City Palace at Kota** abounds in decorations and ornamentation and a small museum shows treasures hitherto in the private collection of the ruler. The most exquisite is in the hall of private audience, with its walls covered with paintings from the Mughal to British periods.

The stunning **Baroli Temple**, 25 miles (40 km) from Kota, has exquisite stone carvings from the 9th century.

For lovers of wildlife, Kota offers the **Dara Wildlife Sanctuary** where tiger, bear, wild boar and spotted deer roam the thick green jungles. The famous hunting paintings from Kota depict this area.

Apart from **Jhalawar's** museum, one should visit the nearby **Jhalra Patan**, the "city of bells" where stand the ruins of one of the finest sun temples in India.

Udaipur: The royal house of Mewar, now better known as **Udaipur**, has two reasons for pride. The first is that it can trace back its recorded history to Bapa Rawal (728 AD), whereas Jaipur and Jodhpur lag behind by 200 and 483 years respectively. The second is pride in being Hindu and not losing honour to the Muslims. Mewar alone resisted such alliances – at least 50 years more than the others. This sense of history and pride persisted during the British period, earning them the highest gun salute in Rajasthan: 19 guns as against the 17 each

Jodhpur Fort.

of Jaipur, Jodhpur, Bundi, Bikaner, Kota and Karauli. Majarana Fateh Singh of Udaipur had the singular distinction of not attending the Delhi Durbar for King George V in 1911.

Udaipur has a profusion of palaces, lakes, temples and cenotaphs. The **City Palace**, now museum, is a labyrinth of courtyards richly decorated with inlaid mirror-work, galleries covered with frescos, temples and kiosks from where one can see the **Pichola Lake.** An island on the lake houses the elegant **Jag Nivas**, built in 1746 as the summer residence of the rulers, and now the **Lake Palace Hotel. Jag Mandir,** another island, is worth a visit at sunset. This is where Prince Khurram, who was later to become Emperor Shah Jahan, took refuge in 1624 and lived for a while.

In the old town the **Jagdish Temple,** built in the mid-17th century, has a remarkable bronze statue of Garuda (a mythical bird) facing his revered Lord Vishnu. The shops and craftsmen's ateliers in the narrow streets of the bazaar justify endless walks. The visitor will marvel at the skill of the artists, their inborn sense of colours and forms and will be tempted to acquire paintings on paper, ivory or cloth.

The temple of Eklingji, the Shaiva patron deity of the Udaipur royal house is 15 miles (24 km) by road from Udaipur. On the way are the ruins of the ancient city of **Nagda** where exquisitely carved temples, both Hindu (10th-century) and Jain (15th-century), are a treat for the eyes. **Eklingji Temple** is carved from marble and even today the Maharana of Udaipur who is the *Diwan* of the temple, makes it a point to visit every Monday.

A remarkable place of worship, **Nathdwara** (30 miles/48 km from Udaipur) is the highly revered temple to Srinathji, a manifestation of Lord Krishna. Non-Hindus are not allowed inside, but images of the Lord painted on cloth are available. These are called *pechwai* and are hung behind the idol.

Another outing from Udaipur takes one 30 miles (50 km) southeast to the welcome sight of **Jaisamand**, the largest artificial lake in Asia. This was constructed by Rana Jai Singh at the end of the 17th century and measures 30 miles (50 km) in circumference. Not far away is a royal hunting ground turned wildlife sanctuary sheltering panther, wild boar and spotted deer.

From Nathdwara, en route to Kumbalgarh, a pleasant stop is at **Rajsamand**, the cool royal lake at Kankroli. From the dam, one gets a magnificent view of the town. The temple too is interesting.

Kumbalgarh and Ranakpur: In the erstwhile princely state of Mewar there were three almost impregnable forts: **Chittor** (70 miles/112 km from Udaipur), **Kumbalgarh** (40 miles/64 km from Udaipur), and **Mandalgarh** (near Kota). Kumbalgarh is not easily accessible, but the adventurous will be well-rewarded. This fort was built by Rana Kumbha in the 15th century. It is surrounded by 13 mountain peaks which keep watch over distant horizons. Seven gateways lead up to the palaces.

In a shaded valley, 100 miles (160 km) northwest from Udaipur, lie the superb Jain temples of **Ranakpur** which were built in the mid-15th century. The

Jodhpur Palace.

Rishabji Temple has 1,444 columns, each different from the others. The nearby **Sun Temple** is worth a visit, both for its carvings and its unusual plan.

Chittor became the first capital of Mewar in the early 13th century under the reign of Jaitra Singh (1213–53). There is told the story of the siege of Chittorgarh in 1303 by the Sultan of Delhi, Ala-ud-din Khilji. The sultan had heard of the beauty of Princess Padmini, the wife of Maharana Rawal Ratan Singh, and was determined to bring her back to his harem. Despite the courage of the brave Rajputs who defended Chittor, the citadel was captured by the sultan's force. Rather than face dishonour, the women chose to die by committing *johar,* mass self immolation, led by Rani Padmini. Chanting verses from the Gita, they threw themselves on the funeral pyre.

Chittor was later recaptured by the Rajputs. But, history repeats itself. Two centuries later, in 1535, Chittor was attacked by the Sultan of Gujarat, Bahadur Shah, and 13,000 Rajput women sacrificed themselves in the flames.

Abu is one of the most sacred places of Jain pilgrimage. According to the Jain tradition, Mahavir, the last of the 24 *Tirthankara* (saints) spent a year there.

Mount Abu, situated at an altitude of 4,000ft (1,220m), is a popular summer resort. Many princes built summer bungalows and small palaces around the Nakki Lake there.

The main attractions are the Dilwara Jain temples of which two, the **Adinath** and **Neminath**, display a profusion of carving in white marble. Adinath was built in 1031 and is dedicated to the first Tirthankar. Neminath was erected in 1230 to celebrate the 22nd Tirthankar. The carving is elaborate and exquisite, creating a lacy effect. The 24 elite Chauhan clans, of which the Hara Chauhans of Bundi and Kota are considered supreme, claim descent from the holy fire that springs from the peak of Mount Abu.

Jodhpur: The Rathors of Kanauj (U.P.) moved in 1211 AD to Marusthal, the hot and blazing desert land of death in the heart of Rajasthan. Their land came to be called Marwar. Two and a half centuries

Jaisalmer Fort with the city in foreground.

passed and, in 1459, Rao Jodha founded **Jodhpur** after the old capital of Mandore had proved too vulnerable. Some five centuries later, Maharaja Umaid Singh had completed for himself one of the largest private homes in the world (with 347 rooms) to create employment as a measure of famine relief. This is now a hotel. Awaiting the visitor are the remains, the symbols of seven centuries of history, begun in hardship, continued in bloodshed and bravery, and culminating in magnificence and decadence.

The **Fort of Jodhpur** sits on a mighty rock 400ft (120metres) tall. A fairly steep climb leads up, winding through seven gateways. The palaces within are carved from a hard sandstone which the sculptors' chisels have carved as if it were soap. An extensive museum displays howdahs, paintings, thrones, banners, doors, weapons and a spectacular 17th century tent. The city of Jodhpur is interesting to walk through, particularly the bazaar.

The old capital of **Mandore,** 5 miles (8 km) from Jodhpur, now has landscaped gardens surrounding temples and the cenotaphs of the Marwar rulers. The **Hall of Heroes**, with larger-than-life figures painted in gaudy colours, as well as the temple of the black Bhairav and the white Bhairav (manifestations of Lord Shiva), where the idols are pasted over the layers of silver paper, are worth visiting.

The **Osian temples** (40 miles/65 km from Jodhpur), both Hindu and Jain, are unique. They date from the 8th to the 12th centuries. Jeep safaris to craft villages are popular.

Jaisalmer: The ancient capitals of Rajasthan, Chittor (Udaipur), Amber (Jaipur), Mandore (Jodhpur) and Lodurva (Jaisalmer) have all become monuments. Of the new habitations, **Jaisalmer,** the land of the Bhatti princes, born of the moon, is by far the oldest and dates back to 1156 AD. The skyline holds kiosks with parapets, balconies and terraces. It is hard to believe that the human hand is capable of executing the intricate stone carvings on these structures. The beauty of the Jain temples (12th–15th centuries) leaves visitors breathless.

Down in the city are the renowned *havelis* of Salim Singh, Nathmalji and the Patwas in the same yellow-gold Jaisalmer stone. These were ready to be dismantled and shipped abroad when they were declared National Treasures. There are remains of a petrified forest at **Aakal,** 10 miles (17 km) from Jaisalmer. All else is sand. Golden turrets, 99 of them, once rose out of the golden Trikuta, the triple-peaked hill which once stood there.

A 10-mile (16-km) drive to the ancient Bhatti capital of **Lodurva** can be fascinating in good weather. The enormous sand dunes make a surrealistic landscape patterned by the wind.

Nagaur: Some 55 miles (90km) from Jodhpur lies **Khimsar.** (En route, the **Balsamand Lake** and bird sanctuary makes a brief stop.) The 15th-century **Khimsar Fort** with carved stone grills is now a charming hotel. If you plan to visit in February or August, get the exact dates for the cattle fairs of Nagaur from the tourist office. In February, Nagaur celebrates the Ramdeoji Fair and in August the Tejaji Cattle Fair, named after local heroes and considered to be among the largest livestock fairs in the world.

Young Rajput.

MADHYA PRADESH, INDIAN HEARTLAND

Madhya Pradesh, literally translated, means "Middle Land". No surprise then that the people of this vast state feel that the whole of India revolves around them.

It is India's largest state, having a land area of approximately 174,000 sq. miles (450,000 sq. km). The next largest state, Rajasthan, is at least 38,600 sq. miles (100,000 sq. km) smaller. If India were to have different time zones, Ramanujganj on the eastern border of the state would be 40 minutes ahead of Jhabua on the western border.

Geographically, Madhya Pradesh is one of the most interesting parts of India. The northern part of the state, with Gwalior as its largest city, lies in the Indo-Gangetic plain. Much of the rest, however, is upland plateaus and hills, interspersed with the deep valleys of rivers which flow east into the Bay of Bengal and west into the Arabian Sea.

The hills are forest-clad. In fact, almost a third of India's forests are located in Madhya Pradesh. They consist of some of the finest deciduous hardwoods in the world – teak, sal, hardwickia, Indian ebony and rosewood. Bamboo is prolific in the hills and there are magnificent fruit and flowering trees. The Mahadeo Hills of the Satpura Range are the home of the tiger, panther, Indian bison and the myriad herbivores which make the jungle their home. Rudyard Kipling's *Jungle Book* was sited in the Mahadeo Hills where the forests, wild life and tribals are today almost exactly as they were in his time.

Travel and food: Madhya Pradesh, though at India's heart by air, is quite easy to reach. One can fly to the state from Delhi, Bombay and Calcutta. Gwalior, Bhopal, Indore, Jabalpur, Raipur and Khajuraho are on the air map. There are excellent train services throughout. Road journeys are interesting because the routes pass through forests and cultivated areas in succession, skirt quaint villages, up hill and down dale.

Most places have adequate, if simple, hotel facilities. But the real joy of travel is in coming to a remote rest house, or "dak bungalow", maintained by the government for its officers on tour or for the weary traveller overtaken by night and in need of shelter.

Dak bungalows generally have two to four bedrooms and baths, austere in furniture, but spotlessly clean and comfortable. Each of them has a *khansama*, or cook-caretaker, who can produce a tasty, hot meal at short notice, cooked as often as not over a fragrant wood-fire. The taste of that first cup of scalding tea drunk at the end of a long drive, sprawled in an easy chair on the verandah of a dak bungalow, will probably be remembered long after the vintage champagne drunk in a smoky drawing room full of chattering socialites is forgotten. The bill at the end of the stay will shock by its very modesty. The style will not be the highest, but the ambience will be unbeatable.

The Madhyadeshis are only too friendly and the danger is the possibility of the visitor being used as a dummy on whom to practise English conversation. Paradoxically, the passing of the Raj has made more people become English-speaking than ever before. Invitations to visit private homes are forthcoming and in the villages the hospitality is overwhelming. Food, milk and tea are pressed on the traveller and a host is hurt by the display of a poor appetite.

The cuisine varies from the wheat-and-meat-based food of northern and western Madhya Pradesh to the rice and fish domination in the south and the east. Gwalior and Indore abound in milk and milk-based preparations. Bhopal produces exquisite meat and fish dishes, of which spicy *rogan josh, korma, keema, biryani* and *kababs* such as *shami* and *seekh*, are the most famous. They are eaten with thin slices of unleavened bread called *roomali roti* ("handkerchief bread") and leavened, flat loaves called *sheermal*. Also interesting are the bafla (wheat cakes), dunked in rich ghee and eaten with dal, a pungent lentil broth, whose tongue-tingling sharpness is moderated by the accompanying *laddoos* (sweet dumplings).

Meals end with fruit – luscious mangoes, juicy melons and watermelons, custard apples, bananas, papayas, guavas and

rotic
culptures at
hajuraho.

oranges. To drink, there is *lassi* (buttermilk), fruit juice, juice from sugarcane, an excellent beer and fine rum from cane. For those with strong heads and a preference for local brews, there is the liquor distilled from the flowers of the mahua tree (Madhuca indica); *sulfi* or the fermented toddy of the sago palm and also date palm toddy – heady drinks for adventurous palates.

The best time to travel in Madhya Pradesh is from the mild autumn of October to the spring of the end of March. April to mid-July are taboo because of the heat. The monsoon months of July, August and September are interesting because the earth bursts into an exuberance of green and the air is fresh and cool. But no matter which season, Madhya Pradesh is fascinating.

Entry point: The northernmost city, **Gwalior** was established in the 8th century AD and named after Saint Gwalipa. The city is dominated by its hill-top fort, one of the most redoubtable in the world. Rajput valour and chivalry are redolent in the very stones of the 15th-century palace of Raja Mansingh located in the citadel.

The fort also houses the **Teli-ka-Mandir,** and ancient temple. **Gujri Mahal** at the foot of the fort has one of the finest museums of sculpture in the country. Gwalior also has the distinction of being a centre of Indian classical music. Miya Tansen, one of the nine jewels of the court of Emperor Akbar the Great, belonged to Gwalior and is buried there. One of the greatest music festivals of India is held here each December to commemorate this great singer.

Gwalior is a good take-off point for two of the loveliest places in Madhya Pradesh, Orchha and Shivpuri. **Orchha,** 75 miles (120 km) from Gwalior, is a medieval city frozen in time and space, existing even today as it must have in the 16th and 17th centuries, when it was built. It was founded in the 16th century by the Bundela king. Rudra Pratap, on the banks of the sparkling **Betwa River**.

The countryside undulates gently between riverine plains and rolling forest-clad hills. The builders of Orchha dotted the landscaped with palace and fortress, temple and cenotaph. The architecture is a **Worshipping Gwalior's ruling family.**

synthesis of traditional Hindu, hybrid Indo-Saracenic and ornate Mughal. One of the finest sights is the view of the cenotaphs from across the river: green hills in the background and the architecturally perfect *chhatries* or cenotaphs sharply etched against an azure sky, with the blue Betwa in between. The 20th century has bypassed Orchha. Palace rooms can be hired overnight.

About 60 miles (100 km) from Gwalior is **Shivpuri,** the former summer capital of the Scindias of Gwalior. One climbs into the Vindhyan plateau at Shivpuri and the contrast with the Gangetic Plain is immediate and marked. Located at Shivpuri are the two lakes of **Sakhia Sagar** and **Madhav Sagar**. Surrounding them is the **Madhav National Park**. It is the home of a wide variety of deer, *chinkara* or Indian gazelle, sambhar, blue bull, black buck, barking deer and four-horned antelope. Also seen in the park are wild dog and sloth bear. Bird life abounds. Peacocks are to be seen in hundreds. In the nearby **Karera Bird Sanctuary** is to be found the Great Indian Bustard, an endangered species that has been rescued by sensitive conservation. The lakes have *muggar,* the Indian crocodile.

Indore and Ujjain: The western metropolis of Madhya Pradesh is Indore. Here, one is well and truly on to the Malwa Plateau, a region of rich black cotton soil of great fertility. Indore is a great industrial centre and has the look of a boom town. On its periphery is the city of **Dewas**, made famous by E.M. Forster in *The Hill of Devi*. It is now becoming one of the fastest growing industrial cities in India.

The land of Malwa is sacred and two of the 12 *jyotir lingas* or Shiva icons, are to be found at **Mahakaleshwar Temple** at Ujjain and **Mandhata** at Omkareshwar. For Hindus, these two places enjoy a sanctity equal to that of Varanasi. Every 12 years Ujjain has the great fair of *Kumbh,* or *Simhastha* as it is locally called. An interesting legend attends this fair, one of four in the country, the other three being held at Allahabad and Haridwar on the Ganga, and Nasik on the Godavari River.

The sacred river at Ujjain is the **Sipra**. The gods and the *asuras* (demons) churned the ocean for the *kumbh* or pot of *amrit,* or nectar. First emerged a pot of *vish,* or poison. Shiva drank it down in a gulp. So strong was it that his divine neck turned blue, giving him one of the names he is known by – "Nilkanth", or the Blue-necked One. Every 12 years, 2½ million Hindus congregate to celebrate the saving of the earth by Shiva.

Ujjain, approximately 35 miles (60 km) from Indore, is not only one of the most sacred cities of the Hindus, but is also a centre of both ancient craft and modern industry. Special mention must be made of the art of the *chhipas,* or dyers and printers of **Bherugarh**, a suburb of Ujjain. Using vegetable dyes and hand-carved teak blocks, with designs and patterns which go back centuries, the *chhipas* produce the most exquisite and colourful block-printed cloth for saris, tapestries and hangings, as well as bedsheets and floor coverings.

Fortress town: A tour of Malwa is incomplete without a visit to **Mandu,** the city of joy. A short 55-mile (90 km) drive from Indore, one approaches the capital of

Gwalior Fort.

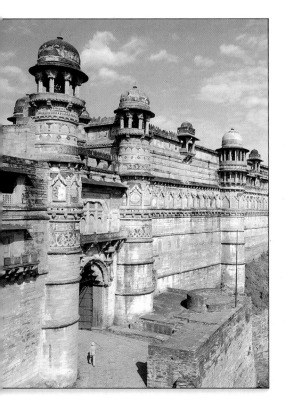

the Sultanate of Malwa either from the plains of Dhar or from the mountain pass at Manpur. Nothing can prepare the visitor for the first sight of Mandu. There is a chasm, a deep wooded ravine which is crossed by a narrow bridge, and piercing the skyline is the largest standing fortified city in the world – Mandu, whose walls have a circumference of more than 45 miles (75 km). These walls stand today almost as they did 300 years ago.

One enters through the **Bhangi Gate**, a portal so designed that it would be a foolhardy enemy who dared a frontal assault. Once inside the gates, vistas of a fairyland open to visitors. There are lakes and groves and gardens and palaces galore. The **Jahaz Mahal**, or ship palace, floats serenely on the bosom of its lake, looking like some heavenly ship sailing into eternity. The **Hindola Mahal**, or swing palace, built of massive stone, appears to sway gently in the breeze.

There is the **Jama Masjid**, with such perfect acoustics that a whisper from the pulpit is heard clearly in the farthest corner of the huge courtyard. There is the **Nikanth Temple**, a standing monument to the secularity and love of all religions of the Emperor Akbar.

Through the green vale of Mandu one comes to **Rewa Kund**, a gem of a lake, said to be filled by the waters of the Narmada River 55 miles (90 km) away and 2,000 ft (600 metres) lower down. Rewa Kund and, in fact, the whole of Mandu, are living monuments to the legend of Sultan Baz Bahadur and his Hindu Queen, Roopmati. Legend has it that she was a commoner whom Baz Bahadur met on the banks of the Narmada River when out hunting. He married her on a promise that he would bring the Narmada to Mandu, and Rewa Kund is the fulfilment of that promise. On its banks he built a palace for himself and, further up, at the very edge of the escarpment, a pavilion for Roopmati, from the terrace of which she could see the Narmada as a silver thread on the horizon. A sheer drop of 2,000ft (610 metres) from the pavilion terrace ends in the plains of Nimar, through which the Narmada flows.

State capital: From paradise back to earth, and one turns to the state capital, *Stupa* with gate, **Sanchi.**

Bhopal was tragically put on the world map by the gas leak from the Union Carbide pesticide plant in 1984, which killed at least 3,500 and affected hundreds of thousands of others. But Bhopal is actually far more than this. The city is in Malwa and enjoys a moderate climate. It is built, like Rome, on seven hills and round three lovely lakes.

Perhaps it is this which inspired architect Charles Correa to design **Bharat Bhavan**, a multi-arts centre without parallel in India. Bhopal has the distinction of being one of the greatest centres of art and culture in the country. A visitor could well spend all his time in the art galleries, museums, theatres and library.

Bhopal's industries give the city an air of briskness. State government is its major occupation. It is a modern city, but it is also a very old one. A scant 18 miles (30 km) away is **Bhim-bethka**, where over 500 caves with neolithic rock painting have been discovered. Five periods have been identified, from the prehistoric upper paleolithic down to the early historical and medieval. The oldest cave paintings are at least as old as those of the Pyrenees. When the earth itself was young, Bhopal was already civilised. Nearby, at **Sanchi**, a great stupa covers relics of Gautama Buddha. Noted for exquisite carvings in honey-coloured stone, Sanchi is a place of Buddhist pilgrimage.

Near Sanchi are **Vidisha**, **Udaygir** and **Gyaraspur**, the cradle of Mauryan civilisation and the rocks on which the tide of ancient Grecian conquest broke. The exquisite sculptured *salbhanjika,* or divine attendant of the gods, is preserved here.

Bhopal, as we see it today, was founded in the 10th century AD by Raja Bhoj. The **Bhojpur Temple**, even in its ruined state, bespeaks the greatness of this king, as also do the remains of the magnificent lake, the **Tal** which once covered 230 sq. miles (600 sq. km) and whose destruction in the 15th century by Sultan Hosang Shah of Malwa altered the climate of the region.

South of Bhopal is Kipling country, with the **Narmada** as the cord which binds the Satpura and Vindhyan Hills together. This is one of the great rivers of India, its water green and foaming as it tumbles from its source at Amarkantak through the gorges and cataracts that it has carved out of the Satpura Hills. It has as yet not been fully polluted by man. Its banks are well-defined and rise to high hills, and the hills themselves are densely wooded. This is tiger country.

Ranging from the low hills of Hoshagabad and rising into the Mahadeo Hills at Pachmarhi, Betul and Chhindwara, the forests explode into exuberance at **Kanha**, one of the finest wildlife sanctuaries in the world. In 1983, Prince Philip, the Duke of Edinburgh, visited Kanha. To reach this 2,700-sq.-mile (7,000 sq. km) park consisting of 400 sq. miles (1,000 sq. km) of core area and 2,300 sq. miles (6,000 sq. km) of forest surround, he drove through 100 miles (160 km) of unbroken forest.

The **Kanha National Park** and its sister sanctuary, **Bandavgarh**, are absolute musts for visitors to the state. These parks have grassy *maidans* or meadows, which are home for deer. The jungles teem with leopard, bear and wildcat, and there are some tigers. In some cases, the numbers are prodigious, with spotted deer alone numbering more than 17,000. Tiger is

Detail
depicting
the Buddha
as a
flaming
pillar.

king, but not set to rule over gaur, the Indian bison. Where the gaur browses, the tiger makes a wide detour. Kanha is home to that unique species of 12-horned swamp deer, the *barasingha (Duvaceli branderi)*, the only swamp deer which has adapted to dwelling on hard ground. It faced extinction till the great naturalist and administrator, M.K.S. Ranjitsinhji, rescued it.

Two places in Madhya Pradesh deserve special mention: Pachmarhi and Bedaghat. **Pachmarhi** is up in the Satpura Hills. It is a paradise for trekkers, rock climbers and nature lovers. **Bedaghat** is near Jabalpur. Here the Narmada river flows through a 2-mile-long (5-km) gorge, between towering white marble cliffs.

Below the gorge are the **Dhuandhar Falls,** literally "Smoky Falls". A row past **Marble Rocks** on a full-moon night is not to be missed. The silence of the night is broken only by the soft plop and squeak of the boatman's oars. The wake trails phosphoresence through the jade waters of the river behind.

Tribal territory: From the almost feminine grace of Marble Rocks to the sheer power and grandeur of the **Chitrakoot Falls** on the Indravati River in Bastar is a long journey of over 400 miles (600 km). But then, remote **Bastar** is a world in itself. It is one of the largest districts in India, covering a land area of over 15,400 sq. miles (40,000 sq. km). Many countries are smaller than Bastar and Switzerland is no larger.

Difficult though it is to reach, Bastar richly repays the visitor for his effort. Here the hills march in ranks and the forests are primeval. In the **Kanger Valley** is India's largest national biosphere reserve, in which nature has been left totally undisturbed by man. **Teerathgarh Falls** decorate the hills with a 820-ft (250-metre) lace of froth, before disappearing into **Kotamsar,** whose limestone rocks produce stalactite and stalagmite caves.

The sheer inaccessibility of Bastar lends enchantment. This is the home of the bisonhorn Madias, who dance and drum at folk festivals in India and abroad. It is also the home of the hill mynah, which imitates the voice of people.

Southern and eastern Madhya Pradesh

Kandariya Mahadev Temple, Khajuraho.

are jungle-clad and remote, but below the surface lie some of the richest mineral deposits in the world. Here is iron ore of unsurpassed purity; copper and tin so pure that it can be smelted in an ordinary earthenware pot: limestone, dolomite, bauxite and coal in almost unlimited quantities. The sleeping giant is already stirring. Mining, huge power plants, steel mills, aluminium factories and copper smelters are here.

A tour of Madhya Pradesh could appropriately end at **Khajuraho.** The period 950 to 1050 AD, a mere hundred years, saw a flowering of architecture in this small village which has no parallel. Here the Chandelas built 85 temples to the glory of God. Today 22 survive. These temples are designed to lead one's eyes from ground level ever upwards to the ultimate heaven, Kailash. They are ornately carved, with each frieze and sculpture depicting the genius of the men who carved it and the king who inspired them to their work.

Khajuraho has achieved fame for the sensual appeal of the erotic sculptures, but these form only a small part of the wealth of the site. Taken in totality, the sculptures of Khajuraho depict the everyday life of the people and the court in the 10th and 11th centuries. This procession of life itself culminates in the inner *sanctum sanctorum*, where one sheds the earthly coil before the deity.

Khajuraho is not something that can be described in words; it has to be experienced. The annual dance festival in March, when India's leading dancers perform on the podium of the **Khandariya Mahadev Temple**, is a good time to visit.

Rich variety: Madhya Pradesh embraces at least four agro-climatic zones and mixes people and ways of life.

The state is home to about 40 percent of India's tribal population. There are three distinct tribal groups. The most numerous are the Gonds, who once ruled much of the state and after whom **Gondwana**, the central portion came to be known. They inhabited the Satpura and Kymore Ranges and their major branches, the Madias and the Muria Gonds live in Bastar.

Western Madhya Pradesh is inhabited by the Bhils, a colourful group of warriors and huntsmen who held even the Mughal army at bay. Eastern Madhya Pradesh is dominated by the Oraons, now almost wholly Christian.

The tribals of Madhya Pradesh have retained their ethnicity and customs, even in the face of modernisation, largely because successive governments have dealt with them with sensitivity. The tribals are often great artists. Wood, bamboo and other forest produce are the media in which they work. In Bastar there is the unmatched art of bell-metal casting, as also the most intricate forms of clay sculpture.

Bharat Bhavan at the capital Bhopal has a museum of tribal art which gives a representative picture of the crafts of these woodsmen.

But craft comes easily to all the people in Madhya Pradesh, ranging from the exquisite weaving of Chanderi and Maheshwar, to the carpet making of Vidisha, Mandsaur and Sarguja. Carpentry, pottery, textile, printing and dyeing, metal working, woodcarving and fine leather work are some of the skilled crafts of Madhya Pradesh.

Marble Rocks on River Narmada.

BIHAR, LAND OF THE BUDDHA

The State of Bihar lies in the eastern Gangetic plain. It was the seat of several of the most famous ancient Indian dynasties and the cradle of Jainism and Buddhism. The name, Bihar, is itself derived from *vihara* (Buddhist monastery).

Patna, the capital of Bihar, is a city of over a million lying along the Ganges in a long strip. Under the name of Pataliputra it was the capital of the Magadha empire.

The Maidan, a large square, divides Patna in two. To the west lies **Bankipur**, a cantonment and administrative area, with colonial buildings: **Raj Bhawan**, the governor's residence; the **Maharaja's Palace,** now the Bihar State Transport Corporation; the **Patna Women's College**, an early 20th-century neo-Mughal complex; and residential bungalows for senior government officers which were built in the 1920s.

The **Patna Museum** near the **High Court** houses a collection of Hindu and Buddhist stone sculptures, bronzes and terracotta sculptures. Among the exhibits is a 49 ft (15 metres) long fossil tree said to be 2,000 million years old and the longest tree fossil in the world. At the entrance of the hall, on the left, is the **Didarganji Yakshi**, a buff-coloured Mauryan sandstone statue of a woman, remarkable for her brilliant polish, her firm rounded breasts, her navel, her aggressive belly and hips, considered to be one of the greatest masterpieces of Indian art of all times.

Between the Maidan and the Ganga stands the **Golghar**, a beehive-shaped structure, built in 1786 as a granary. It is 88ft (27 metres) high and 410 ft (125 metres) wide at its base, with walls almost 13ft (4 metres) thick, and can hold 150,000 tonnes of wheat. Two stairways lead to the top, offering a view of Patna and the other bank of the river.

Old Patna spreads to the east of the Maidan, a narrow strip between the Ganga and the railway line that runs parallel to it. In this district of bazaars, a few buildings stand out: the **Khuda Baksh Oriental**

Preceding pages: the Himalayas from Darjeeling.

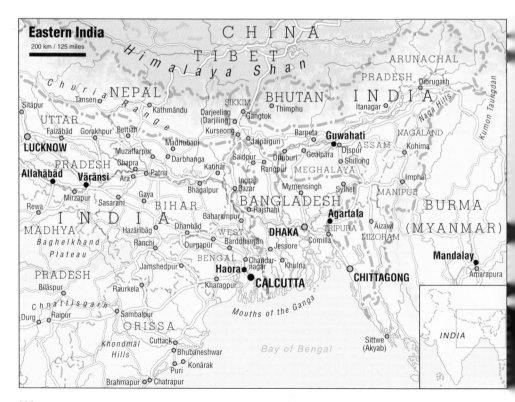

Eastern India
200 km / 125 miles

CHINA
TIBET
Himalaya Shan
NEPAL
BHUTAN
ARUNACHAL PRADESH
INDIA
SIKKIM
Churia Range
Sitapur
Tansen
Kathmandu
Darjeeling (Darjiling)
Gangtok
Thimphu
Itanagar
Dibrugarh
Naga Hills
Kumon Taungdan
UTTAR
Faizabad
Gorakhpur
Bettiah
Kurseong
Jalpaiguri
Barpeta
Guwahati
NAGALAND
LUCKNOW
PRADESH
Muzaffarpur
Chapra
Madhubani
Darbhanga
Katihar
Saidpur
Dhuburi
Rangpur
Goalpara
ASSAM
Shillong
MEGHALAYA
Kohima
Allahabad
Varansi
Ara
Patna
Ganga
Ingraj Bazar
Mymensingh
Sylhet
Imphal
MANIPUR
Mirzapur
Gaya
Bhagalpur
BANGLADESH
Rewa
Sasaram
BIHAR
Baharampur
Rajshahi
Agartala
BURMA
MADHYA
Hazaribag
Dhanbad
WEST
DHAKA
TRIPURA
Aizawl
(MYANMAR)
Baghelkhand Plateau
Ranchi
Durgapur
Barddhaman
Jessore
Comilla
MIZORAM
Bilaspur
Jamshedpur
Chandar-nagar
Khulna
Mandalay
PRADESH
Raurkela
Kharagpur
Haora
CALCUTTA
CHITTAGONG
Amarapura
Chhattisgarh
Durg
Raipur
Sambalpur
Mouths of the Ganga
ORISSA
Khondmal Hills
Cuttack
Bhubaneshwar
Sittwe (Akyab)
INDIA
Puri
Konarak
Brahmapur
Chatrapur
Bay of Bengal

Library, with its rare Islamic manuscripts, including some from the Moorish University of Cordoba in Spain; **Padri-ki-Haveli**, or Saint Mary's Church built in 1775; **Sher Shah Masjid**, and **Patther-ki-Masjid**, mosques erected respectively around 1540 by Sher Sharh, and in 1621 by Parwez Shah, son of Jahangir, and Governor of India.

Haramandirji, a *gurdwara* in old Patna, is one of the holiest places for the Sikhs. Guru Govind Singh, the tenth and last Sikh Guru, was born and died here. The gurdwara, built in the 19th century around the room where the Guru was born, stands at the centre of Patna's Sikh district. It is a tall building in white marble, housing a museum of the Sikh religion. On top is a terrace with white marble kiosks from where one can watch the sun going down over the city while loudspeakers broadcast the recitation from the Holy Granth.

Near the gurdwara, and visited only by appointment with the owner is **Quila House**, a private residence built on the ruins of Sher Shah's fortress, housing a private collection of jade, Chinese paintings, silver filigree work of the Mughal period, and a bed that once belonged to Napoleon.

At **Gulzaribagh**, further east near the Mahabir Ghat, is a former East India Company Factory, now a Government Printing Press. Visitors can visit the opium go-downs, the former ballroom and the hall where Shah Alam II was crowned Emperor of Delhi (under the protection and patronage of the East India Company) on 12 March 1761. In the same area, to the south, at **Kumhrar**, a park has been created around the remains of **Pataliputra**: the foundations of a *vihara* and of Ashoka's palace, wooden beams from structures in the former city, ramparts, and the pond where Emperor Ashoka is said to have thrown the bodies of his 99 brothers whom he had killed to avoid competition from within his family. Needless to say, this was before his conversion to Buddhism. Nearby, at the beginning of the Patna Bypass Road is a well and a shrine to Sitlamata, the goddess of smallpox, a frightening figure dressed in scarlet.

The **Mahatma Gandhi Bridge** crosses the Ganga to the east of the city. On the north bank, near the confluence of the Ganga and the Gandak, at **Sonepur**, a month long animal fair is held every November. Further north, **Vaishali**, 25 miles (40 km) away, is the former capital of the Vajian Confederacy (6th century BC), probably the first republic in Asia. Mahavira was born in Vaishali. The Second Buddhist Council was held here in 383 BC. All that now remains is an Ashoka pillar and ruins of Buddhist *stupas*.

Nepal is not far away. The road beyond Vaishali reaches the India-Nepal border at Raxaul. Near the border, more to the east, and accessible from Patna through Barauni after a seven-hour drive is **Madhubani**, a village famous for its style of folk painting.

Mughal Monuments: Some of the finest monuments in Bihar can be seen west of Patna. At **Maner**, 18 miles (30 km) away, are two mausoleums: **Choti Dargah**, in a small Muslim cemetery, is the grave of Maneri, a Muslim ascetic of the 17th century. **Bari Dargah**, on the high bank of an artificial pond, was built around 1620 by Ibrahim Khan, Governor of Bihar under

The statue of the Buddha, Bodhgaya.

Jahangir, as a mausoleum for Shah Daula, his religious preceptor. At **Sasaram** (96 miles/155 km to the southwest), are some large monuments of the period when there was an interlude of Suri (Afghan) rule in north India: Emperor **Sher Shah's Mausoleum**, built in the 16th century in the middle of a square; a wide tank, and the mausoleums of Hassan Sur Khan, Sher Shah Suri's father, Alawal Khan, the officer in charge of building the mausoleum and the uncompleted one of Salim Shah, Sher Shah's son.

Buxar, 68 miles (110 km) west is the place where Lord Rama is said to have fought the demon Taraka and received, with Lakshman, higher knowledge from the sage Vishvamitra. Lord Ram is said to have left a footprint here at Ram Rekha Ghat. Nearby is the battlefield where, in 1764, the British defeated Mir Kasim, the last independent nawab of Murshidabad and added Bengal and Bihar to their Indian possessions.

The cradle of Buddhism: Fifty-six miles (90km) south of Patna is **Nalanda**, "the place that confers the lotus" (*nalam*) or spiritual knowledge. This is the site of **Sri Mahavihara Arya Bhikshu Sanghasya**, a monastic university that flourished from the 5th century until 1199, when it was ransacked by the Afghan invader, Bakhtiar Khilji. The university, at the height of its activities, had a vast library, 2,000 teachers and more than 10,000 students from as far as Japan, Sumatra, Java and Korea. Legend has it that it contained 9 million volumes and that it burned for six months after the sack of Nalanda. Lord Mahavira, the last Jain Tirthankara, and Lord Buddha taught here. Nalanda developed as a centre of Buddhist learning.

Excavations have yielded nine levels of occupation, six temples (*chaityas*) and 11 monasteries (*viharas*), all built in red brick. The monasteries are on the eastern side. The main ones are Vihara 1 founded in the 9th century by King Balaputradeva of Sumatra, and Viharas 4 and 5, built by King Kumar Gupta in the 1st century AD, with later additions by kings Harshavardan and Devpala. The *viharas* show remains of student cells, lecture halls, bathrooms, kitchens, libraries, storage rooms and wells. To the west are the temples. The

most imposing is the Sariputra Stupa, built by Ashoka in honour of Ananda, the Buddha's first disciple, who was born and died at Nalanda. It is a three-level structure, partly covered with stucco figures of Lord Buddha teaching at Bodhgaya, Nalanda, Rajgir, Sarnath and Vaishali, and surrounded by stupas erected to the memory of students who died during their studies, that could then last a whole lifetime. Steps lead to a platform on top of the stupa, now empty, where a hall once stood housing a statue of Lord Buddha. Nearby are Chaityas 12, 13 and 14, largely ruined, with remains of sculptures.

A new site, Sarai Mound, has been excavated to the northeast. At this site half-faded frescos of horses and elephants have been discovered. East of the ruins, is a museum with Buddhist and Hindu stone and terracotta statues and figurines.

North of Nalanda, a monument in the shape of a Chinese temple has been built to commemorate the memory of Hsuan Tsang, the Chinese traveller who studied at Nalanda in the 7th century.

Leaving Nalanda for Rajgir, the road passes a small Chinese temple, the **Nava Nalanda Mahavira Research Centre on Buddhism and Pali Literature**, set up by the Bihar Government, and **Wat Thai Nalanda**, a small Thai temple of recent construction.

Rajgir, or Rajgriha, the "royal palace," 7 miles (12 km) south, was the capital of the Magadha empire in the 6th century BC. It is a holy place both for Jains and Buddhists. Lord Mahavira taught here for 14 rainy seasons; Muni Suvrata, the 20th Jain Tirthankara, was born here and all of Lord Mahavira's earliest disciples died here. The Buddha too spent five rainy seasons at Rajgir. He had so impressed King Bimbisara at his first visit to Rajgir that, when he returned from Bodhgaya, having attained enlightenment, accompanied by a thousand disciples, the king built a monastery set in a bamboo park for this new order (*sangha*) of monks. The First Buddhist Council, six months after the Buddha's death, was held at Rajgir.

Contemporary Rajgir, a small place, is located north of the ancient site that spreads over seven barren hills surrounding a valley. A 31-mile (50-km) wall with watch-towers built of huge stone blocks used to run round the city. Its remains stand on the hills and at the north and south gates.

Passing by the remains of the **Agatasatru Fort**, built in the 5th century BC, the road reaches a small square lined with shops. On the right is **Venuvana**, the bamboo park where the Buddha and his disciples lived. A small mound, now covered with Muslim graves, marks the site of the *stupa* and *vihara* built by Ajatasatru. In the park are a mini **zoo**; a small **Thai temple**; and **Karanda Tank**, where the Buddha used to bathe.

The **Nipponzan Myohoji** is a large Japanese temple and the Centaur Hokke Club caters to the needs of Japanese pilgrims, offering traditional Japanese meals and accommodation. Burmese Buddhists have also built a temple, to the east of the fort, at the foot of Vipula Hill.

Immediately to the south of Venuvana, at the foot of **Vaibhara Hill** are Jain and Hindu temples built around 22 hot springs. Public baths have been set up where one can relax in hot emerald-green waters. Further up, past the **Pippla Cave** and the **Jarasandha-ki-Baithak**, a monastery built out of large blocks of stone, is the **Saptaparni cave** where the First Buddhist Council was held. Further south, **Manyar Math**, a cylindrical stone structure, is a former temple to Maninaga, a serpent demi-god, referred to in the *Mahabharata*. Turning left the road passes **Jivakamhavana,** the site of the mango grove presented to the Buddha by Jivaka, Bimbisara's physician, and reaches **Maddakuchchi** from where one has to walk to **Gridhrakuta Hill**, probably the holiest place in Rajgir, where the Buddha delivered most of his sermons. From Maddakuchchi, an aerial ropeway chairlift leads to the top of **Ratna Giri**, a hill at the top of which Japanese Buddhists have built the **Vishwa Shanti** (World Peace) **Stupa**, a huge white structure visible from miles around. Four golden statues, one on each side, recall the Buddha's birth, enlightenment, teachings and death.

Places of pilgrimage: Gaya, 56 miles (90 km) southwest of Rajgir, is an important Hindu site. Lord Vishnu is said to have conferred upon Gaya the power to

Paddle steamer on Ganga, Bihar.

cleanse one of one's sins. Devotees flock here to perform ceremonies to clear their dead of the burden of sin they might have carried over to the next world. They take a holy dip in the Phalgu River and lay offerings of *pindas* (sweets) and ritual rice cakes on the ghats along the river, before entering the **Vishnupada Temple** (closed to non-Hindus) built by the Maharani of Indore in 1787 over the footprint Lord Vishnu is believed to have left on a stone. Within the grounds of the temple stands a banyan tree which is said to be the one under which the Buddha spent six years meditating.

The Buddha attained enlightenment in **Bodhgaya**, 7 miles (12 km) south of Gaya, along the Phalgu River. He first meditated in nearby Dungeswari, eating one grain of rice a day for two years, then nothing for four years. Realising that mortification did not bring enlightenment, he moved to a cave where voices told him this was not the place. He then found a *ficus* (banyan) tree and sat under it to meditate, vowing not to rise until he attained enlightenment.

King Ashoka erected a shrine near the *bodhi* tree. This was replaced in the 2nd century by the present **Mahabodhi Temple** with a 177-ft (54-metre) spire which was altered in the 11th century, damaged in the 12th, and restored in the 19th. In the 17th century, Hindus took over the temple as the Buddha is considered an avatar of Vishnu and it is now managed by a joint Buddhist-Hindu committee. Inside is a gilded statue of the Buddha, sitting cross-legged, with his right hand touching the ground in acceptance of enlightenment. Around the temple are votive stupas.

Along the western wall is the *bodhi* tree or rather its latest successor. The original is believed to have been destroyed by Emperor Ashoka before his conversion to Buddhism. The replacement was cut down by Ashoka's jealous wife. The next in the line was destroyed by Shasanka, a Hindu king of Bengal. The immediate predecessor of the present tree withered in the 19th century. Under the tree is the **Vajrasana**, the **Diamond Throne**, a stone slab marking where the Buddha was sitting when he attained enlightenment. A stone railing runs around the temple on three sides, built in place of the original Ashokan one,

part of which is in the nearby museum.

Along the north side of the Mahabodhi Temple, the **Chanka Ramana**, a platform built in the 1st century BC, marks the place where the Buddha walked in meditation. Carved stone lotuses indicate the spots where the lotuses sprung from his feet. South of the temple a statue of the Buddha protected by a cobra stands in the middle of a large lotus pond.

Buddhist communities from all over Asia have built monasteries in Bodhgaya. Each one is a technology centre and most accept foreign students. The archeological museum displays various sculptures, some of them headless and mutilated during the 12th-century Muslim invasion.

On the way back to Patna, **Pawapuri**, 20 miles (32 km) to the southeast, is a holy place for Jains. It was here that Lord Mahavir attained salvation in 477 BC. A white marble temple, the **Jalmandir** in the middle of a lotus pond, marks the place where he was cremated. There are five more Jain temples around the pond.

Southern tribes: South Bihar, called **Chotanagpur**, is very different from the

Remains of the ancient Nalanda University.

north. A large part of the population is tribal, of pre-Dravidian stock, speaking Mon-Khmer languages. The main tribes are the Santal, the Bedia, the Birhor, the No, the Khond, the Munda, and the Oraon. Some are still wanderers, living off hunting, wild fruit and root gathering. The majority have settled to cultivate maize and millet, and raise cattle and fowl. About 60 percent are Christian. Many now work in the new industrial cities that have sprung up in Bihar.

Ranchi, the former summer capital of Bihar, has lost its cool climate with the felling of most of its trees to make room for a new industrial town. A few colonial buildings remain: the **Eastern Railway Hotel,** the **Lutheran Church** and **Saint Paul's Anglican Church**, and some eccentric villas on Kanke Road, near Ranchi Hill – one called PARAVON has been built in the shape of a B-52 aircraft; the house next door has the shape of a warship. Beyond the bazaar area, on top of Ranchi Hill, overlooking Ranchi Lake, stands a **Shiva Temple** of limited interest compared to the 17th-century fortified

Jagannath Temple at Jagannathpur near the airport. It is open to non-Hindus.

Jamshedpur (106 miles/170 km south of Ranchi) is the property of the Tata Iron and Steel Company. The town has grown around the first and most productive steel plant in India built in 1912 by the Parsi industrialist, Sir Jamshedji Tata, after whom the city is named.

Jamshedpur is a well-planned city, with adequate housing, green spaces, medical facilities, and the large Jubilee Park laid out round a lake to celebrate the Golden Jubilee of the township and the steel plant.

East of Ranchi, more easily reached from Calcutta starts "the Indian Ruhr", an industrial zone spreading along the Damodar River into West Bengal. Most of its towns are industrial. To the northwest of Dhanbad, however, the **Parasnath Hill** (4,757 ft/1,450 metres) is a religious centre. Of the 24 Jain Tirthankaras, 20 attained *nirvana* here. On the hill and at the foot of it, are Jain temples of both the Svetambara and Digambara sects, the most interesting ones being the **Samosavan, Bhomia Baba** and **Parasvanath**.

Steel works, Jamshedpur.

ORISSA

Orissa has an ancient tradition of seafaring. At one time, there were Oriya colonies in Burma and Java. Buddhism became the religion of the kingdom of Kalinga, as Orissa was called, soon after the faith was established. Buddhist universities flourished at Nrusinghanath in central Orissa and Ratnagiri near Cuttack.

In 262 BC the Maurya Emperor, Ashoka, defeated Kalinga near Bhubaneshwar, slaying 100,000 people and taking 150,000 captive. This scene of bloodshed is said to have turned Ashoka away from violence and led him to adopt Buddhism. After the collapse of the Mauryan empire, two dynasties ruled in Orissa. The temples of Bhubaneshwar, Konarak and Puri were built during that time. The Kesaris reigned from the 2nd to the 12th centuries. They brought in Brahmins to re-Hinduise Orissa and built the Jagannath Temple at Puri and the Lingaraj Temple at Bhubaneshwar. The Gangas ruled from the 12th to the 15th century. They erected the Sun Temple at Konarak. After a period of confusion, came the Mughals in 1508, succeeded in 1751 by the Marathas.

As in other parts of India, western nations first came to Orissa to trade. The Dutch came to Pipli in the 17th century, and the East India Company at about the same time to Balasore. Bengal, Bihar and Orissa were ceded to the Company in 1765, but it was not until 1803, after a campaign by the Marquis of Wellesley, who took Puri and Cuttack, that British rule was fully established in Orissa.

Orissa is an intensely religious state where fervour is focused on Lord Jagannath, an incarnation of Vishnu. Not surprisingly, Orissan civilisation stemmed from its temples, where the most remarkable erotic statuary can be found and where originated Odissi, a style of religious dancing with definite erotic hues. Odissi was performed previously in temples by resident dancers (maharis) devoting their lives to the temple god. Nearly forgotten during the Muslim rule, Odissi has been revived as a performing art.

City of temples: Capital of Orissa only since 1956, **Bhubaneshwar**, is a city of temples. There were once over a thousand of them; a large number are still active.

An Orissan temple (deul), moving from centre to periphery, usually consists of a sanctum, one or several front porches (jagamohanas), usually with pyramidal roofs, a dancing hall (nata mandir) and a hall of offerings (bhoga mandapa). Deuls with semi-cylindrical roofs are called khakhara deul.

A large number of temples in Bhubaneshwar are located around **Bindu Sarovar**, a tank which is believed to receive water from all the holy rivers of India. The **Lingaraj Temple** to the south, built in 1014 AD to the glory of Shiva, is certainly the most impressive. A massive wall surrounds a 150-ft (45-metre) high deul with a jagamohana, a nata mandir and a bhoga mandapa, as well as minor temples to Parvati, Gopalini and Bhubaneshwari. All are decorated with a profusion of sculptures of deities, nymphs and amorous couples. Entry is prohibited to non-Hindus.

Vaital Deul is a typical 8th-century khakhara deul with an oblong roof. It is decorated with stone figures of Durga, such as the eight-armed Mahishasuramardini, on the northern wall, piercing the left shoulder of Mahishasura, the buffalo-headed demon, with her trident. Within the sanctum, another avatar of Durga, eight-armed Chamunda or Kapalini, often hidden by a drape, sits on a corpse, with an owl and a jackal on each side. Her face is emaciated, her eyes sunken, and she wears a garland of skulls.

Sisiresvara Temple, next to Vaital, has been damaged but has retained sculptures of lions, elephants, the gods Ganesh and Kartikeya, and the Avilokiteshwara Buddha seated cross-legged and accompanied by a deer and a nag (cobra), showing how strong Buddhist influence was in Orissa. The **Uttaresvara Temple** on the north bank of the lake has undergone extensive restoration. Southeast of the lake, the **Ananta-Vasudeva Temple** is one of the few in Bhubaneshwar belonging to the Vaishnava cult.

East of the lake is another group of temples. **Parasuramesvara** is one of the oldest. Built in the 7th century, it is still well preserved and is decorated with a four-

Bondo tribal girl, Orissa.

armed Ganesh, a two-armed Kartikeya mounted on a peacock and killing a snake, amorous couples and rampant lions.

Muktesvara is the gem of Orissan architecture. Entrance to the temple compound is through a sculptured gateway *(torana)*; the *jagamohana* has diamond-shaped latticed windows and a richly decorated interior. Temple, *torana* (gateway) and walls are covered with figures of female warriors, erotic scenes, elephants, maidens, monkeys in various comic scenes, women worshipping *lingas* and *naginis* (half-snakes, half-women). On each side of the *deul* is a grimacing lion face, flanked with smiling dwarfs.

To the east is the **Rajarani Temple**. It is noted for its sculptures of nymphs in extremely sensuous poses, and statues of the *ashta dikpalas,* guardians of the cardinal points of the compass.

Bhubaneshwar has three museums. The **Orissa State Museum** displays Hindu, Buddhist and Jain sculptures, and early Orissan palm manuscripts. The **Handicrafts Museum** has a collection of folk art such as Cuttack silver filigree and *patachitra*

painting on cloth. There is also a **Tribal Research Museum**.

West of Bhubaneshwar, on the immediate outskirts, are two hills **Udayagiri** and **Khandagiri**. Both were once inhabited by Jain ascetics who lived in cells excavated in the rock. Khandagiri has fewer caves than Udayagiri but a small Jain temple still stands on top of this hill.

At **Dhauli**, a hill 5 miles (8 km) south of Bhubaneshwar, there is an example of Emperor Ashoka's edicts. Sculpted elephants mark the site. To commemorate Ashoka's acceptance of Buddhism, substituting the ideal of *dharmavijaya,* spiritual victory, for *digvijaya,* military conquest, Japanese Buddhists have built a huge white **Peace Pagoda** on top of the hill. Some 6 miles (10 km) south is **Pipli**, a small village specialising in a folk form of appliqué work in vivid colours unique to this area.

Puri, 37 miles (60 km) from Bhubaneshwar, is the holiest place in Orissa and one of the biggest pilgrimage centres in India. The city was once a flourishing port identified with ancient Dantpur. Puri is known for its cult of Jagannath, originating some say in

Sun Temple at Konarak.

the times when the people of Orissa worshipped trees and hence the practice of carving his image in wood. According to the more popular legend, however, the Lord appeared in King Indrodyumna's dream and commanded him to build a temple for him. The king complied, getting the images carved out of a single log of wood found floating in the sea, as the Lord had enjoined in the dream. The climax of Jagannath worship is the Rath Yatra festival celebrated every year in June-July at the **Jagannath Temple**.

Known as the "White Pagoda", this temple was built in the 12th century. It lies in the midst of a huge complex of buildings where more than 5,000 priests and other temple staff live. The main building is 213 ft (65 metres) high, surmounted by the mystic wheel or *chakra* and the flag of Vishnu. It is surrounded by a wall 20 ft (6 metres) high. Non-Hindus are not permitted to enter the temple or its grounds.

About two weeks before the festival, the images of Jagannath and his brother, Balabhadra, and his sister, Subhadra, are given a ritual bath. Every 12 years, instead of a bath, the images are replaced by new ones carved afresh from a *daru,* a tree ritually selected by the temple priests. The old images are then buried in a secret ceremony.

On the first day of the festival, the deities are placed on *raths,* ceremonial chariots 40 ft (12 metres) high, with wheels of more than 7 ft (2 metres) in diameter. Jagannath's chariot, the tallest, is yellow-striped. Subhadra has a red chariot. Balabhadra's is bright blue. All three are preceded by four wooden horses but are actually drawn by hundreds of devotees from the temple to Gundicha Mandir, a temple 5 miles (8 km) away, where they will stay for seven days. The rituals completed, the deities ride back to their own temple.

Although the beach at Puri is one of the best in India, the seas can be very rough there, with giant waves and strong and erratic currents. Caution is advised. *Nulia* lifeguards, easily recognissable by their white cone-shaped straw huts, are not always alert. Be sure to watch the fishermen come ashore through the surf.

The Sun Temple: Inland, a few kilome-

tres from Puri, is **Konarak**, a former center of Orissan Buddhism, an active port, now silted, and, in ancient times, a centre for sun worship. A temple to the Sun God was built here in the 9th century. The present **Sun Temple** was erected in the 13th century. It took 16 years to complete; 1,200 artisans were employed on the task. In its original form the temple consisted of a 230-ft (70-metre) high *deul* with a 131-ft (40-metre) *jagamohana*, representing together the Chariot of the Sun, drawn by seven impetuous horses, the chariot having 12 pairs of 8-spoke wheels. The *deul* collapsed in the middle of the 19th century and one horse is missing. The temple used to stand on the shore, but the sea has since receded 2 miles (3 km). However, despite its dilapidated state the Sun Temple stands out as a masterpiece of Orissan architecture.

Both the main *deul* and the *jagamohana*, the ruins of the dancing hall and of the Mayadevi Temple in the Sun Temple compound, are covered with erotic sculptures of couples in a variety of poses, along with depictions of nymphs, war, hunting and court scenes, musicians, floral motifs, and elephants. There are also huge animal statues: two lions guard the pyramidal entrance, and on each side of the temple is a colossal war elephant, and a warhorse trampling on fallen warriors.

South of Bhubaneshwar, along the coast, is **Chilka Lake**, a 425 sq. mile (1,100 sq. km) shallow inland sea, separated from the Bay of Bengal by a sandy ridge, spreading over 47 miles (75 km) from north to south. From Barkul, the Orissa Tourist Development Corporation operates a two-hour cruise to Kalijai Temple, a small shrine on a rock island, and to Nalabar Island. The lake has an abundance of fish and shellfish. From mid-December to mid-January migratory birds spend the winter here.

Further south, 59 miles (95 km) from Bhubaneshwar, **Gopalpur-on-Sea**, has a totally unspoiled beach, probably the best in Eastern India.

Some of Orissa's most interesting tribes live in the district of **Koraput**, the Southern Hills area. Most are from the Austro-Asiatic Munda group, and the Bondos are the least acculturated. Women marry boys half their age and the men, armed with **Puri town.**

arrows, routinely get murderously drunk on sago palm toddy. They dress mostly in beads, though the women wear a stack of nine metal rings around their necks.

In the Northern Hills bordering West Bengal and Bihar, **Simlipal National Park** is one of India's most attractive forests, its 1062 sq. miles (2,750 sq. km) populated with tigers and wild elephants.

North from Bhubaneshwar is **Nandanakanan**, a recreation park set in the middle of Chandka Forest. Animals here are kept in natural surroundings. The main attractions are four white tigers, one-horned rhinos, white-browed gibbons and African lions. A section of the park is a **Botanical Garden**, with a rosarium, a two-storeyed Zen temple and a cactus house.

North of Bhubaneshwar 12 miles (19 km) is **Cuttack**, the former capital of Orissa, the old Abhinaba Bidanasi Katak. There are few remains; ruins of the blue granite **Barabati Maratha** fort, stormed by the British in 1803; **Kadam Rasal**, a walled compound, with corner towers, containing three 18th century mosques and a domed building containing footprints of Prophet Muhammad engraved on a circular stone.

Past Cuttack, off the road to Paradeep, there are more Buddhist remains, the former monasteries of Lalitagiri and Ratnagiri where excavations have uncovered Buddha images, including heads of the Buddha. Rough tracks, hardly motorable, lead through typical Oriya villages.

Further north, **Balasore** is one of the earliest British settlements in India, granted to the East India Company in 1633. Nearby are three shrines. The Kutopokhari Temple at Remuna, is a seat of Vaishnava culture with an 18-arm, 7-ft (2-metre) high granite statue of Durga. Bhudhara Chandi at Sajanagarh, built in the 16th century, contains a three-faced, eight-armed image of Shakti, standing on seven boars. Panchalingeswar on Devagiri Hill, is a temple with five stone *lingams*.

To the east is the small resort of **Chandipur-on-sea**, a beach where the sea recedes by more than 3 miles (5 km) at low tide. Here, in the land of the ancient Sun Temple, the visitor can take a long walk on the beach as he watches the sunrise. Fishermen will take visitors in their catamarans.

Puri beach.

ANDAMAN AND NICOBAR ISLANDS

The Andaman and Nicobar Islands, home of a number of aboriginal tribes, lie 758 miles (1,220 km) southeast of the coast of Bengal and 739 miles (1,190 km) east of Madras. Their existence was reported as early as the 9th century AD by Arab merchants sailing past to enter the Straits to Sumatra, 75 miles (120 km) to the south.

The main aboriginal group are the Onges, who live on Little Andaman. Onges, like other Andamanese tribes, are of Negrito stock. They practise food gathering, hunting, honey-collecting and fishing, and are the only tribe on the islands who freely accept contact with the outside world.

In the Nicobars, the only aboriginals are the Shompens with whom little contact exists. The Nicobarese, the largest group, seem to be of mixed Burmese, Malay, Mon and Shan origin. They are cultivators producing fruit, vegetables, copra and coconut oil. They also raise pigs and cows which were first brought to the islands by erst-

while Danish settlers in the 18th century.

The first westerners to set foot on the islands were the Danes who established a settlement in the Nicobars and then left in 1768 due to poor health conditions. The British surveyed the Andamans in 1789 and established a penal settlement on South Andaman Island but had to abandon it in 1796 because of unhealthy living conditions. The East India Company used the Nicobars in 1816 as a base to launch an attack on Rangoon during the Anglo-Burmese Wars, and reoccupied the Andamans in 1858. Finally, the British Indian Government annexed both groups of islands in 1872, along with Great and Little Cocos that lie off Burma. The only point of settlement developed by the British was Port Blair, where a penitentiary was built for prisoners serving life terms.

Until World War II, the islands remained untouched by time. In 1942, however, they became the westernmost point reached by the Japanese. Their occupation ended in 1945. During that period, in December 1943, Subhas Bose, the Indian nationalist leader who was then working with the Japanese

Early photo of an Andaman tribal group.

against the British rulers of India, landed at Port Blair for two days, and there unfurled the *Triranghi Jhanda,* the Indian national tricolor. But he could not, as he had wished, establish an Indian Provisional Government Administration there nor garrison the islands with the Indian National Army that he had raised.

Port Blair, the capital, on South Andaman, was named after Lt. Reginald Blair who conducted a survey of the area in 1789. Until World War II it had remained essentially a penal settlement.

The **Cellular Jail,** now a museum, where a total of 400 freedom fighters were held during the struggle for independence, is a massive whitewashed 18th-century building that faces the sea.

The **zoo** on Haddo Promontory has saltwater crocodiles, hornbills and crab-eating monkeys. Other places of interest are the **Anthropological Museum** (exhibiting mini-reproductions of villages of local tribes), a Burmese temple at **Phoenix Bay,** the Ghol Ghar spice stores, and the **Cottage Industries Emporium.**

From Marine Jetty, ferries ply across the harbour to **Aberdeen Market, Vyper Island**, where executions used to take place, or past the **Chattam Saw Mill**, situated on an island off Haddo. Cruises are organised by the Department of Information, Publicity and Tourism, as well as hotels during the day, and at sunset.

The closest beach is **Corbyn's Cove,** 4 miles (6 km) from town. There is a hotel offering various facilities, including windsurfing. There are beaches too at **Wandoor** (15 miles/25 km) and **Shirya Tapu** at the southern tip of the island. Excursions can be arranged from Port Blair to the **Botanical Gardens** (9 miles/14 km), **Burmah Nullah** and the **Wimberlygunj lumbering centres,** in the jungle.

As most of the islands are reserves where tribes are protected from contact with the outside world, only a limited number are open to visitors. Most hotels and tour operators in Port Blair propose one-day picnics, scuba-diving and snorkeling trips to Bird, Grub, Jolly Boy, Red Skin and Snob Islands, as well as an overnight excursion to Cinque Island that includes a small trek through the forest offering much scope for birdwatching.

Aboriginals by the beach.

CALCUTTA, CULTURAL CAPITAL

In 1686, Job Charnock, chief of the East India Company's factory in Hooghly, looking for new factory sites, selected a group of three villages – Kalikata, Govindapur and Sutanuti – where Armenian and Portuguese traders had already settled. A factory was established in Kalikata on 24 August 1690, and Calcutta was born. A fort was built, named after King William I. With poor defences, surrounded by a maze of narrow lanes, it was easily taken on 20 June 1756, by Siraj-ud-Daula, the Nawab of Bengal. Those English residents who did not escape were crammed into a small room with only one small window. Overnight, 113 of the 146 prisoners died. This is the incident recorded as the tragedy of the Black Hole of Calcutta. Calcutta was retaken on 2 January 1757 by Robert Clive, Governor of Madras. Fort William was rebuilt in 1773.

Life in the early days had been austere. Company staff lived in thatched mud houses and ate at common tables. There were no distractions and the mortality ran at times at one-third of the expatriate community. The lifestyle evolved rapidly with the development of Calcutta and was distinctly marked by the profile of the European population, most of whom were bachelors in their twenties and thirties. Punch houses made their appearance. Brawls and duels were common. When they were not out, the young "writers," as Company employees were called, would stay home smoking the hookah or watching dances performed by "nautch girls," usually prostitutes. Marriages were few. Writers usually lived with local mistresses, their "sleeping dictionaries".

Things progressively changed. In 1773, Calcutta became the headquarters (potentially, the capital) of the British administration in India. By that time, the European population had swollen from a few hundred to 100,000 through the arrival of new writers, traders, soldiers and what the administration called "cargoes of females". The decline of Calcutta started when the capital of British India was moved to Delhi in 1911. Then with the partition of

the Indian subcontinent when India became an independent country and the flow of refugees across the newly created borders, Calcutta had to make room for a substantial addition to its population. Again in 1971, in the wake of the Bangladesh war, there was a further sudden increase. This, in addition to rapid growth overburdened the city, and brought services to the verge of collapse. Two recent developments have helped the transport situation: the metro is operational after many problems in construction, and there is now a new suspension bridge over the river at Hasting which relieves some of the pressure on the Howrah bridge.

Calcutta is the largest city in India, with a population of over 10 million. Recent descriptions of its misery, however, are exaggerated. It is a lively city where something is always happening, be it religious celebrations, concerts, cricket matches, theatre or movie festivals, or political demonstrations; and although decaying, the architectural heritage is still there.

Downtown: Calcutta was built around **Fort William.** On the western side of the

fort is the **Strand** and the **Hoogly River,** a branch of the holy Ganga, on the eastern side is the Maidan.

The **Maidan** is a huge open park surrounding Fort William. For a long time, to ensure that the fort's guns had a free field of fire in all directions, no buildings were permitted here. Today the main construction on the Maidan is the **Victoria Memorial**, a massive domed building of white marble from Rajasthan. It was inaugurated in 1921 by the Prince of Wales (later, briefly, Edward VIII). It houses a collection of Victorian memorabilia and also history-related objects on Bengal.

In the park in which the memorial stands are statues of Queen Victoria, Lord Curzon and other Raj figures. Here, on weekends, people picnic, families meet for matchmaking, and transiting pilgrims bring flowers to the statue of "Maharani Victoria".

Behind the Memorial, on Lower Circular Road, is the **Presidency General Hospital** where, in 1898, Sir Ronald Ross identified the carrier of malaria, the female anopheles mosquito.

The **Racecourse**, opened in 1819, is the largest in the East. In its central oval are the Calcutta Polo Club grounds where the game has been played since 1861.

To the southeast is Cathedral Road starting at **Rabindra Sadan,** a concert hall named after Rabindranath Tagore, which is active all the year round. The nearby **Academy of Fine Arts** has a collection of old textiles, miniatures, Mughal swords, Tagore memorabilia and modern Bengali art. The adjacent **St Paul's Cathedral** was consecrated in 1847. It is a tall white Gothic building with rows of fans hanging from a wooden ceiling, stalls and pews of heavy wood, and a stained-glass window by Burne-Jones. On the walls are interesting commemorative slabs to the British killed during the Mutiny and those who lost their lives in various wars.

Near the Cathedral are the **Birla Planetarium** and the **Nehru Children's Museum.** The latter displays a collection of toys from all over the world and two remarkable dioramas of the *Ramayana* and the *Mahabharata* shown in 61 scenes.

At the northern end of the Maidan, the 158-ft (48-metre) high **Ochterlony Monu-**

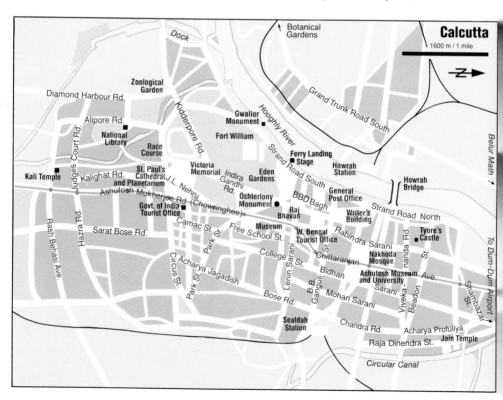

ment was erected to celebrate Sir David Ochterlony's victories in the Nepal wars. In the 19th century the monument was used by Young Bengal nationalists to hoist the French flag as a sign of rebellion against the British Raj. The monument has been recently renamed **Shaheed Minar** to honour martyred freedom fighters.

Describing the **Maidan** in terms of its monuments does not show how lively it is. In the 19th century, nationalists organised a fair, the Hindu Mela, on the Maidan, with concerts of music and dance and also plays and lectures. It was here that Tagore, aged 15, made his first public appearance. Nowadays, the Maidan Mela is a daily 24-hour show. At sunrise, joggers make their appearance; the West Bengal Mounted Police hack their horses; Army units do their morning drills; goats and sheep browse on the course of the Calcutta Golf Club, before being led to slaughter. Later, tramways start plying, bringing people to work. Football or cricket then takes over, and *sadhus* and bards gather audiences under trees near the **Gandhi Statue** and the **War Memorial**. At night, action concentrates around **Sri Aurobindo's Statue** opposite the Victoria Memorial.

Along the Maidan, **Chowringhee,** once a jungle path leading to the Kali Temple, and the **Esplanade** symbolise Calcutta's past grandeur with late 19th Century buildings such as the **Oberoi Grand** and the **Indian Museum**, opened in 1814. Chowringhee's glory has, however, departed. Most of the facades are decaying; hawkers, shoe-shine boys, beggars and touts now crowd the pavement.

Raj Bhavan was built in 1803 by Governor-General Wellesley, who believed that India should be governed "from a palace, not from a counting-house". Towards the river are the **Assembly House**, the old **Town Hall** and the **High Court** built in 1872 on the model of the Gothic belfry of Ypres in Flanders.

To the west is **St John's Church**, built in 1784. It is reputed to have the best organ in India. Job Charnock was buried here. In the garden stands a monument to the victims of the "Black Hole" tragedy. Beyond is **Dalhousie Square**, renamed **B.B.D. Bag** in memory of three brothers, Binoy,

Badal and Dinesh, who were hanged for having conspired to kill Lord Dalhousie. Facing the tank that once used to be Calcutta's only source of drinking water, stands **Writers Building**, the seat of the West Bengal Government. It was built in the late 19th century. The first Writers Buildings that stood here housed "writers" (clerks) of the East India Company, hence its name. Opposite stands **St Andrew's Kirk,** opened in 1818. The offices of Calcutta's most prestigious companies – tall Victorian buildings, with art nouveau staircases, brass signs, marble floors and wood panelling – are the old **Clive Row,** now **Netaji Subhas Road**.

These streets are now choked with hawkers, cars and taxis. Even the Stock Exchange has spilled over onto the street opposite Jardine Henderson's. The present **General Post Office** is on the site of the first Fort William and a plaque near the main entrance marks the location of the notorious "Black Hole of Calcutta".

In India Exchange Lane, near the **Jute Balers Association**, speculators on the jute market operate from booths equipped with telephones, projecting a couple of feet from the walls of the buildings along the street. Buyers in the booths shout their orders to sellers who stand in the street. Nearby is a small tomb, ironical memorial to the Dead Telephone.

The Bazaars: Starting at the northeastern corner of the Maidan, in **Bentinck Street** there is a succession of Chinese shoemakers, Muslim tailors and sweet and tea shops. **Tiretta Market** nearby, named after its former owner, a friend of Casanova's who had to flee Venice, sells dry fish, vegetable and meat.

Chinatown is in Tiretta where the Chinese settled at the end of the 18th century. A whole area in Calcutta once was a Cantonese town, but since 1962, when Indian and Chinese troops clashed at the frontier, it has been greatly reduced. There are still some 30,000 Chinese citizens, but most of the Chinese buildings have disappeared, except the **Nanking Restaurant** on Blackburn Lane, the **Sea Ip Temple** on Chatawala Gully, a few clubs, and the **Kuomintang Press,** on Metcalfe Street, publishing two daily papers in Chinese.

St Paul's Cathedral.

238

In **Old China Bazaar,** west of Brabourne Road, Parsis have an agiary (fire temple), the Ismailites have a mosque, and the Gujarati Jains a temple, probably one of the most charming in Calcutta, in this area. There are also three synagogues. One of them, Magen David, was built in 1884. Calcutta's Jews came from Iraq in the 19th century and formed a prosperous community but emigration since the end of World War II has drastically reduced their number to about 200.

Off Old China Bazaar Lane, stands the **Armenian Church of Our Lady of Nazareth**. It was built in 1724. Coming from Isfahan, the Armenians were already here and in Chinsura, upriver on the Hooghly, when Job Charnock founded Calcutta. A grave in the church cemetery is dated 1630. In and around Calcutta, the Armenians have several churches, a school, a club and also one of India's best rugby teams.

Along Chitpur Road, now Rabindra Sarani, stands the **Nakhoda Mosque**, built in red sandstone with four floors on the model of Akbar's tomb near Agra. It has room for a congregation of 10,000.

Stately homes: Joransanko with verandahed houses on Sir Hariram Goenka Street and mansions around Kali Krishna Nagore and Jadulal Mullick streets, has a character all its own. The most eccentric of the mansions is **Tagore's Castle** on Darpanarain Tagore Lane built in 1867 and reminiscent of Sleeping Beauty's castle at Disneyland. Overbuilt structures have, unfortunately, altered its silhouette.

At the end of Dwarkanath Tagore Lane is **Rabindra Mancha**, an 18th century house where the poet Rabindranath Tagore was born in 1861, and where he died in 1941. It is now a museum devoted to the poet's life and to the Young Bengal Movement. Adjoining the house is a library and **Rabindra Bharati**, the Tagore Academy.

In **Kumarthuli**, further north, live a community of artisans making clay images of goddesses Durga, Lakshmi or Saraswati for festivals.

In Rajabazar on Badni Das Temple Road are three Jain temples of the Svetambara sect, built at the end of the 19th century. Their architecture is a mixture of Mughal, baroque, neo-classical and local styles,

akhoda
losque.

and their interiors are decorated with mosaics, coloured glass, mirrors, coloured stones, crystal and marble.

At Chorebagan ("the thieves' garden"), the **Marble Palace** on Muktaram Babu Street was built in 1835 by Raja Mullick in Italian marble. The Raja's descendants still live here, but most of it can be visited. In dark halls are assembled paintings, clocks, statues, crystal and china. Among them there is said to be a Napoleon by Houdon, one Arnold, one Gainsborough, three Rubens and a statue by Michelangelo. In the yard is the family temple, and a collection of parrots, doves and mynahs.

Calcutta University on College Square was founded in 1873. It has, in the past, been the scene of many demonstrations and most of its walls are still covered with political grafitti. In the **University Senate** building is the **Asutosh Museum**, presenting a collection of Pala sculptures, terracotta, bronzes, *thankas* (Buddhist religious paintings on cloth) and Bengali folk art. The **Albert Hall coffee shop**, on Bankim Chatterjee Street, is the main meeting place for all who matter in the city's intellectual and the student circles.

Behind Chowringhee is where the Europeans used to live. It is an area of mansions slowly being replaced by modern buildings. **Park Street,** the main thoroughfare, was laid during the first quarter of this century. The **Freemason's Hall** on this street was built in the 19th century. It houses the Star of the East Lodge, the oldest outside Britain. The **Asiatic Society,** also at the beginning of Park Street, was founded in 1784. The present building houses a permanent exhibition of oriental manuscripts, prints, and paintings that can be visited on request.

Another landmark is **La Martinière College** on Lower Circular Road, founded by a Frenchman, Claude Martin, born in Lyons. A former bodyguard to the French Governor of Pondicherry, Martin later joined the service of the East India Company and ended his career as a Major-General. He died in 1800, bequeathing his fortune to set up schools in Lyons, Calcutta and Lucknow, and Rs. 50,000 to the Church of the Sacred Heart at Chandernagore with instructions that the interest

Contemporary image of Goddess Kali.

earned be distributed every day to the poor, for all time to come.

Park Street used to be called European Burial Road and once ended at the **South Park Street Cemetery**, the oldest extant in Calcutta. It was opened in 1767. Here are buried Major General Charles "Hindoo" Stuart, an Irishman who adopted the Hindu religion; Robert Kyd, founder of the Botanical Gardens; William Makepeace Thackeray's father; Rose Aylmer "who died of eating too many pineapples"; the poet Henry Derozio, founder of the Young Bengal Movement; and Sir William Jones, the father of the Asiatic Society.

Nearby, in the suburb of Bhowanipore, is **Netaji Bhawan** on Elgin Road, the house from which Netaji Subhas Bose, the nationalist leader escaped during the World War II to establish the Indian National Army in Japanese-occupied Southeast Asia. It is now a museum.

South Calcutta: This is essentially residential, with upper-class alternating with middle-class neighbourhoods. Warren Hastings' first residence, at Alipore, now an institute of education, is said to be haunted by its former owner. The **National Library**, on Belvedere Road, was once the Winter Viceregal Lodge.

The **Zoological Gardens** were established in 1876. In wintertime thousands of migratory birds stay on the lake. Among the animals are bizarre specimens such as the Tigon, the result of crossing a tiger and an African lioness.

Kalighat is a middle-class neighbourhood on **Tolly's Nullah**, a canal also called Adiganga, "the real Ganga", because it is believed to be the original bed of the Hooghly. In 1775 a Colonel Tolly drained the silted canal to bring Ganga water to the **Kali Temple**.

The present Kali Temple was built in 1809 although there's been one here since early times. Thugs used to come to pray before setting out in search of victims. Human sacrifices are known to have taken place, but today only goats, and, on occasions, buffaloes, are sacrificed while pilgrims make offerings to Kali of milk mixed with Ganga water and *bhang* (cannabis).

Next door, Mother Teresa's **Home for**

The Writers Building.

the **Destitute and Dying** is the first of several missions run by her Sisters of Charity in the city. Volunteers should check directly with the Mother House, a bus ride away at 54A Lower Circular Road (Tel: 224 7115), and arrive early enough for morning mass. The nuns in white saris will dispatch you to where your services are most needed.

There are more temples further south on Alipore Chetla and Tollygunge roads. Nearby, is the **Tollygunge Club**. Once an indigo plantation was located here. Later the Maharaja of Mysore built his Calcutta mansion on the site. It became the Tollygunge Club in 1895 and offers its facilities (golf, tennis and squash) to visitors on a daily basis.

East of Tollygunge, around **Rabindra Sarovar lake**, are rowing clubs and the **Birla Art Academy** on Southern Avenue, a museum which is never crowded, with a whole floor of miniatures from all schools, a modern art gallery, and old statues.

The **Birla Industrial and Technological Museum** has on display a life-size model of part of a working coal mine.

The **Ramakrishna Mission Institute of Culture** on Gol Park, near the lake, is a branch of the Ramakrishna Mission of Belur Math. It has a school of languages, a library, a museum of Indian art and a Universal Prayer Room.

Ghats on the Ganga: From the ghat near the Garden Reach shipyard, a ferry crosses to the **Botanical Gardens** in Howrah. Set up in 1786, these once boasted the largest banyan tree in the world. The trunk was, however, struck by lightning in 1919 and was subsequently removed. About 1,500 off-shoots remain, forming a circle with a diameter of more than 33 ft (10 metres).

The **Metiaburuz Shiite Mosque** on Garden Reach Road was built and lavishly decorated by the royal family of Oudh in the 19th century.

The riverside ghats off Strand Road, like any on the Ganga, are most active at dawn and sunset. During festivals thousands of devotees converge on **Babu**, **Outram** and **Princep Ghats** to immerse clay images of Durga, Kali, Lakshmi or Saraswati into the river. Other communities hold festivals too. On Chaat, Biharis dip fruit in the river and Sindhis, on Chetti Chand, immerse statues of the god Jhulelal. On Strand Road, in January, a transit camp is arranged for the thousands of pilgrims on their way to the holy island of Sagardwip. Every morning, the ghats swarm with people washing and praying.

On the riverfront promenade, families and lovers stroll near the **Gwalior Monument**, called the "Pepper Pot" because of its shape, and erected to commemorate a British victory in the Maratha Wars. At Princep Ghat dinghies are available for hire on an hourly basis. Behind Babu Ghat are **Eden Gardens**, a park created in 1877, with a kiosk and a pagoda brought to Calcutta from Prome in Burma by Lord Curzon. Eden Gardens Stadium is the Mecca of Indian Cricket.

The **Howrah Bridge**, over the Hooghly, now a Calcutta landmark, was built in 1941. It has 8 lanes for traffic, which is not enough for the daily flow of trams, buses, trucks, trishaws, pedestrians, buffaloes, sheep, goats, taxis and bullock-carts. On hot days its length can increase by one metre. It has recently been supplemented by a new suspension bridge at Hastings.

Left, new bridge on the Hooghly. **Right**, Lord Curzon, creator of the Victoria Memorial behind him.

BENGAL, GANGA'S BOUNTY

West Bengal stretches from the Himalaya to the Bay of Bengal. Before the partition of the subcontinent, the province of Bengal included what is now Bangladesh, with which the Indian Union State of West Bengal shares its languages, culture and historical background.

Early mention of Bengal can be found in the *Mahabharata* and in Ptolemy's geography. Bengal was then a seafaring nation, sending traders to Sri Lanka, Sumatra and Java and being visited by Greeks, Chinese and Persians either by sea or over land.

From the end of the 19th century onwards Bengal was one of the most prosperous territories of the British Empire. A new Bengali culture developed under the Raj. Temples were built, the Bengali language was enriched by poets and writers such as Bankim Chandra Chatterjee and Rabindranath Tagore. Major religious philosophers like Ramakrishna and Vivekananda appeared. A sense of Bengali and all-India nationalism developed. The attempted partition of Bengal in 1904 by Lord Curzon into a Hindu West and a Muslim East, and the removal of the capital to New Delhi inflamed nationalist feelings.

Early colonisers: On the right bank of the Hooghly, less than 37 miles (60 km) from Calcutta, along the Grand Trunk Road, are sleepy little towns with palaces, old churches, riverfront promenades and colonial houses and cemeteries – remains of the old Danish, Dutch and French settlements. The Grand Trunk Road is reached by the Bally Bridge crossing the Hooghly at **Dakshineshwar**, where, on the left bank, stands the 9th century **Kali Bhavatarini Temple** complex containing a central temple to Kali, one to Radha-Krishna and 12 small temples to Shiva. The philosopher Ramakrishna lived here: his room is now a museum.

Downstream across the river, is **Belur Math**, headquarters of the Ramakrishna Mission, founded in 1938 by Ramakrishna's disciple Vivekananda. The main building, the **Sri Ramakrishna Temple**, 246ft (75 metres) long and 115ft (35 metres) high, reflects Ramakrishna's call for harmony between religions. The gate is Buddhist, the structure above the entrance, South Indian, the windows and balconies, Mughal and Rajput, and the floorplan is that of a Christian cross.

The first erstwhile foreign settlement north of Calcutta is **Serampore**. The Danish East India Company carried on trade here from the late 17th century till 1845, when the Danes sold to Britain all their possessions in India. Under the Danes, Serampore became an important cultural centre. In 1799 William Carey, an Englishman, and two fellow Baptist missionaries, established a press here and were pioneers of printing in several oriental languages.

In 1819 Carey founded the **Serampore College**, incorporated in 1827 as a university by Danish Royal Charter. This was the first modern university in Asia. Still active, the college is now a Baptist theological institute. It stands on the bank of the Hooghly, among other 18th and 19th century mansions. Slightly inland is **Saint Olaf's Church**, built in 1747.

A gate bearing the motto of the French Republic *Liberté, Egalité, Fraternité*, marks the entrance to **Chandernagore,** a French *Etablissement* almost continuously from 1673 to 1952. Hardly anybody speaks French there now but a French atmosphere still persists along the shaded Quai Dupleix, now Strand Road, with its public benches exactly like those in Paris parks. The **Eglise du Sacré Coeur** could well be a French village church with its statue of Joan of Arc and a Lourdes grotto.

To the northwest, at **Palpara** and **Narwah**, are groups of Shiva temples. The most important is the 18th century **Nandadulal Temple** at Lal Bagan dedicated to Krishna, a good example of flat-roofed Bengali architecture.

The Dutch settled at **Chinsura** further north in 1625 and ceded it to Britain in 1826 against Bencoolen in Sumatra. A Dutch barracks, a church and a cemetery still remain from that period. Chinsura's Armenian community built **St John's Church** in 1695 and, once a year, on Saint John's day, in January, the Armenians of Calcutta gather here to hold religious services. To the north, on the riverside, is the

Imambara, a Shiite mosque with a clock tower donated by Queen Victoria.

The Portuguese founded nearby Bandel de Ugolim, now **Hooghly**, in 1580, and controlled most of the Mughal Empire's foreign trade passing through Bengal, until the arrival of other European nations. In 1632, after a three-month siege, Hooghly was destroyed by the Mughal Emperor Shah Jahan.

The **Church of Our Lady of Bandel** is all that remains of the Portuguese past. Consecrated in 1599 it was rebuilt after it was destroyed by Shah Jahan in 1632, but without the usual exuberance of Portuguese churches. It has remained a pilgrimage centre. Even today, each Christmas Eve, a mass is celebrated, drawing extra trainloads of Catholics from Calcutta.

Holy cities: North of Hooghly, at **Bansberia**, are two temples. The small **Vasudeva Temple** built in the 17th century has sculptured terracotta tiles representing ships, Portuguese soldiers and scenes from the *Ramayana*. **Hangseshwari Temple,** with its 13 towers, was founded in the early 19th century. Rajah Deb started building it after a dream but died before completion. His widow was about to commit *sati* (self-immolation) but was saved at the last moment by the religious reformer, Ram Mohan Roy, founder of the Brahmo Samaj movement. She lived on and finished the temple.

Beyond Bansberia, **Tribeni** is a holy place at the confluence of two rivers, the Saraswati and the Yamuna with the Ganga. Twice a year, at Dussera and during the festival of Varuna, the god of water, pilgrims visit the little **Benimadhava Temple** complex and take a bath in the Ganga. On the southern side of the Saraswati is the **Darya Zafar Khan,** Bengal's oldest Muslim building, erected in the 13th century using material from dismantled Buddhist and Hindu temples.

Nawadwip, 78 miles (125 km) north of Calcutta, also known as **Nadia**, is built on nine formerly distinct islands on the Ganga, called Bhagirathi here. It was the capital of Bengal in the 11th and 12th centuries and is among the holiest of places in West Bengal. Chaitanya Mahaprabhu, said to be an incarnation of Vishnu, taught the

Vaishnava philosophy here in the 16th century. Every year in March, over 500,000 pilgrims come to Nadia for the *padikrama,* a pilgrimage on foot, that takes them along a 30-mile (50-km) loop around places and temples associated with Chaitanya. Nearby is Sri Mayapur, the headquarters of the International Society for Krishna Consciousness (ISKON).

At Mayapur, ISKON is now building a Vedic City, the future "spiritual capital of the world". There is already a temple, a guest house, gardens with lotus-shaped fountains, a museum in the house where the founder of the movement, Swami Prabhupada, lived, and a souvenir shop selling books, T-shirts, clothes, cassettes and discs. From its Calcutta centre, ISKON organises bus trips to Mayapur at least twice a week with a video programme on the movement and a colour movie on Rama and Sita aboard the bus.

Murshidabad and Malda: Some 30 miles (50 km) north of the battlefield of Plassey, **Murshidabad** was the capital of Bengal in 1705, when the Diwan (Mughal Viceroy) of Bengal, Bihar and Orissa, Murshid Kuli Khan, transferred his capital here from Dacca. Most of the monuments are ruined but Siraj-ud-Daula's grave at Khusbagh (across the river), Murshid Kuli Khan's tomb inside the Katra Mosque and the Jaffraganj cemetery can still be seen. There are also palaces like the Jaffraganj Deorhi palace, where Siraj-ud-Daula was assassinated; Hazarduari, the Nawab's palace, built in 1837 in Gothic style, now a museum containing old arms, china and special plates used by the nawab that, it was believed, would conveniently crack if the food were poisoned. Murshidabad is still well-known for its fine silk and ivory carving.

Nearby, at **Baranagar** are 18th century terracotta temples. Further north, 210 miles (340 km) from Calcutta, is **Malda**, formerly called English Bazaar, a foreign settlement dating from 1680, where the Dutch, the French, and then the East India Company carried on trade. Gaur, nearby, was the capital of the Pala and Sen dynasties. Under the names of Ramvati and then Lakshmanavati, the city was destroyed by the Afghan rulers of Bengal. Elements from the Hindu monuments were used to

build the new capital of **Pandua** where the most important remains are the Barasona Baroduari Mosque completed in 1526; Feroze Minar, a minaret built in 1486; the ruined Chika Mosque with Hindu idols on the doors and lintels; and the now dilapilated Lattina and Adina Mosques.

To the south: South of Calcutta start the **Sunderbans,** "beautiful forest" in Bengali, formed by the delta of the Ganga and the Brahmaputra, and extending across the entire northern shore of the Bay of Bengal. Two-thirds of this area is in Bangladesh. This Sunderban is a marshy mangrove jungle, the largest estuarine forest in the world. Nature is extremely hostile. The land is saturated with salt, sustaining a poor single crop a year; it is also the land of the man-eating Royal Bengal Tiger which swims and often attacks fishermen in their boats, killing altogether more than 200 persons each year.

There are few roads, and water transport is often the only way of communication. A permit is required to enter this area. Check with the West Bengal Tourist Promotion Board, particularly for the **Sudhanyakali** and **Sajankali** wildlife sanctuaries. The chances of seeing a tiger are slim, but there are estuarine crocodiles, the largest in the world, usually seen sleeping on mud flats along the river.

At **Bratacharingam**, 9 miles (15 km) south of Calcutta, on the road to Diamond Harbour, is Gurusaday Museum, a collection of Bengali folk art: terracotta temple plaques, clay figurines, wood sculptures, Kalighat folk paintings, scroll painting and *kanthas* (used cotton saris, stitched together and embroidered).

On the Hooghly, at the end of Budge-Budge Road, branching off Diamond Harbour Road, is **Achipur** named after Ah-Chi, the first Chinese to migrate to Bengal in modern times (end of the 18th century). His red-painted grave facing the river is probably the only Chinese tomb along the Ganga. There is also a Taoist temple. On every Lunar New Year, the Chinese community of Calcutta comes here on pilgrimage, transforming this Bengali village into a Chinese town for one day.

Diamond Harbour, 30 miles (50 km) down the Hooghly from Calcutta, a natural harbour, is a former stronghold of the Portuguese pirates. Remains of their fort can still be seen along the riverfront. This small port has a Conradian flavour.

The last island before the ocean is **Sagardwip**, where the Ganga meets the sea. The place is so sacred that dying at Sagardwip is believed to be enough to ensure the attainment of *nirvana*. Every year, in mid-January, a religious festival, Gangasagar Mela, is celebrated here. Over half-a-million pilgrims take a holy dip that washes them clean of all sins and then converge at the Kapil Muni Temple, built in memory of Kapila, a philosopher who taught and died on the island. An independent trip to Sagardwip can be arranged with accommodation on board the boat.

On the west coast of the Bay of Bengal 150 miles (240 km) south-east of Calcutta, on the Orissa border, is Digha, the only seaside resort with proper hotel accommodation in West Bengal. Rich Calcuttans have built villas here, but the place has since considerably decayed.

Famous hill station: Every year, at the beginning of the monsoon, the Viceroys of India, and after 1911 the Lieutenant Governors of Bengal, would move, lock, stock and barrel, to **Darjeeling**, situated at an altitude of 7,000ft (2,134 metres), facing the Himalaya.

The British developed Darjeeling into a pleasant resort. In the 1840s tea planting was introduced in the area. Darjeeling "orthodox" tea is now famous and among the most expensive.

Darjeeling is a three-hour drive up a winding road from Bagdogra airport near Siliguri. It first ascends mild slopes covered with tea gardens, then climbs steeply 5,000ft (1,500 metres) over a distance of 20 miles (35 km). It can also be reached from New Jalpaiguri railway station by Toy Train. The ride on the 2ft (600mm) gauge track takes seven hours through almost the same landscape as the road.

Darjeeling is an abrupt change from the plains and Calcutta. The population is Nepali, Lepcha, Tibetan and Bhutia. There is no pollution, there are no crowds, and the pace of life is slow. At the town centre is the Mall, Darjeeling's commercial street, lined with souvenir shops. Photo-stores sell prints of old black-and-white pictures from the early 1900s. The Mall leads to Chaurastha, a square with a bandstand, a bookshop with old books on India and Tibet, and antique shops.

On Observatory Hill is perhaps the oldest built-up site in Darjeeling. A Red Hat Buddhist monastery, Dorjeling, "the place of the thunderbolt" once stood here but was destroyed by the Nepalis in the 19th century. A Shiva temple and an old-fashioned hotel now occupy the site.

On Birch Hill to the north, stands the Shrubbery, the residence of the Governor of West Bengal, and further down along Birch Hill Road, the Himalayan Mountaineering Institute once headed by the late Tenzing Norgay, the Sherpa guide who conquered the Everest with Sir Edmund Hillary on 29 May 1953. A museum displays the equipment used.

The nearby Zoological Park specialises in high-altitude wildlife – yaks, Himalayan black bears, pandas, but it also has four Siberian Tigers. Below, the tea estate of Happy Valley is one of the best in Darjeeling. It can be visited every day except Sunday and Monday.

Tea gardens at Darjeeling.

Dominating the Mall is the **Planters' Club**, which visitors can join and where they can stay on a daily basis. The club becomes very lively on Sunday when planters meet for lunch.

The **Lloyd Botanical Gardens** were laid out in 1878 on land donated by the owners of Lloyd's Bank. They present a collection of Himalayan and Alpine flora. Nearby is the Tibetan Refugee Self-Help Centre with its temple, school, hospital, and a shop selling carpets, textiles and jewellery.

Mount Kanchenjunga can be seen from Observatory Hill, but a much better view of the peak is that from **Tiger Hill**, 6 miles (10 km) south of Darjeeling. Taxis take visitors there to watch the sunrise. On most winter days, the range can be clearly seen, with **Kanchenjunga** (28,208 ft/ 8,598 metres) in the middle, flanked by **Kabru** (24,074 ft/7,338 mwtres) and **Pandim** (21,952ft/6,691 metres).

To the right are the Three Sisters, **Everest** (29,009 ft/8,842 metres), **Makalu** (27,828 ft/8,482 m) and the **Lhotse** (27,887 ft/8,500 metres), and to the east, Tibetan peaks. On the way back the taxis stop at Ghoom. The small Tibetan monastery by the roadside is often mistaken for the nearby **Yiga Cholang Yellow Hat Buddhist Temple**, built in 1875 and hosting a 16-ft (5-metre) statue of Lord Buddha.

Along the top: With a plunging view of the plains of Bangladesh below, **Kurseong** (4,783 ft/1,458 metres), 22 miles (35 km) south of Darjeeling, marks the point where the Toy Train starts running parallel to the road. It goes so slowly here that one can buy from the hawkers alongside.

Branching off at Ghoom, a road leads to **Mirik** 25 miles (40km) southwest of Darjeeling, an artificial lake in a small valley where tourist facilities and mountain river fishing are being introduced. Here the road from Darjeeling runs along the border between India and Nepal.

West of Darjeeling, Dandakphu, a five-hour drive from Darjeeling and situated 80 miles (130 km) from Everest as the crow flies, is a centre for trekking. Dandakphu deserves a visit by itself as it commands a better view of the main Himalayan range than Tiger Hill does since it is closer and higher.

Kalimpong, east of Darjeeling, is reached after a two-hour journey. Driving among forests and tea gardens, the road descends to about 650 ft (200 metres) above sea-level and crosses the one-lane bridge over the Teesta River, near its confluence with the Rangeet at Pashoke, and climbs back to an altitude of 4,078 ft (1,243 metres), finally reaching Kalimpong 32 miles (51 km) from Darjeeling. The Lepchas have a legend about the meeting of the Rangeet and the Teesta. They say the two rivers are lovers who fled the mountains to hide their love. One came down in a straight line, led by a partridge, the other zigzagged, led by a cobra, and they were united at Pashoke.

Kalimpong has a population of 25,000. It was once the starting point for the land route to Tibet. Twice a week, on Wednesday and Saturday, a market, a *haat,* is still held here selling spices, fruit and traditional Tibetan medicines, textiles, wool and musk.

There are two Yellow Hat Buddhist monasteries in Kalimpong. **Tharpa Choling** at Tirpai, the largest one, houses a

Temple at Vishnupur.

248

library of Tibetan manuscripts and *thankas.* **Zang-dog Palrifo Brang Monastery,** on Durpin Dara Hill, is smaller and of more recent construction.

East of Kalimpong, bordering Bhutan, are the **Dooars,** a tea-garden and jungle area little known to tourists. It lies in the valley formed by the lower Teesta River and its tributaries in the foothills of the Himalaya. The Dooars can be reached by metre-gauge railway from New Jalpaiguri and by plane through Cooch Behar or Bagdogra. At **Jaldapara** there is a Wildlife Sanctuary, with one-horned rhinos, elephants, deer, gaur and wild boar. The Tourist Lodge at nearby **Madarihat** is a villa on stilts built entirely in timber. Nearby is Phuntsholing, across the border, in Bhutan.

West of Calcutta: The **Tarakeshwar Temple** built around a black stone *lingam* of Tarakeshwar Babu, an avatar of Shiva, 35 miles (57 km) west of Calcutta, has little architectural interest but is one of West Bengal's most active pilgrimage centres. At Shivaratri in February and Kasta-mela in August, barefooted pilgrims carry Ganga water from Calcutta to the temple in earthen pots decorated with flowers and pour it over the *lingam.*

Further west, **Kamarpukur,** a group of three hamlets surrounded by paddy fields, is religious philosopher Ramakrishna Paramhansdeb's birthplace. There is a temple with a marble statue of Ramakrishna where he was born, and another next to it devoted to Raghubir, an avatar of Rama, Ramakrishna's family deity.

Vishnupur, still further west (125 miles/ 200 km from Calcutta), was the capital of the Malla kings. In the 17th and 18th centuries Vishnupur became an important cultural centre, developing its distinct style of temple architecture, drawing its inspiration from the curved roofs of Bengali village huts, with facades covered with terracotta tiles depicting various scenes from the *Ramayana.*

The most impressive building in Vishnupur is **Rashmancha,** a flat pyramid-like structure resting on the arches of three circumambulatory galleries. Nearby, opposite the Tourist Lodge, is **Dalmadal,** a huge cannon, almost 13ft (4 metres) long, whose boom saved the city from the Mar-

atha armies in 1742. There are temples all over the city. The most remarkable ones are **Kalachand Sri Mandir**; **Shamroy Mandir,** perhaps the finest terracotta temple of Bengal, with scenes from the *Ramayana* and the *Mahabharata*; **Jore Bangla,** covered with tiles depicting naval battles and hunting scenes; **Madan Mohan**; and **Madan Gopal,** resembling a church more than a temple, with its five towers.

North of Vishnupur, and at about 85 miles (136 km) from Calcutta, is **Shantiniketan.** In 1861 Rabindranath Tagore's father founded an ashram here. The poet spent most of his Nobel Prize money to make it an educational institution in 1902. Then, with the help of the Maharaja of Tripura, he upgraded it to the level of a university in 1921. Here the poet revived the traditional Indian way of teaching in the open air, under a tree, in close contact with nature.

At each change of season, and on Shantiniketan foundation day, festivals are held, with dances, songs and plays by Tagore which are performed by students of the university.

Shantiniketan soon became one of the hubs of intellectual life of India. The University's most famous alumnus is probably the late Indira Gandhi.

An annual festival is celebrated near Shantiniketan, at **Kendubilwa,** the birthplace of Jaidev, another great Bengali poet and propagator of Vaishnava philosophy. In mid-January, Bengali bards, known as *bauls,* gather here and hold a four-day non-stop recital of the poet's compositions.

To the north of Shantiniketan are two pilgrimage centres. **Bakreshwar,** 36 miles (58 km) towards the Bihar border, is a place of Shiva and Kali worship, where the space between the goddess's eyebrows is said to have fallen when she was cut in 51 pieces. Bakreshwar is famous as well for its hot sulfurous springs.

The other centre is **Tarapith,** 50 miles (80 km) from Shantiniketan, which is a small village dominated by a temple to Tara, an avatar of Kali, whose third eye is said to have landed here. Festivals are held here several times a year, the most important being Tara and Lakshmi Pujas in October.

SIKKIM, BUDDHIST STATE

Sikkim is among India's smallest states but it is the highest, with peaks above 21,000ft (6,330 metres). Kanchenjunga (28,200ft/ 8,500 metres), the second highest summit in the world, is believed to be the abode of a god of the same name, a fiery character with a red face who wears a crown made of five skulls and rides a snow lion. Legend has it that, at the peak, this god buried five sacred treasures – salt, gems, sacred books, medicines and a suit of armour.

Until the 18th century, the inhabitants of Sikkim were mainly Lepchas, cultivators of Mongol origin who came from Tibet in the 8th century, followed by Bhotias, also from Tibet, sheep and yak breeders who carried on a caravan trade between China and India.

The first kings of Sikkim were the Namgyals descended from the Minyaks of Tibet. Khye-Bumsa, a Namgyal prince helped in the building of the Sa-Kya Monastery in Central Tibet in 1268. He befriended the Lepchas, the original inhabitants, and swore a blood brotherhood with their chief, Thekongtek. When Thekongtek died, the Lepchas turned for leadership to Guru Tashi, Khye-Bumsa's fourth son, who was consecrated king (Chogyal) by three lamas in 1642.

In 1700, the Bhutanese invaded and occupied Sikkim and the young Chogyal, Chador was forced into exile, to return only eight years later, but at the cost of losing Kalimpong and Rhenock.

Chador Namgyal built monasteries at Pemayangtse and Tashiding. He invented the Lepcha alphabet. He was assassinated in 1717 on the orders of his pro-Bhutanese half-sister, Pei Womgmo. His successors had to fight the Bhutanese and the Nepalis with the help of Tibet and China.

The early 19th century saw the East India Company entering the Himalaya with a view to opening up trade with Tibet. In 1814, in the Anglo-Nepal wars, Sikkim sided with the Company and received, as a reward, in 1816, parts of the Nepali Terai. As a friendly gesture, King Tsugphud Namgyal gave the East India Company the hill of Darjeeling for development as a resort. Then, relations soured and after a quarrel over the illegal collection of taxes by the British in Sikkim, the British annexed the Terai and established a protectorate over the kingdom. Since the 18th century there has been a steady flow of Nepalis into Sikkim and they now constitute 75 percent of the population.

When British rule in India ended on 15 August 1947, the government of independent India entered into a similar arrangement with the Chogyal as it had with the British until 1975. Sikkim was not wholly merged with the Indian Union. In 1975, however, the Sikkim Parliament, controlled by the Sikkim National Congress, voted for the incorporation of the kingdom into India. The monarchy was abolished and Sikkim became a state of the Indian Union of 26 April 1975.

The capital, **Gangtok**, "the hill made flat", lies at an altitude of 5,400ft (1,640 metres), facing Kanchenjunga. It is reached by road from Darjeeling, Bagdogra airport (70 miles/110 km), or New Siliguri railway station (77 miles/125 km). Access to Sikkim is restricted, although individuals may visit. The eastern part of the state, the Nathu-la **Gangtok.**

and Jelep-la passes leading to Tibet, and the north, are closed to tourists.

The most important building in Gangtok is the **Chogyal's Palace**, usually closed to visitors except for the Tsuklakhang Royal Chapel, where festivals and ceremonies are held. The palace itself opens once a year, during the last week of December, for the Pong Labsal festival during which lamas wearing masks perform a dance to Kanchenjunga around a banner-pole.

Most of Gangtok's places of interest are in the southern part of the town. The **Research Institute of Tibetology**, built in 1958 by the last Chogyal to preserve Tibetan culture, houses a library of more than 30,000 books on Buddhism, astrology, medicine and philosophy, as well as a collection of *thankas* (Tibetan religious paintings on cloth). The **Deer Park** is set up on the model of a similar one in Sarnath in homage to the Bodhisattva who was reincarnated as a musk deer. The **Orchid Sanctuary** is where over 250 different types of orchids bloom. Nearby is also a **Tibetan Refugee Craft Centre** and the celebrated **Hotel Tashi Delek**.

The **Rumtek Monastery**, 14 miles (23 km) west of Gangtok, belongs to the Yellow Hat Karmapa Sect, a reformist branch of Tantric Buddhism, founded in the 15th century. The monastery, built in the 1960s, is a replica of one in Tibet destroyed at the time of the Chinese takeover.

Further to the west, **Pemayangtse** (1.3 miles/2.1 km) has a **Red Hat Ningma Monastery**, which the original sect built in 1705. Its walls and ceilings bear frescos of gods and demons. A one-day trek leads to **Tashiding Ningma Monastery** (1706) in the north. Another longer trek can be organised from Pemayangtse. As the bridle path approaches Kanchenjunga, the altitude rises to 10,000 ft, then 14,000 ft and terraced rice-paddies and barley fields give way to apple-orchards, then fir trees, and mountain lakes.

Yakshun, reached after six hours, is a small town where the first Chogyal was crowned in 1642. There is also the **Himalayan Montaineering Institute**.

The next stages are **Bakkhin** (5 hours) and **Dzongri** (6 hours) with a close-up view of Kanchenjunga.

Lamas at a Sikkim Tibetan monastery.

ASSAM, BRAHMA'S GIFT

Assam probably derives its name from Ahoms, the name of the dynasty that ruled here from the 13th to the early 19th century. Assam today covers the plain of the Brahmaputra River along its whole course south of the hill state of Arunachal Pradesh and the kingdom of Bhutan, till it turns south into Bangladesh.

The origins of the Assamese and their early history are obscure and mixed with legend. The first legendary king of Assam, then called Kamarupa, was Naraksur, a son of Vishnu and Dharitri (Mother Earth). He invited Brahmins from Gaur in Bengal to settle down in his capital Pragjyotishpur, now Guwahati, to spread their teachings and way of life. Naraksur was, however, killed later on by Vishnu for his unreligious behaviour. His son, Bhagadatta, was defeated by the *Mahabharata* hero, Arjuna. From then on, until the 13th century, Assam was a melting-pot of Aryan, Dravidian and Mongoloid races.

In 1228, the Ahoms, a Buddhist Tai tribe from North Thailand, entered Assam, defeated the Kamrupa ruler and established a kingdom which came to be called Assam, with its capital at Sibsagar. The Ahoms adopted the Hindu Vaishnava religion and the kingdom rapidly became a powerful one. The Mughals sent expeditions to subdue "the rats of Assam", without success, in 1478, 1553 and 1672. Progressively, Assam expanded east, establishing its authority over the Naga kingdom of Cachar, destroying its capital, Dimapur, in 1536. The kingdom was annexed to Assam.

Burmese invasions: Ahom power started weakening in the 17th century. Then, in 1792, Burma invaded Assam. The king, Gaurianath Singh, asked the East India Company for assistance. The Burmese were repelled but came back in 1816. After the Anglo-Burmese war of 1824–26, Burma ceded Assam to the East India Company by the Treaty of Yandaboo, on 26 January 1826.

A revolt, the Khamti rebellion, in 1839, followed by another led by Maniran Barb-

Chital, the swift-footed Indian Spotted Deer.

hander Barua, who was a former spy for the East India Company, were both crushed.

During World War II Assam played a major role, providing a supply route to China and Burma. The Japanese Kohima offensive of 1944 was an attempt to occupy this strategic area both to cut off supplies to China and to open the way to the Indian plains.

Today, Assam's major problem is the growing imbalance between the Assamese and immigrants – Bengali Hindus displaced by partition of the subcontinent in 1947; Bihari Muslims after the 1971 Bangladesh War, and Bangladeshis fleeing poverty. Between 1980 and 1983 there was widespread agitation over this issue and there were attacks on immigrants. ULFA and Bodo separatists stalk the hills today.

During the disturbances Assam was closed to foreign tourists. Access is forbidden by road or rail, although visitors can now fly in.

Main town: The former capital of the Kamrup kings **Guwahati** has a population of 500,000. Its beauty derives from its location on the south bank of the Brahmaputra. On a cliff to the east of the city are **Raj Bhavan**, the governor's residence, and the **Belle Vue Hotel**, commanding a spectacular view of the river both east and west.

The municipal area is immediately below, where the Legislative Assembly, the Public Works Department Bungalow and the Chief Justice's residence are located. Behind these buildings, near the Dighali Pukuri tank, is the **State Museum** housing rare stone sculptures dating from the Kamrupa period.

In and around Guwahati there are several temples. On a small promontory along the river, the **Sulkeswar Janardhan Temple**, consecrated in the 10th century and rebuilt in the 17th, has a statue of the Lord Buddha facing the river, a rare coexistence with a Hindu deity found in very few temples in India.

Nearby, in the middle of the river on **Peacock Island**, is a small Shiva temple that can be reached by boat from the *ghat* next to the High Court. **Navagraha**

Sunrise over the river Brahmaputra, Assam.

Mandir, the Temple of the Nine Planets, east of the city on Chitrachala Hill, is probably the birth site of Guwahati. The temple was an important astrological centre, hence Guwahati's earlier name, Pragjyotishpur, the City of Eastern Astrology, which is the name that will be given to the new capital now under construction near Dispur, the current capital of Assam.

To the south, at the confluence of three mountain streams is the **Vashistha Ashram,** a small temple founded by a sage. It is now both a pilgrimage centre and a picnic spot.

To the West, **Kamakhya Mandir,** Guwahati's most important temple, is on the top of Nichala Hill. The legend goes that to stop Lord Shiva's fearful dance of destruction, provoked by the sight of the dead body of his consort, goddess Shakti, the lesser gods stealthily dismembered and scattered her body far and wide. Shakti's *yoni* (reproductive organ) landed on the top of Nichala Hill, said to be Lord Shiva's *lingam* (phallic symbol).

This temple is one of India's main centres of the tantric cult. In former times 5,000 *devadasis* (temple dancers) were reputedly attached to it and in 1553, it was destroyed by Kalapahar, a Brahmin who had converted to Islam, after being rejected by his caste because of his marriage to a Muslim princess. Its ruins can still be seen around the water tank.

The present structure, with its high beehive spire, bas-reliefs of nymphs, and long turtle-back hall, is typical of Assamese religious architecture.

Outside Guwahati, on the north bank, at Hajo, the **Hayagribha Madadeva Mahdap Temple** is believed by the Bhotias to be the place where the Buddha attained *nirvana.* This temple, located on a hill, was also destroyed by Kalapahar and later rebuilt. It is finely decorated with bas-reliefs of nymphs, elephants and scenes from the *Ramayana.*

Near Hajo is **Pao Mecca,** a mosque on a hill. A pilgrimage here is believed to be the equivalent of one-fourth of a *Haj* to Mecca.

The **Kaziranga National Park** on the south bank of the Brahmaputra, 145 miles (233 km) northeast of Guwahati, the main sanctuary for the Indian one-horned rhinoceros, was declared a game sanctuary in 1926.

The Indian rhinoceros *(Rhinoceros unicornis)* is one of nature's last relics from the prehistoric world. Marco Polo mistook it for the mythical unicorn. Nearing extinction at the turn of the century, it has now been rehabilitated primarily due to efforts in Assam.

There are now about 1,100 rhinos in the park, over half the world's population. At least 20 are killed by poachers each year in spite of stringent protective measures. The horn is removed and sent to Hong Kong or Singapore.

Elephants take visitors early in the morning to a few points from where rhinoceros may be viewed. They may also be watched from viewing towers. The best viewing season is March as the elephant grass has dried and lies flat.

To the northwest, 110 miles (176 km) from Guwahati, is the **Manas Wildlife Sanctuary**, set in thick jungle along the Bhutanese border. One-horned rhinoceros, tigers, gaurs, the pygmy hog and the rare golden langur live there but are hardly seen due to the thick foliage. Above all, however, Manas is known as an angler's paradise where the *mahaseer,* a local variety of carp, abounds.

Further north starts Upper Assam, an oil and tea garden. **Duliajan,** a new well-planned town in the midst of the jungle, is the capital of northeast India's oil country. Assamese oil contributes more than 10 percent of the country's production. Derricks and rigs can be seen standing among tea gardens and paddies. They are an old feature of the Assamese landscape since oil was first struck here in 1867.

Between Jorhat and Duliajan, in and around **Sibsagar,** on the Assam Trunk Road, is the former capital of the Ahoms. Only a few monuments remain: the water tank, along with Devi, Shiva and Vishnu temples; the Rang Ghar, an original oval-shaped pavilion from where kings watched elephant fights; Charaideo, the necropolis of Ahom Kings; and a place at Gurgaon.

In this area there are still scattered isolated village communities where Shan Thai is still spoken and the Buddhist religion is still practised.

Rhinoceros unicornis, the Greater One-horned Indian Rhinoceros.

254

NORTHEASTERN STATES

Meghalaya, "the abode of clouds", south of Assam, was previously part of Assam. It became a separate state of the Indian Union in 1972. It is a hilly region, very foggy in winter, and traffic police dress in fluorescent gear. It is inhabited by three tribal groups, the Garos in the west, the Khasis in the centre, and the Jaintias in the east. They originally constituted independent little township kingdoms, the Seiyams, which the British annexed one by one to British India in the 19th century.

The Garos are of Tibetan stock. They were animists and once practised human sacrifice. In 1848, under a treaty with the British, they agreed to stop displaying skulls in their houses. Archery stakes, a peculiar local form of gambling using arrows, is still a common amusement.

The Khasis are Mon-Khmers related to the Shans of Burma. Their religion, Seng Khasi, is simple: God is everywhere and should not be represented or adored in a specific form. There are no churches, just prayer-halls for specific celebrations.

The Khasis love gold and amber, the two basic components of their jewellery. To commemorate their dead, they erect *mawbynnas,* monoliths of various heights, arranged in groups of three or more that can be seen in most villages. The Pnars, generally known as Jaintias are closely related to the Khasis.

The three tribes have a matrilineal and matrilocal family system. Missionaries in the 19th century converted most of them to Christianity but the old traditions persist, especially their folk dances. A major dance festival, the Shad Suk Myasiem, the Festival of the Joyful Heart, is held in Shillong in April. In November, the Garo 100-drum festival in Tura celebrates the end of the harvesting season.

Shillong, the capital of Assam until 1972 and of Meghalaya since then, lies 60 miles (100 km) south of Guwahati, a three-hour drive through hills covered with pineapple and betel plantations, and pine forests. It passes along the **Umiam Lake**, formed by a recently built dam.

Shillong has been called the "Scotland of the East" because of its climate and its location at an altitude of 4,900ft (1,500 metres). The climate is so temperate that its founder is said to have wanted the town to become the breeding ground for potential British soldiers to serve and police the expanding Raj!

Here the British and rich Bengalis built cottages, a golf course and polo grounds. It is a small city with a market, **Bara Bazaar,** selling Nepali silver and Khasi gold jewellery, spices and textiles. Shillong spreads on hills covered with English-style country houses, the largest being **Raj Bhavan**, the summer residence of the Governor of Assam and Meghalaya, and the **Pinewood Hotel**. Nearby are the **Ward Lake** and the **Botanical Garden**.

Cherrapunji, 35 miles (56 km) to the south, is reputedly the world's wettest place with 45 inches (1,150mm) of rain each year. The most interesting spot however is **Mawphluang**, 15 miles (24 km) further south, a barren and windy plateau covered with monoliths.

On the way back, visitors stop at **Shillong Peak** which offers a fine view of the neighbouring hills, and at the **Elephant Waterfall**.

Access to Garo country is difficult. A road from Shillong is being built but, at present, the only way to reach it is to drive to Guwahati and then southwest to Tura. The villages have retained their traditional architecture and some traditional buildings like the bachelors' dormitory at Rongreng.

Arunachal Pradesh: To the north of Assam lies **Arunachal Pradesh**. Its strategic location on the frontier between India and China kept it isolated for years, even after local headhunters reformed. Only organised groups can get permits.

The area has 600,000 inhabitants divided into 82 Mongoloid and Tibeto-Burmese tribes, the main ones being the Apatanis, the Khamptis, the Padmas and the Miris. Most are Buddhists. At **Tawang**, at an altitude of 10,000ft (3,048 metres) is India's largest Buddhist monastery, over 350 years old, where the 6th Dalai Lama was born. Some areas, like the **Chetak Pass** (14,000ft/4,267 metres), are so remote that an Indian Army

Left, tribal dancer.

expedition recently found a community there that still live in caves and eat their food raw, not having yet discovered fire.

To the east, near the border with China and Burma, the Brahmaputra forms a lake called **Brahmakund**, before entering the plains of Assam. Bathing here is believed to wash away one's sins and Hindus come here by the thousands on Makar Sankranti day in mid-January. At **Ledo** starts the old road to Mandalay, crossing the Burmese border at the Pangso Pass. Beyond this is the "lake of no return" where retreating British troops in 1942 got lost in quicksand.

Nagaland: With similar visitor restrictions to Arunachal Pradesh, Nagaland is inhabited by a variety of Tibeto-Burmese tribes, speaking more than 20 different dialects, the main ones being the Aos, the Angamis and the Konyaks. These Nagas were once headhunters, but the practice was abandoned years ago.

The Cacharis, one of the Naga tribes once established a Hindu kingdom at Dimapur from where they used to raid Assam and Burma. The Ahoms of As-sam established their authority over Cachar at the end of the 17th century, but as soon as Burma invaded Assam in 1816, the Naga raids on the plains were resumed. In 1832, the British, while establishing a road link between Assam and Manipur, encountered the Nagas for the first time. For a few years they made attempts to control them, Naga raids being followed by punitive expeditions. In 1879 the British outpost at Kohima came under Naga siege for a whole month. A state of permanent peace was finally reached in 1889.

During the World War II the Japanese and the Indian National Army launched an attack on Kohima, taking half of the city in 1943. The objective was to reach Dimapur, a vital rail-head for supplies to British Army units in forward areas. Kohima proved to be the furthest point west reached by the Japanese.

In the war against the Japanese, the Nagas were of great help to the allied forces, carrying supplies to the front, evacuating the wounded, and spying behind the enemy lines. After Indian inde-

Monoliths erected by Khasi tribals, Meghalaya.

pendence, some Nagas grouped in a Naga National Council demanded autonomy but soon extremist elements were asking for independence. In November 1975, at Shillong, the Government of India and Naga leaders reached an agreement, whereby the Nagas accepted the Indian Constitution, but there are still occasional outbreaks of violence.

Kohima has a War Cemetery with Commonwealth Graves, and a memorial with a famous inscription: "When you go home tell them of us and say ' For your tomorrow we gave our today.'"

Naga villages are usually perched on hills and are surrounded by a stone wall. One, Barra Basti, is a suburb of Kohima.

To the east of Kohima, at Dimapur, are the remains of the former capital of the Cachar Hills razed by the Ahoms in 1536.

Manipur: This is another former princely state on the Burmese border but it is easier to visit. Meitheis, a Tibeto-Burmese tribe related to the Shans, form 60 percent of the population. They live in the valleys and have developed Jagoi, a Manipuri school of Indian classical dance.

The 29 other tribes, most of them Tibeto-Burmese and now mostly Christian, form one-third of the population and live in the hills. The largest of these groups are the Lotha, the Konyak and the Nagas.

The Manipuris have a reputation as fierce fighters. They excel in such martial arts as the spear dance (*takhousarol*), sword fight (*thanghaicol*) and wrestling (*mukna*). They are also good riders. Polo, the game that spread over the Mughal Empire in the 16th century, is said to have originated here.

As a nation of warriors, Manipuris have a history of conflict with their neighbours in Arakan and other border regions of Burma, which they invaded in 1738. In 1819, the Raja of Manipur who previously had paid tribute to the Burmese crown did not attend the coronation of Burma's new King Bagyidaw. The Burmese sent out a punitive expedition. The Anglo-Burmese War was caused partly by this incursion.

Burma was defeated, and by the Treaty of Yandaboo, on 24 February 1826, recognised British sovereignty over Mani-

Manipuri dancers.

pur. After years of relative peace, a revolt took place in 1891 during which the British chief commissioner of Assam was killed. The rising was crushed and its leader, Tikenderjit Singh, the Maharaja's brother, hanged. There was trouble again in 1930, when a self-styled prophet, Jadonang, announced the imminent departure of the British. He was executed and the priestess of his cult, Rani Gaidiniliou, then aged 17, was sentenced to life imprisonment. She was released when India gained independence.

In 1944, the Indian National Army and the Japanese put Imphal under siege from March to June. They were repulsed and in March 1945, General Slim's 14th Army marched to Mandalay from the Manipur hills. In 1949 Manipur became Union Territory and a fully fledged State of the Indian Union in 1972.

Imphal, the capital, can be reached by road from Kohima after a 80-mile (130-km) drive along the famous road to Mandalay. It has two war cemeteries, a museum displaying tribal artifacts, Kwairamb Bazaar, a women's market, the Rajah's Palace, the Royal Polo Grounds and, nearby at Langthabal, the Raja's Summer Palace. Tribes live in the Ukhrul area, some 35 miles (60 km) to the northeast, a restricted area in view of occasional insurgency.

Mizoram and Tripura: The former Lushai Hills District, **Mizoram** is bordered by Bangladesh on one side and Burma on the other. Related to the Shan, Mizos are a group of tribes (Lushais, Hmars, Pawis) that came relatively recently to India. They started raiding tea plantations in 1871. The British retaliated and established control over the area in 1872, but could not establish peace until 1892.

The British then introduced the Inner Line system. Only missionaries were allowed through. As a result, 95 percent of the population is Christian and literacy has reached 86 percent in some tribes. At the time of Indian independence Mizoram became a Union Territory and was granted full statehood in 1987.

Tripura is the former princely state of Tipperah. The population, mostly of Tibeto–Burmese origin, took up Vaishnava Hinduism early, and was ruled by rajas until Indian independence. Other major ethnic groups in Tripura are the Kukis, related to the Shans of Burma, Chakmas, Moghs, Lusharis and Riangs.

Tripura had been permanently at war with her neighbours when the British, taking advantage of a feud between Maharajah Krishna Manikya and the Nawabs of Bengal, intervened and established a protectorate.

After independence, Tripura joined the Indian Union in 1949 and became a State in 1972. There is no visitor access.

Agartala is a small town of 60,000 people, surrounded by hills on three sides, with a palace erected in 1940 by Maharaja Bikram, a philanthropist who helped Rabindranath Tagore finance the Shantiniketan University in Bengal. The palace set in "Mughal Gardens" is now the State Assembly House. It is said that the old cannons on display used to be fired in salute once a year, until the 16th century, when 1,000 human sacrifices were held in Agartala. In Udaipur, the ancient capital of Tripura, is a ruined temple, **Tripura Sundari**.

Tribals from Madhya Pradesh.

TEA

Chinese tradition points to India as the original home of tea. A Brahmin, Dharma, went as a missionary to China. He was so tired that he fell asleep on reaching his destination. When he awoke, he was so angry at his own weakness that he tore out his eyebrows. The hair took root and became tea plants, the leaves of which he ate and fell into meditation.

Tea had been identified in Assam by English travellers as early as in the last years of the 18th century. When the East Indian Company's monopoly of importing tea into Britain from China was abolished in 1823, the Honourable Company decided to look into the possibility of growing tea in India.

Expeditions were sent to Assam which confirmed previous reports. In 1826, after the Burmese wars, the Company's troops brought back a tea bush as evidence of the existence of tea in the area. Then, on Christmas Eve, 1844, the Governor General, Lord Bentinck, officially announced the discovery of tea in India and called for the development of the industry. Production started in Assam in 1836, in Bengal in 1839, and in the Nilgiris in the south, in 1863. Plantations were introduced into the Darjeeling area in the early 1840s. The bushes were not indigenous. They had been smuggled out of China.

The first Indian teas were of low quality and Chinese experts were brought to Assam to supervise the processing of tea leaves. India soon became a major grower and, by 1900, was supplying Britain with 150 million pounds of tea against 15 million brought from China.

Today, India is the world's largest producer of the fragrant leaf, with an output of 635,000 tonnes against a total world production of 2 million tonnes. India's area under tea (400,000 hectares) is the largest in the world. More than half of Indian tea is grown in Assam, one fourth in West Bengal and about a fifth in the southern Nilgiris.

There are two sorts of Indian tea. CTC tea, the most common, takes its name from the Crush-Tear-Cool process in which the leaf is broken. It constitutes 75 percent of the total output. It gives a strong liquid of dark colour. Most CTC production is for the home market.

"Orthodox" teas have a lighter colour (they are said to be "bright") and yield a weaker liquid: one kilo makes 350 cups against 500 for CTC tea. Most of the Orthodox tea is exported, the best varieties being Darjeeling and Assam Golden Flower Orange Pekoe.

Some 60 percent of the Indian production is sold through auctions, including all export teas. Auction centres exist at Guwahati, in Assam; at Cochin, Coimbatore and Coonoor, in the south; at Siliguri and Calcutta, in West Bengal. The largest centre is the one in Calcutta run by the firm of J. Thomas. The centre has two auction rooms (one for the home market, the other for exports), and the largest tea tasting room in the world, where purchasing agents can taste all possible varieties of tea available in West Bengal and Assam.

From having been consumed only by the hill tribes 150 years ago, tea has become the national drink of India. However, on average, each cup of tea consumed by an Indian is matched by approximately six consumed by an Englishman.

Tea gardens can be easily visited in Darjeeling and in the south, where the whole process of tea preparation can be observed. ∎

Tea pickers, Darjeeling.

BOMBAY – BUSY AND BURSTING

The story of Bombay city is a fascinating rags to riches one, and so urbanised has the city become that visitors often forget that they are on an island. From obscure, humble beginnings as a set of seven small islands with tidal creeks and marshes between them, the city has risen to such eminence that, today, it is India's most important commercial and industrial centre. The seven islands have been merged by land reclamation into one.

Preceding pages: Ganesh festival at Chowpatti Beach, Bombay. **Left**, Victoria Terminus. **Below**, Terminus detail.

Today Bombay is booming. Home to the wealthy and the glamorous, it has long been India's Hollywood ("Bollywood"), producing more films each year than any other city in the world. Nowadays it is also the home of India's own fast-growing satellite and television industries.

Like all big cities, Bombay has its seamy side, its slums and its overcrowding, the foothills of poverty on which are built towering skyscrapers. And like all success stories, there have been chapters of

intrigue, violence, happiness and calm, and the struggles of the pre-independence years, when Bombay became the political capital of nationalist India.

The Good Bay: Bombay is part of India's beautiful west coast that runs down from Gujarat, through Bombay to Goa, Karnataka and Kerala. South of Bombay, narrow beaches and plains sweep up into the forested hills of the Western Ghats. The city boasts a perfect natural harbour which was developed by the British and, once the Suez Canal opened in the 19th century, the port of Bombay never knew a dull moment. Today it handles more than 40 percent of India's maritime trade.

Bombay summers are hot and humid, and the winters cool, the sea breeze bringing relief throughout the year. The monsoon that hits the coast between June and September brings down curtains of heavy rain which obscure the view and flood the roads, and when they occasionally part in patches some spectacular sunsets are to be seen over the sea.

Today Bombay's seven islands survive only as names of localities like Colaba, Mahim, Mazgaon, Parel, Worli, Girgaum and Dongri. The tidal swamps have all been reclaimed and, later, even large expanses of the open sea have been filled in, for example, the Churchgate and Nariman Point Reclamations.

The name Bombay (*Mumbai* in the local language, Marathi) is said to be derived from the name of the local deity, Mumba Devi, whose temple, though rebuilt and re-located, still stands. The Portuguese predecessors of the British preferred to think of the name as *Bom Baim,* the Good Bay, an equally apt name for this excellent port. The city now stretches 14 miles (22 km) into the Arabian Sea to its south, west and east.

The maximum width of the composite island that now constitutes metropolitan Bombay is no more than 3 miles (5 km). Into this narrow strip are squeezed the majority of Bombay's 12½ million people, its major business and commercial establishments, its docks and warehouses, and much of its industry – including almost the whole of its major textile industry which alone employs some 40–50,000 workers.

A melting pot: Bombay is home to all Indian creeds and cultures. The Bombay Municipal Corporation provides primary and secondary education in at least 10 languages, including English. Bombay has developed a *lingua franca* entirely peculiar to itself – "Bombay Hindustani", which regular Hindi/Urdu speakers find rather comic. It is often caricatured in Indian films and plays.

Local Muslim nawabs ruled this region for some time, but handed it over to the Portuguese in 1534 in exchange for support against the Mughals. This was the beginning of Bombay's large Christian (largely Roman Catholic) population and its numerous churches, which led to two separate areas in Bombay coming to be known as "Portuguese Church".

Until recently, a number of the older churches retained their Portuguese facades, but most of these have been lost to modernisation. **St Andrew's** in the suburb of Bandra is a fine example of an original, Portuguese-style facade.

There are also minor remains of Portuguese fortifications both on the main island and the much larger island of Salsette north of the city and now mostly incorporated in Greater Bombay. (Also being developed is a New Bombay on the mainland, a few miles across Bombay harbour.) At Bassein (Vasai is the actual name), there are ruins of a Portuguese walled settlement which include a large church. Bassein is some 30 miles (50 km) from Bombay and is easily accessible by local train and bus.

In 1662 Charles II of England married Catherine of Braganza, a Portuguese princess. As part of the dowry, the British crown received the islands of Bombay. They were leased to the British East India Company in 1668 at the princely rent of $10 per annum.

This company of merchant-adventurers had for some time felt the need for an additional west-coast port, to supplement and ultimately to supplant Surat in Gujarat. Far-sighted governors of this period, like Gerald Augiers, began the construction of the city and harbour, inviting the settlement of Gujarati merchants and Parsi, Muslim and Hindu manufacturers and trad-

Waterfront, with the Taj Hotel (left) and Gateway of India (right).

ers to help develop the city. This led to the settlement of all these communities in Bombay.

Gujaratis from the state north of Bombay constitute a very substantial proportion of the city's population, and especially of its business community. Fleeing persecution in Persia, the Parsis migrated to Gujarat and moved to Bombay in large numbers in the 17th century. Being Zoroastrians, they built Fire Temples and a "Tower of Silence" on Malabar Hill.

The tower is an isolated facility for the disposal of the dead by exposure to the elements and vultures (*dokhura*). Burial and cremation are ruled out for Zoroastrians, since they hold both fire and earth sacred. However, where *dokhura* facilities are not available, modern Parsis permit burial.

Another ancient but miniscule minority Indian community, that of the Jews, is also based in Bombay. Seven synagogues in the city still serve their dwindling numbers. The house of the Sassoons, Iraqi in origin and no longer Bombay-based since the 1940s, has also left its mark through endowments for educational and charitable purposes. Bombay still has a Sassoon Dock (now used by the fishing fleet) and a Sassoon Library.

The Hindu population of Bombay is largely Maharashtrian though most non-Maharashtrian Bombayites are also Hindus, with a fair number of Jains among the Gujaratis, and also neo-Buddhists among the ex-untouchables.

The Muslims of Bombay, like the Parsis and Gujaratis, have merged with the rest in the melting pot of urban culture. Yet there are areas in Bombay where their unique contributions to Indian life can still be observed and enjoyed. On Mohammed Ali Road, one can get kababs rolled up in *rotis* (unleavened bread) or hot *jalebi* sweets, at all hours.

The slow transformation of the swampy islands during the 17th and 18th centuries gave way in the 19th century to rapid changes. In 1858, the Honourable East India Company returned the islands to the British crown. In the 1850s came the "Fire Carriage", (steam engine) and by the end of the century Bombay was linked with

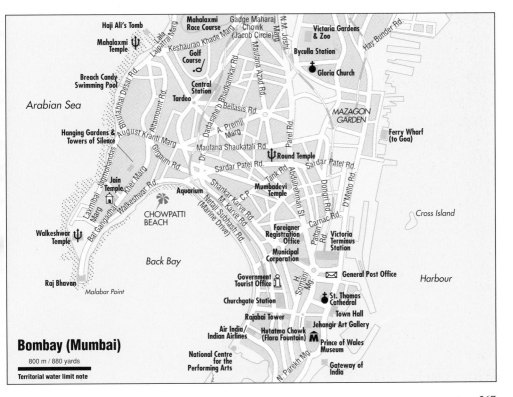

Bombay (Mumbai)

800 m / 880 yards

Territorial water limit note

central and northern India by the Great Indian Peninsular Railway, and, some time later, with eastern India too. During this period, Bombay became a most important "cotton-polis", Raw cotton from Gujarat was shipped to Lancashire, spun and woven into cloth, and brought back to Bombay for sale all over the country. Notwithstanding this, Bombay's cotton textile industry was established in this period, thanks to the grit and persistence of Bombay's entrepreneurs.

The outbreak of the American Civil War in 1861 and the opening of the Suez Canal gave further impetus to cotton exports from India. During the cotton boom, Bombay was given a facelift. The newfound wealth was poured into the construction of impressive commercial and civic buildings in the second half of the 19th century.

The **Afghan Memorial Church** of St John the Evangelist is in the Colaba area, which is the long arm of South Bombay that stretches into the sea. The church was established in 1847 and consecrated 11 years later as a memorial to those who fell in the First Afghan War. It is a lovely piece of architecture with Gothic arches and stained-glass windows.

The **Old Secretariat** and the **Public Works Department Secretariat** were designed and built by Colonel Orel Henry St Clair Wilkins during 1867–74, and are High Victorian Gothic in style.

The building of the **University Hall** and **Elphinstone College**, with its central tower and canopied balconies, was funded by Sir Cowasjee Jehangir Readymoney and, along with the Library and Clock Tower (now called **Rajabai Tower**), was completed in 1878.

The **School of Art** was also built at this time. Rudyard Kipling was born and spent his early years here. His father, John Lockwood Kipling, was principal of the school and, under his guidance many local artisans received training and prepared sculptured panels and motifs to adorn the buildings that were then being built in Bombay.

Crawford Market, designed by William Emerson, has bas-reliefs by J.L. Kipling. Today, the reliefs are hardly no-

The celebrated Bombay dabbawallas.

ticed as they stand high above the crowd and bustle of this market area.

Flora Fountain stands in another crowded square at the heart of the Fort area, now called **Hutatma Chowk** (Martyrs' Square). The fountain is a landmark in itself and was erected in honour of the Governor, Sir Henry Bartle Edward Frere, who built new Bombay in the 1860s. The memorial that has given the square its new name – Hutatma – commemorates those who lost their lives in the cause of setting up a separate Maharashtra state in the Indian Union. This has traditionally been the business centre of Bombay, with major banks and airline offices.

The **Fort** (downtown) area in South Bombay derives its name from the fact that the area fell within the former walled city, of which only a small fragment survives as part of the eastern boundary wall of **St. George's Hospital**.

Memories of this walled area were preserved in such names as Churchgate, Bazaargate and Rampart Row, all renamed in recent years. Within the Fort was the Castle, the headquarters of the Bombay Government. Until India became independent, government orders were issued as from "Bombay Castle", though the castle itself had long ceased to exist.

The finest High Victorian Gothic structure in Bombay, designed by Frederick William Stevens, is **Victoria Terminus** (V.T.) and the adjoining headquarters building of the **Central Railway**, known originally as the Great Indian Peninsular Railway. It was built over 1878-87. The structure is of yellow sandstone and granite combined with polychromatic stones and blue-gray basalt for decorations in the interior.

The **Municipal Corporation Building** opposite V.T. is another Stevens masterpiece, especially the domed central staircase and the cuspated arches in the arcaded stories. The imposing **Western Railway Central** office building at Churchgate, built in grey-blue basalt with bands of white in 1890 has towers with oriental domes.

The foundation stone of the **Prince of Wales Museum** was laid by George V in 1905 during his visit to India as Prince of

Bombay's red light district.

Wales. George Wittet designed this building with its dome and other oriental features in blue-grey basalt and yellow sandstone. The museum contains some excellent examples of Indian miniature painting of the Mughal and Rajasthan Schools. There are also collections of artifacts of jade and chinaware. The museum is one of the most important in India.

Another Wittet building of note is the **General Post Office** near V.T. Wittet also left his mark in the **Ballard Estate** area, where, however, his office buildings reflect similar 19th-century structures in London.

George Wittet will be remembered most, however, for his **Gateway of India** on the waterfront at Apollo Bunder. It was conceived as a triumphal arch to commemorate the visit of George V and Queen Mary for the Delhi Darbar in 1911. The honey-coloured basalt of the arch, facing the sea, catches the light of the rising and setting sun and changes from shades of gold to orange and pink. It was through this arch that the last of the British troops left India by sea.

While Bombay city boasts no ancient or even medieval monuments, an hour's ride away by motor launch, within the waters of the harbour, is the island of **Gharapuri** or **Elephanta,** site of a magnificent series of rock-cut cave temples with large sculptured interiors. These were excavated in the 7th and 8th centuries. The centrepiece is a massive 18-ft (5-metre) three-headed bust of Shiva, representing his manifestations as Creator, Preserver and Destroyer. The Portuguese called the island Elephanta after a massive elephant sculpture that once stood in one of the excavated courtyards there. It now stands in the garden of the Bombay city zoo.

Some 25 miles (40 km) from the Fort area, near Borivali station of the Western Railway suburban line, is a National Park within which lie the 2nd-century Buddhist hill caves of **Kanheri**. Sculpture here, too, is on a large scale and matches that of the better known Ajanta and Ellora caves in eastern Maharashtra.

Surrounded as it is on three sides by the sea, life in Bombay draws much of its character from the beaches, seaside prom-

Three-headed Shiva, Elephanta Island.

enades and coastline. Beyond the central city are the beaches of **Juhu, Versova, Madh Island, Marve, Manori** and **Gorai**, one-time secluded seaside resorts. Today, Juhu is crowded with residential apartments, its beach swarming with picnickers and hawkers.

Gillian Tindall called her historical study of Bombay *City of Gold* and, certainly, the pursuit of wealth is a major occupation here. But Bombayites do not forget the "temples of their gods" though, perhaps, as often as not, in pursuit of equally material aims. Appropriately, a major shrine near the racecourse is dedicated to Mahalakshmi, goddess of wealth and prosperity.

The cosmopolitan Bombayite believes in the efficacy of offerings at holy shrines, whether of their own religion or of others. Peoples of all faiths queue up patiently in their thousands on fixed days of the week to make their offerings, whether at the tomb of the Muslim saint, Haji Ali, on the tidal island off the shore opposite the racecourse at Mahalakshmi; or for the Wednesday "Novenas" at St Michael's Church at Mahim; or at the Siddhivinayak Temple at Prabhadevi on Tuesdays.

Bandra Fair, in celebration of the feast of St Mary, is centred on an image of St Mary at the Mount Mary Shrine and attracts thousands of seekers of succour and favours – with no particular distinction of caste or creed.

Marine Drive (otherwise known as Netaji Subhash Road) links Malabar Hill to Fort and Colaba. This long gracefully curving road along the buttressed seacoast, viewed from the Hanging Gardens on Malabar Hill or the high-rise buildings at Nariman Point, provides at night a view of the glittering Queen's Necklace, and, by day and night, a panorama of Bombay's skyline.

Along Marine Drive runs a wide sidewalk, ideal for the early morning jogger, evening walker and late night stroller. During the monsoons the turbulent waves splash over the parapets.

Chowpatti, at the north end of Marine Drive, is a stretch of sandy beach. In the evenings, it is crowded with people enjoying the cool sea breeze and stalls selling delicious Bombay *bhelpuri* and other snacks. Chowpatti is famous also for its *kulfi* and ice creams. During the Ganesh Chaturthi festival, processions from the city meet here with images of Ganesh, which are then immersed in the sea.

The **Taraporevala Aquarium** is also on Marine Drive. It has a good collection of tropical fish. More disturbing, however, is the fish-and-chips stall just outside the main building.

Feeding the millions: With more than 3 million people pouring into metropolitan Bombay, especially the southern half of the island, every day by the three local railway lines and by bus, cab and private car, for work and business, there is an enormous demand for soft drinks, snacks and quick lunches which Bombay was geared to meet long before the newfangled fast food establishments were thought of. Long queues form at food kiosks and restaurants for favourite low-cost meals, but everything, from *vada sambar* or *biryani* in little roadside restaurants to Mandarin Chinese and all varieties of western cuisine are available.

However, the large numbers of office goers prefer a warm, home-cooked lunch, and this is made possible by Bombay's unique city-wide organisation of *dabbawallas*. These *dhoti*-clad, Gandhi-capped men collect *dabbas* ("ever-hot" lunchboxes) from residences early in the forenoon.

Each is identified as to ownership and locations (from and to) by markings decipherable by the *dabbawallas* alone, even the illiterate among them. These are assembled and sorted by destination and carried off by local train. At various stations appropriate batches of *dabbas* are handed to other teams for delivery. In the afternoon, the process is reversed.

The heat and rush of the day does not cramp the style of Bombayites. Once the day's work is done, they can be seen walking the gardens, children riding on horses at the old bandstand, and pavement hawkers doing their evening business. Cinema and theatre halls are crowded; the sea-faces from Marine Drive to Juhu come alive. The city sleeps late. The streets are never empty. As some people move homewards in cars, others lay out their humble beds on the pavements and try to catch a good night's sleep.

MAHARASHTRA, SERMONS IN STONES

Bombay's pre-eminence may lead you to think that it represents the soul of Maharashtra. But the city is only Maharashtra's avaricious heart; its soul, true to Hindu belief, lies south of it, nearer its navel.

Bombay, because it is the commercial centre of the country, contains a cross-section of India's diverse population. But its Maharashtrian element is very cross; it feels done out of the riches which should rightfully belong to "sons of the soil". This theory reasserts itself at times of economic stress. Its principal beneficiary is a local political party, the Shiv Sena, which makes the issue its central plank. The rest of Maharashtra, secure in its parochial cohesiveness, does not bother about the Sena at all.

The Sena is named after the 17th century Maratha warrior Shivaji, who was anti-imperialist when the empire-builders were the Mughals. It's no wonder then that there is a Hindu-Muslim communal edge to much of the politics of the area.

In Puné you will find the proprietary pride in Shivaji even more pronounced. There are those who feel that this constant harking back to a glorious past ensures a less than glorious present, that the Maharashtrians' relative lack of initiative and entrepreneurship is partly a result of this habit of lapsing into the past.

But this glorious past has left behind a treasure for the visitor. The best approach is to use five cities (Puné, Kolhapur, Aurangabad, Nagpur and Nasik) as bases for exploratory trips to nearby places of interest. If you *have* to choose only one, choose Aurangabad: the caves of Ajanta and Ellora offer riches comparable to those of the Taj Mahal.

Once called Poona by the British, **Puné** has now reclaimed its original Marathi name. It is 105 miles (170 km) from Bombay, approachable by road, rail or air. The air journey is short (around half an hour) and gives a magical view of Bombay's vast expanse of lights, especially at night on the return route from Puné. Below, beyond the flash of the Osho Commune – known by wags as "Club Meditation",

you can sometimes make out the race-course lights during the thoroughbred racing season. Both Puné and Bombay have celebrated tracks.

The road journey from Bombay over the Western Ghats is marked by hair-raising bends over steep inclines, in the company of truck-convoys. The roads are good; your driver had better be too.

The best journey is undoubtedly by one of the fast trains, especially *The Deccan Queen,* which takes four hours each way through many mountain tunnels and past scenic vistas. The journey is particularly picturesque, if a little wet, during the monsoon when the hills are green and small waterfalls cascade down them.

Puné, once the capital of the Maratha Empire and captured by the British at the Battle of Koregaon in 1818, was developed in the 18th century along the lines of an archetypal army town. The British passion for order – though passion's not quite the word for such meticulousness – resulted in the usual army cantonment areas, uncluttered and well-served by broad roads, in distinct contrast to the busy and crowded old city.

Puné became the centre of many Hindu social reform movements; it also became for a time, during the heyday of Bal Gangadhar Tilak, the epicentre of India's independence movement. Rapid industrialisation has changed its character considerably; its clutter now spares no one; even then a certain old-world charm occasionally asserts itself.

Well worth a visit in Puné is the **Raja Kelkar Museum,** the private collection of Dinkar Kelkar. Its focus is on traditional Indian arts. It has 36 sections which include carved palace and temple doors, 2,000-year-old excavated pottery, traditional Indian lamps, and 17th-century miniature paintings. Of special interest are a collection of brass nutcrackers (some of them explicitly erotic) and brass padlocks (including a scorpion-shaped padlock whose: "pincers" lock together). Mr Kelkar, a benign if loquacious old gentleman, often greets visitors. His collection is so large that the exhibits have to be shown by rotation.

The **Agha Khan Palace**, with its Italianate arches and spacious well-mannered lawns, was an unlikely place for a prison, but at one time the British interned Mahatma Gandhi and his wife Kasturba here along with other leaders of the Congress Party. Kasturba died in the palace and a memorial has been erected in the grounds.

Mahadji Scindia, one of the Maratha ruling princes, constructed the small blackstone Shiva temple **Shinde Chhatri** in the 18th century. His descendant, Madhavrao II, built an annex in Mahadji's memory. But his architectural inspiration was not Indian, like Mahadji's, but Southern European. The contrast in the two styles is a kind of monument to the assimilative powers of Indian culture.

Mahadji's *samadhi* (mausoleum) stands across a courtyard. There is a likeness of him in silver, topped by a flame-coloured turban. A nearby sign, excessively haughty, warns you not to open an umbrella as that would be insulting to Scindia's memory.

Maratha forts and temples: Simha Gad, whose literal translation is fortress of the lion, stands on a hilltop 15 miles (25 km) from Puné. Around 300 years ago Shivaji's right-hand-man, General Tanaji Malsure, with a group of trusted lieutenants, scaled its sheer precipice with the help of ropes and giant lizards especially trained for the purpose. Shivaji won the fortress but lost his general, killed during the action. Today, most of the fort's battlements are overgrown with weeds.

Other Shivaji forts within easy reach of Puné are **Rajgadh**, **Torna**, **Purander** and **Shivneri**.

Shanwarwada, built in 1736, was once the palace of the Peshwa rulers who succeeded to Shivaji's empire, after having served it as ministers. A massive fire in 1827 destroyed most of the palace, leaving behind only its old fortified walls, large brass-studded gates, 18th century lotus pools, and the elaborate foundations of the palace.

The 8th-century rock-cut **Temple of Pataleshwar** stands in the middle of Puné. It has been carved into a single boulder of awe-inspiring size. The temple is used by worshippers even today.

There are many other fine temples in Puné, the best known, the **Parvati Tem-**

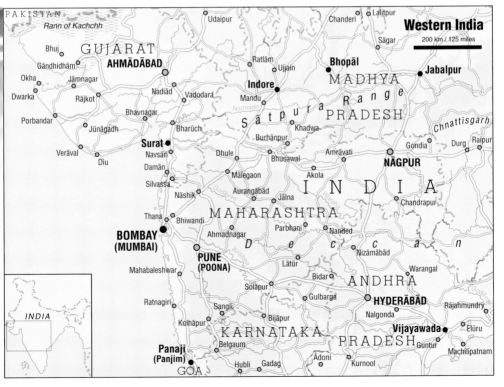

ple on a hilltop on the outskirts of the city. This was once the private shrine of Peshwa rulers. A Muslim shrine, the **Qamarali Darvesh**, contains a celebrated "levitating" stone, which you might be tempted to investigate.

From Puné you can go to hill resorts, which were called hill stations because the British always "stationed" themselves, even when they were on holiday. Notable amongst these are **Lonavala** (45 miles/70 km from Puné).

Three miles (5 km) away is an even smaller and quieter hill station called **Khandala**. **Mahableshwar** (60 miles/100 km) and **Panchgani** (55 miles/90 km) are cool hill stations which lend themselves to quiet walks amidst unspoilt natural beauty and panoramic views. Horse-riding is *de rigueur;* horses and ponies of varying spirit are available on hire.

Matheran (72 miles/116 km from Puné), accessible also from Bombay from which it is only 58 miles (94 km), has the added attraction of being inaccessible to automobiles, prohibited by law. You either walk the last 12 miles (20 km) up a steep hill or take a toy-train from Neral. (It's a *slow* toy-train, taking 1½ hours.)

Kolhapur: One of the most important pilgrimage centres in Maharashtra is Kolhapur (245 miles/395 km from Bombay). In fact, it's often called **Dakshina Kashi** (the Benares of the South). Not unexpectedly, it has many temples, the one held in highest esteem being the **Mahalaxmi Temple** (also called **Ambabai Temple**), built in the 9th century. To the east of the city is **Kotiteerth**, a temple of Mahadev in the centre of a wide expanse of water.

Kolhapur was also the capital of a former princely state and therefore has some splendid palaces and royal homes. These include an **Old Palace** of the 18th century and a **New Palace** with an octagonal clock tower and museum. There is also **Shalini Palace**, an example of Indo-Saracenic architecture.

Kolhapur, is also known for its wrestlers (it boasts a stadium which can hold 20,000 people) and is *the* place if you are looking for Kolhapur *chappals* (sandals).

Panhala, 9 miles (15 km) away, is not

Ellora Caves

only a hill station but is also of historical interest, being the scene of a famous Shivaji escape. **Sangli**, 30 miles (50 km) away, was also the capital of a former principality. It has a well-known museum and a fine temple. **Ratnagiri**, 80 miles (125 km) from Kolhapur, is the gateway to the beaches of Southern Konkan. Ratnagiri itself has a fine beach but is better known for its succulent Alphonso mangoes, indisputably the best in India. **Ganpatipule**, 95 miles (155 km) from Kolhapur, is an old pilgrimage centre, now being developed as a major beach resort. **Pandharpur** (125 miles/200 km) draws pilgrims from all over Maharashtra to its famous **Shrine of Vithal** in July and August each year. **Sholapur** (140 miles/225 km) is now a teeming textile town. It has a formidable fort as well as a temple in the middle of an expanse of water.

Monuments and caves: As its name suggests, **Aurangabad** (230 miles/370 km from Bombay) has a strong Muslim flavour. This dates back from the time of the Mughal Emperor Aurangzeb. The mausoleum of Aurangzeb's Begum (**Bibi ka Maqbara**), may seem familiar. It should be: it was intended to be a replica of the Taj Mahal, but suffers from all the defects of second-hand art.

Aurangabad also has a Buddhist legacy in its caves. Just 1½ miles (3 km) behind the Bibi ka Maqbara, there are 12 caves which were excavated between the 3rd and 11th century AD. The most interesting are caves 3, 6 and 7. Carry a torch.

The **Sunehri Maha** (the golden palace) and **Panchakki**, an old water-mill, were both built by Malik Amber.

At **Daulatabad** (9 miles/15 km from Aurangabad) is a massive hilltop fort, often described as totally impregnable. Conquerors usually bribed the sentry. Many other monuments from the Mughal era survive here.

Ellora, 15 miles (25 km) away from Aurangabad, has 34 rock-cut temples representing the Buddhist, Jain and Hindu Brahmanic faiths. Amongst the most important historical monuments in India, these caves were scooped out of the rocks 10 centuries ago. The term "cave temple" cannot convey the magnitude of the Ellora achievement. The feat could be compared to carving a whole cathedral out of solid rock, interior and exterior.

All the caves are man-made. The artists who flocked to these remote areas from vast distances, literally hammered monuments out of rock. Their technique needed a profound knowledge of rock formations and their structure. The work was usually started from the top of the temple and moved downwards to eliminate the need for scaffolding.

The centrepiece at Ellora is the **Kailash Temple**. Its architects were not modest about their ambitions; Kailash is after all the mythical mountain where the gods live. The total area scooped out is nearly 70,000 sq. ft (6,500 sq. metres), while the 100-ft-high (30-metre) shrine itself occupies an area of about 18,300 sq. ft (1,700 sq. metres). In its galleries are recreated various scenes from Shiva myths. One of them represents the eternal struggle between the forces of evil represented by Ravana, the demon king of Sri Lanka, and the forces of good represented by Shiva and Parvati. Ravana violently rocks the throne of Shiva and Parvati, but Shiva and Parvati sit calm and unimpressed.

Although the carvings at Ellora are of three religions, the structures are often similar, probably due to the demands of the rock formations. Within, differences are discernible: the Jain caves are ascetic; the Buddhist caves, inspired by Buddhism's 2nd-century attempt at populism, show an austere richness.

The 30 Buddhist caves of **Ajanta**, 60 miles (100 km) from Aurangabad, not only contain sculptures but remarkably preserved frescos as well. The Ajanta caves are secluded and were discovered accidentally only in the 19th century. This probably explains why the monuments escaped the depredations of invading armies.

Buddhism was a religion of denial. That's how Gautama Buddha saw it; he was against the worshipping of idols and forbade his followers from making images of himself. He did not even favour the wearing of colourful clothing or any ornamentation which might excite desire.

After the Buddha's death, as Buddhism spread wider, its preachers felt the need for giving a representational form to its teachings. Buddhist monks began to tell stories of Buddha's earlier incarnations; paintings and sculptures of these stories began to proliferate. Thus began the process of Buddhism acquiring some of the sensuousness of Hinduism.

The frescos and sculptures of Ajanta are from that heady period and the westerner, used to the idea of religion being essentially a negation of the senses, will be startled by the voluptuousness of much of the imagery. The most important caves are 1, 2, 9, 10, 16, 17, 19, 21 and 26.

Other destinations: Nagpur was the capital of the Bhosle branch of the Maratha Empire. Its imperial glory is now revived every winter when today's rulers – cabinet ministers and elected representatives – move from Bombay to this winter capital of Maharashtra. Nagpur derives additional satisfaction from being located at the geographical centre of India. It is also famous for being orange-growing country.

Ramtek, which is 165 miles/265 km from Nagpur, is so named because Rama, the popular incarnation of Lord Vishnu, stopped here with his wife Sita and brother Lakshman when they were banished from Ayodhya.

Wardha, which is 45 miles (75 km) from Nagpur, is the alighting point for **Sevagram** and **Paunar**. The former is the village where Mahatma Gandhi lived in an ashram. This has been well-preserved and is a place of modern pilgrimage. Paunar was made famous by one of Gandhi's disciples, Acharya Vinoba Bhave, who lived and died there.

Nagzira, 70 miles (115 km) from Nagpur, is a game sanctuary in a beautiful setting. The Nagzira forests have two all-year-round water tanks which provide an ideal habitat for wildlife

Nawegaon National Park, 85 miles (135 km) from Nagpur, is a forest rich in wildlife. It has an 18th century artificial lake. The man who made it has been deified as Kolasur Dev and his shrine lies by the lake.

Chandrapur, 100 miles (160 km) from Nagpur boasts a fort and several temples. From Chandrapur you can head for Tadoba, undoubtedly Maharashtra's best known sanctuary. In the park is a lake held to be sacred by the tribals. Its sanctity

must suit the crocodiles which thrive in it in large numbers.

Chikalda 135 miles (220 km) from Nagpur is the hill station of the region. It is approached through a thick jungle teeming with wildlife.

Nasik is a holy city; it stands on the banks of the river Godavari, venerated by Hindus. Two thousand temples and many bathing ghats testify to its sanctity. An incident in the *Ramayana* features Nasik: when Lakshman, Rama's younger brother, tiring of the efforts of the demon Shoorpanakha to persuade him to marry her, chopped off her nose, it fell where Nasik now stands.

The Sinhastha Mela, held once every 12 years, is the high point of a pilgrimage to Nasik. The crush of people at this time is best seen from a distance.

In **Trimbakeshwar** (18 miles/30 km from Nasik), according to legend, a dispute arose between the gods and the demons over the possession of a pot of nectar. In the melée, the nectar spilled. One of the places where some drops fell was Trimbakeshwar. The river Godavari rises here from a hill called **Brahmagiri**. The **Trimbakeshwar Temple** is an imposing monument with splendid carvings.

Shirdhi (46 miles/75 km from Nasik) is where Sai Baba, the Muslim teacher whose wisdom and miraculous powers made him a saint for people of all religions, including Hindus, lived and died. His followers come in great numbers through the year to pay their respects to his memory.

Some people may want nothing more cultural from Maharashtra than a quiet beach. There are many in and around Bombay, but they are not quiet. For that you will have to go further afield. Try **Kihim** (85 miles/136 km) from Bombay or Murud (135 miles/216 km) which has a breathtaking approach, an old palace and an island fort less than a mile offshore. **Ganapathipule** (230 miles/375 km) has white sand amidst much greenery. It has an old temple of Ganapati on a colossal rock on the shore. The idol inside the temple is said to have been made by nature. A sea-tossed Ganapati found on white sand and placed in a rock-based temple: nature, religion, monument.

Which sums up Maharashtra.

Detail of fresco, Ajanta Caves.

GOA: GOLDEN SANDS, WHITE CHURCHES

It was almost dusk. Afonso de Albuquerque stood on a grassy hillock overlooking the Mandovi River. To the north stretched miles of fertile green fields edged by an undulating fringe of verdant hills. The wide river lazily slithered away into the horizon. Below him smoke and billowing sails marked the area of battle. It had been a bitter fight, but now the enemy navy lay all but decimated. Albuquerque felt good. This bountiful land was now his – wrested from Yusuf Adilshah, Sultan of Bijapur.

It was 25 November 1510, the feast of St Catherine. Overwhelmed, Albuquerque knelt and gave thanks and ordered a shrine to be built in the saint's honour. Thus began four centuries of Portuguese influence on this tiny land. The Portuguese came looking for spices; they stayed on to make Goa the capital of their empire in the east.

It is the Iberian aura, the cultural alloy of Latin and Oriental, the coexistence of Hinduism and Christianity, that gives Goa its identity. The Portuguese invested a hitherto predominantly Hindu society with their religion, attitudes and lifestyles, and Goa's ethos and élan are consequences of this encounter.

Like the stained-glass windows on the churches that punctuate the hillsides, Goa's fabric is a mosaic of bright and variegated colours – the flamboyant designs of Latin exuberance set against the russet hues of traditional Indian attitudes and lifestyles.

Nature too, has in no mean manner contributed to this symbiotic tapestry. Tucked away snugly between the hills of the Western Ghats and the Arabian Sea, this tiny territory of 1,350 sq. miles (3,500 sq. km), about halfway down the west coast of the Indian peninsula, is verdant with bottlegreen hills wooded with jackfruit, mango and cashew groves, cut across by rivers and edged by miles of sun-drenched beaches. A warm, languid climate, and a gentle unspoilt people, complete this compelling kaleidoscope.

Left, Mapusa Cow Market, Goa. Below, looking out.

Cocooned within its natural boundaries and the colonial cloisters of Portuguese rule, this tiny pocket of the Indian subcontinent lay slumbering for several centuries, bypassed by history. While the rest of the country progressed towards independence and the 20th century, Goa remained a Portuguese colony, suspended in a web of nostalgia.

Iberian legacy: Since Goa's absorption into the Indian Union in 1961, there have been many changes. Yet, sleepy villages and myriad white churches still characterise this lotus-eater's paradise, where the romance of the past lingers on and the mood is gentle and unhurried.

One can drive through peaceful towns with their Iberian-style villas, stop at a small *taverna* (bar) for a drink of *feni* – a locally brewed drink made from cashew or coconut, listen to the sounds of a *mando* (love song) and the strains of a guitar mingling with the sensuous lapping of the waves, or bask on the golden sands of idyllic beaches.

There is a Mediterranean atmosphere in the quaint towns with their red-tiled roofs and narrow streets and the charming fishing villages snuggled among coconut groves. Fishermen with faces weathered to mahogany by sun, salt and wind, catch mackerel, shark, crab, lobster and shrimp. And on Sundays, and feast days, the local folk – the women often in European dress and with lace mantillas on their heads, the men in black suits – file into the baroque-styled churches for service.

Most of Goa's larger towns are situated in the coastal belt where the Portuguese first settled. They are small urbanisations, certainly by Indian standards, but the mainstream of Goan life flows largely in its villages.

Capital town: Panjim (now Panaji), the capital of Goa situated on the southern bank of the Mandovi River, has a population of about 40,000 and, like most other Goan towns, is centred on a church and the square in front of it.

Largo da Igreja (Church Square) is an impressive ensemble: a dazzling white-balustraded stairway in front of the **Church of the Immaculate Conception** heightens the proportions of the baroque facade

tatue of
ouis De
amoes,
ld Goa
athedral.

which dominates the square. Built in 1541, its tall, twin towers were the first signs of "home" for the sailors who made the long voyage from Lisbon.

Panjim, in fact, has several squares, the houses lining them rising directly above the wide streets. Most of these villas, painted in pale yellow, green or deep rose, with their embellishments picked out in white or some contrasting colour, display French windows opening on to wrought-iron balconies which overlook the street below.

Particularly quaint is the old residential area of **Fountainahas** which lies behind the church and where narrow cobbled alleys weave through a miscellany of closely-knit houses with tiled roofs, over-hanging balconies and carved pillars, much as one would expect to find in any provincial town in Portugal or Spain.

Down winding streets which echo the sputter of motorcycles and scooters, inter-spersed among rows of tiny stores, are innumerable cafés which cater to the re-laxed temperament of the locals. There is never too little time here to prevent stop-ping for a drink or a chat. Shops close for siesta and the whole town dozes away the golden hours.

Facing the river, along the broad river-side boulevard, are some of Panjim's pub-lic buildings, including the **Secretariat**, built in 1615 by the Portuguese on the site of the Palacio Idalcao (palace of the Sul-tan of Bijapur, Yusuf Adil Khan, called the Idalcan by the Portuguese), a many-shuttered edifice which was once the vice-roy's residence.

Beyond **Largo da Palacio** (Palace Square) lies the quay which bursts into feverish activity every morning when the steamer from Bombay spills its contents onto the pier. The ship which plies back and forth from Bombay every day, except for the monsoon months (June to Septem-ber), provides the most enjoyable means of travel to Goa – slow and relaxed, in-dicative of the Goan way of life.

The **Campal,** as the riverside boulevard is called, is one of the most picturesque spots in Panjim. If you stand somewhat seaward and look towards the river, you can see in a single glance an astounding **The riverside at Panjim.**

chunk of history: in the far distance, the ramparts of the **Aguada Fort** – once one of the main bastions commanding the entrance into the Mandovi – with powder rooms, barracks, a church and a lighthouse, and now used as a prison; along the water's edge the white-gabled facade of a church tucked in between the folds of the shoreline; and sailing past on the river a reminder of the present, the slow continuous procession of barges carrying iron ore from mines in the interior to Marmagoa harbour for export.

Margao, the second largest town in Goa and the principal commercial centre, is one of the few linked to the rest of India by a railway line. In the heart of one of the most fertile districts, Salcete, Margao is the home of several prominent landowning families who have built themselves town as well as country houses, even while their roots remained in the villages.

A few other towns are sprinkled around the territory: **Vasco da Gama** is slowly developing into an industrial centre; **Marmagoa,** Goa's port, is one of India's finest natural harbours; **Mapusa** in the north is an interesting traditional market town. But the true voice of Goan culture is much more audible in the villages and outlying regions. Rich and poor alike live in the villages, visiting the towns for business or trade.

Village houses in Goa are impressive structures. Patterned around a central courtyard or patio, usually overgrown with banana trees, the village house derives its style from a combination of Indian elements and the Italianate form prevalent in Europe two centuries ago.

An open verandah surrounds the patio and leads into airy, spacious rooms, which display carved, rosewood furniture, ornate mirrors, chandeliers and a profusion of blue and white porcelain.

Some of the larger homes also maintain their own private chapels with baroque-styled altars, similar to those in the churches. The houses are built of red laterite stone found all over Goa while window panes are traditionally covered with small rectangles of translucent oyster shell, instead of glass.

Churches and carnivals: As one drives through Goa's villages, one is struck by the deep imprint of four and a half centuries of Latin Catholicism. The Portuguese came not only to conquer, but also to preach: colonisation and proselytisation went hand in hand. Presiding over every village, commanding the heights at hilltops, hugging the shores of rivers, sparkling white churches, crosses and small shrines indicate Christian ubiquity; religion is never more than a bend away.

Built mostly in the 16th and 17th centuries, the churches of Goa have been architecturally influenced by the Gothic styles of the Middle Ages and the baroque styles of the Renaissance.

On the feast day of the patron saint – and every village has one – the whole village is in attendance. The image of the saint, brightly decorated, is carried in procession by priests and laity to the chanting of prayers and litanies, recited or sung, accompanied by a violin or even a brass band. A fair normally provides the finale – refreshments, such as black gram, cashew nuts, coconut and jaggery sweets, fancy goods and even utensils are on display for sale.

MAHARASHTRA

Vengurla

Belgaum

KARNATAKA

Pernem

Vagator Beach
Calangute Beach
Aguada Fort

Mapuca
Saligao
Old Goa
Banasterim
Bicholim
Valpoi

Panaji
(Panjim)

Talaulim
Agacaim
Mangesh Temple

Londa

Marmagao
Vasco da Gama
Dabolim Airport

Cortalim
Ponda
Lautolim

Madgaon
Colva Beach
Rachol
Chandor

Arabian Sea

Territorial water limit note

Betul Beach

Cabo de Rama

KARNATAKA

INDIA

Goa

Karwar

Goa

16 km / 10 miles

Often, music and dance accompany such festivities, the Christian religion having been thoroughly mingled with traditional Indian practices of folk worship. Carnival in Goa is comparable to Rio's Mardi Gras, when for three days towns and villages rock under the wildest spirits. Masqueraders dance in the streets, and *feni* flows freely everywhere.

Beaches: Strung along Goa's 60-mile (100-km) coastline, like a lace frill on the edge of a colourful skirt, are some of the most beautiful beaches in the world – dazzling stretches of golden sand and surf edging the vast aquamarine expanse of the Arabian Sea.

An unbroken 4-mile (7-km) crescent of sun-drenched sand marks the twin beaches of **Candolim** and **Calangute**, north of Panjim and the Aguada headland.

Wake earlier than usual and walk along the crumbly sands towards the gold-speckled silken sheet of an early morning ocean. You may come upon fishermen singing as they heave in their catch. You may be invited to share a steaming cup of tea. Later, souvenir hawkers will arrive and rather alter the atmosphere, reminding you that you are in a tourist resort.

Farther north, past estuaries of the many streams that gurgle through the land, are a series of secluded beaches. **Anjuna**, a haven for the faded flower children from the West; **Vagator** beneath the soaring backdrop of **Chapora Fort**; and the many hidden coves and creeks awaiting discovery by the more intrepid visitor.

A raw beauty characterises the beaches of the southern coast of Goa. While **Siridao**, near the Zuari estuary, is a shell-collector's haven with its assortment of oyster and mother-of-pearl shells, it is **Colva**, with its broad brow of silver-grey, powder-fine sand that has been the inspiration for many folk tales and songs.

A drive south from Margao through heavily wooded teak plantations and deep green ravines brings the visitor to **Betul** village where a varied and almost inexhaustible supply of seafood, including some of Goa's largest mussels, can be obtained. Accessible only by boat from Betul and with a particular quality of remoteness is the enchanting and pictur-

Vagator beach.

esque Betul beach, all but unmarked by the footprints of tourists.

Old Golden Goa: No visit to Goa is complete without a visit to **Old Goa**, the Golden Goa (*Goa Doirada*) of the 16th century, when it was the "Rome of the Orient".

The best way to come to Old Goa is by boat as the Portuguese did, and through the Viceregal Arch, the ceremonial entry point where Vasco da Gama gazes out from his niche.

From here one can look back to the 16th century when Goa Doirada boasted a larger population than London or Paris. That was the time when the city reached its apogee, just before the Dutch and the English successfully challenged Portugal's maritime pretensions.

Magnificent churches, sumptuous buildings, stately mansions and broad streets once characterised the 3 sq. miles (8 sq. km) of Old Goa (it was called just Goa then). A "noble city full of beautiful buildings and palaces," wrote Albert de Mandelslo, a Dutch traveller who visited Goa in 1639. So magnificent was the city that it was said, "*Quem vin Goa excuse de ver Lisboa*" ("Whoever has seen Goa need not see Lisbon").

Among the many splendid buildings of Old Goa, the **Sé Cathedral** (Cathedral of St Catherine) remains one of the greatest monuments of the period. Completed in 1619, it is the largest Christian church in Asia, and a grand example of Renaissance architecture. The Cathedral's 260-ft (80-metre) long aisle culminates in a richly carved gilt altarpiece – one of the finest in India. There is a font in the church, possibly a vessel of Hindu origin, said to have been used by Goa's patron saint, St Francis Xavier, who came to Goa in 1542 and converted large numbers of its inhabitants to Christianity.

Within the compound of the cathedral but facing the opposite direction, is the Church of St Francis of Assisi with a stucco ceiling and a profusion of carvings. The inner sides of the buttressed walls have frescos of intricate floral designs painted in a hybrid style combining Indian and European elements.

A similar style can be detected in the frescoes in the Basilica of Bom Jesus. The

The Church of St Francis of Assisi in Old Goa.

basilica, where the mortal remains of St Francis Xavier are enshrined, is indeed the best specimen of baroque architecture in India. The chapel attracts large numbers of pilgrims. St Francis's body which was brought to Goa almost 150 years after his death, now lies in an airtight glass coffin, placed inside a silver casket fashioned by a 17th-century Florentine jeweller. It was glassed in after a devotee made off with a toe centuries ago.

The tomb, which came from Italy, donated by the Grand Duke of Tuscany, is made from alabaster and Florentine marble and inlaid with semi-precious stones and bronze panels depicting scenes from the life of the saint. The interior of the chapel which houses the mausoleum is richly adorned with paintings and wood carvings, and over the south door hangs a picture which is believed to be the likeness of the saint.

There are many more churches in Old Goa in varying stages of deterioration. The **Church of St Cajetan**, near the ferry wharf, with its two belfries and cupola in the centre was modelled in miniature on the Basilica of St Peter in Rome by its Italian architect. Also near the river bank stands the **Chapel of St Catherine** built on the site of the bitterest fighting during Albuquerque's conquest of Goa in 1510.

A few minutes' walk up the road from the basilica is **Monte Santo** (Holy Hill) where one haunted tower of the **Church of the Augustinian Monastery** is all that remains of a once splendid vaulted structure. Adjacent to the ruins stands the **Convent of St Monica**, once one of the largest nunneries in the Portuguese empire.

Past the flying buttresses of the convent, on a grassy mound at the edge of a steep cliff, stands the shell of the **Church of Our Lady of the Rosary**, one of the earliest to be built in Goa. It represents a fusion of European and Indian elements; while the wall frescos reveal Hindu designs, those on the alabaster tomb of Dona Caterina, wife of the 10th viceroy and the first Portuguese woman to hazard the arduous voyage to the Indies, demonstrate the impact of the Muslim-Bijapur style.

There is hardly a temple to be seen in the coastal areas. Over the years, the Portu-

Stately home, Portuguese-style.

guese zeal for propagating their religion became rigid and intolerant. Conversions were forcibly imposed, temples were demolished and churches built in their place; and the practice of any religion other than pure Roman Catholicism was severely punished. Those who were determined to preserve their ancient faith removed their deities from the shrines and fled to the interior, where the arm of the law could not reach them. It is therefore only in the mountainous interior regions to the east that Hindu temples can be seen.

It was not until 1814, when the Inquisition died down, that Hindu temples were rebuilt in sylvan surroundings, on gentle slopes of verdant hills or in valleys sheltered by thick groves of palm trees. Though influenced by the style of Maratha temple architecture and to some extent by Islamic and Christian elements, the styles in these temples represent a purely distinctive idiom of Hindu architecture. Several temples have Islamic domes, while the plan of the structure is often similar to Christian architectural patterns.

The **Shri Mangesh Temple** (dedicated to Lord Shiva), and the Shanta-Durga (to goddess Parvati) and Nagesh Temples in the Ponda neighbourhood are among the most frequented in Goa. Ornate, baroque interiors and several storied *deepmals* – elaborate lamp towers – are unique features of these Goan Hindu shrines.

Considerable changes are shaking the somnolence of Goa – long suspended as it was in a fossilised world of 18th-century Portugal. Reunion with the rest of India has brought water and electricity to the villages, communication with the outside world and the charter flights of westerners. Tourism has grown steadily, and substantial resorts are being created.

The inflow of migrant labour has aggravated the pressures on domestic resources and brought about the growth of a new culture. Goans fear that the very elements constituting the unique identity of the land are likely to be diluted by the pace of its integration with the rest of the country. Possibly a new identity will emerge. But the image that will nevertheless endure, will be of a fascinating tapestry of legend and myth, of mists and dreams.

GUJARAT: A DELICATE BALANCE

Through the blaring cacophony of bicycles, autorickshaws, cars and bullock carts, a motorcycle with large milk cans tied astride darts through the streets of Ahmedabad with its rider bedecked in a brilliant red turban, flashing golden earrings and a fierce moustache. He is a *Rabari* from the milk-vending community, who has adopted modern transportation while continuing to wear his traditional dress. He is the essence of Gujarat.

In some parts of India tradition is linked with backwardness, and modernity with technology. If you have television in your home, you wear trousers; a bullock-cart is driven only by someone who wears a *dhoti* and a turban. Gujarat, in its vibrant, dynamic and characteristic fashion turns the whole thing topsy turvy and yet lands comfortably on all fours every time.

The archeological finds at Lothal near Dhandhuka in Ahmedabad district and Rozadi in Saurashtra carry the history of Gujarat back to the age of Harappa and Mohenjodaro, 3,500 years ago. In legend, the epics and Puranas tell of how Lord Krishna and his brother Balarama left Mathura and settled at Kusathali or Dwarka on Gujarat's western coast. The name "Gujarat" derives from the Prakrit "Gujaratta" or "Gurjara Rastra" which means "land of the Gurjaras". The Gurjaras were an immigrant tribe who entered India through the northern passes along with the Hunas, passed through the Punjab and settled in lands that came to be known as Gujarat, a name that became popular only around the 10th century.

Traders by tradition: Gujarat has always been a field for conquering and colonising races. Ethnic and linguistic movements from the northern plains and the western ocean brought with them their own languages, arts and crafts, poetry, thought forms, social practices, historical traditions, religious practices and philosophy. Gujarat therefore has the greatest number of sub-divisions of communities in India.

Proximity to the sea and the Gujaratis' consequent flair for maritime and mercantile pursuits developed a strong spirit of enterprise, practical wisdom and catholicity of taste among them. Continuous seafaring activities produced a well-to-do middle-class which wielded considerable influence. Traders and artisans formed powerful guilds and made business, trade and the acquisition of wealth a strong tradition in Gujarat.

Gujarat spreads itself into the regions of Kutch, Saurashtra and the verdant territories between the rivers Banas and Damanganga. These are fertile lands of wheat, cotton, groundnut and banana plantations kept green by the Banas, Sabarmati, Mali, Tapi and Narmada Rivers on the coastal plains and the Bhadar, Setrunji and Bhogavo on the peninsular plains. The southern border is hilly, and Diu island is an escape into holiday ambience.

Ahmedabad's belligerent, swerving autorickshaws, modern Ashram Road with its hotels, shops and cinemas, the heavily populated industrial sections of town, are all manifestations of its character as the great textile and commercial city of Western India. Omnipresent is the Sabarmati River over which four bridges connect the old city with the new.

On one side are the crowded streets leading to **Manek Chowk**, where rows of traders dealing in silver jewellery or printed fabrics lean against spotless white bolster-pillows, waiting for customers. On the upper floors of the buildings on this street are exquisitely carved wooden balconies, windows and doorways of old *havelis* (family homes). They are fast being dismantled and sold as antiques or placed in museums. The most beautiful ones stand in **Doshiwada-ni-Pol**. Gujarat wood sculpture is usually part of the decoration of temples and private buildings. Much of it is religious in significance and depicts the deities of old legends.

Mosques, bazaars, museums: The reign of Sultan Allauddin Khalji of Delhi witnessed the creation of the first Muslim empire in India and one of his earliest conquests was the wealthy kingdom of Gujarat in 1300. Ahmed Shah I founded Ahmedabad on the site of the ancient city of Karnavati in 1411.

The Indo-Saracen architecture of Ahmedabad blends Hindu and Muslim styles. **Sidi Saiyad's Mosque** near Relief Road is Ahmedabad's most eloquent example of the finest such work in sandstone. Its twin windows of pierced stone with a design of an almost lyrical tree with palm leaves and curving tendrils must be seen. The shaking minarets of **Rajpur Bibi's Mosque** at Gomtipur and **Sidi Bashir's Mosque** at Kalipur are fun. Pressure exerted on the inner walls of the minarets sets them vibrating, to the delight of both visitor and tourist guide.

On Sundays, the edge of the Sabarmati River below Ellis Bridge comes alive with the **Khanmasa Bazaar**, a sprawling market of the most fascinating and sometimes preposterous wares to be found by any collector enterprising enough to wander on the dusty banks.

There is, of course, no "nightlife" in Ahmedabad, but the substitute it offers is, again, typical of the essence of Gujarat. A 15-minute drive out of Ahmedabad on the main highway to Vadodara (Baroda) is the **Vechaar Utensil Museum** and **Vishalla Restaurant**. Vechaar should be visited in the cool of the evening. It houses a remarkable collection of metalware; utensils of every imaginable shape and size in bronze, brass and other alloys have been collected from every corner of Gujarat. Housed in a building made of mud walls and with a central water tank, the atmosphere is both rustic and evocative of the old Gujarat.

A traditional Gujarati meal at the **Vishalla Restaurant** appropriately rounds off the visit to the museum. Vegetarian favourites, baked breads in a variety of cereals, fresh, white butter, jaggery and yogurt are served on large brass dishes by rural waiters to the accompaniment of folk music or puppet shows, in a decor recreating a village ambience. The local potter moulds the drinking pots and dishes which are used by the restaurant.

The grace of Ahmedabad's modern architecture and institutions must be seen to understand the Gujarati's appreciation of his own culture and aesthetic sensibilities. The **Indian Institute of Management** in Vastrapur provides a comprehensive education to those aspiring to be managers. The buildings, designed by Louis Kahn,

Indian Institute of Management, Ahmedabad.

are a fascinating display of the sense of drama that can be created by light and shade, angles and arches, and the stark lines of lengthy corridors.

The **Calico Museum of Textiles** in Shahibag is located in the Sarabhai Foundation which is a public charitable trust. The Museum has an exquisite collection of fabrics from all over India. Rich brocades and fine embroideries from Kashmir, Gujarat and the southern states are laid out with aesthetic simplicity. Free guided tours in English, Gujarati and Hindi are provided twice a day.

The **Shreyas Folk Museum** in Ambavadi and the **Tribal Museum** on Ashram Road portray the rural heritage of Gujarat. Tattoos and kites carry stylised folk designs outdoors.

Hridey Kunj, Mahatma Gandhi's Ashram at Sabarmati is a set of austere yet beautiful buildings nestling amidst mango trees. It was from here that Gandhi experimented in non-violent methods of political struggle. The museum, added later, is stunningly simple and a fitting tribute to the great man. Designed by Charles Correa, a well-known Indian architect, it displays Gandhi's spectacles, spinning wheel, sandals, photographs, and cloth spun by him as part of the movement for *swadeshi* (self-sufficiency).

Gujarat Vidyapith, a university established by Mahatma Gandhi, has a vast collection of books, a museum, a research centre and the Navjivan Press which holds the copyright of Gandhi's works. It is located on the busy Ashram Road and visitors can shop for *khadi* (hand-spun) fabrics and other handmade village industry products at the nearby Khadi Gramudyog Bhandar, another institution established by Gandhi.

Some 10 miles (17 km) to the north of Ahmedabad is **Adalaj Vava**, a 15th-century step-well, an architectural delight with its geometric and floral patterns on the stone pillars and lintels that line the steps that lead down to the rectangular well. The steps are accessible from three sides. Tanks and wells have always been artistically treated in Gujarat and Adalaj has been created with as much care as any memorable temple. This step-well was built during the most glorious period of the Indo-Saracenic style of architecture.

The **Sun Temple** at **Modhera** is a three-hour journey by road north of Ahmedabad. It is one of the finest examples of Indian temple architecture. Built in 1026, during the reign of King Bhima of the Solanki dynasty, the temple is dedicated to the Sun God, Surya, and stands on a plinth overlooking a deep stone-stepped tank. Every inch of the edifice is elaborately carved with figures of gods, flowers and animals.

Rann of Kutch: It is a fairly long drive onwards to Bhuj across the **Little Rann of Kutch** but a traveller with a spirit of discovery should not leave Kutch out of his itinerary. From Ahmedabad there are overnight trains and buses but it is more convenient to take a car right through.

Kutch (Kaccha), best visited between October and February, covers 3,350 sq. miles (8,750 sq. km), bounded by the Gulf of Kutch, the Indian Ocean and the Rann of Kutch, a peculiar region described by one Lt. Burnes in his memoirs as "a space without a counterpart in the globe". The word rann derives from the Sanskrit word *irina*, meaning a waste. The expanse is

The Asiatic Lion, an endangered species.

hard, dry, saline and flat and, as the summer heat intensifies, the salt in the baked and blistered earth shines with mirages of dazzling whiteness; herds of galloping wild ass can be seen.

Bhuj town is partly surrounded by walls built in 1723. In 1865 Rao Pragmalji built an imposing and intricate palace at one of the gates. Its Aina Mahal has walls of marble covered with mirrors separated by gilded ornaments with shades of Venetian glass. There are ingenious pumps and siphons to fill the pond which has a fountain spraying water in various patterns. There are collections of ornaments and paintings, both European and Indian, and exquisite inlaid ivory doors made in 1708.

From Bhuj, half a day and an auto-rickshaw is what is required for a visit to a street of potters where men mould and fire the local white clay into pots for daily use in the villages. Women paint fine geometric designs on them. Hand block-printing and the techniques of tying and dyeing fabric known as *bandhani* can be seen in tiny shops and workplaces called *karkhanas.*

Village fair in Gujarat.

The **Kutch Museum,** which overlooks the Hamirsar water tank, is the oldest in Gujarat, opened in 1877. It has the largest collection of Kshatrapa (Indo-Scythian) inscriptions, the oldest dated 89 AD. The silverwork of Kaccha is distinctive and the museum has a fine collection of coins and jewellery, apart from gold and enamel work, textiles, woodwork, old utensils, arms and accoutrements and a section on the communities peculiar to Kaccha. The Rabaris, Debariyas, Gracias, Sodhas and others still wear dresses bejewelled with mirrorwork.

Village handicrafts: Visiting one of these communities involves a two-hour bus or taxi ride from the centre of Bhuj to **Hodka** or **Dhorodo** in the Rann area known as **Banni**. The villages consist of round mud huts called *bhungas* with a single central support pole, and a thatched or tiled roof, all surrounding a large community courtyard. Women are shy of male visitors but they are hospitable if anyone wishes to see the inside of their houses. They have exquisite personal collections of embroidered quilts and garments, as well as some for sale. Walls, shelves, grain containers and cupboards are fashioned in mud with decorative designs washed with lime paste and embedded with mirrors which throw back hundreds of shimmering reflections when a candle is lit.

For the less intrepid, **Bhujodi,** 6 miles (10 km) short of Bhuj, just off the main road, displays the life and styles of a weaving community. It is a small village with narrow winding lanes, and a pit-loom in almost every home. Visitors can buy brilliantly woven *dhablas* (blankets), shawls and woollen stoles decorated with *bandhani* designs from the weavers.

The Indian Airlines flight from Bhuj across the Gulf of Kutch to Jamnagar is an astonishing 13 minutes and certainly saves time. **Jamnagar**, the district headquarters, is a walled city with several gateways, typical of traditional towns. The older parts are bursting at the seams but many areas were scientifically planned, as recently as 1914, and have a systematic layout of facades, squares, circles and broad streets. Textile mill and tie-dyed fabrics both roll out of Jamnagar.

The Kotho Bastion of **Lakhota Palace**

is located in the middle of a tank and is approached over a stone bridge. It could accommodate a thousand soldiers, and now houses a fine museum.

Jamnagar has a solarium which was built in 1933. With the destruction of two similar solaria in France during World War II this is probably now the only one of its kind in the world, and certainly in Asia.

Five jewels: "There are five jewels in Saurashtra, namely rivers, women, horses, the fourth being Somnath and the fifth is the *darshan* of the idol of Hari or Lord Krishna." *The Puranas.*

Dwarka, 85 miles (137 km) west of Jamnagar was a flourishing port in ancient times and a famed holy spot. It is said that Krishna established Dwarka 5,000 years ago. The **Temple of Dwarkadish** on the northern bank of the Gomti Creek is typical of the architecture of ancient Hindu temples. It has a shrine, a large hall, a roof supported by 60 columns of granite and sandstone, and a conical spire about 160ft (50 metres) high. The temple has seven floors. Its exterior is profusely carved while the inside is extremely simple. The shrine is elaborately ornamented and has a sculpted figure of Ganesh, the elephant deity, over the entrance. Across the creek of salt water are five sweet-water springs.

Gandhi's birthplace: For those who have a special interest in the life of Mahatma Gandhi, a visit to **Porbandar**, his birthplace, farther down the coast is a pilgrimage worth planning. It is a quiet coastal town. Gandhi was born here in 1869 in his ancestral home, a quarter of a mile from the sea. With its small rooms, trellised windows and carved balconies, niches in the walls for kerosene lamps, the house has an air of peace and tranquility.

Nearby is **Kirti Mandir** which has a Gandhian library, some of Gandhi's personal effects, a photographic exhibition on his life and times, and a spinning and prayer hall.

The crowded parts of Porbandar will remind the visitor of the older Ahmedabad and a walk down the long beach will be undisturbed by the usual trappings of a popular seaside resort.

Driving along quiet coastal roads through Chorwad and Verawal you will

Jain temples at Palitana, Gujarat.

reach **Somnath**, one of the 12 most sacred Shiva shrines in India. It stands majestically washed by the Arabian Sea. Ransacked repeatedly by northern invaders and rebuilt over and over, successively in gold, silver, wood and finally in stone, it is said to have been built by Soma, the Moon God, in penance and worship of the wrathful Lord Shiva who had laid a curse on him.

Much of the temple was destroyed by Mohammed Ghazni in 1026 and parts of the present temple have been reconstructed in the old style. Nearby is a temple marking the spot where Lord Krishna is said to have been accidentally killed by a hunter's arrow. Rhythmic cymbals clash at dusk to mark the time for special prayers.

Three miles (5 km) from Junagadh is the only place in the world, apart from Africa, where the lion can be seen in its natural habitat. In the **Gir Forest** began one of the earliest efforts at conservation. In 1900 the Nawab of Junagadh, in whose territory most of the Gir Forest lay, had invited Lord Curzon, viceroy at that time, for a lion shikar (hunt). When the viceroy accepted, a newspaper published an anonymous letter which questioned the propriety of an important person doing further damage to an endangered species. Lord Curzon not only cancelled his shikar but also advised the nawab to protect the remaining lions, which the nawab and his successors dutifully did. Now the Gir Forest is one of the largest and most important game preserves in India.

Lions in the Gir: The Gir lion is a majestic animal with a bigger tail tassle, bushier elbow tufts and a smaller mane than its African cousin. Early in the 20th century there were only a hundred lions left in the Gir; now they number over 250. A dozen randy males were sterilised recently after lions strayed from the sanctuary. The forest is one of the few remaining places where a visitor can drive through open scrub country, dry tropical thorn forests and an evergreen corridor along the riverside. It harbours a variety of smaller animals and birds. There is also a newly developed crocodile farm, panthers and striped hyena.

Temple City: Palitana in Bhavanagar district almost completes the full circle of Saurashtra. A mile (2km) from town is the **Shatrunjaya Hill**, the most important centre of Jain pilgrimage, with an incredible 863 Jain temples atop its twin peaks.

Palitana is a major marketing centre for chillies, cereals and pulses and has a bustling market for farmers.

It is worth heading back in the direction of Ahmedabad via **Surendranagar** and **Wadhwan**. The ancestors of the stone carvers of Wadhwan built Dwarka and Somnath. Skilled stone carvers live and work near **Hawa Mahal**, a finely conceived but unfinished palace at the edge of the town. Today some travel on assignments to build temples even in distant Kenya and Uganda.

In the village of **Chitravara** the remarkable technique of dot weaving is used to make wool wraps for women. Traders in Surendranagar town have a vast collection of old embroideries and artefacts from all over Saurashtra.

The "industrial corridor" of Gujarat is due south of Ahmedabad. Tools used by prehistoric man were found in **Vadodara** now booming with an oil refinery, petrochemical complex and other industries. Its **Lakshmi Vilas Palace**, **Baroda Museum** and **University of Fine Arts** take the bite off the side effects of industrialisation.

In its hinterland lies the exclusively tribal belt of Gujarat with its tribal architecture and lifestyle untouched by "progress".

Surat was the first outpost established by the British East India Company and was on one of the old trade routes for silks, embroideries and spices. Despite a dominant Parsi and Muslim influence, its architecture is mostly Portuguese and British. Today it is the centre of the diamond-cutting and *zari* (gold thread) industry. It was also the unfortunate focal point for an outbreak of plague in the early 1990s.

A group of farmers wearing heavy silver jewellery, bright turbans and shawls, stand around a video screen in the town square watching imitation spaghetti westerns. This cultural parallelism, typical of Gujarat, is delicately balanced today; of tomorrow, who knows?

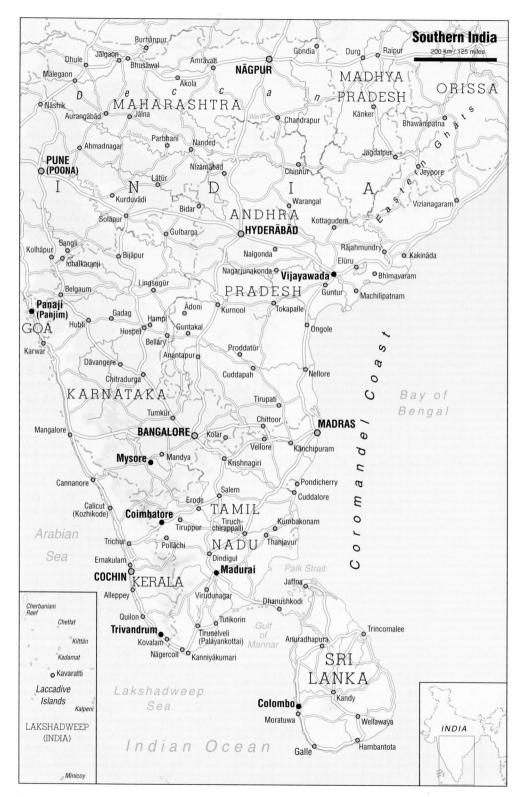

Southern India

200 km / 125 miles

MADRAS, CULTURE AND CHANGE

Situated on the east coast, Madras (population 5.3 million) is the fourth largest of the Indian cities, after Bombay, Calcutta and Delhi. It is the most convenient entry point for people wishing to travel in southern India. There are convenient connections by plane, bus and train from Madras to all parts of Tamil Nadu – to the temple cities of Chidambaram, Thanjavur and Rameshwaram, or for day trips to Mahabalipuram and Kanchipuram.

Trips to hill resorts like Ootacamund, Kodaikanal and the game sanctuaries can also be conveniently made from Madras. The city is well linked with other parts of India and with Sri Lanka, Burma and the Far East.

Madras city is aligned north to south along the coast at the northern tip of Tamil Nadu. It has spread far beyond its original site in the north and west to encompass later colonial buildings, the coach factory, cycle and car factories and other industries.

The city has a number of rivers and canals, such as the Adyar River and the Cooum, along which are gardens and facilities for boat rides. On the Adyar are some fine buildings like the Madras Club, the Madras Boat Club, the Chettinad Palace and the Theosophical Society buildings and gardens.

Dosas and dance drama: Climatically, Madras goes from hot to hotter and hottest, with relief brought by the northwest monsoon in June–July and the southeast monsoon in December–January. Palm and casuarina trees trim the coastline, sea breezes bring a cool freshness to the land and the beaches are beautiful in the early hours of the day and in the late evenings. The sea here, on the east coast, is not as inviting for the swimmer as the Arabian Sea, but the beach resorts are always humming with picnickers and holidaymakers. At night, lights from fishermen's boats and catamarans can be seen glowing over the dark waters.

Madras is the gateway to Tamil Nadu, and serves as an introduction to Tamil culture, food, customs and people. Excellent vegetarian Brahmin food is available in restaurants like **Woodlands** and Dasaprakash. They serve delicious, hot *thali* meals with limitless boiled rice, lentil curries and a dozen tiny portions of vegetables. The crisp fried *dosa* and the steamed *idli* are famous rice-powder preparations and have come to be identified with Tamil Nadu worldwide.

The Tamil language is an ancient, beautiful, and poetic one, often spoken at breathtaking speed. The richness of Tamil literature offers endless scope for interpretation in dance and theatre and is the very soul of the culture of Tamil Nadu.

The colours and clothing that women wear in Tamil Nadu cannot be compared with that of any others in India, except, perhaps, Rajasthan. The Kanchipuram silk and cotton saris worn at home and for religious and social occasions are characterised by a combination of brilliant contrasting colours – orange with purple, parrot-green with pink. The older generation of Tamil Brahmin women drape their saris in the traditional style, drawing one end between the legs and the other over the shoulder. The men wear *lungis* or *dhotis,* a length of cloth fastened at the waist and hanging down to the ankles sarong-style. A marriage or a religious procession in Madras provides a glittering display of colourful clothes and heavy jewellery.

Madras has a large Christian population of all denominations. The British occupation from the 17th century onwards has also left an Anglo-Indian population. Though well amalgamated in Indian society, their religion, clothes and culture make them distinct.

Madras today is a curious mixture. While it retains the old legacy of the British East India Company, and is, in some ways, a conservative bastion in social and religious matters, it is also the Hollywood of South India and, simultaneously, a stronghold of traditional Tamil culture. There are churchyards, staid residential areas and prim gardens side by side with high cinema posters with giant-size cutouts of heros and heroines rising out of them, painted in gaudy colours and dotted with flashy sequins. These occupy prime positions and clutter up the skyline.

Preceding pages: Gopuram, Kumbeshwara Temple at Kumbakonam, Tamil Nadu.

"Nothing is impossible" is the motto of the Madras film industry – no plot too unrealistic, no stunt too difficult to engineer, no costume too daring. Legends, myths, historical and social themes, served with glamour, is the fare. There are heroines who you wouldn't believe could dance and heroes who you thought had gone out of style. Everything goes.

But Tamil film stars have always aspired for even greater glory than celluloid could bring them. Politicians, chief ministers of states, members of parliament, social and political leaders, religious gurus and philanthropists spring out of the silver screen into the real world and survive and prosper in it.

The British East India Company established one of its earliest seats of power in India in Madras. Unlike Bombay and Calcutta, Madras does not have a natural harbour. The present breakwaters were built in the 19th century. The construction of **Fort St George** was begun around 1640. In the city, white and black areas were once clearly demarcated. The Fort was often attacked by Indian and French forces, yet it continued to expand. Today the old buildings in Fort St George house the Tamil Nadu Government **Secretariat and the Legislative Assembly**. A charming feature of the East India Company architecture is the use of Madras *chunam*, a glittering whitewash of limestone mixed with crushed sea shells. The *chunam*-coated walls of the buildings are a dazzling sight in summer.

Within the Fort, a number of other early buildings still stand, of which **St Mary's Church** is the most interesting. It is the earliest English building surviving intact in India and the oldest Anglican church in the east. It was consecrated in 1680. The interior of the church is whitewashed, but there are also elaborate carved wooden panels. It was at this church that Robert Clive, victor of the Battle of Plassey in 1759, which is taken as the beginning of British rule in India, was married in 1753. Elihu Yale, who later founded the university bearing his name in America, was also associated with this church.

The **Fort St George Museum** con-

Madras, an early view.

tains some fascinating items belonging to the early days of the East India Company and the colonial period. Coins, weapons, pictures and books form part of the interesting collection. Other buildings of importance in the Fort are the **Old Government House**, the **Banqueting Hall** (now called Rajaji Hall) built by Goldingham for the Governor's official entertainment during the Clive period, when British power and prestige in India were in the ascendant. The architectural style of this period drew inspiration from the glory of the classical Greeks and Romans with Doric, Corinthian and Tuscan pillars, entablatures and friezes.

Two beautiful churches in Madras that still have regular services are **St George's Cathedral** and **St Andrew's Kirk**. The latter is said to resemble St Martin-in-the-Fields in London. It was built by James Gibbs. The towering steeples and the strength of the pillars of the facade make it a city landmark. St George's Cathedral, consecrated in 1816, was designed by Captain James Caldwell and Thomas Fiott de Havillard. The interior

here has slim Ionic pillars, plasterwork and stained-glass windows.

The "**ice factory**" on Marina Beach, near the old building of the University was built in 1842. This circular structure was built to store ice imported from America. Later it was converted into a home for widows. The **San Thome Church** on the Main Beach Road is associated with the Apostle, St Thomas. It is believed that he was martyred on what is called **St Thomas's Mount** in Madras (near the airport) and that his remains were enshrined in this church. The San Thome was first built in the 16th century and has been rebuilt over the years.

Outdoors, the attractions around Madras are the **Guindy Deer Park** and the **Snake Park**. The former has species of black buck, spotted deer, monkeys and other animals. The Snake Park is the only major reptilium in India. It was started by an American, Romulus Whitaker, who worked towards educating visitors on the types of snakes in India, to prevent the thoughtless killing of the reptile.

The **Theosophical Society** has its head-

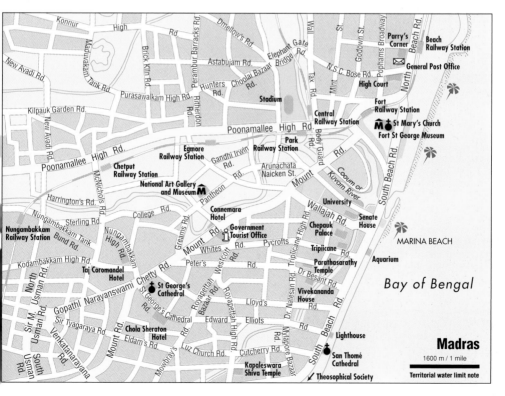

quarters on the banks of the Adyar River. It boasts a vast library of books on religion; in the gardens that lead up to the river and the sea is a sprawling banyan tree, said to be one of the largest in India.

The **Marina**, almost 8 miles (13 km) long, is a wide sandy beach with a drive along it fringed with palms and casuarinas, running along the whole length of Madras. The Marina has an aquarium, located opposite the 19th century building of the **Presidency College** and the **Senate House** of the University. The University building and its grounds are interesting examples of the adoption of an Indo-Islamic style for Indian public buildings that was in vogue in the second half of the 19th century. North of the University building and its grounds are other interesting structures such as Egmore Railway Station, the Madras Medical College, Ripon Building and Victoria Public Hall.

One of the most important localities of Madras is **Mylapore**, where the **Kapaleswara Shiva Temple**, the tank, market area and old Brahmin residential houses are situated. Mylapore is a unified complex and is best viewed as such. At the evening bazaar, crowds of women, freshly bathed, adorned with sweet-smelling jasmine flowers in their hair, make their way to the Kapaleswara Temple. Another ancient and important temple is the **Krishna Parathasarathy Temple** on the Triplicane High Road.

The **State Government Museum** in Madras includes a Museum Theatre and Art Gallery. The museum was established in 1846 and has departments of Natural History and Art. It houses a rare collection of sculptures from Amaravati in Andhra Pradesh, belonging to the Buddhist period, 2nd century AD. The white limestone sculptured medallions and panels tell the story of the life of the Buddha.

The Bronze Gallery of the museum has the finest collection of Chola bronzes (9–13th centuries AD), apart from the Thanjavur Art Gallery and some temple collections. Some are hardly two inches high and others are over two feet tall, all perfectly modelled, iconographically sophisticated, and dramatic. The dancing **Fort St George, Madras.**

298

Shivas, Durgas and Ganeshes and the famous Rama, Lakshman and Sita group are the pride of this museum.

In performing arts, the **Music Academy of Madras** is well known. Each winter there are music and dance programmes by eminent artists. Audiences are very discerning and this inspires the performers, whether of Karnatak music or Bharata Natyam dancing.

Down the coastal road, towards Mahabalipuram, is **Kalakshetra**, an academy of music and dance set up by Rukmini Devi, the doyenne of Indian dance. Her efforts to re-establish classical dance in a modern context have given India a good number of leading dancers. Students are trained in the performing arts and related subjects. Artists from all over the world also come to Kalakshetra to share in this experience. Experimentation and innovation are the rule in this school run on the lines of the *gurukuls*, where teachers teach and live together in simplicity, amidst natural greenery. Kalakshetra organises annual dance-drama programmes worth attending.

On the same road, leading from Madras to Mahabalipuram, is **Cholamandalam**, the artists' village. There are residential huts, and workshop areas, kilns and furnaces where the artists work. Cholamandalam artists organise exhibitions, poetry readings and other programmes throughout the year.

Shopping: Almost anything is available in Madras. **Moore Market** near the railway station (recently extensively damaged by fire) once sold secondhand furniture and books. The **Burma Bazaar** towards the port area on North Beach Road is a haven for the trader in smuggled goods – from French perfumes to electronic goods from Japan. Madras, however, is most famous for its silk emporia where silk saris, scarves and material for suiting and dresses are available by the yard at well-known shops. Silks woven in Kanchipuram and other centres are world famous for their quality and vibrant colours. The **Victoria Technical Institute** (VTI) sells handmade items like lace and embroidery, and **Poompuhar**, the Government Handicrafts Emporium, has articles of sandal-wood, *papier maché* and bronze. Both these are on Mount Road (Anna Salai as it is now called).

Pondicherry: This formerly French-ruled town is now one of India's Union Territories. It lies on the coast, 93 miles (150 km) south of Madras. It first came under French rule in the mid 18th century, but over the years it repeatedly became a battlefield and, on many occasions, changed hands. The town was finally restored to the French by the British under the Treaty of Paris in 1763. It returned to India only in 1954.

The town was originally divided by a canal. One side used to be the *Ville Blanche* (white town) and the other the *Ville Noire* (black town) for the Indian population. The heart of the city used to be the **Government Park**, around which are now the **Raj Nivas** (residence of the lieutenant governor) and other official buildings. Near the Railway Station is the Gothic-style **Sacred Heart Church**.

Pondicherry streets, in the old French area, are cobbled and the seaside pavements and beaches are designed to resemble those at Nice or any other waterfront town of Southern France.

Some 6 miles (10 km) from the town are the Sri Aurobindo Ashram and the new city **Auroville**. The ashram was established by Sri Aurobindo, an important Indian religious philosopher, who had once played an active role in the Indian independence movement. In conformity with his philosophy and teachings, the city of Auroville was designed by a French architect, Roger Auger, as a model universal city, where man can live close to nature and in harmony with his fellow beings. The ashram, its orchards, workshops and activity centres attract a number of foreigners who share the beliefs of Aurobindo and of the "Mother", who succeeded him. Wealthy patronage and an opportunity to experiment with a different lifestyle attracts many.

Outside Pondicherry is **Arikamedu**, an important archeological site, where excavations have revealed a Greco-Roman trading centre of the early years of the Christian era. The remains indicate a flourishing trade with the Romans in dyed muslins and spices.

TAMIL NADU

If the truth be told, contemporary Tamil culture is defined by hot blood, hot food, hot colours, hot music and hot coffee. Overripe film actresses dancing with quivering thighs across film hoardings and the aroma of roasting coffee beans are sights and smells which confront the traveller everywhere. Yet tourist itineraries usually substitute a more "brahminical" perception of local culture in which defunct stone temples, elitist South Indian classical dance and music performances and mild vegetarian Brahmin *thalis* are the main attractions.

With good reason perhaps. A visitor who suddenly finds himself entangled in a jumble of traffic in the capital Madras (which sometimes resembles a garbage dump the tide left behind) might benefit from a more genteel introduction to Dravidian civilisation today.

At one of the city's many *Bharatanatyam* (classical dance) concerts, however, he may be surprised to discover that the "divine Lord" to whom almost all dance compositions are dedicated often makes a personal appearance in emotional "conjugal unions" on stage. The dancers once came from a highly civilised community of courtesans referred to as "Devadasis" or "servants of god", but now mostly hail from urban middle class backgrounds, because of the social status a dancing daughter has come to confer on conservative families. At the Madras Festival – Mid December to early January – India's leading classical dancers and singers perform for the nation's most discriminating audience.

Adventurous travellers are also advised to visit a "military restaurant" (as non-vegetarian restaurants are traditionally called) and quite literally explode the notion that only mild vegetarian *thalis* are available in South India. Fiery Chettinad cuisine uses rabbit, quail, crab plus many exotic spices and lichens for flavouring.

Vellu's Military is Madras's oldest Chettinad restaurant. Though its interiors have been renovated, it still uses a traditional wood-burning stove and the prices

are very reasonable. At the other end of the price spectrum The Raintree, at the Taj Connemara Hotel, offers relatively authentic Chettinad food despite the modulation of spices to suit western palates. (The Chettinad area of South-eastern Tamil Nadu is also famous for its merchant traders' palatial house with woodwork in carved Burma teak.)

The temple trail: Temple hopping across Tamil Nadu, the conventional post-Madras option for must visitors, need not be too dry and academic if balanced with less demanding pursuits. A good place to start exploring the confluence of ancient heritage with contemporary hedonism is **Mahabalipuram** or **Mamallapuram**, within easy driving distance of Madras.

This ancient Hindu town with a superb frieze dates back to the 5th century and a clean beach put it on the original hippy trail in the 1960s. As a result the big decision a traveller must take while in Mahabalipuram today is: "Which shall I try first – the rock carving or the fritters?"

Leaving the shade of a fritter-café close to the beach to walk, sweating profusely,

Left, Tamilian belle. Right, sculptor at work in Tamil Nadu.

past a lotus-covered communal bath, one encounters stone carvers still at work to the staccato rhythm of chisels. A few hundred metres down a gauntlet of antique and handicraft shops, turn right and be confronted by several guides and an epic frieze well worth having delayed a cold beer for. The *Descent of the Ganga* or *Arjuna's Penance* captures the tension between flesh and spirit with great immediacy. These bas relief images are unlike those seen anywhere else in this stone carving-ridden country.

From Mahabalipuram it is also possible to begin tracing the evolution of South Indian temple architecture. Its rock cuts are an architectural improvement on the caves of Hindu and Jain ascetics and evolved during the reign of the Pallavas, who emerged by the 6th century AD as the rulers of a kingdom centred around **Kanchipuram**. The free-standing *rathas* or chariots at Mahabalipuram also display the first (now common) temple features such as *garbagrihas*, or womb-like sanctums, capped by modest spires or *vimanas*. Kanchipuram is a typical temple town,

within comfortable driving distance of Mahabalipuram in a north-westerly direction inland. **Kailasanatha**, the finest structural Pallavas temple, is located here. This temple has an added courtyard, and the *vimana* crowning the inner sanctum is higher. Prototype carvings of Shiva, accompanied by his consort and mythical lions known as *yalis* set the standard for carvers. The town's silk saris are renowned for colour and intricate patterns.

Temple architecture buffs should travel on to Thanjavur, Srirangam and Madurai, much further south. In **Thanjavur**, the former Chola capital set in the Kaveri delta paddy fields, the **Brihadeshwara** temple dominates the landscape. It was constructed in the 10th century by Rajaraja I to appear bigger and better that anything the Pallavas built. It features a *vimana* over 200 ft (60 metres) high and entrance towers known as *gopuras*, built amongst other innovations. Subsequent Chola temples add subsidiary shrines and extended *mandapas* or pavilions to the architectural plan. Chola bronzes and Tanjore paintings, made with uncut gems, are worth

Temple complex, Kanchipuram.

seeking out here. Regular buses ply from Madras, Pondicherry and Madurai.

Leap-frogging over a few centuries, one arrives at **Srirangam** and **Madurai** – within easy driving distance – to see the work of the Vijaynagar Kings. Temples now had to support an increasing number of social functions. Here royal one up-manship has been taken further. For marriages, for example, the 1,000 pillared pavilions were added. The *gopuras* have been made taller and water tanks were also introduced.

Although each temple town has a distinct character, there is a redundancy of sensations after a while. The strident call of *nagaswarams* (a reed pipe loosely comparable to the oboe), the overpowering fragrance of jasmine and marigold garlands; the sight of hundreds of slippers piled up outside temple *gopuras* and the odour of thousands of superstitious pilgrims pressing forward for a better view of a idol being paraded on a palanquin; these are common to all temple complexes. Also, from a spiritual standpoint, the architectural evolution reflects a steady

bureaucratisation of the powerful religious energy which once animated the land.

A good way to put this in context would be to visit the **Ramalingeswara** temple on **Rameswaram** island, severed from the mainland by a cyclone in the 15th century. Walk away from blaring, devotional songs playing on loudspeakers and catch a bus as far as it will go to the extreme tip of the island for a holy bath at **Danushkodi,** the site of the confluence of the Indian ocean with the Bay of Bengal. Later while walking back to the bus stop 2 miles (3 km) across a perfect circle of sand, sprinkled with dunes which turn purple in the twilight, a traveller might recollect that a pilgrimage to Varanasi was once said to be complete only after bathing at Danushkodi. Danushkodi, incidentally, was a thriving port linking India to Sri Lanka, only 12 miles (20 km) away across the Gulf of Mannar, until it was devastated by a cyclone in 1964.

There was a time when the Ramalingeswara temple was a thatched shack in a hermit's charge. Today it is famous almost only for its 1,212 pillar corridors and practically no one bothers to walk out of Danushkodi or Rama's Bow for a swim in Rama's legendary bathing pool.

A feature of Tamil temples are the presiding orthodox Brahmins, who still dress in white loincloths and display forehead markings, half shaven scalps and long hair at the back twisted into single plaits. A sacred thread always stands out against their bare chests. Although a minority community, the Tamilian Brahmins continue to exert much influence in national and international affairs. Their relatively fair skin and aquiline features have led them to claim Aryan ancestry.

In reaction to centuries of Brahmin rule, a pro-Dravidian party championed lower castes and won power in 1967. The matinee idol, MG Ramachandran (MGR) took over a decade later, still speaking for the masses. The current Chief Minister Jayalalitha Jayaram, who ascended the throne after his death, is also a former film star and just goes to show how routine the transition from sex symbol to ruling divinity has become for modern Tamil Nadu.

In Tamil Nadu today MGR survives largely as a gigantic cut out in the pres-

Arjuna's Penance, carvings at Mahabali-puram.

ence of his former "companion" Jayalalitha or as a hideously painted statue. (Watch out for the guy in dark glasses, a white fur cap and pink lips.) Meanwhile Jayalalitha has seen her airbrush aura grow since MGR's demise. Today she rules the state with a heart which seems to have no need for the bullet-proof vest concealed beneath her maternity cape – and evokes hysterical support from her fans, including a walk across burning coals by a group of sycophants and ruling party ministers.

Amongst the state's other quirks are its attitude to skin colour and language. The ebony-skinned Tamils are perhaps the most colour-conscious people in the world. Relatively light-skinned men, women and babies being a definite talking point for proud family members.

In the hills Tamil Nadu preserves vintage British colonial hedonism. A traveller may arrive at the former summer retreats of **Coonoor**, **Wellington** and **Ooty** in the Nilgiri hills (Western Ghats) by an antique hill train which climbs through steep forests past butterflies and jungle fowl. The occasional wild elephant trumpets in response to the engines hooting.

Long walks, golf, angling, riding and just reading by a fire are the usual Nilgiri pastimes. Many of the anglicised Indian gentlemen in these parts tog up in red coats and ride with slobbering hounds in pursuit of jackals. The fact that typically Tamilian *dosas* – rice pancakes – are often served at post-hunt breakfasts only emphasises just how well other British rituals adapt to Dravidian conditions. Gorse, imported from Scotland, now grows wild and expatriate trout are taken on a fly local gillies refer to as *Kakibandoo* from the Welsh *coch y bondhu*. Snooker was first played at the Ootacamund Club, one of the last bastions of suet pudding.

In addition to hill stations in the Nilgiris, **Kodaikanal** in the Palani hills and **Yercaud** in the Shevaroy hills are former colonial summer-escapes located in Tamil Nadu. Yercaud has the advantage of being less popular with tourists and Kodaikanal that of being close to Madurai, and thus on the regular temple beat.

On the coast: Tamil Nadu's long coastline is washed by diverse influences.

Left, a Tamil does his penance. **Below**, Meenakshi Temple, Madurai.

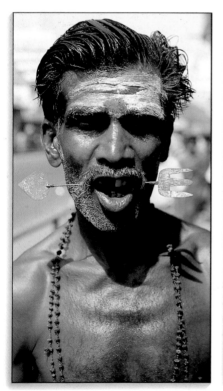

Pondicherry, the former French colony, is listed as a Union Territory for administrative purposes. All this implies for a traveller is that beer is cheaper. In addition to Le Club – arguably the best French restaurant in India – Pondicherry has French-speaking rickshaw drivers, Vietnamese restaurants and Goubert Salai, the cleanest seaside promenade in the country. It is also one of the very few towns in India where woman may freely bare their legs. Mirra Alfissa, French-born spiritual companion to the Bengali philosopher Sri Aurobindo, put her disciples in shorts in the 1950s. To this day turbanned matrons of epic proportions still pedal their bikes unencumbered.

Alfissa, known as The Mother, also believed that if men have evolved from apes, then supermen could evolve from men. **Auroville**, the city conceived to breed such supermen and India's only officially sanctioned global village commune, lies a short bicycle ride from Pondicherry. In this community it is possible to find people of Tamilian village background who dress and work like European executives and Europeans who live and work like Tamilian villagers!

Some European settlements on the Tamil Nadu coast are more obscure. A committed traveller can experience what is left of the former Danish settlement of **Tranquebar** by walking through the old gate, with its coat-of-arms, down to the sea. A memorial to the first protestant missionaries to visit India remembers Bartholomew Ziegenbalg and Heinrich Plutschau. On the right Dansborg Fort overlooks a deserted beach. (The state government is said to have negotiated with the Taj Group of hotels to turn Tranquebar into a heritage resort, but there is no sign of anything happening yet.)

Unfortunately there is no place to stay in Tranquebar or many of the small beach towns on the Coromandel coast. Apart from **Covelong** and **Mahabalipuram** near Madras, Tamil Nadu is yet to exploit its coastline for tourism. The exception is Hotel Tamil Nadu's ugly beach-side cottages at **Mandapam**. This marine research town on the mainland is within easy driving distance of the Rameswaram temple.

Ritual bathing at the seaside, Tamil Nadu.

Jungle: As might be expected from a state bounded by the Western and Eastern ghat mountains and the Coromandel coast, there are still a few pockets of natural jungle, coastal wetland and coral islands where wild animals, birds and intrepid tourists can thrive.

On the coast, **Vedanthangla** and **Point Calimere** play host to a large number of migratory birds during the winter monsoon. **Mudumalai**, in the Nilgiri foothills is the home of the gaur (Indian bison), wild elephants and a handful of tigers. The Anamalai sanctuary near Kodaikanal harbours lion-tailed macaques. Access to these sanctuaries is easily granted upon arrival, though it is wise to book accommodation, elephants and jeeps in advance.

Lesser known sanctuaries (which require special government permits) offer the naturalist an extraordinary chance to view rare species.

Mannar Marine Park, for example, is clustered around 21 low-lying, uninhabited coral islands drawn into the Gulf of Mannar as if with a sharp eyebrow pencil.

The sanctuary is the home of the endangered sea cow, or Dugong dugong. Myriad other aquatic life forms are also supported by the park's coral reef and more than a hundred varieties of seaweed and grass which changes the depths of green in the sea bed. Permission to land on the island can be granted only by the Chief Conservator of Forests in Madras, if you convince him that you have a genuine professional reason for visiting.

The Mukurti sanctuary, home of the Nilgiri Tahr (an endangered species of mountain goat) located high in the Nilgiri, is restricted access. Permission may be routinely obtained from the Nilgiri Wildlife Association in Ootacamund, but can take a few days. **Mukurti** is a little known paradise where clefts of tropical rain forests called sholas combine with grassland in a primeval garden. At this altitude (6–7,000 ft/1,800–2,100 metres) one has the surreal benefit of a temperate climate and tropical colours straight off a beach shirt. Here tigers in flaming mountain coats prove that Tamil Nadu has more to set fire to its landscape than billboard starlets.

Tamil Nadu farm.

306

ASHRAMS

The ashram circuit is the key to the secret heart of India. North to South the country is rich in opportunities to experience a wide heritage of disciplines for body and mind. The stretching and breathing exercises of hatha yoga are now ubiquitous in the West, but in India the interested traveller can go to the source.

Some ashrams heavily emphasise physical culture, while others combine yogic exercises and diet with meditation and study of philosophy. There are holistic healing centres where yoga, massage, diet, ayurvedic medicine and naturopathy are employed to relieve a variety of ailments, and at least a week or two of your time is required.

Institutions that concentrate on yoga have a Hindu orientation, and are the most numerous in largely Hindu India, but there are also Buddhist, Jain and Sikh centres. Most ashrams are located at important pilgrimage places, and are sometimes called *dharamsalas*, a Sanskrit term meaning "pilgrim's rest house". Often the same holy spot is honoured by several religions.

Some modern-day gurus have become jet-setters who spend more time abroad than at home. Bogus gurus are legion, particularly attracted to the extra rupees foreign travellers bring, so going along with a known thing is a good idea. Contact organisations at home or reliable sources in India for recommendations.

High profile ashrams include Sai Baba's centre in Puttaparthi near Bangalore in South India and the late Swami Muktananda's ashram in Ganeshpuri near Bombay. The Muktananda ashram is now headed by one of his successors, Swami Chidvilasananda, or Gurumayi, and prospective guests must apply months in advance.

The International Society for Krishna Consciousness (ISKON) operates ashrams in various places sacred to Krishna, such as Vrindaban and Varanasi. ISKON centres which draw Hare Krishna devotees, have restaurants attached where food is good, clean and reasonably priced.

Those after a slick, new-age, Club Meditation approach may prefer the pricey (for India) Osho-Rajneesh centre in Puné, Maharashtra. Now run by an "inner circle" of Westerners, the ashram offers a broad selection of psycho-spiritual courses, food at Western prices. Visitors stay at nearby hotels and an Aids test is required.

The Satyananda Yoga ashram in Monghyr, Bihar offers good facilities and instruction. If you are staying in Bombay, try the yoga institute in Santa Cruz, which runs week-long courses and teaches yoga with an emphasis on health and healing. Yoga ashrams provide vegetarian food only.

Hill stations near sacred sites on the river Ganga are likely places to find low-key, restful ashrams. Rishikesh, in Uttar Pradesh, is one such. It had brief fame in the 1960 when the Beatles flirted with Transcendental Meditation at Maharishi Mahesh Yogi's ashram there. Swami Sivananda founded his Divine Life Society there in 1936, and today a large ashram invites study of yoga and Hindu philosophy.

There are possibilities amongst many small temples along the Beas River in Himachal Pradesh. Numerous Tibetan Buddhist monasteries range along the route from Dharamsala to Manali. Some monasteries have teachers in residence and accommodation for students who wish to study and practise Tibetan Buddhism. There are also Tibetan Buddhist monasteries at Darjeeling and Sikkim and at Bylekuppe and Mungod in the South. Some of these areas require special entry permits. ∎

ANDHRA PRADESH

South India starts in Andhra Pradesh. Geologically it is one of the most ancient parts of peninsular India. In historical times, the region was divided into three major segments, namely the coastal Circars, Telengana and the hinterland Rayalaseema. These are indeed three distinctive geographical tracts, the first being the rich fertile riparian and deltaic parts of the Godavari and the Krishna; the second, the forested and hilly tract of the north, between the Vindhya range and the Godavari River; and the third, the southwestern part of the lower Deccan in the districts of Cuddappah, Kurnool, Chittoor and Anantapur – hilly, plateau land with hot, arid valleys. Telengana is Andhra's core region and Telugu, the name of the language of the Andhras, is derived from its name.

Kingdoms in Andhra have also followed this regional pattern, with the most ancient Vishnukundins and the Vengi Chalukyas and the Matharas in the Vijayanagar kings in Rayalaseema, and the Kakatiyas in Telengana.

The Telugu language has the vocabulary and richness of classical Sanskrit usage, with the result that, despite its basic Dravidian matrix, it is almost overwhelmingly "spoken Sanskrit" in style. The rural traditions are notable for their *padyam*s – rolling, sonorous prose narrations of rural life, customs, *characteritcs* and festivities. Telugu is one of the sweetest among the Indian tongues, and has rich epic and Puranic literature, created by a galaxy of poets like Potana, Vemana, Srinatha and Nannayya.

Telugu culture absorbed the best of Vedic Aryan felicities of the north into its Dravidian base and expressed it in art, music and dance. Under the Satavahanas (2nd century BC to the 2nd century AD) it had played a notable part in shaping and defining the Southern Indian ethos, besides protecting the zone from the onslaughts of medieval Islamic thrusts into the south. Nevertheless, the Telengana region has been continuously exposed to Islam since medieval times and Hyder-abad, the captial of Andhra Pradesh, was the capital of the Muslim Nizam of Hyderabad until independence.

The Andhras are excellent craftsmen, making lacquer toys, Anakapalli articles, Nirmal painted pottery, *bidri* – lead-inlaid back-metal trinkets and palm-leaf and slate articles, besides the Gadhwal, Pochampad and Dharmavaram silk saris.

Kucchipudi is the classical Andhra dance form. It is essentially a narrative dance of Puranic legends, branching off in its essential grammar and gestures from the pristine *Bharata Natyam* of Tamil Nadu.

A modern city: The Qutb Shahais, who ruled the area in the 16th and 17th centuries had their capital city in the fortress city of Golconda. The capital was shifted to **Hyderabad** only in 1590. The later offshoot of this dynasty, the Asaf Jahi Nizams, ruled from Hyderabad. Their dominions spread over the whole of Telengana, Vidarbha and Marathwada of the present-day Maharashtra, and the districts of Bidar and Gulbarga of the present-day Karnataka.

Alone among the Indian princes, the Nizam was given the distinction of being called His Exalted Highness by the British. The last of the clan was Nizam VII, Osman Ali Khan, the owner of fabulous royal jewellery and gems of inestimable value. The Nizam left several palaces in and around Hyderabad, like the Falaknuma Palace on the Banjara Hills and the main King Kothi Palace in the heart of Hyderabad city, which lies forlorn today.

One of the early generals of the clan, Salar Jung, was noted for his voluminous collections of antiques and rare art treasures which were housed in a showpiece landmark of Hyderabad, the **Salar Jung Museum**, now given the status of a National Museum and housed in a new building. It has a unique collection of miniature paintings and illuminated manuscripts of the Koran as well as gems.

The original town of Bhagyangara, located on the Musi River, has been built into modern Hyderabad, linking it with the adjacent area of its twin city of Secunderabad at the other end of **Hussain Sagar** lake which connects the two townships and which has become a favourite evening promenade.

Charminar, Hyderabad landmark.

On a rocky plateau with access to both the Krishna and Godavari Rivers, Hyderabad has become the centre of a transport and communication network and a market for crafts, grains, tobacco and the *anabshahi* variety of large-sized seedless grapes that thrive in the climate and on the soil of Telengana and Rayalaseema.

The famed **Charminar**, built at the end of the 16th century, is one of the landmarks of the city. It rises to four storeys and has space for a mosque on its topmost floor. Built in typical Qutb-Shahi style, with carefully finished stucco ornamentation and *gul-dasta* style minars, and miniature minarets at the corners and the fringes, it maintains the architectural tradition seen at Golconda.

Around Charminar is an interesting bazaar area where some of the best bargains can be struck in goods from silk, metalwork, pearls and bangles, to rare Urdu books and manuscripts. Adjacent to the Charminar is the impressive **Mecca Mosque**, among the largest in the world. Its construction proceeded in stages over almost the whole 17th century.

The twin city, **Hyderabad-Secunderabad**, is among the seven largest cities of India. Secunderabad, till India became independent, remained separated from Hyderabad though adjacent to it, because it was the seat of the British "Resident" in Hyderabad State. Parts of the town are still typical of that type of British-Indian township – the Secunderabad Club and the old Residency are excellent examples.

By tradition, Hyderabad has always been a cosmopolitan and gracious city, a centre of learning and the arts. It enjoys mild cool winters.

Fortress city: Now almost part of sprawling Hyderabad, **Golconda** has grand fortifications, a Citadel, numerous mosques, tombs, pavilions and *baradaris* and the remarkable tomb cluster of the Qutb Shahi royal cemetery at the foot of the fort. The fortress held out for eight long months when it was besieged by the mighty Mughal Emperor Aurangzeb in 1687 and fell only when it was treacherously betrayed. The main citadel is situated on a hill and is surrounded by walls of solid stone. The outer wall, surround-

Golconda Fort.

ing the whole township, is about 8 miles (13 km) long and is also strongly fortified. In its heyday, the 6-mile (10-km) long road from Golconda to Hyderabad was a fabulous bazaar selling jewellery, diamonds, pearls and other gems and trinkets which were world famous. Marco Polo came here to bargain.

Going north to south in Andhra Pradesh, there are the coastal districts of the Northern Circars. There, at a wooded site near Gara is the group of temples at **Mukhalingam**, built by Ganga kings. Across the Rishikilya and Vamsadhra rivers is **Srikurmam**, where there is a unique representation of a zooanthropomorphic incarnation of Vishnu as tortoise-man in the sanctum of the Vishnu Temple. This valley is rich in Buddhist *stupa* sites, as at **Salihundam** and the ancient port of **Kalingapatnam**.

To the south on the Godavari estuary is **Rajamahendrapuram** on the route to **Vengi**, the site of the capital of the Eastern Chalukyas in Eluru District, and also to the delightful coastal group of temples at **Biccavolu** and **Masulipatnam**.

Further south is **Vijayawada**, an ancient city with a large number of 6th–13th century AD rock-cut and structural temples along the banks of the River Krishna. **Amaravati**, the celebrated Buddhist site, with its museums and temples, is 16 miles (26 km) away.

Northeast of Hyderabad, in the Telengana region, is **Warangal**, a reputedly impregnable fortress, which was under continuous attack from the Delhi Sultans in the 13th and 14th centuries. It has four massive *toranas* (gates). Nearby is the spectacular **Hanumankonda Temple** of the Kakatiyas built of blocks of granite. A little further, in Palampet on the banks of a lake is **Ramappa Temple**, embellished with sculptures of women dancers.

Across the bridge over the Godavari near Khammam and Kottagudem, is the **temple of the god Bhadrachalam** who is supposed to have descended to earth in human form to ransom Ramadasa, a saint being held by a Qutb Shahi king.

Leaving the Telengana region and turning south towards the Krishna Valley, one reaches **Kurnool**, passing on the way the

Sketch of Amravati bas-relief.

NAGA PEOPLE WORSHIPPING THE TRISUL EMBLEM OF BUDDHA, ON A FIERY PILLAR.

From a bas-relief at Amaravati.

magnificent group of Navabrahma Temples near Alampur. Further south, along the Nallamalai Hills, past the Ahobilam Hill Temple, and the Chola temples at Attirala on the Pennar River, one reaches **Tirupati**, the great pilgrim centre which draws a stream of bald pilgrims from north, south, east and west to its shrine of **Shri Venkateswara**. Non-Hindus may visit. More people come here than visit Mecca, and it is India's wealthiest temple.

Close to Tirupati is the **Chandagiri Mahal and Fort**. It was here that the last Vijayanagar king, Ranga Raya, approved of the sale to the East India Company of the land on which Fort St George at Madras was built.

In the opening centuries of the Christian era, the entire coastal belt, and more especially the Krishna River delta and lower reaches, hummed with activity and sea-going vessels reached as far upstream as Amaravati (or Dhanyakataka), the capital city of the southern wing of the Satavahanas, and beyond up to Nagarjunakonda. Further upstream, the Krishna runs in a long serpentine gorge across the Srisailam Ranges from the upper plateau stretches, after its confluence with the Tungabhadra at Sangamesvaram and the environs of Alampur.

This whole area had been subjected to several excavations over the years, especially at **Nagarjunakonda**, near **Nagarjunasagar** dam which will eventually submerge this whole valley. Most archeological remains have been moved to an island museum reached by boat.

Digging revealed several Buddhist monastic settlements with *stupas* (Buddhist reliquaries), *chaityas* (Buddhist temples), and *viharas* (monasteries) and records quoting clergy and scholars participating in these centres, and coming from as far as Kashmir, Gandhara, China and Kamarupa (now Assam).

Crystal reliquaries placed within stone caskets and containing gold, flowers and bone fragments have been found. Carved *Buddhapadas* (replicas of the feet of the Buddha) also often contained relics in a receptacle cavity cut between the big toes.

Along with Buddhism and Hinduism, Jainism had also flourished in Andhra

Left, a devotee at Tirupati Temple. Below, celebrating Pongal, a southern festival.

Pradesh but was mostly confined to the central and southwestern parts of the state, as at Tumbalam in the Cuddappah District, near Adoni.

Moving island towards the border with Orissa, the landscape begins to alter. No longer do isolated mounds rise from the plain, framed by areca palms like a vision from Gauguin painting. Mango groves, coffee plantations and waterfalls groves appear, with swift streams flowing through them. Approaching the wooded eastern Ghats, the roads roughen and climb.

The Araku Valley is tribal territory, with 17 groups spread out in 70 small villages. The people like to wear several nose rings at once and carry rattan umbrellas to protect against rain or sun. Dances and hunting festivals may be open to visitors, and rustic shrines devoted to ancestor worship can be photographed. The ox carts have huge wheels. During Pongal, the winter festival, the oxen's horns are painted bright colours. Naxalite guerillas sometimes hide out in the hills, but travel is generally safe, though slow.

The highest point in Andhra rises to 5,511ft (1,680 metres) in the midst of the **Chintapalli Forest**, known for exotic birds and flying squirrels. **Sankaram** some 28 miles (45 km) distant, has rock pinnacles where Buddhists carved and worshipped in caves and monasteries between 300 BC and 700 AD. They are known today as the ten million *lingams*, or Kotilingams.

Vizianagaram, once capital of the Kalinga kingdom, has a spectacular fort dating from the 2nd century. At the old temple, the King Deva Raya had a vision in 1509 which inspired the classic Telugu memoirs, "Amakutamalyada".

Although the industrial port of **Visakhapatnam** boast a long beach, it is rough and none too clean. Better swimming, without the threat of sharks, is possible at the mouth of Gostari River, 15 miles (24 km) away, at **Bhimunipatnam**. Since cyclones can come unexpectedly anytime between October and December, always check local weather forecasts before setting out. Nearby, bananas and palms line **Hollanders Green**, or Vallanda Bhoomi, where a Dutch East Indies Company left a cemetery, fort and armoury.

Consulting an astrologer.

KARNATAKA

Accounting for a sixteenth of the total land mass of India, Karnataka, with a population of about 45 million, consists of three distinct regions: a narrow fertile coastal strip, comprising of the two districts of North and South Kanara along the Arabian Sea; the hilly uplands dominated by the Western Ghats whose peaks stand like stern sentinels barring the entry of monsoon clouds into the third area, the Deccan Plateau east of the Ghats where the landscape becomes rock-strewn and bare. No three regions could be more strikingly different.

Coastal Karnataka is about 40 miles (65 km) broad at its widest. A dozen rivers flow through this coastal strip, their banks swollen during the three monsoon months (July–September) of torrential rain. This is when the red soil of Kanara decks itself with brilliant greenery for miles at a stretch.

Malnad, in the foothills of the Ghats, one of the wettest region in India, is celebrated for its teak and rosewood, its areca and bamboo, its pepperving and cardamom. In the southern region of the Ghats, amidst the profusion of tropical rainforests, roams the Indian elephant, as do the stately gaur and the long-tailed langur, the latter frequently breaking into the silence of the freckled forest with gossipy chatter.

The Deccan plateau is reputed to be one of the oldest land formations on earth – the so-called Gondwana Plate, which emerged when geological time theoretically began.

Unlike the rivers of coastal Karnataka, the upland rivers are in no great hurry to rush to the sea. The one exception is the Sharavati, which plunges down a yawning chasm in a glorious spectacle of cascading water and flying spray. **Jog Falls** is visited by thousands all the year round, especially in the winter months, when the water flows fullest. The Honnemardu eco-project offers watersports nearby.

As varied as the land is its people. In Karnataka's southern corner, amidst the **The palace at Mysore.**

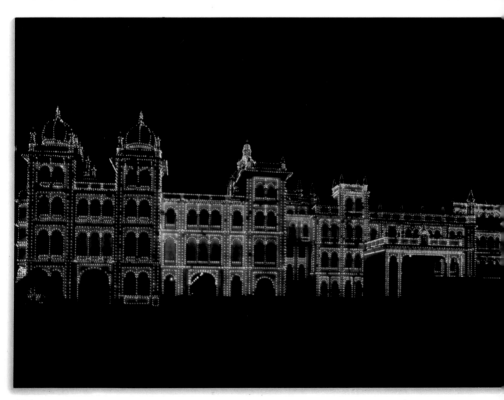

314

hills and valleys of **Coorg**, live the tall and sinewy Kodagu people whose picturesque costumes are in striking contrast to the simpler lifestyle of the people on the coast.

North of Coorg, in the flatland of what was the former state of Mysore, live the Vokkaligas whose rich farms are watered by the river Kaveri. The local accent has a musical cadence and falls softly on the ear, in contrast to the Kannada spoken farther north, which is harsh and guttural.

The dividing line between the two regions is the river Tungabhadra, which is also the dividing line between the black and red soils of the state. Incidentally, the word "Kannada" is derived from *kari* (black) and *nadu* (land).

The people of the north are mostly Lingayats, followers of that great scholar-saint, Basava (12th century), whose masculine vigour in the handling of the Kannada language and whose uncompromising preaching of the equality of all people mark him out as one of Karnataka's notable personalities.

Coastal Karnataka is inhabited, among others, by fisherfolk who have plied their boats for generations and whose forefathers traded with ancient Mesopotamia. Even the Greeks are known to have come to Karnataka's shores in the pre-Christian era. Spoken in this coastal strip are Kannada, the dominant language of the state; Tulu, one of the five Dravidian languages; and Konkani, which belongs to the Indo-Aryan group. Konkani, in its many accents, is spoken by Hindus, Christians and Muslims alike.

The Christians of Kanara are among the oldest converts to the faith, with some of their churches dating back to the 16th century. The Church of the Most Holy Rosary at Bolar, in Mangalore, was established in 1526.

A cursory look at the past: Karnataka's history is a turbulent one. First in recorded memory is the dynasty of the Chalukyas, who were replaced by the Rashtrakutas, one of whom, the great Amoghavarsha Nripatunga (814–880 AD), wrote a magnificent treatise on poetics. The Rashtrakutas were the premier

High Court, Bangalore.

power in the India of their day. It was they who had the massive monolithic Kailash Temple at Ellora in Maharashtra carved from solid rock.

After the Rashtrakutas came the Chalukyas of Kalyana. There were other princely houses, too, like the Kadambas of Hangal, the Sindas of Sindavadi, and the Silaharas of north Konkan. Later came the Hoysalas and the Rayas of the Vijayanagar Empire.

For several centuries, between the end of the Rashtrakuta rule and the rise of the Vijayanagar kingdom, seers and saint singers of compelling power and truth, rather than warriors, were to dominate the scene. With the downfall of the Vijayanagar kingdom, Karnataka did not emerge on the national scene again till Hyder Ali and his son Tipu Sultan were to galvanise the country with their military prowess and administrative acumen. When the British finally overpowered Tipu in 1799 at the famous Battle of Seringapatam, they dismembered his kingdom with thoroughness. Karnataka thereafter was parcelled out among various political groupings, leaving the core of Tipu's empire to be ruled by a successor of an earlier deposed dynasty, with his capital in Mysore.

But even before the advent of Hyder Ali, other Muslim rulers had established themselves in north Karnataka, in **Bijapur**. The founder of the kingdom of Bijapur, Yusuf Adil Shah, was born in Constantinople in 1443. His successors were to enrich the city with such splendid mosques as to rival anything Islam could raise elsewhere. Outstanding is **Gol Gumbaz**, whose dome is comparable to that of St Peter's in Rome.

At **Gulbarga** are the remnants of a fort originally built by a Raja Gulchand and later developed by Allauddin Bahmani, founder of the kingdom of that name. The fort covers several hectares and includes the **Jami Mosque** with 37,600 sq. feet (35,000 sq. metres) of built-up area in the style of the mosque at Cordova in Spain. The interior arches are so designed and the pillars placed that the pulpit can be seen unobstructed from any part of the hall. The acoustics too are perfect.

Gol Gumbaz, Bijapur.

316

The capital of modern Karnataka is **Bangalore**, whose beginnings go back to 1537, when a petty chieftain, Kempe Gowda, built a mud fort on a hill. Today, it is a sprawling city, one of the fastest growing in India, covering some 50 sq. miles (130 sq. km) and attracting computer software firms, aerospace and commerce. Located here are some of the largest industrial plants in India. Winston Churchill once lived here in one of the earliest clubs set up by the British. Indeed, at one time, Bangalore was a little British island in the south, and Raj connections remain in such names as Richmond Town, Cox Town and Fraser Town.

There are many attractive places within 18–25 miles (30–40 km) of Bangalore: the **Nandi Hills** are famous for their salubrious climate, and **Bannarghatta** is an hour's drive from Bangalore and has been made a national park for protected wildlife. Seen here are over a hundred varieties of birds, besides monkeys, bison, wild boar, elephants, panthers, spotted deer and sloth bears.

Mysore, capital of the erstwhile princely state of that name, is famous for its jasmine, known locally as Mysore Mallige, whose fragrance has been widely celebrated in song. It is also famous for its silk and sandalwood, its palaces and its leisurely way of life.

About 8 miles (14 km) from Mysore is the battle-scarred town of **Shrirangapattam**, once Tipu Sultan's capital. It was here that the Tiger of Mysore, as Tipu was called, fought and died. Outside the ruins of the old fort is **Daria Daulat** (Splendour of the Sea), Tipu's summer palace, set in an exquisite garden and still in good shape though it was built in 1784. About 30 miles (48 km) from Mysore is the lovely temple of **Somnathpur** built by the renowned architect, Jakanachari. Around its exterior base are portrayed in sequence the main incidents from the *Ramayana* and *Mahabharata*, India's great epics.

But Somnathpur is only hors d'oeuvre to the main architectural course – there are still the temples at Halebid, Belur, **Badami**, **Aihole** and Pattadakal. It wasn't for nothing that Karnataka has been called

Below, dancing Shiva, Halebid. Right, colossus of Jain saint at Gomateswara, Shravan Belgola.

the cradle of India's temple architecture. Some are freestanding structures, others have been carved out of granite hills.

First were the cave temples of Badami and Aihole, carved in the second half of the 6th century AD. By the beginning of the 7th century, the transition from the rock-cut medium to structural techniques was already underway. **Belur** is a striking example of the latter, as is **Halebid** about 11 miles (17 km) east of Belur. But easily the most remarkable work of art – though not necessarily the most beautiful – is the 57-ft (17-metre) statue of a Jain saint, Gomateswara, raised on a granite hill, itself 394 ft (120 metres) above ground level. The statue was erected in 983 AD and there is nothing comparable to it in the world. Of this, the historian Fergusson wrote: "One is astonished at the amount of labour such a work must have entailed and puzzled to know whether it was part of the hill or had been moved to the spot where it now stands."

In north Karnataka is **Hampi,** the site of the capital of the old Vijayanagar Empire. These medieval ruins cover some 10 sq. miles (26 sq. km). Hampi is 8 miles (14 km) from Tungabhadra Dam and on the outskirts of Hospet, a town connected to other cities by an excellent train service. The ruins of Hampi, which are most impressive even today, include the **Virupaksha Temple** where worship continues to be offered as it was when it was first built. Its central hall was raised by the emperor Krishnadevaraya to commemorate his coronation in 1509–10. The Portuguese traveller Paes, who saw Hampi in its heyday, described it as being as large as Rome, with the palaces of its king more spacious than the castles of Lisbon. Hampi was destroyed in 1565, after the Battle of Talikota, in which the Vijayanagar army was defeated by the forces of the Bijapur confederacy.

The Kannada personality: Karnataka has been described as the crucible in which races, classes, religions and cultures have acted and interacted to produce the Kannada personality – generous, liberal in the understanding of value systems other than its own, and distrustful of fanaticism and flamboyance. One distinguished Kannada writer, V. Sitaramiah,

has asserted that "the long-range value preference, the pride and grateful memory of Kannada poets, has been, by and large, for tolerance and the art of peace."

And what are these "arts of peace?" The weavers of silk in Mysore, of saris in Irkal, the patient carvers in ivory and sandalwood who have made Karnataka famous, the Yakshagana dancers of Kanara and a whole school of musical articulation that embraces the entire south, but centred at Dharwad. The red clay tiles made in Mangalore on the coast are not only used all over India but have, for decades, been exported to East Africa and elsewhere – east and west.

Savoury delights: Karnataka's culinary genius has peacefully conquered cities all over India and has even established footholds in London, Paris, Frankfurt, Tokyo and New York. If the Kanara coast specialises in a variety of seafood, it is also responsible for the making of the polysyllabic *bisi bele huli anna* (created, as much as made out of lentil, tamarind, chilli powder and *dalchini)* and the even more famous *idli* (rice cakes) and *dosai* (a kind of pancake, hot and spicy, often with potato fillings). Lesser known among the gastronomic delights of Karnataka are *uppittu* (made of wheat flour, shredded coconut, green chillis and lemon) and *hoalige* (a flat pancake-like wafer about six inches across, filled with molasses and shredded coconut, or copra and sugar, or a variety of lentils and molasses, and fried lightly in a flat skillet).

One of the pleasures of Karnataka is the variety of its offerings of fruit. There are some 25 varieties of mango alone, from the humble *neelam* to the royal *Bennet Alphonso.* In coastal Karnataka, every household has its mini orchard, with mango, banana, chickoo, mangosteen and jackfruit trees, and cashew trees with their delicious nuts. One can get drunk, they say, just on cashew fruit and, indeed, one of the best drinks is a brand of cashew liquor called *feni.* Like vodka, it has to be drunk for its potency.

One has to spend time in Karnataka to savour its many delights. For sheer beauty, there are few places that can excel the string of lakes that constitute the **Sharavati** system or the confluence of the **Hemavati** and the **Kaveri** rivers, just above the **Krishnaraja Sagar**. To the people of Karnataka, the Kaveri is *Mother Kaveri,* the giver of wealth.

The beaches of Karnataka are something else again. From Karwar in the north to Ullal in the south, it is one long stretch of sparkling white. The poet Rabindranath Tagore thought there never was another beach more beautiful than the one at **Karwar**, but he probably had not seen **Thandrabail** or **Suratkal**. Lying there, on a moonlit night, amidst the gathering sounds of the waves scudding against the black basalt shore, and listening to the whisper of winds through the casuarinas, or sitting in the shade of a coconut grove, sipping the tender-coconut water, time flows untroubled.

Drama and buffalo races: But nothing can be more memorable than a night spent in a field, sitting on a straw mat watching *bayalata* (field play), the folk drama of the people. This is not for anyone in a hurry, for the drama depicting the exploits of heroes and heroines from India's epics will run from early night till the rising of the sun. It has everything: music, dance, drama, and, of course, there is the easy camaraderie of people who know what it is all about and are willing to share their knowledge with you.

When the fields are flush with water, there is another sight not to be missed: the *kambala* or the buffalo race that is unique to Kanara. Run in a paddy field by pairs of buffaloes, egged on by strong-muscled men in a highly charged atmosphere, the *kambala* is an annual event.

Here is a man crouching behind the buffaloes on a stout wooden shaft yoked to the animals. Not a muscle moves. Only the wind is playing on his locks of hair. Suddenly the scene explodes, the man springs up, his hand cocked, his whip held high, and huge animals lunge forward, bellowing, their hooves churning the muddy waters and sending their wet spray into the hot air, their eyes wide, wild and white – man and beast engaged with one aim: victory.

This is Karnataka where every day brings adventure and joy. *Banni, bega banni!* or Come, come soon!

Chariot Temple amongst the remains of Hampi.

KERALA

Long ago a demon called Darikan sought invincibility by undergoing an arduous penance. His dedication forced Brahma, the Lord of Creation, to grant him his wish. Revelling in his immortality, Darikan proceeded on a wave of destruction so terrible that the whole world trembled and even the gods felt threatened. They prostrated before Lord Shiva and beseeched him to save the Universe.

As the all-powerful God knew Darikan had contemptuously rejected Brahma's offer of immunity from women, he summoned up his divine energy to create, from his third eye, a goddess. Called Bhadrakali, this warrior-goddess fought with the demon in a war which only ended when Darikan paid for his arrogance with his life. When the victorious Bhadrakali returned to Lord Shiva, he requested her to select a place on earth and reside there as the protector of mankind.

The goddess did not hesitate; she left her father's heavenly abode and came to the land now known as Kerala in the southwestern corner of India. She is the presiding deity in most of the villages of her chosen land and the *thattakkam*, Kerala's local equivalent of a parish, is always under the divine jurisdiction of a goddess.

Kerala's divine attractions are tucked away in the Cardamon Hills and along the Malabar Coast, laced between 41 rivers and plantations of teak, pepper and rubber, all kept green by two monsoons each year. But they are also plentiful in Thiruvanthapuram (**Trivandrum**), former seat of the Maharajahs of Travancore.

Although the temple of **Sri Padmanabhaswamy** that they built to honour Lord Vishnu still physically dominates the bustling city, Trivandrum's secular and political importance is enough to warrant an international airport. The crowds and the bazaars of the new, and growing, urban India can also be seen in the busy sprawling towns of Cochin, Quilon, Trichur, Calicut and Cannanore. These towns are linked by trains and

Temple elephants Trichur, Kerala.

320

buses which pass through a different Kerala – a Kerala of natural beauty bordered by a shoreline where fishermen land their catch to more ancient and timeless rhythms. Whilst the wealth of the sea satisfies the tastes of fish-loving Keralites, the land that it laps against is tilled to yield an equally generous harvest.

Coconuts and coffee: Much of the landscape and wealth of Kerala is dominated by tall, elegant coconut palms. No part of this tree is wasted and a flourishing coir (fibre) industry exists because of its plentiful presence. Coffee plantations spread across the foothills of the Western Ghats, tea grows at higher altitudes and, in southern Kerala, acres of rubber trees stand in lines of military precision.

When Columbus sailed from Spain he sought a route to the land of spices – Kerala. The Malabar coast grows the world's best pepper, known as Black Gold, which induced half of Europe into power struggles to command supplies of this small, pungent berry. The fragrant cardamom and the sweet cashew nut are other important cash crops and no compound is without a few banana trees. The flatter, fertile land supports two or three annual harvests of rice, an essential ingredient in a Keralite's diet.

Rural Kerala is a traditional land with beautiful old houses blending into the contours; with the scholarly and religious dedication of the great 9th-Century Hindu teacher, Adi Shankaracharya, born at Kaladi; with the necessary stamina to master temple arts such as Kathakali; with the austere spiritual magnificence of temples such as those at Ettumanoor, Irinjalakuda and Trichur, and with the stark, white elegance of traditional Kerala dress. In traditional Kerala there is no abuse, waste or vulgarity; there is, instead, along with respect, appreciation and restraint, a deep understanding and reverence for the land which eventually supplies all needs.

Modern values: Today there is also another, newer, Kerala where many of these old values are ridiculed or ignored. Houses are concrete structures built in defiance of the climate and environment; towns like Chavakad have become "little Dubais",

Kovalam Beach, Kerala.

brash and vulgar with the new wealth of thousands of migrant workers to the Gulf states.

The Kerala of today is a mixed land of calm and noise, honesty and corruption, beauty and ugliness, tradition and progress, faith and atheism, learning and ignorance. This is also the Kerala with not only Hindus, Muslims, Christians and Jews but many different castes and communities – all with their own customs and traditions and styles of dress, food, jewellery and marriage.

Many of these different factors blend together: for instance, a Marxist politician might prostrate before a Hindu shrine; a Muslim contribute to a temple festival; or a Christian make a Hindu pilgrimage; and buses display the religious icons of three faiths.

However confusing as it may be for outsiders, Malayalis, the people of Kerala, find nothing contradictory in either their behaviour or their nature. A high-caste Namboodiri brahmin, trained in the priestly *Vedas*, but teaching college mathematics, was amused that his existence could be considered schizophrenic: "Why do you mention two levels? – I live on at least six."

Originally, worship in Kerala revolved around the great mysteries of Nature, a natural respect for one's ancestors and a strong attraction towards the concept of a Mother Goddess.

Over the centuries, the early strains of religious beliefs flowed into the mainstream of Hindu philosophy, so that now the most evolved and austere of Hindu ritual flourishes alongside an ancient and darker Dravidian style of worship.

God is conceived in the most formless, fathomless way by the same people who find the divine in a snake, a tree or a stone. Ghosts, demons and evil spirits are a reality in India's most literate state – the same state that saw, in 1957, the world's first freely elected Communist government.

The temple of **Chottanikkara**, near Cochin, attracts a growing number of faithful pilgrims/patients who seek release from evil spirits, and the long iron nails driven into the huge tree near the sanctum of the goddess testify to their

Preparing for "snake boat" races in the Onam festival.

successful exorcism.

Maybe these contrasting elements explain the genuine religious tolerance found in Kerala, a state remarkably free from the communal violence which still haunts other parts of India.

According to popular belief, the oldest of the Christian denominations, the Syrian Christians, was established by the apostle St Thomas in 50 AD. The followers of the Prophet Muhammad also came early to Kerala, and although the exterior of the mosque at Kodungallur is a brash, modern concrete structure, its interior is still the cool and serene original of India's oldest mosque.

The mosque was built on land given by Kodungallur's Hindu ruler; a gesture echoed by the Rajah of Cochin when he welcomed the Jews, followers of a faith unaccustomed to tolerance elsewhere. Although recent emigration to Israel has reduced the community to a handful, their magnificent synagogue at Cochin still stands.

Christians, Muslims and Jews all found a welcome in Kerala, as did the early Phoenician, Greek and Roman traders. However, when the Zamorin of Calicut greeted Portugal's Vasco da Gama in 1498 he unwittingly received the first European greedy for Indian wealth. Over the centuries, Kerala witnessed and played its part in the colonising struggles of the Portuguese, the French, the Dutch and, finally, the British.

The Raj left a deep and lasting impression on Kerala's social institutions and legal procedures but the Malayali never surrendered his individual identity or passionate awareness of his own culture. There is little colonial architecture and even though the famous Matancherry Palace at Cochin was built by the Portuguese and repaired by the Dutch (renaming it the Dutch Palace), its architectural style is of Kerala.

Exquisite carvings: Kerala's contribution to the cultural wealth of India has been enormous. The palaces are stunning with intricate wood carvings and murals. At **Padmanabhjapuram**, window panes of mica cast a magic light into the carved rooms cooled with natural air-condition-

On Kerala's backwaters.

ing using inner courtyards. An imposing royal bed, a single granite slab, is placed atop a gleaming black floor made from egg whites and burnt coconut shell. Paintings at Krishnapuram are similar to those in the temples at Vaikom and Tripprayyar, but gods and men usually dwell in more austere and restrained houses.

Any list of Indian writers, poets and musicians features Malayalis prominently: people like the diplomat turned writer K.P.S. Menon, the poet Vallathol Narayana Menon (also famous as the man who revived Kathakali and founded the Kalamandalam School near Shoranur), and the great singer of Karnatak music, the late Chembai Vaidyanatha Bhagavatar.

The major cultural contribution of this small state, which covers a mere 15,000 sq. miles (38,850 sq. km) is probably its theatre – some of the world's greatest. There is the highly classical art of Koodiyattam, the lyrically sensuous dance of Mohiniattam, the religious fervour of Krishnanattam and, above all, the spectacular magnificence of Kathakali.

Deep within all these highly developed and refined art forms beats the generating spirit which gives them their existence: an extraordinarily rich folk theatre, a theatre which evolved out of the religious beliefs of its participants and, despite its highly dramatic presentation, is less a theatrical performance than an act of worship. The spectacular *theyyams* of Malabar demonstrate this concept when the fantastically costumed god-actors dance before small shrines, possessed with the spirit and power of their ancient Dravidian deities.

Only during the monsoon months of June to August is it difficult to find some ritual, ceremony or festival taking place. Although the non-Hindu is not usually permitted to enter a temple and witness the most sacred rites, temple festivals are accessible and visible to all.

In central Kerala the use of elephants brings a fairytale quality; there can be few sights to beat that of 30 great caparisoned tuskers assembled before the Vadakkunathan temple on the day of the Trichur Pooram.

Although legend declares that the land of Kerala was formed when Parsurama,

Teyattam dancer is possessed by the god Bhagavati in north Kerala.

an incarnation of Lord Vishnu, threw his mighty battle-axe into the Arabian Sea, the fertile land that emerged was established as the state of Kerala as recently as 1956, with the integration of three Malayalam speaking areas – Malabar and the two former princely states of Cochin and Travancore. Between the ancient creation myth and the modern political fact is a land of lush, physical beauty which contains a rich and unique storehouse of legend, romance, history, culture and tradition.

The open air: Among Kerala's excellent beaches, the best known is Kovalam, located some 10 miles (16 km) south of Trivandrum, where facilities at all levels are available. But for the tourist amenities in the vicinity of the beach itself, in the countryside around and the fishing settlements in the area, life goes on very much as in the rest of rural Kerala. Ayurvedic massage is relaxing after a swim in rough waters.

Varkala, 32 miles (54 km) north of Trivandrum, has a fine beach at the base of cliffs. Watch out for fishing lines or nets which are dragged from the calm water at around sunset.

Close by is **Kollam** (Quilon), a cashew nut port which is the southern gateway to the backwaters. Travellers can journey through a network of narrow canals and wide lakes where people paddle to their daily tasks.

Unlike the wave-tossed western seashore, which runs roughly parallel, the backwaters are calm. Boats of all descriptions are punted or sailed along the shallow green waterways with palms arching overhead. Tidy bungalows line up on either side, to give way to great heaps of coconut fibre or clusters of Chinese fishing nets, lit up at night to attract shrimps.

Where the waters widen, villagers sometimes can be found up to their necks, picking up fish from the muddy bottom with their toes and flinging them into terracotta pots which float beside them on the surface.

Most tourists take the steamers between Kollam (Quilon) and Alappuzha (Alleppey) for a trip which can be done under two hours in the broad passages, or closer

Chinese-style fishing nets off Cochin.

to eight hours when stopping off in the narrow passages. Two companies run them: the state Water Transport Department boats are usually slower than Alleppey Tourism. At Karunagapalli, shipbuilders fashion *kettu vallam*, (literally, tied boats) out of jackwood planks sewn together with coir rope. Several cruising houseboats made in this style, complete with rattan-thatched canopies, can be hired for two-day trips.

At night, they moor amidst the Chinese fishing nets. With 100 percent literacy in the state, constant requests for "one pen" echo across the water, and many a ubiquitous bic is tossed in to float over to the far shore. During winter holidays, paper star lanterns are strung in every window and reflections shimmer in the shallows.

Cochin (Kochi) can be reached from Alleppey by water, but boat traffic on the way to this major port and naval base is extremely heavy, and many prefer to travel by road or rail. Ferries connect the islands **Willingdon**, **Bolgatty**, **Gundu** and **Vypeen** to the southern peninsula of Fort Cochin and Matancherry and also to the commercial centre, **Ernakulum**, on the mainland. Semitic traders from Yemen and Babylon used to import dates and olive oil in exchange for peacocks and spices.

Jew Town, a settlement which dates back a millennium, still thrives with antique and spice shops. The small synagogue there is used by the diminishing Jewish community; many families, originally refugees from Spain in the 15th century when the Rajah of Cochin offered protection, have left for Israel.

There is little trace of the Arabs, Phoenician, Chinese, Romans, and Greeks who traded at this tropical port, except in the bloodlines of the present inhabitants. Old colonial churches and warehouses recall the Portuguese, Dutch, and British settlers with faded elegance. The frescoes in the Matancherry Palace date from the 17th century and depict Indian epics in extraordinary vegetable colours. Dolphins sometimes romp in the current beside the boats near the harbour entrance.

The **Periyar Game Sanctuary**, 50 miles (80 km) from Kottayam, surrounds the

Spices from Kerala.

Periyar Lake formed by a dam across the Periyar River. In its 299 sq. miles (775 sq. km) area, a variety of wildlife, from elephants, bison, leopards and tigers to monkeys, may be seen, either from lodges or viewing huts or from a launch cruising down the lake which meanders through the jungle-covered hills that surround it.

Lakshadweep: Scattered some 124-248 miles (200-400 km) west of the Kerala coast lie the islands of the Union (centrally administered) Territory of Lakshadweep, a name anglicised earlier to Laccadive Islands.

Some speculate that the name derives from the estimates of early sailors, who must have imagined at least 100,000 (a lakh) of these coral islands and atolls. In fact there are only 27, of which just 10 are inhabited by some 40,000 people, though some of the others serve as fishing stations. The people resemble Kerala mainlanders and, like them, speak Malayalam. Most are Sunni Muslims.

Coconut farming and fishing are the main occupations, along with dairy and poultry farming. Links with the mainland and between the islands have improved.

The headquarters of the Administration of Lakshadweep is on **Kavaratti Island** and the smallest of the inhabited islands is Bitra (0.1 sq. km) with a meagre population of 181.

Barracudas and sharks patrol beyond the reefs, and provide exciting deep sea fishing. Glassbottom boats, snorkels or scuba gear are available for close-up encounters with sea turtles, dolphins, eagle rays, parrot fish and lion fish.

Foreign tourists can use kayaks, catamarans, or a small sailboat on **Bangaram**, the pricey island developed especially for them. It is difficult to get a permit to stay elsewhere, unless booked on a cruise. A 20-seater plane from Cochin arrives in Agatti, then a two hour boat ride connects to the island. Arrangements should be made at Cochin's Casino Hotel on Willingdon Island.

The visitor should ascertain the current situation, availability of accommodation and other details from the Secretary to the Administrator, Lakshadweep, Harbour Road, Cochin 3, Kerala.

Offshore.

INSIGHT GUIDES
Travel Tips

Your vacation.

Your vacation after losing your wallet in the ocean.

Lose your cash and it's lost forever. Lose American Express®
Travelers Cheques and get them replaced. They can mean
the difference between the vacation of your dreams and
your worst nightmare. And, they are accepted like cash
worldwide. Available at participating banks, credit unions, AAA offices
and American Express Travel locations. *Don't take chances. Take American Express
Travelers Cheques.*

do more AMERICAN EXPRESS

**Travelers
Cheques**

Getting Acquainted

The Place

India lies between latitude 8° north and 36° north and longitude 68° east and 97° east. It is surrounded by the Arabian Sea on the west, the Bay of Bengal on the east and the Indian Ocean at its southern tip at Cape Cormorin. It shares borders with Pakistan, China, Nepal, Bhutan and Bangladesh.

Time Zones: India is five and a half hours ahead of Greenwich Mean Time.

Dialling Codes: to call India from abroad, dial the international access code, followed by 91 for India, the local code less the initial zero, then the number you want. For local dialling codes, see the list under Telecoms.

Area: India covers an area of 3,287,590 sq. km (1,269,346 sq. miles).

Topography

The Indian sub-continent is divided into seven major regions: Himalayas, Indo-Gangetic Plain, Central Highlands, Peninsular Plateau, Western Ghats, Eastern Ghats and the bordering seas and islands.

The Himalayas: The Himalayas form a natural boundary in the north. They are not a single range, but a number of parallel chains of mountains with deep valleys between them. They form the watershed of three major Indian rivers, the Indus, Ganga (Ganges) and Brahmaputra.

The Indo-Gangetic Plain: This lies at the foot of the Himalayas. To the far west, in Pakistan, it becomes the Indus plain, to the southwest it becomes the Great Indian or Thar Desert.

The Central Highlands: South of the Indo-Gangetic plain, the land rises in ranges to the Central Highlands. The Aravallis are considered one of the oldest mountain ranges in the world. They lie on a northeast to southwest axis on a line from the city of Ahmedabad (Gujarat) to Jaipur (Rajasthan) about 1,200 metres–1,700 metres (3,900 ft–5,500 ft) above sea level. The foreland of the Central Highlands is interrupted by the basin of the north-flowing Chambal River, which joins the Ganga-Yamuna system in the plains, then to Bundlekhand and its hills which rise to about 500 metres (1,600 ft); the foreland continues eastward with the Baghelkhand and Chotanagar plateaux. Southwards the Vindhyachal, with an average height of 300 metres (984 ft), traverses almost the whole peninsula, including the ancient cities of Indore and Ujjain. The Narmada River marks the end of the Central Highlands, sometimes called the Malwa Plateau.

The Peninsular Plateau: This consists of the Deccan Plateau which is mostly arid and barren, and the Eastern and Western Ghats, the long steps of hills along the coasts. The Deccan actually consists of a number of linked plateaux like the Teladgama near Hyderabad, and the Karnatakan plateau to the southwest. Karnataka has many strange, boulder-strewn hills geologically termed "granite inselbergs".

The Western Ghats: These hills form the western border of the Deccan, running from the Tapti river down the coast to Cape Comorin in the extreme south; their average height is about 1,200 metres (3,900 ft). This range intercepts the monsoon winds from the southwest and causes heavy rainfull on the western slopes, while the eastern slopes are relatively arid and bare.

The Eastern Ghats: These form an irregular eastern border to the Deccan and are broken up by large rivers such as the Krishna and the Godavari. In the far south, the Ghats end in the lovely Nilgiri Hills, or blue mountains, famous for the hill station of Ootacamund (Ooty); to the east and south is the Tamilnadu Plateau and the basin of the Cauvery, the great river of the south. The Southern Ghats, a continuation of the Western Ghats, stretch southwards to Cape Comorin.

The Bordering Seas and Islands: The Arabian Ocean, Bay of Bengal, Indian Ocean and Andaman Sea touch Indian shores. The Andamans and Nicobar, a string of 300 islands, have been formed by a submarine mountain range which divides the Bay of Bengal from the Andaman Sea. The Lakshadweep, Minicoy and Amindivi islands comprise 22 coral islands and five islets off the Kerala coast.

Environmental Diversity

Vegetation: India has a wide range of environments, from high, snow-capped mountains to tropical rainforests, from hot and cold deserts and scrubland to lush, fertile plains and valleys providing a great variety of habitats for a rich animal and plant life.

Northern India has trees of the broad-leafed variety including alder, laurel, birch and maple and conifers such as juniper. There are rhododendrons, bamboo and dwarf willow. Silver birch, fir and silver fir, spruce and cedar (deodar) forests cover the upper regions and sal forests can be found in the lower hills. Tall grasses and forests of bamboo grow in Assam.

In southern India various kinds of palm grow on the Deccan plateau. Tropical plants grow in western India. Commercial crops of the region include bananas, betel nuts, cardamoms, citrus fruits, coconuts, coffee and tea, ginger, pepper and rubber. Ironwood, rosewood and teak are plentiful in the forests here.

Until recently, India was covered by trees, ranging from dense tropical forests, as found on the wet slopes of the Western Ghats, to open deciduous forests in the drier interior. Now, however, much of this is cultivated land or has been degraded by heavy grazing, collection of firewood and other uses.

Wildlife: There are about 20 national parks and more than 200 sanctuaries in India, home to 500 species of mammals and hundreds of species of birds and reptiles. Gujarat's Gir Forest is famous for Asiatic lions, Periyar (in Kerala) for elephants, Manas and Kaziranga for one-horned rhinoceroses, Manipur's Keibul Lamjao Park for Thiamin deer, Corbett and Khana for tigers.

Independent travellers who want to see wild game should refer to the section on Entry Regulations. A selection of wildlife sanctuaries follows, but avid naturalists should consult the *Insight Guide: Indian Wildlife* for a definitive listing of national parks, reserves, forests and sanctuaries.

Outside these parks, local adventure-sport institutes offer the latest advice, particularly on routes through the Himalayas or Ghats. There are a host of private trekking and rafting firms. Leading outdoor experts with official government ties include:

The Adventurers, a Wilderness School plus Indian Institute for Adventure Applications (IIAA), 142 69th Cross, 5th Block, Rajajinagar, Bangalore, KA, tel: (91) 80-330 5508; fax: 80-332 4338.

Himalayan Mountaineering Institute, Jawahar Parbat, Darjeeling, WB, tel: (91) 0354 2378 or 3478.

Indian Institute of Skiing and Mountaineering, Dept of Tourism, C-1 Hutments, Dalhousie Rd, New Delhi, tel: (91) 301 6179.

National Institute of Water Sport, E-3 Dramila Apts, Mangor Hill, Vasco da Gama, Goa, tel: (91) 08354 513 507.

Nehru Institute of Mountaineering, Uttarkashi, Uttar Pradesh, tel: (91) 01374 21 or 22/23.

Western Himalayan Institute of Mountaineering and Allied Sports, Manali, HP, tel: (91) 01902 2342 or 2206.

Wildlife and Bird Parks

The top 15 wildlife and bird parks (in alphabetical order):

Bhandhavgarh (Madhya Pradesh): Excellent game viewing and birdlife. Tiger, leopard, gaur, chital, sambar, dhole, nilgai, wild boar, sloth bear, chinkara. Elephant riding. Best time to visit: November–June. Contact: Director, Bandhavgarh National Park, PO Umaria, Dist: Shadol, Madhya Pradesh 484661.

Corbett (Uttar Pradesh): Tiger, mugger, gharial, deer, most species. Mahseer and other sporting fish in Ramganga river. Best time: February–May. Contact: Field director, Project Tiger, Corbett National Park, PO Ramnagar, Dist: Nainital, Uttar Pradesh.

Dudhwa (Uttar Pradesh): Tiger, leopard, sloth bear, rhinoceros, swamp deer, hog deer, chital and an excellent range of birdlife. Best time: December–June. Contact: Director, Dudhwa National Park, Lakhimpur, Kheri, Uttar Pradesh.

Gir (Gujarat): Last home of the Asiatic lion and Indian wild ass. Forty species of animals and more than 450 species of birds, some migrant from Africa. Best time: December-April. Contact: Conservator of Forests, Sardar Baug, Junagadh, Gujarat 362001.

Jawahar National Park (Bandipur Tiger Reserve, Karnataka): The park has one of the best-planned road systems among Indian parks which provides excellent opportunities for game viewing, especially for elephant, leopard and gaur. Best times: March–July, September–October. Contact: Field Director, Project Tiger, Bandipur Tiger Reserve, Mysore 570004.

Kanha (Madhya Pradesh): Considered by some to be India's greatest national park, the area is certainly an excellent place to see many species in their natural habitat. Barasingha (swamp deer), tiger and other species. Best time: February–June (closed July–November). Contact: Field Director, Project Tiger, PO Mandla, Madhya Pradesh.

Kaziranga (Assam): Famous for rhinoceros, wild buffalo, swamp deer and hog deer. Tiger, wild boar, Hoolock gibbon, capped langur and ratel (hog badger) can also be seen. Well-trained elephants can be hired. Best time: November–March. Contact: Director, Kaziranga National Park, PO Bokakhat, Dist: Jorhat, Assam 785612.

Kumbalgarh (Rajasthan): This large sanctuary in the Aravalli hills is perhaps the only area in India where the highly-endangered wolf is breeding successfully. Other animals include leopard, sloth bear, chinkara, chousingha, ratel and flying squirrel. Best time: September–November. Contact: Wildlife Warden, Kumbalgarh Sanctuary, Dist: Udaipur, Rajasthan.

Namdapha (Arunachal Pradesh): Fascinating mix of Indo-Burmese, Indo-Chinese and Himalayan wildlife. Tiger, leopard, (clouded leopard, snow leopard), gaur, goral, takin, musk deer, Hoolock gibbons, slow loris, binturong and red panda. Hornbills and pheasants are among the great range of birds. Best time: October–March. Contact: Field-Director, Project Tiger, PO Miao, Dist: Tirap, Arunachal Pradesh.

Nanda Devi (Uttar Pradesh): A natural sanctuary and the site of India's second-highest mountain, Nanda Devi Peak (7,816 metres/25,675 ft). Mountain goat, snow leopard, musk deer. Best time: April–October. Contact: DCF, Nanda Devi National Park, Joshimath, Dist: Chamoli, Uttar Pradesh.

Periyar (Kerala): India's southernmost tiger reserve. Elephant viewing excellent, some tiger, monkey. Woodland birds in abundance. Boats and dugouts available. Best time: September–May. Contact: The Field Director, Project Tiger, Kanjikuzhi, Kottayam, Kerala.

Ranthambore (Rajasthan): An impressive range of animal species including sambar, chital, nilgai, chinkara, monkey, wild boar, sloth bear, hyena, jackal, leopard and tiger. Excellent birdlife including crested serpent eagle. Best time: October–April. Contact: The Field Director, Ranthambore National Park, Sawai Madhopur, Rajasthan.

Sunderbans (West Bengal): Most of the area is estuarine mangrove forest and swamp where crocodiles and turtles can be seen. The park holds more tigers than any other reserve. Best time: December–February. Contact: Field Director, Sunderbans Tiger Reserve, PO Canning, Dist: 24 Parganas, West Bengal.

Birdlife

Chilka (Orissa): Lake, shore and hinterland on the Bay of Bengal coast supporting white chital and blackbuck. Extensive birdlife includes wading birds and flamingo. Dolphins can sometimes be seen. Best time: December–March. Contact: DFO, Ghunar South, PO Khurda, Dist: Puri, Orissa.

Keoladeo Ghana (Uttar Pradesh): One of the world's greatest heronries. Famous for waterbirds including crane and migratory fowl. Mammals include sambar, blackbuck, chital, nilgai, fishing cat, jungle cat, otter and mongoose. Best times: breeding, August–October; migrants, October–February. Contact: Chief Wildlife Warden, Keoladeo National Park, Bharatpur, Uttar Pradesh.

Climate

When talking about a country of such tremendous size and geographical diversity as India, it is difficult to make a general statement concerning the climate. It ranges from the eternal snows of the Himalayas and the temperate conditions along the coasts, to the continental climate of inland areas. There are also many regional and seasonal variations. The best time to visit is after the monsoons.

October to March is the cool season

and therefore the best time of year in Peninsular India. On the whole, the weather is beautifully predictable in winter, with blue skies and bright sunshine in most areas. Some parts of the south and east see a brief spell of rain from the northeast monsoon, while snow and sleet make the extreme north very cold and often inaccessible.

Summer, from April to June, is hot and dry for most of the country, and humid along the coasts. Kashmir and the hill stations of Himachal and Uttar Pradesh are particularly lovely at this time of the year.

The southwest monsoon begins to set in along the western coast towards the end of May, bringing welcome respite from the heat, and varying amounts of rain as it moves across the rest of the country through June and July and withdraws by late September. Northeastern India has heavy rain during this season, and is one of the world's wettest regions.

The People

Population size: (1991) 865 million/ 263 per sq. km. The decennial growth rate is 24 percent, a decrease of just over 1 percent since 1971–81. Life expectancy is 58 years for men and 59 for women. There are 929 women for every 1,000 men, a difference which has steadily increased since the beginning of the century.

Ethnic mix: Indo-Aryan and Dravadian (90 percent); Tibtan; Chinese.

Religion: Hindu (80 percent); Muslim (11 percent); Christian (2 percent); Sikh (2 percent), Jain, Buddhist.

Daily life: Removing one's shoes before entering temples, mosques or gurdwara (sikh temple) is essential. Overshoes are provided in some places at a nominal cost and stockinged feet are usually permissible. Avoid taking leather goods of any kind into temples as these can often cause offence.

Photography is prohibited inside the inner sanctum of many places of worship. Do obtain permission before using a camera. Visitors are usually welcome to look around at their leisure and can sometimes stay during religious rituals. For visits to places of worship, modest clothing, rather than brief skirts and skimpy tops or shorts, would be appropriate. In Sikh temples,

your head should be covered. In mosques, women should cover their heads and arms and wear long skirts. A small contribution to the donation box is customary.

The *namaste*, the greeting with folded hands, is the Indian form of greeting and its use will be appreciated, though men, especially in the cities, will not hesitate to shake hands with you if you are a man. A handshake would even be appreciated as a gesture of special friendliness. Most Indian women would be taken aback at the informality of interaction between the sexes common in the West and physical contact with women is to be avoided. Do not shake hands with a woman (unless she first offers to), or put your hand on her shoulder.

In private, visitors are received as honoured guests and your unfamiliarity with Indian ways will be accepted and understood. If you want to experience eating with your fingers, remember to use only the right hand.

Avoid pointing the soles of your feet towards anyone as this is considered a sign of disrespect. Don't point with your index finger: use either your extended hand or your chin.

Try never to shout or lose control with Indians. If you do, they may become more unco-operative and it will lead you nowhere.

The Economy

With a well-developed, democratic political and administrative structure, a large skilled labour force and an adequate communications system, the country has made considerable progress since independence.

The national debt reached US$70 billion by the 1990s and inflation 10 percent, partly due to the disastrous effects of the Gulf War, political instability and to the security problems facing the country.

Of the labour force, 70 percent is employed in agriculture, 13 percent in industry and 17 percent in services. The rural population represents about 75 percent of the total with 12 cities having more than one million people. Greater Bombay is the largest with 12 million inhabitants.

Despite the agrarian bias of its economy, industry has grown enormously, placing India among the 15

top industrial nations of the world. Her relatively low level of exports is partly due to a large volume of domestic consumption. The per capital national income, although meagre in comparison with the rest of the world, is a considerable improvement over 1947. In the matter of production of foodgrains in particular, the advance has been spectacular – once a chronically deficit area, India can now export foodgrains. However, 37 percent of the population remains below the poverty line.

Sixty-four percent of the villages now have electricity. The literacy rate from seven years and above is 52 percent, 64 percent for men and 39 percent for women. This shows a considerable improvement from 18 percent in 1951 just after Independence.

Government

The Indian Union is a federation comprising 25 states and six union territories. Each state, and some union territories, has its own legislative assembly and government, headed by a chief minister. The central (federal) government is headed by a prime minister and council of ministers (cabinet) responsible to the two houses of parliament: the Lok Sabha (Council of the People) and the Rajya Sabha (Council of State). The Lok Sabha is composed of 543 members directly elected by the people on the basis of adult franchise (530 seats for the states and 13 for the union territories), plus two nominated members.

The Rajya Sabha is an indirectly elected body of 232 members renewed every two years, which functions somewhat like the British House of Lords. The president is elected for a five-year term by an electoral college consisting of members of parliament and members of the state legislatures. Since 1992 the president has been Dr Shankar Dayal Sharma. Each state has its own legislature and is responsible for a number of administrative functions such as health, education, forests and surface transport (except railways).

Elections are normally held every five years but can, in certain situations, be called earlier. India has had nine general elections since it became an independent country in 1947. There are six national parties, 37 state parties and 301 registered parties. The recognised national parties are: Bharatiya Janata (BJP); The Communist Party of India (Marxist); The Communist Party of India; Indian National Congress; Janata Party (JP); and Janata Dal.

Planning the Trip

Clothing

The golden rule of travelling light applies. Travelling in southern India, or the north during summer, is "shirt-sleeve weather" and it is best to wear cotton. In the north during winter, sweaters and jackets are required. Cotton shirts, blouses and skirts are inexpensive and easily available throughout the country. Remember to bring underwear (especially bras) and swimwear.

Plan your wardrobe according to your itinerary and the season of your visit. In winter a sweater, preferably two, one light and one heavy, as well as a jacket or an anorak are necessary, especially in the north where daily temperature differentials can be quite wide. Lighter clothing would be adequate in the south and along the coast. Cottons are ideal for summer. Avoid synthetics. Comfortable footwear, trainers for winter and sandals for summer, make walking on uneven surfaces easier.

For their own convenience, women should avoid sleeveless blouses, mini skirts and provocative dressing.

Electrical adaptors

The voltage system in India is 220V AC, 50 cycle system. DC supplies also exist, so check first. Sockets are of the two round-pin variety normally, but do vary. Take a universal adaptor for British, Irish and Australasian plugs. American and Canadian appliances will need a transformer, too, unless multi-voltage.

Film

Colour print film, developing and printing facilities are available in all big cities. Colour slide film can only be found in major cities and it may be safer to bring your own.

There are few places where prompt and reliable camera servicing can be done, so photographic equipment should be checked before the trip. Protect both your camera and film from excessive exposure to heat, dust and humidity. Do not leave them in direct sun or in a locked car (which can get incredibly hot) as heat affects film.

Carry film by hand in a plastic bag which can be given to airport security officers for inspection rather than being put through X-ray machines.

Other Essentials

If travelling away from the major cities or big hotels, take a sheet sleeping bag, pillowcases, medical kit, padlock, sewing kit and ear-plugs among other items. Sun cream, sun block (vital in the mountains) and insect repellent are not readily available so they should be brought with you. A hat is a sensible item. A basin/bath plug is also useful in smaller hotels which often do not have them. Western cosmetics and tampons are not easily available, so it is best to carry your own supply.

Obtaining good maps of India, in India, can be difficult; the government forbids the sale of detailed maps in border areas, which includes the entire coastline, for security reasons. Some good maps to bring are: *Bartholomew's* 1:4,000,000 map of South Asia; *Lascelles* map of the same scale and *Nelles Verlag* maps. If larger scale city maps are needed, the tourist offices can supply them. State and city maps are also published by the TT company, 328 GST Road, Chromepet, Madras, Tamilnadu 600044, or try the Survey of India, Janpath Barracks A, New Delhi 110001.

Entry Regulations

Tourist visas for all nationalities are issued either for one month from the date of entry, with that entry having to be within a month of issue (this visa is not available by post), or for six months from the date of issue (not entry). It is safer to take a multiple-entry visa, to have an option on visiting a neighbouring country.

The best place to obtain a visa is from the embassy or high commission in your country of residence, rather than risk the complications and delays involved in applying for one in neighbouring countries. It is also possible, and sometimes faster, to pay a visa agency to obtain one on your behalf. Tourist visas can be extended by three months at the foreigner's registration offices in Delhi, Bombay, Calcutta and Madras, or with the superintendant of police at any district headquarters.

Five-year visas are also issued to businessmen and students. Check with the embassy for current details.

If you stay for more than 180 days, before leaving the country you must have a tax clearance certificate. These can be obtained from the foreigner's section of the income tax department in every city. They are free, but take bank receipts to show you have changed money legally.

In addition to visas, special permits are required for certain specific areas, while other areas are out of bounds to foreigners. Applications for the special permits should be made at least one month in advance to the Ministry for Home Affairs Foreigner's Section, Lok Nayak Bhawan, Khan Market, New Delhi 110003.

Restricted Areas

The following is a list of places one *can* visit in restricted areas. Only tour groups are permitted to visit these areas, however, and the length of stay is also restricted. Permits are usually obtainable from Indian missions abroad; the Ministry of Home Affairs; Foreign Residents' Registration Offices; home commissioners; district magistrates; and for some destinations from the chief immigration officers at New Delhi, Bombay, Calcutta and Madras airports.

Assam: Kaziranga National Park, Manas Bird Sanctuary, Guwahati City, Kamakhya Temple, Sibasgar, Jatinga Bird Sanctuary.

Meghalaya: Shillong, Barapani, Cherapunji, Mawsyram, Jakeran, Ranikor, Thadlaskein, Nartiang, Tura, Siju.

Manipur: Loktak Lake, Imphal, Moirang INA Memorial, Keibul Deer Sanctuary and Waithe Lake.

Andaman and Nicobar Islands: Municipal Area, Port Blair, Havelock Island, Long, Neil Island, Mayabunder, Diglipur and Rangat Jolly Buoy, South Cinque, Red Skin, Mount Harriet, Madhuban.

Lakshadweep: Bangaram.

Sikkim: Gangtok, Rumtek, Phodang, Pemayangste, Zongri. For Taangu, Mangan, Singhik, Chungthang, Lachung and Yumthang permits are available from the Home and Tourism secretaries, Government of Sikkim.

Mizoram: Vairangte, Thindawl, Aizawl.

Himachal Pradesh: Poo, Khab, Sumdho, Dhankar, Tabo, Gompa, Kaza. For Morang-Dabling contact the Government of Himachal Pradesh, New Delhi.

Arunachal Pradesh: Itanagar, Ziro, Along, Pasighat, Miao, Namdapha.

Uttar Pradesh: Nanda Devi Sanctuary, Niti Ghati and Kalindi Khal in Chamoli, Uttar Kashi districts, and adjoining areas of Milam Glacier.

Customs

Customs procedures have recently been simplified. Visitors fill in declaration forms on the plane, and then proceed to the relevant red or green channels. Tourists seldom have any trouble. Occasionally, customs officials ask to see one suitcase at random and make a quick check. Prohibited articles include certain dangerous drugs, live plants, gold and silver bullion and coins not in current use. Firearms require possession licences (valid for six months) issued by Indian embassies or consulates abroad, or, on arrival in India, by a district magistrate. For further details, check with the issuing authority. All checked luggage arriving at Delhi airport is X-rayed before reaching the baggage collection area in the arrival hall.

Duty-free imports include 200 cigarettes (or 50 cigars), 0.95 litre (1 pint) of alcohol, a camera with five rolls of film and a reasonable amount of personal effects, including binoculars, a portable typewriter, sound recording instruments and so on. Professional equipment and high-value articles must be declared or listed on arrival with a written undertaking to re-export them. Both the list and the articles must be produced on departure. As this formality can be a lengthy process, allow extra time, both on arrival and at departure. For unaccompanied baggage or baggage misplaced by the airline, make sure you get a landing certificate from customs on arrival.

To avoid last-minute departure problems, remember that the export of antiques (over 100 years old), all animal products, and jewellery valued at over Rs. 2,000/- (in the case of gold) and Rs. 10,000/- (in the case of articles not made of gold) are banned. When in doubt about the age of semi-antiques, contact the office of the Archaeological Survey of India in Delhi, Bombay, Calcutta, Madras or Srinagar.

Currency Declaration forms for amounts of cash in excess of US$1,000 must be completed at customs on arrival.

Health

No inoculations are legally required to enter India, but meningitis, typhoid and hepatitis A shots are recommended, also cholera, polio, tetanus and anti-malaria pills. Vaccinations can be obtained in the major cities, but ensure the needle is new.

It would be useful to bring along a personal medical kit to take care of minor ailments. Anti-diarrhoea medication, a broad spectrum antibiotic, aspirin and something for throat infections and allergies would be a good idea. Also include bandaids, antiseptic cream, insect repellent and water purification tablets. Salt pills to combat heat exhaustion are necessary if your visit is in summer. A locally available powder (Vijay Electrolyte) containing salts and dextrose is an ideal additive to water, especially when travelling in the summer months or when suffering from diarrhoea.

"Delhi Belly" can be avoided with a little care. When you arrive, rest on your first day and only eat simple food; well-cooked vegetarian dishes, a south Indian *thali* and peeled fruits are perhaps best. An upset stomach is often caused by eating too many rich Indian meat dishes (often cooked with vast amounts of oil and spices) and failing to let your body acclimatise. Drink plenty of fluids but never drink unboiled or unfiltered water. When in doubt, stick to soda, mineral water, or aerated drinks of standard brands. In smaller towns, avoid factory ice as this is often made with unboiled water. All food should be cooked and eaten hot. Avoid salads and always peel fruits.

Currency

All encashments of traveller's cheques and exchange of foreign currency used to have to be recorded on the currency declaration form, or receipts kept as proof of legal conversion. The laws have eased, but some businesses and hotels still insist. Visitors leaving after a stay of 90 days or more will have to produce proof of encashment of traveller's cheques or exchange of currency for income tax exemption and to show that they have been self-supporting.

Indian currency is based on the decimal system, with 100 paise to the rupee. Coins are in denominations of 5, 10, 20, 25 and 50 paise. One and two rupee coins are also in use. Notes are in 1, 2, 5, 10, 20, 50, 100 and the rarer 500 rupee denominations. Indian rupees may not be brought in nor taken out of the country. Exchange rates fluctuate against other currencies.

Traveller's cheques should be well-known brands like Thomas Cook, American Express and Visa. A slightly better exchange rate is offered by banks, but not all banks will accept them.

Credit cards are increasingly accepted by hotels, restaurants, large shops, tourist emporia and airlines. Again, it is preferable to have a well-known card like American Express, Access/Mastercard, Visa, Diners Club. The Bank of Baroda issues rupees against a Visa card at all its branches and Amex issues rupees or traveller's cheques to cardholders against a cheque at their offices.

Public Holidays

There are many festivals in India, but only a few of these are full public holidays:

26 January	Republic Day
15 August	Independence Day
2 October	Mahatma Gandhi's Birthday
25 December	Christmas Day

See also Festivals.

Getting There

By Air

The majority of visitors now arrive in India by air. Bombay and Delhi airports are the major entry points with fewer international flights using Calcutta and Madras. Other "international" airports are Patna and Varanasi with daily flights to/from Kathmandu (Nepal); Hyderabad and Trivandrum with flights to/from the Gulf region; Dabolin (Goa) with charters to/from Germany, France and UK. There are occasional flights from Bangalore to Singapore. Trivandrum also has flights to/from Male (Maldives) and Colombo.

Delhi and Bombay are well served with flights from most parts of the world. Discounts are often available during the off-peak season, so it is worth making enquiries. Many long-haul flights unfortunately arrive between midnight and 6am, apparently to suit the night landing regulations of European and Far Eastern cities but, in reality, often because of weight restrictions for a full plane taking off in the thin air of an Indian summer.

Once you have bought a ticket, check with the airline to confirm your booking then note down the ticket number, flight number, computer reference code and other details, and keep them separate from the ticket so, in case of loss or theft, you can obtain a replacement.

The four major airports are constantly improving and all have left-luggage facilities. Porters and licensed taxis are available. Delhi, Bombay, Calcutta and Madras all have duty-free shops in both the arrival and departure halls.

By Sea

A few cruise ships such as Cunard's *QE II* do call, but India is not a regular cruise destination. Some freighters offer passage to India and excellent accommodation is still available. The American President Line, British India Steam Navigation Company, Eastern Shipping, Lloyd Triestino and the Shipping Corporation of India are among the lines with regular sailings to and from Bombay, Calcutta and Madras.

By Rail

There is a train from Lahore in Pakistan to Amritsar in India which crosses the Wagah-Attari border. It stops for a couple of hours for customs and immigration at the border.

By Road

The border crossing from Pakistan to India is from Wagah to Attari. To cross, you have to travel to Wagah by public transport, cross the border on foot and take another bus or taxi to the nearest town. The border with Nepal is only open for non-Indian or Nepalese nationals at Birganj/Raxhal, Bairwa and Kakarbitta/Naxalbari.

The "hippy trail" through Turkey, Iran, Afghanistan and Pakistan is little used by tourists now, but when peace returns to this fascinating area, it might again become popular with the more adventurous traveller. Some companies in the UK and Germany do, however, still operate a few departures. In London, Trailfinders (42-48 Earls Court Road, London W8 6EJ, tel: 0171-937 5400) can give advice.

Insurance

It is always advisable to obtain good travel insurance to cover the worst possible scenario. Take a copy of your policy to keep separately as a safeguard.

Special Facilities

Travelling with Children

Indians love children and are very tolerant and indulgent with them. The problem is that children can be more easily affected by the heat, unsafe drinking water, unfamiliar food seasoned with chillies and spices. In case of diarrhoea, rehydration salts are vital for the child. Keep them away from stray animals, especially dogs and monkeys. To avoid rabies it may be safer to take an anti-rabies vaccine.

For infants, it is difficult to find nappies and places to change them. Consider bringing a supply of disposables, or changing to washables. A changing mat is essential, as is powdered milk of a familiar brand.

For touring, walking and hiking, child-carrier backpacks or a folding buggy or pram is worth its weight.

Disabled Travellers

Although disability is common in India, there are very few provisions for wheelchairs and special toilets. The roads are full of potholes, kerbs are often high and without ramps. If you have difficulty walking, it may be hard to negotiate street obstacles, beggars, or steep staircases. On the other hand, Indians will always be willing to help you in and out of buses or cars, or up stairs. Taxis and rickshaws are cheap and the driver, with a little baksheesh, will probably help.

You could employ a guide who will be prepared to help with obstacles. Another option is to go with a paid companion. In the UK, the Holiday Care Service, 2 Old Bank Chambers, Station Road, Horley, Surrey RH6 9HW (tel: 01293-774535), could put you in touch with someone.

Some package holiday operators cater for travellers with disabilities, but first ensure that your needs have been understood before making a booking. Contact an organisation for the disabled for information.

Women Travelling Alone

Take the normal precautions such as avoiding crowded places, night travel, local public transport which can become crowded very quickly (crowds are a haven for gropers).

"Eve-teasing" is the Indian word for sexual harassment. Avoid wearing clothes that expose legs, arms and cleavage – a large scarf is handy to use as a cover-all when required. More serious sexual assaults on tourists are rare, but in case something should happen call for help from passers-by. On the up-side, there are ladies-only queues at train and bus stations, ladies-only waiting rooms and compartments on trains.

Useful Addresses

Embassies

Great Britain: High Commission of India, India House, Aldwych, London WC2B 4NA, tel: 0891-880 800 (24-hours recorded visa information); 0171-836 0990 (specific visa enquiries); 0171-836 8484 (general).
US: Embassy of India, 2107 Massachusetts Avenue NW, Washington DC 20008, tel: (202) 939 7000; fax: (202) 939 7027.

Tourist Offices

Indian Government Tourist Offices abroad:
Australia: Level 5, 65 Elizabeth Street, Sydney, NSW 2000, tel: 02-232 1600/1796.
Canada: 60 Bloor Street West, 1003, Toronto, Ontario M4W 3B8, tel: 416-962 3788.
France: 8 Bd de la Madeleine, 75009 Paris, tel: 1-42 65 83 86.
Germany: Kaiserstrasse 77-111, 6000 Frankfurt Main-1, tel: 069-23 54 23 or 23 54 24.
Great Britain: 7 Cork Street, London W1X 2LN, tel: 0181-812 0929 (24-hour tourist information); 0171-437 3677; fax: 0171-494 1048.
Italy: Via Albricci 9, 21022 Milano, tel: 02-80 49 52.
Spain: Av Pio XII 30, 28016 Madrid, tel: 91-345 7339.
US: 30 Rockefeller Plaza, Room 15, North Mezzanine, New York, NY 10020, tel: (212) 586 4901/4902.

Practical Tips

Emergencies

Generally speaking, India is a safe place to travel, but a tourist is a natural target for thieves and pick-pockets, so take the usual precautions and keep money, credit cards, valuables and passport in a money belt or pouch well secured with a cord around your neck. A protective hand over this in a crowded place could save you a lot of heartache and hassle. Do not leave belongings unattended, especially on a beach. Invest in good strong locks for all stages of travel, chaining luggage to the berth on a train, or to your seat on a bus, is another precaution which travelling Indians often take. Watch your luggage carefully during loading and unloading especially.

Credit card frauds do exist so make sure that shops and restaurants process your card in front of you.

Another sensible precaution is to keep a photocopy of your passport and visa, traveller's cheque numbers and receipts, ticket details, insurance policy number and telephone claims number, and some emergency money in a bag or case separate from your other cash and documents.

If you are robbed, report the incident immediately to a police station (be patient, this can take hours).

Weights & Measures

The metric system is uniformly used all over India. Precious metals, especially gold, are often sold by the traditional tola, which is equivalent to 11.5 grams. Gems are weighed in carats (0.2 grams). Financial outlays and population are usually expressed in *lakhs* (100 thousand) and *crores* (100 *lakhs* or 10 million).

Business Hours

Government offices: officially 9.30am–6pm Monday–Friday, but most business is done between 10am and 5pm with a long lunch break.
Post Offices: 10am–4.30pm Monday–Friday, and until 12 noon on Saturday. However, in most of the larger cities, the Central Post Office is open until 6.30pm on weekdays, 4.30pm on Saturday. On Sunday some open until noon. Major telegraph offices are open 24 hours.
Shops: 10am–7pm. Some shops close for lunch. Although Sunday is an official holiday, different localities in major cities have staggered days off so that there are always some shopping areas open.
Restaurants: until 11pm. Some nightclubs and discotheques close very much later. Hotel coffee shops are often open around the clock.
Banks: 10am–2pm Monday–Friday, 10am–noon Saturday for most foreign banks and nationalised Indian banks (of which the State Bank is the largest). Some banks operate evening branches, while others remain open on Sunday and close on another day of the week, and some open 9am–1pm. All banks are closed on national holidays, on 30 June and 31 December.

Most businesses close on public holidays.

Tipping

There is no harm expressing your appreciation with a small tip. Depending on services rendered and the type of establishment, this could range from Rs. 2/- to Rs. 10/-. In restaurants, the tip is customarily 10–15 percent of the bill. Leading hotels add a 10 percent service surcharge and tipping in such places is therefore optional.

Although tipping taxis and three-wheelers is not an established norm, it does not go amiss. Here again, 10 percent of the fare or leaving the change, if substantial, would be adequate. Porters at railway stations would expect around Rs. 2/- a bag. At airports, a rupee per bag in addition to the fee charged by the airport authority, though not essential, would be welcome.

If you have been a house guest, check with your host whether he has any objections to your tipping any of his domestic helpers (e.g. a chauffeur who may have driven you around) before doing so.

Religious Services

There are few towns in India that are without a church, mosque, or Hindu temple. There are Sikh *gurdwaras* in major towns; a number of synagogues in Bombay, two in Calcutta and one each in New Delhi and Puné. Your hotel can supply information on the religious institution you are seeking.

Media

Newspapers & Magazines

With a large number of English-language dailies and hundreds of newspapers in Indian languages, the press in India provides a wide and critical coverage of national and international events.

Among the better known national English language dailies are the *Times of India*, *The Indian Express*, *The Hindu*, *The Statesman*, *The Telegraph*, *The Hindustan Times* and *The Indian Post*. There are also two Sunday papers, *The Sunday Observer* and *The Sunday Mail*. The main newspapers in Delhi are *Asian Age* and *Pioneer*.

The top news magazines include *India Today*, *Sunday* and *Frontline*. There are also excellent general-interest magazines such as *Sanctuary* (specialising in South Asian natural history) and *The India Magazine*. Travel magazines like *Travel Links* and city magazines like *Delhi Diary* give current information on internal travel and local cultural events.

International newspapers are available in Bombay and New Delhi within 24 hours and most international magazines are also readily available.

There are several glossy magazines in English, including *Society*, *Bombay* and *First City*, and women's magazines such as *Savvy* and *Femina*.

Television & Radio Stations

Doordarshan is the government television company and broadcasts programmes in English, Hindi and regional languages. Local timings vary, but generally the news in English can be heard daily at 7.50am and 9.30pm.

Satellite television is available almost everywhere, including Star TV's five-channel network incorporating BBC World Service and MTV. Other stations include VTV (local youth-orientated music channel) and Zee TV (Hindi). There are channels showing sport, American soaps and sitcoms and English-language movies. Up to 30 stations can be picked up, given the right equipment.

Monthly video magazines can be bought or hired (from "video parlours") in most towns. The most successful is *Newstrack*, produced by Living Media (which publishes the magazine *India Today*), providing 90 minutes of news and background that would never be shown on television.

All India Radio (AIR) broadcasts on the short-wave, medium-wave and in Delhi, Bombay and Madras on FM (UHF). The frequencies vary, so check with your hotel.

Postal Services

The internal mail service is efficient in most areas. It is advisable to personally affix stamps to letters or postcards and hand them over to the post office counter for immediate franking rather than to post them in a letterbox. Sending a registered parcel overseas is a complicated and time-consuming process. Most parcels should be stitched into cheap cotton cloth and then sealed (there are people outside major post offices offering this service). Two customs forms need to be completed. Once the parcel has been weighed and stamps affixed, make sure it is franked and a receipt of registration is issued. Important or valuable material should be registered.

Many shops offer to dispatch goods, but not all of them are reliable. It is usually only safe when handled by one of the government-run emporiums. Airfreighting purchases is possible but can be equally time-consuming. You will need to produce the bill and receipt, encashment certificate, passport and onward airline ticket. There are many airfreight agents throughout India and most travel agents can provide assistance.

Courier Services

Most of the major international courier networks have agency agreements with Indian companies; DHL, Skypak, IML all work under their own brand names while Federal Express operates as Blue Dart. All these companies have offices in the major towns and, in addition to linking into the international networks, operate extensive domestic networks.

Poste Restante

Generally this works well, but make sure your name is clearly written. Most towns have only one main post office but there is often confusion between Delhi and New Delhi. New Delhi's main post office is near Connaught Circus while Delhi's main post office is between the Red Fort and Kashmir Gate in "Old" Delhi.

Telecoms

The overloaded exchanges make telephone communication frustrating. However, in the major cities with the introduction of electronic exchanges, the telephone system is improving. Long-distance calls to most parts of India can be made direct or booked through the operator. A demand service (not person-to-person) is available between some towns and to the United Kingdom. Satellite calls are the quickest but cost eight times as much as regular calls.

International calls can now be dialled to most parts of the world or booked through the operator. Calling from hotels can be extremely expensive, with surcharges up to 300 percent, so check rates first.

Privately-run telephone services with international direct-dialling facilities are very widespread. Advertising themselves with the acronyms STD/ISD (standard trunk dialling/international subscriber dialling), they are quick and easy to use. Some stay open 24 hours a day. Both national and international calls are dialled direct. To call abroad, dial the international access code (00), the code for the country you want (44 for the UK, 1 for the US or Canada), the appropriate area code (leaving out any initial zeros), and the number you want. Some booths have an electronic screen that keeps time and calculates cost during the call. Prices are similar to those at official telecommunications centres.

Home country direct services are now available from any telephone to the UK, US, Canada, Australia, New Zealand and a number of other countries. These allow you to make a collect or telephone credit card call to that country via the operator there. If you cannot find a telephone with home country direct buttons, you can use any phone toll-free by dialling 000, your country code and 17 (except Canada which is 000-167).

Many privately-run telephone services have fax machines and most large hotels offer a fax service in their business centres. Telex services, both domestic and international, are good and reasonably priced.

Telephone Codes

Note: Some towns and villages are remote and do not yet have an STD dialling code, so calls will have to be connected via the operator.

Agra, Uttar Pradesh: 0562
Ahmedabad, Gujarat: 0272
Allahabad, Uttar Pradesh: 0532
Alleppey, Kerala: 0477
Amritsar, Punjab: 0183
Aurangabad, Maharashtra: 02432
Bangalore, Karnataka: 080
Bharatpur, Rajasthan: 05644
Bhavnagar, Gujarat: 0278
Bhopal, Madhaya Pradesh: 0755
Bhubaneshwar, Orissa: 0674
Bhuj, Gujarat: 02832
Bikaner, Rajasthan: 0151
Bodh Gaya, Bihar: 063181
Bombay, Maharashtra: 022
Calcutta, West Bengal: 033
Calicut, Kozhikode: 0495
Chandigarh: 0172
Cochin, Kerala: 0484
Coimbatore, Tamil Nadu: 0422
Dalhousie, Himachal Pradesh: 01892
Daman: 02636
Darjeeling, West Bengal: 0354
Dehra Dun, Uttar Pradesh: 0135
Delhi/New Delhi: 011
Dharamsala, Himachal Pradesh: 01892
Diu, Gujarat: 028758
Gangtok, Sikkim: 0359
Goa, Calangute: 083227
Goa, Panjim: 0832
Gondal, Gujarat: 02825
Gopalpur-On-Sea, Orissa: 0681281
Gwalior, Madhya Pradesh: 0751
Guwahati, Assam: 0361
Haridwar, Uttar Pradesh: 0133
Hassan, Karnataka: 08172
Hospet, Karnataka: 08394
Hyderabad/Secunderabad, Andhra Pradesh: 0842
Indore, Madhya Pradesh: 0731
Jaipur, Rajasthan: 0141

Jaisalmer, Rajasthan: 02992
Jammu, Jammu & Kashmir: 0191
Jhansi, Uttar Pradesh: 0517
Jodhpur, Rajasthan: 0291
Kanniyakumari, Tamil Nadu: 04653
Kangra, Himachal Pradesh: 018926
Kasauli, Himachal Pradesh: 01793
Khajuraho, Madhya Pradesh: 076861
Kodaikanal, Tamil Nadu: 04542
Kota, Rajasthan: 0744
Kottayam, Kerala: 0481
Kovalam, Kerala: 0471
Kulu, Himachal Pradesh: 01902
Leh, Ladakh: via operator
Lucknow, Uttar Pradesh: 0522
Madras, Tamil Nadu: 044
Madurai, Tamil Nadu: 0452
Manali, Himachal Pradesh: via operator
Mandu, Madhya Pradesh: via operator
Mangalore, Karnataka: 0832
Mussoorie, Uttar Pradesh: 01362
Mysore, Karnataka: 0821
Nainital, Uttar Pradesh: 05942
Ootacamund (Ooty), Nilgris, Tamil Nadu: 0423
Pondicherry: 0413
Port Blair, Andaman Islands: 03192
Pune (Poona), Maharastra: 0212
Puri, Orissa: 06752
Quilon, Kerala: 0474
Rishikesh, Uttar Pradesh: via operator
Sanchi, Madhya Pradesh: via operator
Shimla, Himachal Pradesh: 0177
Shivpuri, Madhya Pradesh: via operator
Srinagar, Kashmir: 0194
Thanjavur (Tanjore), Tamil Nadu: 04362
Thrissur/Trichur, Kerala: 0487
Tiruchirapalli (Trichy), Tamil Nadu: 0431
Trivandrum/Thiruvananthapuram, Kerala: 0471
Udaipur, Rajasthan: 0294
Vadodara/Baroda, Gujarat: 0265
Varanasi (Benares), Uttar Pradesh: 0542
Vishakhapatnam, Andhra Pradesh: 0891

Tourist Offices

The Government of India has tourist offices in these cities and towns:
New Delhi: 88 Janpath, New Delhi 110001, tel: 3320005/3320008/ 3320109/3320266/3320342. Domestic airport information counter, tel: 3295296. International airport information counter, tel: 3291171.
Agra: 191 The Mall, Agra 282001,

Uttar Pradesh, tel: 363377/363959.
Aurangabad: Krishna Vilas, Station Road, Aurangabad 431005, Maharashtra, tel: 31217.
Bangalore: KFC Building, 48 Church Street, Bangalore 560001, Karnataka, tel: 5585417.
Bhubaneshwar: B-20 Kalpana Area, Bhubaneshwar 751014, Orissa, tel: 54203.
Bombay/Mumbai: 123 M. Karve Road, Opp. Churchgate, Bombay 400020, Maharashtra, tel: 2032932/ 2033144/2033145/2036854; fax: 91-22-2014496.
Calcutta: "Embassy", 4 Shakespeare Sarani, Calcutta 700071, West Bengal, tel: 2421402/2425813/242 1475; fax: 91-33-2423521.
Cochin/Kochi: Willingdon Island, Kochi 682009, Kerala, tel: 668352.
Guwahati: B.K. Kakati Road, Ulubari, Guwahati 781007, Assam, tel: 547407.
Hyderabad: 3-6-369/A-30, Sandozi Building, 2nd floor, 26 Himayat Nagar, Hyderabad 500029, Andhra Pradesh, tel: 660037.
Imphal: Old Lambulane, Jail Road, Imphal 795001, Manipur, tel: 21131.
Jaipur: State Hotel, Khasa Kothi, Jaipur 302001, Rajasthan, tel: 372200.
Khajuraho: Near Western Group of Temples, Khajuraho 471606, Madhya Pradesh, tel: 2047/2048.
Madras: 154 Anna Salai, Madras 600002, Tamil Nadu, tel: 8269685/ 8269695; fax: 91-44-8266893.
Goa (Panaji): Communidade Building, Church Square, Panaji 403001, Goa, tel: 43412.
Patna: Paryatan Bhawan, Birchand Patel Path, Patna 800001, Bihar, tel: 226721.
Port Blair: VIP Road, Junglighat, P.O. Port Blair 744103, Andaman & Nicobar Islands, tel: 21006.
Shillong: Tirot Singh Syiem Road, Police Bazar, Shillong 793001, Meghalaya, tel: 225632.
Trivandrum (Thiruvananthapuram): Airport, Thiruvananthapuram, Kerala, tel: 451498.
Varanasi: 15B The Mall, Varanasi 221002, Uttar Pradesh, tel: 43744.

Embassies

United Kingdom: New Delhi, Shanti Path, Chanakyapuri, tel: 601371.

Bombay, Maker Chambers IV, 2nd floor, 222 Jamnalal Bajaj Marg, Nariman Point, tel: 2830517, 2832330. **Calcutta**, Ho Chi Minh Sarani, tel: 2425171/75. **Madras**, 24 Anderson Road, tel: 473136/7.
US: **New Delhi**, Shanti Path, Chanakyapuri, tel: 600651.

Getting Around
On Arrival

Once through customs the visitor is often besieged by porters, taxi drivers and others. Choose one porter and stick to him. There is a system of paying porters a fixed amount per piece of baggage before leaving the termina, a tip of Rs. 5/-, once the bags are aboard the taxi or bus, is sufficient. If a travel agent or a friend is meeting you, he or she may be waiting outside the building. When taking a taxi or bus into town, it is advisable to change money in the arrival hall.

In Delhi, Bombay and Bangalore, a system of prepayment for taxis into the city is operated by the traffic police. This saves considerable anguish when the occasional unscrupulous driver takes a long route or tries to overcharge. Elsewhere, enquire at the information desk for the going rate for a journey to your destination before getting into the taxi; make sure the meter is "down" before you start the journey. It is all right to share a taxi even if the destination may not be the same (although in the same area). In some cities, taxis have fare charts which, when applied to the amount on the meter, give the correct fare. There is often a night surcharge of 10 percent between 11pm and 6am and a rate of Rs. 1/- to Rs. 2/- per piece of baggage.

Some major hotels operate courtesy buses, and a public service known as EATS (Ex-Serviceman's Transport Service) operates an airport bus sevice in Delhi, Bombay and Calcutta with stops at hotels and major points en route to the city centre.

Public Transport
By Air

Indian Airlines (not to be confused with the international carrier, Air India), has one of the world's largest domestic networks. The reservations system has been improved by the introduction of computers. For travel during the peak season (September–March), try and make reservations in advance as flights are usually heavily booked.

With time-consuming check-in and security procedures, you must be at the airport an hour before departure time. Coach services from some city terminals are available. In-flight service is adequate. Alcohol is only available on international flights. Indian Airlines has a good safety record. Its fares are often lower than those charged for comparable distances elsewhere. The baggage allowance per adult is 20kg and 30kg in business class.

Cancellation charges on tickets purchased locally are extremely high, but none are applicable for domestic sectors issued on international tickets.

The Discover India fare valid for 21 days of travel all over the country and the Tour India Scheme valid for 14 days and limited to six flight coupons are both particulary attractive. These tickets must be purchased abroad, or paid for in India using foreign currency. For details, contact your travel agent or an Air India office abroad, or write to: Traffic Manager, Indian Airlines House, Parliament Street, New Delhi.

Air India carries domestic passengers on its linking flights between Bombay and Delhi, Calcutta, Madras and Bangalore. These flights leave from the international terminals in the respective cities.

Privately-operated airlines such as Jagsons, Modiluft, Jet Airways, East-West Airlines and Sahara fly certain domestic sectors.

Airline timetables are published in *Divan* and *Excel* magazines and are shown on teletext. They are also available at travel agents and counters at all major airports. A local travel magazine, *Travel Links*, also publishes air and rail timetables.

AIRLINE ADDRESSES

Air India: **Bombay:** Air India Building, Nariman Point, tel: 202 4142/202 3747. **Calcutta:** 50 Chowringhee Road, tel: 442356. **New Delhi:** Jeevan Bharti LIC Building, Connaught Circus, tel: 331 1225. **Madras:** 19 Marshalls Road, Egmore, tel: 847799/848899.
Archana Airways: 41-AE, Friends Colony, New Delhi 110065, tel: 637403.

British Airways: **Bombay:** 202 Vir Nariman Road, tel: 220888. **Calcutta:** 41 Chowringhee Road, tel: 293430. **New Delhi:** 1-A Connaught Circus, tel: 332 7428. **Madras:** Fagun Mansions, 26 Cinc Road, tel: 474272/477388.
East-West Airlines: DCM Building, 16 Barakhamba Road, New Delhi 110001, tel: 331 0936/46/56/66.
Damania Airlines: Somdutt Chambers 1, Bhikaji Cama Place, New Delhi, tel: 688 8955/687 7319.
Indian Airlines: **Bombay:** Air India Building, Nariman Point, tel: 202 3131; reservations 202 3031; airport 611 6633; flight arr/dep 611 4433. **Calcutta:** 39 Chittranjan Avenue, tel: 264433; reservations 263135; airport 220 4433; flight arr/dep 552 9841. **New Delhi:** Main Booking Office, Sofdarjang Airport, tel: 462 4332; reservations 462 0566; flight arr/dep 301 4433. **Madras:** 19 Marshalls Road, Egmore, tel: 825 1677; reservations 827 7888; airport 234 3131; flight arr/dep 234 4433.
Jet Airways: C-28, Connaught Place, New Delhi 110001, tel: 372 1356.
Modiluft: Vandana Building (Ground Floor), Tolstoy Marg, Connaught Place, New Delhi 110001, tel: 335 4446/ 4447/4450/371 2069.
Sahara Airways: 7th Floor, Ambadeep Building, Kasturba Gandhi Marg, New Delhi 110001, tel: 332 7727/332 7748.

By Rail

Rail travel is safe and comfortable, but can be confusing. Of the many different categories of accommodation available, those recommended are air-conditioned first class (the most expensive and comparable with the best anywhere); two-tier air-conditioned sleeper and air-conditioned chair car (both second class). Travel by non-air-conditioned first and second class can be dusty and uncomfortable and is best avoided.

Advance reservation is strongly recommended. Many stations have computerised booking counters. In the larger cities, the major stations have tourist sections with English-speaking staff to reduce the queues for foreigners and non-resident Indians buying tickets; however payment is in pounds sterling or US dollars (traveller's cheques or cash). If reservations are not available, talk to the stationmaster about other options such as the tourist quota and reservation against cancellation (RAC).

You are advised to buy your departure tickets on arrival in each town to avoid delays. At most large stations it is possible to reserve tickets for journeys starting elsewhere in the country. Indian Railways representatives abroad accept bookings up to six months ahead, with a minimum of one month for first class, three months for second.

Trains are slow compared to those in the west, so if you are in a hurry, stick to the expresses. Fares are generally low. The Indrail Pass, available to foreign nationals and Indians resident abroad and paid for in foreign currency, offers particularly good value (it is not valid for the Palace on Wheels and Royal Orient). In the UK the pass can be obtained through S.D. Enterprises, 103 Wembley Park Drive, Wembley, Middlesex HA9 8HG, tel: 0181-903 3411; fax: 0181-903 0392. It can also be bought in India at Railway Central Reservations Offices.

RESERVATION OFFICES

Bombay Central, tel: 292122, 222126, 292042, 291952.
Bombay VT, tel: 4150079.
Calcutta, tel: 280370/74, 202025.
Madras, tel: (advance): 564455, 563545; (current): 567585, 566565.
New Delhi, tel: 344877, 345080, 345181.

Tourist Guide Offices at railway reservation centres are helpful in planning itineraries and obtaining reservations. Tourist Guides are available at **New Delhi** (tel: 352164), **Bombay**, Churchgate (tel: 298016-4577), **Calcutta**, Fairlie Place (tel: 202789), **Madras Central** (tel: 563816). Railway timetables available at Indian Tourist Offices abroad also contain much useful information. For the railway enthusiast, the more detailed *All India Railway Time-Table* or the concise but comprehensive *Trains At A Glance*, can be bought at most railway stations.

Remember to check which station your train departs from and do allow at least an hour to find your seat/berth. Lists of passengers with the compartment and seat/berth numbers allotted to them are displayed on platforms and on each compartment an hour before departure. The station superintendent and the conductor attached to the train are usually available for assistance.

Food can usually be ordered through the coach attendant and, on some trains, the fare covers food as well. Bed rolls are available on payment on certain routes in first and second class provided this request is made at the time of reservation. Bedding is provided in the air-conditioned first class.

Retiring rooms (for short-term occupation only) are available at over 1,100 stations on a first-come first-served basis, but these are usually heavily booked. All first class waiting rooms have *couches* for passengers using their own bedding. At both New Delhi and Calcutta stations, a Rail Yatri Niwas has been built for transit passengers. Rooms can be booked in advance.

Cloakrooms are available at most stations where travellers can leave their luggage, but bags must be locked, and don't lose the reclaim ticket. Check opening times of the cloakroom for collection.

RAILWAY TOURS

Butterfields Indian Railway Tours: This company runs its own specially converted carriages attached to a series of scheduled train services. Butterfields Indian Railway Tours, Burton Fleming, Driffield, Yorks YO25 0PQ, tel: 01262 470230.

Maharaja Saloons: Many of the princely states had their own carriages for maharajas and officials to travel in. Some of these are available for hire and can be attached to certain scheduled trains. The most successful and best organised service uses the Maharaja of Jodhpur's saloons and connects Jodhpur with Jaisalmer. It is important to note that these are not luxury saloons, having been built in 1942 and they are not air-conditioned. Contact PRO, Northern Railway, Baroda House, New Delhi 110001.

The Royal Orient: Utilising the famous picturesque carriages of the Palace on Wheels, this is a luxury, refurbished, air-conditioned, metre-gauge train. Accommodation is mainly in coupés, with each carriage having a mini-bar, kitchenette and modern toilets. It departs from Delhi Cantonment Station on Wednesdays at 2.30pm and travels through Udaipur, Palitana, Somnath/Ahmedpur-Mandvi, Sasan Gir, Ahmedabad and Jaipur over the next six days, arriving back in Delhi at 6am the following Wednesday. Bookings can be made through travel agents abroad or in India at the Tourism Corporation of Gujarat, Nigam Bhavan, Sector 16, Gandhinagar, 382016, tel: 22029/22645/22528; fax: 02712/22029.

The Palace on Wheels: Many of the tracks in Rajasthan are being converted to broad gauge and on completion will accommodate a brand new Palace on Wheels train running from Delhi to Jaipur, Udaipur, Jaisalmer, Jodhpur and Agra between September and April. For further information contact your travel agent or Central Reservations Office, Palace on Wheels, Tourist Reception Centre, Rajasthan Tourism, Bikaner House, Pandara Road, New Delhi 110003, tel: 381884; fax: 382823.

By Bus

Almost every part of the country is connected by an extensive and well-developed bus system with the railway stations being the natural hubs for both local and regional services. Some of the more rural routes are serviced by noisy dilapidated vehicles, but an increasing number of deluxe and air-conditioned expresses ply the trunk routes. Unfortunately, many of the trunk routes are now operated by video coaches – if you have never been to an Indian cinema, a night bus journey is an introduction to the low-brow popular brand of Hindi or regional film.

There are many parts of the country where the bus service is the only means of public transport – the Himalayas in particular. Buses are also more convenient than trains on sectors such as Delhi–Jaipur, Jaipur–Agra, Bangalore–Mysore and Bombay–Goa.

On many routes, even local ones, reservations can be made. Most baggage is carried on the bus roof, so all bags should be locked and checked on at intermediate stops.

Most cities have a bus service; Bombay's bus service is excellent whereas Delhi's is inadequate and crowded. In cities it is preferable to use taxis or three-wheeled "auto-rickshaws".

By Taxi

Chauffeur-driven cars can be hired through major agencies and most hotels. Taxis are air-conditioned and non-air-conditioned. Charges vary, ranging from Rs. 325/- for eight hours and 80 km (50 miles) to Rs. 450/- for an air-conditioned car. For out of town travel, there is a per km charge, usually between Rs. 2.30–Rs. 3/- per km in the plains (in the hills this rate is often Rs. 6/- per km), with an overnight charge of Rs. 100/-. Package tours, sold by travel agencies and hotels, include assistance, guides, hotel accommodation, in addition to taxi charges.

The local yellow-top black taxis are metered, but with constant hikes in fuel prices, charges may often be higher than indicated on the meter. If so, this will be prominently stated in the taxi and the driver will have a card showing the excess over the meter reading that can be legitimately charged. The fare for three-wheelers is about half that of taxis. Do not forget to ensure that the meter in the three-wheeler is flagged down to the minimum fare.

By Boat

Apart from the river ferries there are very few boat services in India. The Andaman Islands are connected to Calcutta and Madras by boat, as well as to each other. There are luxury services between Kochi and Lakshadweep. Kerala has a regular passenger boat system and a number of services operate from Alappuzha and Kollam (formerly Alleppey and Quilon), including the popular backwater trip between the two.

Private Transport
Driving in India

You will need your domestic licence, liability insurance, an international driver's permit and your vehicle's registration papers.

This is not, however, an easy country in which to drive and it is definitely not recommended for beginners and those of a nervous disposition. Most highways are danger zones where it is best to expect the unexpected, since most drivers ignore traffic regulations. City traffic is heavy and undisciplined, vehicles cut in and out without warn-

ing, pedestrians, cyclists, stray dogs, cows, pot-holes, speed-breakers, slow-moving carts, vehicles parked in the middle of the road and other obstacles have to be overcome. The monsoons play havoc with roads and bridges. Don't be tempted to calculate travel times by mileage, since you may average 45 kph (28 mph) on some drives. Accident rates are high, especially at night when not everyone uses lights. In case of accident, it is advisable to report to the local police station with haste since mobs assemble quickly and the scene can turn ugly.

Fuel is quite inexpensive, but it is advisable to start a journey with a full tank, refuelling wherever possible, and to keep a five-litre spare can for emergencies. Roadside mechanics will fix a puncture, but carry a spare and a jack, a tow rope and extra fan belt. Remember that in India you drive on the left.

Full information regarding road conditions can be obtained from the automobile associations listed below which periodically issue regional motoring maps, general information regarding roads and detailed route charts.

Automobile Association of Upper India, Lilaram Building, 14-F Connaught Circus, New Delhi 110001, tel: 331 4071, 331 2323/4/5.
Western India Automobile Association, Lalji Narainji Memorial Building, 76 Veer Nariman Road, Bombay 400020, tel: 291085, 291192.
Automobile Association of Eastern India, 13 Promothosh Barna Sarani, Calcutta 700019, tel: 474804.
Automobile Association of Southern India, 187 Anna Salai, Madras 600006, tel: 86121/2/3.
UP Automobile Assiciation, 32-A Mahatma Gandhi Marg, Allahabad, tel: 2445.

Chauffeur-driven cars, costing about US$20 a day, can be arranged through tourist offices, hotels, local car rental firms, or branches of Hertz, Budget or Europcar.

The big international chains are best for **self-drive car rental**. They charge 30 percent less than for chauffeur-driven cars with about a Rs. 1,000/- deposit against damage if paid in India, more if paid in country of residence. In some places motorbikes or mopeds are available for hire.

On Foot

It is generally unsafe to hitchhike in India, except in emergencies. Even then only a bus or truck is likely to stop and the ride would be slow and uncomfortable.

On Departure

Remember to reconfirm your reservations for departure well in advance to avoid any last-minute difficulties. Security procedures can be intensive and time-consuming, so allow two hours for check-in. An airport/seaport tax is charged on departure and must be paid prior to check-in (check the cost with your airline at the time of booking). Do ensure that the name of your outward-bound carrier is endorsed on the tax receipt.

For visitors with entry permits, exit endorsements are necessary from the office where they were registered. Should a stay exceed 90 days, an income tax exemption certificate must be obtained from the Foreign Section of the Income Tax Department in Delhi, Bombay, Calcutta or Madras.

India
A to Z

Where to Stay

EXPENSIVE

Welcomgroup Mughal Sheraton, Taj Ganj, Fatehbad Road, tel: 361701; fax: 361730. Luxury hotel, built and furnished in Moghul style with good, but expensive restaurants, gardens, bar, pool. Some rooms have a view of the Taj Mahal.

Agra Ashok (ITDC), 6-B The Mall, tel: 361 2233. A government hotel, 3km (5 miles) from the Taj Mahal. Spacious rooms, restaurants, gardens, pool.

Clarks Shiraz, 54 Taj Road, tel: 362421. Comfortable hotel on a large estate with facilities for golf, croquet, tennis and swimming. Good shops, restaurants (especially the rooftop one), bar, travel services, banks.

Taj View, Taj Ganj, Fatehbad Road, tel: 361171; fax: 361179. Rooms with a view, twin pools, exquisite shops within a functional exterior. All five-star amenities.

MODERATE

Amar, Fatehbad Road, tel: 360695. Modern hotel with restaurant, bar, health club and pool.

Grand, 237 Station Road, Agra Cant, tel: 364014. Popular hotel in large grounds with facilities for camping, tennis and badminton. Nice garden, restaurant and bar.

Lauries, M.G. Road, tel: 364536. A well-known hotel with facilities for camping. Pleasant grounds, restaurant, bar and pool.

BUDGET

There are a number of hotels in the Taj Ganj, the crowded area around the Taj Mahal, convenient for a short stay. Try **India Guest House**, **Shah Jahan** and **Kamal** (good rooftop restaurant) near the South Gate and **Sheela** or **Hotel Pink** near the East Gate.

Further south try **Akbar International**, Fatehbad Road, or **Safari** on Shamsahbad Road.

In the Sadar Bazaar and Cantonement area, try the **Tourist Rest House** at Baluganj, the **Rose** or **Sakura** at Old Idgah colony.

Where to Eat

Apart from the restaurants in the large hotels, Agra has several moderate to cheap places to eat, try **Zorba**, the **Buddha** for vegetarian food (Indian and Western), **Chung-Wah** for Chinese, **Gaylords**, **Kwality**, **Sonam** or **Prakash** in the Sadar area and **Joney's Place** (vegetarian) or **Saeed's Place** (Israeli food) near the South Gate.

Attractions

CULTURAL

The Gallery, Fatehbad Road, tel: 365714. Folk and classical dances, daily 7pm.

Akbar International, tel: 360749. Concerts.

Where to Stay

EXPENSIVE

The Cama, Lady Vidyagauri Road, tel: 353244. The city's top hotel, situated in the elegant Khanpur area. It has restaurants, bar, a garden terrace with pool and rooms with a view of the river.

MODERATE

The Stay Inn, Lady Vidyagauri Road, tel: 354127. At Khanpur gate, a clean, modern hotel with some a/c rooms.

Embassy, behind the bank of Maharashtra, Lal Darwaja. Good mid-budget choice. Comfortable and all amenities.

BUDGET

Gujarat, 3rd floor, Sneha Complex, Dr Tankaria Road, Lal Darwaja, tel: 356627. A pleasant, clean and reasonably priced option.

Cadillac, Dr Tankaria Road, Lal Darwaja, tel: 351481. Small rooms, attached/common baths and a men's dormitory.

Natraj, Dada Mavlankar Road, Bhadra, tel: 350048. Comfortable rooms with baths and balconies.

Where to Eat

Kalapi, Dr Tankaria Road. Excellent and reasonably priced vegetarian food.

Where to Stay

EXPENSIVE

Allahabad Regency, 16 Tashkent Marg, Civil Lines, tel: 601519. Elegantly furnished, clean, comfortable hotel, with pool, health club, sauna, Jacuzzi and good gym.

Presidency, 19-D Sarojini Naidu Marg, Civil Lines, tel: 623308. Advance booking required for this pleasant, comfortable, moderate-priced guest house with pool and foreign exchange.

Yatrik, 33 Sardar Patel Marg, Civil Lines, tel: 601713. Popular, well-managed hotel with lovely tropical garden.

BUDGET

NC Continental, Katju Road, tel: 56431. Pleasant, simple rooms, close to the railway station.

Where to Eat

El Chico, MG Marg, Civil Lines. Good deluxe restaurant with a choice of Indian, Western and Chinese dishes and an adjacent snack shop.

Jade Garden, MG Marg, Civil Lines. Good Chinese food.

Hot Stuff, 15 Elgin Road, Civil Lines. Popular for Western fast food, milkshakes and ice-creams.

Where to Stay

Alleppey Prince, AS Road, tel: 3752. The best in town with a/c rooms, restaurant and pool. Kathakali dance performances are hosted occasionally and backwater tours are organised from here.

Kuttanad Tourist Home, near KSRTC bus stand, tel: 61354. Good value budget rooms with a rooftop restaurant and bar.

Where to Stay

Mohan International Hotel, Albert Road, tel: 27801. Centrally air-conditioned, deluxe hotel with restaurant, coffee shop and pool.

Ritz, 45 The Mall, tel: 226606. Elegant, old-style hotel in quiet locality with lawns, gym and pool.

Mrs Bhandari's Guest House, 10 Cantonement, tel: 64247. Recommended, unusual lodging in a colonial house with camping and parking.

Sita Niwas, near the Golden Temple, tel: 43092. A good budget option, central and with a range of rooms.

Where to Eat

Mrs Bhandari's (above) serves colonial-style three-course meals followed by dessert. Reservations are essential for non-residents.

Kwality, Mall Road. South Indian snack bar and ice-cream parlour with an adjoining a/c restaurant.

Aurangabad, Maharashtra

Where to Stay

EXPENSIVE

Ajanta Ambassador, Chikalthana, tel: 82211, 82451; fax: 84367. Luxury five-star hotel with pseudo-ethnic interiors and all amenities. Good sports facilities.

Rama International, R-3 Chikalthana, tel: 82455/7, 82241. Luxury five-star hotel near to airport with all amenities, tennis courts and shopping arcade.

MODERATE

MTDC Holiday Resort, Station Road, tel: 23298. Large, old, but comfortable rooms, garden and a good restaurant.

BUDGET

Youth Hostel, Padampura, off Station Road, tel: 29801. Rooms and dormitories with full-board. Best budget option.

Bangalore, Karnataka

Where to Stay

EXPENSIVE

Taj Residency, 14 Mahatma Gandhi Road, tel: 558 4444; fax: 558 4748. A Taj group luxury hotel with an interesting club-style bar and good South Indian coffee shop.

West End (Taj Group), Race Course Road, tel: 226 9281. Beautiful old garden hotel. The cottages here are recommended.

Windsor Manor, 25 Sankey Road, tel:

226 9898; fax: 226 4941. Elegant five-star hotel with good restaurants, bar and pool.

Gateway Hotel (Taj Group), 66 Residency Road, tel: 544545. A new hotel, centrally located.

Holiday Inn, 28 Sankey Road, tel: 226 2233; fax: 226 7676. Located near the golf course. Luxury suites available.

MODERATE

Ashok, High Grounds, tel: 558 4444; fax: 260023. Comfortable, with a pleasant garden and pool. Convenient for the railway station.

Bangalore International, 2-A/B Crescent Road, High Grounds, tel: 226 8011. Good mid-budget a/c rooms, cable TV, restaurant and bar.

Victoria, 47–48 Residency Road, tel: 558 4077; fax: 221 3281. Best mid-budget option. Old-world hotel in a pleasant environment. Good restaurant. Book in advance.

BUDGET

YMCA, Neru Pathanga Road, Cubbon Park, tel: 221 1848. Accommodation for men only. Book in advance.

YWCA Guest House, 86 Infantry Road, tel: 570997. Accommodation for women only. Advanced booking advised.

Where to Eat

Casa Piccola, Residency Road. American-style fast food. Imaginative, informal decor and easy prices. Recommended.

Chalukya, near racecourse. Udupi fare, good quality.

Chinese Hut, Palace Road. Excellent fare, mainly Cantonese.

Coconut Grove, Spencer's Oakshott Place (behind MG Road). Excellent Malabar, Konkan, Coorg and Chettinad dishes. Draught beer available.

Kamat's. There are several in Bangalore, where the chain began.

Mavalli Tiffin Rooms, Lalbagh Road. The finest Udupi-style food in the South, but be prepared to queue. Breakfast here, especially before 7am, should not be missed.

Memories of China, Taj Residency, MG Road. The lunch buffet is among the best Chinese lunches anywhere in the country.

Prince's, Brigade Road. This upmarket restaurant stands out for quality, value for money, service and ambience. Ex-

cellent steaks. Table bookings advised. Diners – if couples – have free access to the popular disco next door.

Bharatpur, Rajasthan

Where to Stay

EXPENSIVE

Bharatpur Forest Lodge, Bharatpur Bird Sanctuary, tel: 2722/2760. Situated inside the park, this offers luxury rooms with balconies, excellent buffet restaurant and bar. Book in advance.

MODERATE

Forest Rest House, tel: 2777. Situated in the forest, popular rooms with bath, restaurant and gardens. Book in advance.

BUDGET

Tourist Complex, near Goverdhan Gate, tel: 3546. Simple rooms near railway station. Restaurant.

Bhavnagar, Gujarat

Where to Stay

Nilambagh Palace, Station Road, tel: 24241. The best hotel in town, formerly a palace. It has large, comfortable rooms.

Blue Hill, opposite Pil Gardens, tel: 26951. Good, efficient, mid-budget hotel with a roof terrace.

Vrindavan, Darbargarh, tel: 27391. Clean, simple, cheap accommodation in the city centre.

Where to Eat

All the large hotels have acceptable restaurants. Try:

Nilgiri, Blue Hill Hotel. Indian, Western and Chinese cuisine.

Gokul, Blue Hill Hotel. Gujarati cuisine and thalis.

Manali, Apollo Hotel, ST Station Road. Standard Indian fare, not too greasy.

Natraj, near Ganga Devi Mandir. Good vegetarian food (South Indian and Punjabi) and a selection of ice-creams.

Bhopal, Madhya Pradesh

Where to Stay

EXPENSIVE

Jehan Numa Palace, 57 Shamla Hills, tel: 540107; fax: 551992. Bhopal's best hotel, set in pleasant grounds with gardens, pool, coffee shop, bars and a good restaurant.

MODERATE

MPTDC Palash, TT Nagar, near New Market, tel: 553006. Large rooms set around a pleasant lawn with good restaurant, bar and coffee shop. Popular option, so book in advance.

BUDGET

Ranjit, Hamidia Road, tel: 75211. Simple rooms with baths, terrace bar and vegetarian restaurant.

Where to Eat

India Coffee House, New Market, and **Jyoti**, 53 Hamidia Road, are good budget food options.

Shopping

New Market: handicrafts, handlooms and garments (closed Sunday, Monday).
Chowk: silver jewellery, crafts and silk (closed Monday, Friday).
The MP State Emporium, Hamidia Road: traditional textiles.

Bhubaneshwar, Orissa
Where to Stay

EXPENSIVE

Kalinga Ashok, Gautam Nagar, tel: 53318. All five-star amenities; no pool.
Oberoi Bhubaneshwar, Nagapalli, tel: 56116. The best luxury hotel in the city. All amenities, two restaurants, coffee shop and pool. Located far from the centre.
Prachi, tel: 751001. A well-established luxury hotel with good restaurants and pool.
Swosti, 103 Janpath, tel: 404178. Highly recommended luxury hotel with two excellent restaurants and a bar.

MODERATE

Bhubaneshwar, Cuttack Road, tel: 51977. Good value, with clean, comfortable rooms and a restaurant.
Meghdoot, 5-B Sahid Nagar, tel: 55802. Wide range of rooms, restaurant and coffee shop.

BUDGET

Pushpak, Kalpana Square, tel: 50545. Large rooms with balconies and a decent restaurant.
Bhagwat Niwas, 9 Buddha Nagar, tel:

51808. Behind the Pushpak, its basic, clean rooms are good value.

Where to Eat

Hare Krishna, Janpath. Posh, a/c restaurant serving excellent pure vegetarian food. Pricey.
Swosti, 103 Janpath. A very good restaurant with Orissan cuisine and specialities. Book in advance.

Bhuj, Gujarat
Where to Stay

MODERATE

Prince, New Station Road, tel: 20370. The best place in town. A/c rooms with bath, TV and a good multi-cuisine restaurant.
Anam, New Station Road, tel: 23397. Clean, comfortable rooms with bath. Popular vegetarian restaurant.

BUDGET

Annapurna, Bhid Gate, tel: 20831. Good budget option with clean rooms, friendly atmosphere and inexpensive restaurant for excellent Kutch thalis.

Where to Eat

Apart from the hotels above, try:
Green Hotel, Shroff Bazaar. Punjabi and South Indian food, milk-shakes, ice-cream.
Noorani, Dada Bazaar. Good, inexpensive non-vegetarian food.
Bharat Juice Stall, ST Station Road. Excellent range of ice-creams, milk-shakes and cold drinks.

Bikaner, Rajasthan
Where to Stay

EXPENSIVE

Lalgarh Palace Hotel, tel: 23263/25963. A number of the 34 rooms still have the original furnishings and carpets made in a local prison. Part of the palace houses a museum, another part is a private residence. Golf course and squash court.

BUDGET

Dholamaru Tourist, near Major Puran Singh Circle, tel: 28621. A range of decent rooms from dormitory to mid-budget. Good, inexpensive food.

Bodhgaya, Bihar
Where to Stay

EXPENSIVE

ITDC Bodhgaya Ashok, tel: 725. The only deluxe hotel. Pleasant ambience and a good restaurant.

BUDGET

Daijokyo Buddhist House, tel: 747. Preference is given to Japanese pilgrims. Excellent Japanese restaurant.
Root Institute, near Thai temple. A meditation retreat. Huts and dormitory accommodation and meals.

Bombay, Maharashtra
Where to Stay

EXPENSIVE

Taj Mahal/Taj Intercontinental, PJ Ramchandani Road, tel: 202 3366; fax: 287 2711. India's most famous hotel, situated opposite the Gateway of India. It is very grand and very expensive with beautiful rooms in both the old and new wings. Excellent restaurants and bars, outdoor pool, disco, shopping arcades, beauty parlour.
Oberoi Towers, Nariman Point, tel: 202 4343. Luxurious five-star hotel with great sea-view rooms. Several restaurants and bars, terrace garden pool on the 9th floor, large shopping arcade, disco.
The Oberoi, Nariman Point, tel: 202 5757; fax: 204 3282. Next door to the Oberoi Towers. Chic, modern with good restaurants, health club, pool and shops.
Leela Kempinski, Sahar Airport, tel: 636 3636; fax: 836 0606. Ultra deluxe, new hotel. Best for sports facilities. Some great restaurants.
President, 90 Cuffe Parade, tel: 215 0808; fax: 215 1201. Centrally located, five-star hotel with good restaurants (the Italian one in particular), pool, shops, beauty parlour.
Sun-n-Sand, 39 Juhu Beach, tel: 620 1811. One of Bombay's oldest, well-established five-star hotels located on Juhu Beach. Pleasant pool and poolside restaurant, water-sports facilities.
Holiday Inn, Balraj Sahni Marg, tel: 620 4444. Five-star with terrace garden, two pools, shops and several sea-view rooms.

MODERATE

In the Colaba area:

Kerawala Chambers, 25 PJ Ramchandani Marg, tel: 241197.

The Strand, 30 PJ Ramchandani Marg, tel: 241624.

Chateau Windsor, 86 VN Road, tel: 202 3676.

Norman's, 127 Marine Drive, tel: 203 4234.

Sea Green, 145 Marine Drive, tel: 222284.

Oasis, 272 SBS Marg, tel: 261 7886.

Balwas International, 265 E Bellasis Road, opposite BEST bus depot, tel: 308 1481.

Bombay Palace, Syed Villa, off YMCA Road, tel: 308 6118.

YMCA, 18 YMCA Road, tel: 307 0601.

Seaside, 39/2 Juhu Beach, tel: 620 0293.

BUDGET

Lawrence, 3rd floor, 33 Rope Walk Lane, tel: 243618. Located opposite the Jehangir Art Gallery, it has a few great value rooms, but reservations are essential.

Salvation Army Hostel, Red Shield House, 30 Merriweather Road, tel: 241824. Located behind the Taj Mahal Hotel. Double rooms and dormitories (lockers available), canteen.

YWCA, 18 Madam Cama Road, tel: 202 0445. Doubles, family rooms and dormitories. Rates include membership, breakfast and buffet. Try to make a cash booking well in advance.

Highway Inn, Vishal Shopping Centre, Andheri-Kurla Road, Andheri East, tel: 832 0021. Located near Andheri suburban station and not far from Sahar Airport, it offers fair accommodation for transit passengers.

Where to Eat

Bombay is full of excellent eating options to suit different budgets. Most good, expensive restaurants are located in the luxury hotels. Apart from Indian food, they serve Italian, Thai, Chinese, French and Polynesian cuisine. Other recommendations are:

EXPENSIVE

Golden Gate, Madam Cama Road (near the YWCA), tel: 202 6306. Seafood, Chinese and Indian cuisine. Great Salad Bar lunch.

Palkhi, Walton Road, tel: 240079.

Mughlai specialities and vegetarian cuisine.

China Garden, Om Chambers, 123 August Kranti Marg, tel: 828 0841. Chinese, Korean, Thai and Japanese cuisine.

Khyber, Kala Ghoda (opposite Jehangir Art Gallery), tel: 273227. Very rich Mughlai and Punjabi cuisine.

Copper Chimney, K Dubash Marg, tel: 204 1661. Tandoori and North Indian specialities.

MODERATE

Delhi Darbar, Colaba Causeway, tel: 202 0235. Authentic Mughlai cuisine and traditional biryanis.

Fab Bistro, 2/5 Kamal Mansion, Arthur Bunder Road, tel: 241459. Western cuisine including steak sizlers, and Chinese.

Chetana, 34 K Dubash Road, tel: 244968. Excellent vegetarian Gujarati and Rajasthani cuisine.

Kamling, VN Road, tel: 204 2618. Authentic Chinese cuisine with Cantonese and seafood specials.

Samovar, Jehangir Art Gallery, MG Road. The gallery café, popular for snacks and lunch.

BUDGET

Café Royal, opposite Regal cinema. Western, Indian and Chinese cuisine. Draught beer available.

Majestic, near Regal Cinema. Traditional South Indian cuisine.

New Martin, near Strand Cinema. Goan specialities and seafood.

Bade Mian, behind Taj Mahal Hotel. Open-air pavement grill, famous for kebabs.

Piccolo, Homi Mody Street, tel: 274537. Authentic Parsi cuisine.

Landmark, 35 S Patkar Road, opposite RTI Building, tel: 8226077. A branch of Piccolo with Parsi cuisine and good desserts.

Purohit's, VN Road, tel: 2046241. Traditional Indian cuisine with great thalis.

Attractions

LIBRARIES

Asiatic Society, SBS Marg, Horniman Circle, Ballard Estate, tel: 266 0956. Monday–Saturday 10am–5pm.

British Council, A Wing Mittal Towers, Nariman Point, tel: 223560.

Alliance Française, Theosophy Hall, 40 New Marine Lines, tel: 203 1867.

Max Mueller Bhavan, Prince of Wales Annexe, off MG Road, tel: 202 7542.

Bombay Natural History Society, Hornbill House, tel: 243421. Monday–Friday 10am–5pm, Saturday 10am–1pm.

KR Cama Oriental Institute, 136 Bombay Samachar Marg, tel: 243893. Monday–Friday 10am–5pm, Saturday 10am–1pm.

BARS

Leopolds Pub, Colaba Causeway.

London Pub, 39D Chowpatty Seaface.

Tiger Tim's, near the market in Fort.

DISCOTHEQUES

In town, discos are in some luxury hotels, but entry is restricted to members and hotel residents/guests. Try **The Cellar** at Hotel Oberoi (couples only), or head for the suburbs to **Razberry Rhinoceros**, Juhu Hotel, Juhu Beach, (couples only), **Wild Orchid**, Chembur, (couples only), and **Sheetal Again**, Juhu.

Shopping

Monday–Saturday 10am–7pm, closed Sunday. Some bazaars remain open until 9pm.

CLOTHES

Colaba Causeway: leather items, clothes.

Fashion Street, MG Road: export surplus Western clothes shops.

HANDICRAFTS

Handicrafts are available from different State Emporia in the **World Trade Centre**, Cuffe Parade, and **Sir PM Road**, Fort. **The Central Cottage Industries Emporium**, 34 Shivaji Marg (near Gateway of India) has the widest range of handicrafts and souvenirs.

BOOKS

Crossword, Mahalakshmi Chambers, 22 Bhulabhai Desai Road, Breach Candy, tel: 492 2458; and **Strand**, near HMV, off PM Road, Fort, are the biggest and the best. Try also **Pustak Bharati**, Bharatiya Vidhya Bhavan, KM Munshi Marg, tel: 363 4462, for Hindu philosophy and literature.

Sports

The Breach Candy, expat sports club, offers day membership to use its facilities.

Where to Stay

EXPENSIVE

Oberoi Grand, 15 Jawaharlal Nehru Road, Chowringhee, tel: 292323; fax: 291217. Classic, well-established luxury hotel with all amenities.

Taj Bengal, 34B Belvedere Road, Alipore, tel: 248 3939; fax: 248 1766. Five-star Taj Group hotel with excellent restaurants.

MODERATE

Airport Ashok, near Calcutta Airport, tel: 569111/29; fax: 5529137. Selection of suites, double and single rooms. Convenient for the airport.

Fairlawn, 13A Sudder Street, tel: 244 4460; fax: 244 1835. Well managed hotel. Raj era ambience.

Kenilworth, 2 Little Russell Street, tel: 242 1373; fax: 242 5136. Good value rooms in the new wing. Restaurant, bar and garden.

Astor, 15 Shakespeare Sarani, tel: 242 9950. An old Victorian house, garden, good restaurant and bar.

BUDGET

Great Eastern, 1–3 Old Court House Street, tel: 248 2331/2311. Range of rooms, some with bath.

Diplomat, 10 Sudder Street. Double and single rooms.

Salvation Army Red Shield Guest House, 2 Sudder Street, tel: 242895. Good value. Dormitories and a few double rooms.

Shilton, 5A Sudder Street, tel: 245 1512. Good value rooms with breakfast.

YMCA, 25 Chowringhee, tel: 292192. Double rooms including breakfast and dinner.

YMCA, 42 Surendra Nath Banerjee Road, tel: 2443814.

The Youth Hostel, 10 J.B. Ananda Dutta Lane, tel: 290260. Dormitories.

Where to Eat

There are numerous restaurants in Calcutta serving Mughlai, Bengali, Continental, South Indian, Chinese and vegetarian food, in addition to fast food restaurants, hotel coffee shops and patisseries and cafes selling pastries and ice-creams. Here is a selection:

Peter Cat, 18 Park Street, near Park Street – Middleton Row crossing, tel: 298841. Mughlai cuisine, bar. 10.30am–11.30pm.

Suruchi, 89 Elliot Road, near A.G. School, tel: 293292. Bengali cuisine. 10am–8pm, closed half day Sunday.

Jyothi Vihar, 3A Ho Chi Minh Sarani, tel: 449791. South Indian cuisine.

La Rotisserie, 15 J.L. Nehru Road, in Oberoi Grand, tel: 292323. Continental cuisine. 7.30pm–midnight, closed Sunday.

Ming Court, Oberoi Grand, and **Chinoiserie**, Taj Bengal, both serve Chinese food.

Gupta Brothers, 18B Park Street, tel: 299687. Vegetarian fare.

Fish for Dish, 13A Shyamsquare. Good for fast food.

Flury's, 18 Park Street. Coffee shop serving pastries and ice-creams.

Attractions

For information on daily conducted excursions around Calcutta and tours in and around the city, contact the **Tourist Bureau of the Government of West Bengal**, 3/2 BBD Bagh East, Calcutta 700001, tel: 288271/248 8271. For information on car, coach and launch rental, tel: 288272.

Calcutta has a wealth of art galleries, museums and permanent exhibitions in addition to the largest concentration of concert halls of all Indian cities. Here is a selection:

MUSEUMS & ART GALLERIES

Academy of Fine Arts, Cathedral Road, tel: 444205. 3–6pm, closed Monday.

Birla Academy of Art and Culture, 108–109 Southern Avenue, tel: 469802. 3.30–6pm, closed Monday.

Calcutta Art Gallery, 10E Ho Chi Minh Sarani, tel: 477668. 10am–1pm, 4–8pm.

Indian Museum, 27 Jawaharlal Nehru Road, tel: 239855. March–November 10am–5pm; December–February 10am–4.30pm; closed Mondays and public holidays.

National Library, Alipore, tel: 455381. Monday–Friday 10am–5pm.

Nehru Children's Museum, 94/1 Chowringhee Road, tel: 443516. 11am–7pm, closed Monday.

State Archives of West Bengal, 6 Bhowani Dutta Lane, tel: 347182. 10.30am–5.30pm, closed Sunday and public holidays.

Museum and Art Gallery, Institute Chandernagore, The Residency, Chandernagore. Monday–Friday, 4–6.30pm, Sunday 11am–5pm, closed Thursday.

CONCERT HALLS

Rabindra Sadan, AJC Bose Road, tel: 449937.

Kala Mandir, 48 Shakespeare Sarani, tel: 449086.

Calcutta School of Music, 6B Sunny Park, tel: 471375.

Academy of Fine Arts, Cathedral Road, tel: 284302.

Oberoi Grand, 15 Jawaharlal Nehru Road, tel: 290181.

THEATRES

Plays in English are usually performed at **Kala Mandir**, 48 Shakespeare Sarani, tel: 449086.

FILMS

Newspapers publish a daily list of what's on.

BARS

There are a few watering places in Calcutta: the **Esplanade** at the Taj Bengal and the **Chowringhee Bar** at the Oberoi Grand (15 JL Nehru Road, tel: 290181). For a sunset drink try the **Tippu Sultan Bar** at the Tollygunge Club (120 Deshpran Sasmal Road, tel: 463141), or the **Verandah** at the Calcutta Club (241 Acharya Jagadish Chandra Bose Road, tel: 443318).

DISCOTHEQUES

The only decent disco in town is the **Pink Elephant** at the Oberoi Grand. Admission is restricted to members, their guests and visitors staying at the hotel.

CABARETS

Calcutta had great cabarets and nightclubs. The remaining three, **Blue Fox**, **Trinca's** and **Moklin Rouge** on Park Street, are pale reflections of what they used to be.

Shopping

Calcutta has many shopping areas. In the White Town, the Government Emporium offers local handicrafts; antique shops sell Rajasthani jewellery, old prints and postcards; Tibetan handicrafts can be found at Chamba Lama, New Market; toys, Hobby Centre; linen, Good Companion; chic ethnic clothes, Sacha's Ritu's.

The bazaar area in North Calcutta spreads over a third of the city with individual streets devoted to one item. There are shops and *gaddies*, smaller shops with an elevated floor where the owner and his staff sit, and street hawkers selling bags, secondhand books and records, pets and animals (Natibagan), secondhand furniture (Mullick Bazar), firecrackers (Old China Bazar), electrical goods (Paddar Court), shoes (Bentinck Street), jewellery (PB Sakar, PC Chandra, Dharamtola Street, Bowbazar).

At Kidderpore, the Five Star Market on Circular Garden Beach Road is the largest smuggled goods market in town.

GOVERNMENT EMPORIA

Cauvery, Karnataka State Arts and Crafts, 7 J.L. Nehru Road.
Central Cottage Industries Emporium, 7 J.L. Nehru Road.
Handloom House, 2 Lindsay Street.
Assam Emporium, 8 Russell Street.
Bihar Emporium, 145 Rashbehari Avenue.
Kashmir Art Emporium, 12 J.L. Nehru Road.
Manjusha, West Bengal handicrafts, 7/1D Lindsay Street.
Phulkari, Punjab handicrafts, 26B Camac Street.
Rajasthali, 30E, J.L. Nehru Road.
Uttar Pradesh Handicrafts, 12B Lindsay Street.

SILKS

Indian Silk House, Gangadeen Gupta, 1 Shakespeare Sarani, G/F Air-Conditioned Market.

BOOKS

Every year, at the end of January, the Calcutta Book Fair on Cathedral Road on the Meridan attracts over a million visitors.
Oxford Book and Stationery, 17 Park Street, tel: 240831.
Modern Book Depot, 78 Chowringhee Centre, opposite New Empire Cinema, tel: 290933.

Sport

There is an active social and sports life revolving around the clubs. Most will accept visitors as temporary guests on introduction by a resident

permanent member. Visitors without local aquaintances may contact the club secretary.
Calcutta Polo Club, 51 J.L. Nehru Road, tel: 442031.
Calcutta Racquet Club, Maidan, tel: 441152.
Calcutta Rowing Club, 15 Rabindra Sarobar, tel: 463343.
Calcutta Swimming Club, 1 Strand Road, tel: 282894.
Mohan Bagan Athletic Club, Maidan, tel: 281634.
Royal Calcutta Turf Club, 1 Russell Street, tel: 291103.
The Calcutta Club, Acharya Jagadish Chandra Bose Road, tel: 443318.
Tollygunge Club, 120 Deshpran Sasmal Road, tel: 463141.

Calicut, Kozhikode
Where to Stay

Sea Queen, Beach Road, tel: 58504. Comfortable mid-budget choice with some a/c rooms, restaurant and bar. Close to the beach.
Alakapuri Guest House, Moulana Mohd, Ali Road, tel: 73361. Colonial designed guest house, large rooms with bath, restaurant and cafe.

Chandigarh
Where to Stay

EXPENSIVE

Shivalik View, Sector 17, tel: 702150. Large, posh, central hotel with rooftop Chinese restaurant, 24-hour coffee shop and a variety of shops.
Mount View, Sector 10, tel: 547126; fax: 42111. Well-established luxury hotel with modern amenities and pool.
Sunbeam, Udyog Path, Sector 22B, tel: 41335. Modern, comfortable a/c hotel with coffee shop and foreign exchange facility.

BUDGET

Chandigarh Tourist Bungalow, 97 Sector 21A, tel: 23321. Near the bus-stand. Clean, comfortable rooms.

Where to Eat

Bhoj, 1090-1, sector 22B. Recommended for pure vegetarian thalis.
Mehfil, Sector 17, tel: 544224. Good North Indian cuisine. Popular, book in advance.

Amrit, Punjabi & Vinee, opposite the bus-stand. Good, hygienic North and South Indian food at budget rates.

Shopping

Sector 17 Shopping Complex, Haryana State Emporium Phulkari. Embroidered silk, woodwork, Punjabi shoes.
Khadi Gramodyog, Uttar Pradesh State Emporium, Hotel Shivalik View. Handlooms and block-printed garments.

Sport

Rowing: Sukhna Lake has rowing and pedal boats for hire.
Swimming: Pools in Sectors 14 (university campus) and 23.

Cochin, Kerala
Where to Stay

Taj Malabar, Willingdon Island, tel: 340010. One of the best hotels in the state, an old-style hostelry renovated. Gardens, restaurants and pool. Recommended.
KTDC Bolgatty Palace, Bolgatty Island, tel: 355003.
Basoto Lodge, Press Club Road, tel: 352140. Popular budget option with basic, clean rooms.

Coimbatore, Tamil Nadu
Where to Stay

MODERATE

Surya International, 105 Race Course Road, tel: 37751/5. Restaurant, bar, shops, foreign exchange. Ideal for early-morning travel to Ooty.
Sri Annapoorna, 47 East Arokiasamy Road, R.S. Puram, tel: 47722. Some a/c rooms, vegetarian restaurant, bar.
Sri Aarvee, 311-A Bharathiar Road, Sidhapudur, tel: 43677. Comfortable hotel with a good Andhra restaurant.

BUDGET

Sri Shakti, 11/148 Shastri Road, tel: 34225. Near the bus-stand. Good value budget rooms.

Cuttack, Orissa

See Bhubaneshwar for accommodation.

Dalhousie, Himachal Pradesh

Where to Stay

MODERATE

Aroma & Claire, Court Road, The Mall, tel: 2199. Sprawling old-fashioned hotel with character and comfort.
Grand View, Bus Stand, tel: 2623. Colonial building with Raj ambience, good suites and a decent bar.

BUDGET

Youth Hostel, tel: 2189. Basic accommodation and dormitories.

Where to Eat

For budget food, try the vegetarian snacks in the market area.

Daman

Where to Stay

MODERATE

Hotel Gurukripa, Seaface Road, tel: 2846. Best in town. Good rooms, roof garden, bar and restaurant.

BUDGET

Sovereign, Seaface Road, tel: 2823. Large, efficient and near the beach.

Where to Eat

Gurukripa (above). Seafood, tandoori, Chinese.
Samrat, Seaface Road. Vegetarian. Special Gujarati thalis.
Sovereign, Seaface Road. Indoor/outdoor restaurant with a choice of beers and snacks.

Darjeeling, West Bengal

Where to Stay

EXPENSIVE

Windermere, Observatory Hill, tel: 2397. A legendary hotel with famous clientele and old-fashioned grandeur.
New Elgin, Robertson Road, tel: 3314. Good, elegant, old-world hotel.
Central, Robertson Road, tel: 2033. Well established and comfortable. Good restaurant.

MODERATE

Bellevue, The Mall, tel: 2129. Very central, decent rooms, restaurant and bar.
Shangrila, The Mall, tel: 3349. Wood-

panelled rooms with fireplaces. Good restaurant.

BUDGET

Shamrock, Upper Beechwood Road. Popular, friendly place with food. Good value.
Youth Hostel, Zakir Hussein Road, tel: 2290. Popular place. Dormitories, some rooms. Good views.
Flora, 7 Dr S.M. Das Road, tel: 3458. Simple, basic and budget-friendly accommodation.

Where to Eat

New Dish, J.P. Sharma Road. Famous both for its Chinese food and the chef who formerly cooked for the Bhutanese royal family.
Glenary's, The Mall. Well-established restaurant, bar and cafe with a bakery and confectionary. Good for Raj-style "high tea".
Aliment, Zakir Hussein Road. Good, inexpensive Chinese and Tibetan food. Convenient for Youth Hostel nearby.

Dehra Dun, Uttar Pradesh

Where to Stay

MODERATE

Madhuban, 97 Rajpur Road, tel: 24094. Best hotel in town. All amenities; pool, bar, two good restaurants.
Osho Resorts, 111 Rajpur Road, tel: 29544. Located on the Mussoorie road, this is a hotel/ashram with a good multi-cuisine restaurant owned by the Rajneesh Trust (now Osho).

BUDGET

GMVN Drona, 45 Ghandi Road, tel: 24371. Simple and central. Rooms and dormitories.
Victoria, near the railway station. Good value budget rooms.

Where to Eat

Apart from the restaurants mentioned above, try:
Kundan Palace, opposite Madhuban Hotel. Popular, open-air, multi-cuisine.

Delhi/New Delhi

Where to Stay

EXPENSIVE & MODERATE

Ambassador, Sujan Singh Marg, tel: 463 2600; fax: 463 2252. Old-fash-

ioned hotel near Khan Market with spacious rooms and good South Indian restaurant.
Centaur, near IGI Airport, tel: 548 1411; fax: 545 2256. The most convenient location for catching early morning flights and for transit passengers, 24-hour coffee shop.
Claridges, 12 Aurangzed Road, tel: 301 0211; fax: 301 0625. Elegant, old-fashioned hotel with great restaurants, good pool, beauty parlour.
Hilton Hotel, Barakhamba Road, tel: 332 0101; fax: 3325335. Another modern, luxury hotel located near Connaught Place circle. Good restaurants, bar, pool and disco.
Hyatt Regency, Bhikaji Cama Place, Ring Road, tel: 688 1234; fax: 688 6833. Luxury hotel in South Delhi. Pleasant environment, excellent restaurants, especially La Piazza for Italian food. Very good pastry shop, airy bar with live jazz, good pool. Disco is free for women every Wednesday.
Imperial, Janpath, tel: 332 5332; fax: 332 4542. Colonial-style hotel, centrally located, with a popular open-air restaurant, large bar, nice pool, shopping arcade. Down-at-heel charm reflected in its moderate price.
Le Meridien, Windsor Place, tel: 371 0101; fax: 371 4545. Five-star ultramodern hotel south of India Gate, off Janpath. A variety of restaurants, bars, swimming pool on the fourth floor, disco.
Maurya Sheraton, Sardar Patel Marg, tel: 301 0101; fax: 301 0908. Luxury hotel, great restaurants and the best lap-swimming pool. Small disco, popular with the younger crowd.
Oberoi (Intercontinental), Dr Zakir Hussain Marg, tel/fax: 436 3030. Centrally located, elegant and exclusive. Restaurants, bars, shops, pool, beauty parlour, health club.
Oberoi Maidens, 7 Sham Nath Marg, tel: 252 5464; fax: 291 5134. Colonial-style hotel in old Delhi. Large rooms, personal service, pleasant gardens, pool and restaurant.
Taj Mahal, Man Singh Road, tel: 301 6162; fax: 301 7299. The flagship of the Taj Group. Luxurious and comfortable with good restaurants, popular coffee shop, pool and beauty parlour.
Taj Palace, Sardar Patel Marg, tel: 301 0404; fax: 301 1252. Another luxury Taj Group hotel. Large and comfortable, all five-star facilities, disco.

BUDGET

Around Connaught Place there are several good guest houses and cheaper dormitory accommodation. Try: **Hotel Fifty-Five** (tel: 332 1244), **Nirula's Guest House** (tel: 332 2419), **Palace Heights** (tel: 332 1419), **YMCA Tourist Hostel** (Jai Singh Road), **YWCA International Guest House** (10 Sansad Marg, Parliament Street).

Budget travellers could try **Mrs Colaco's**, **Ringo's Guest House**, **Mr S.C. Jain's**, or **Sunny Guest House** around Janpath Lane, off Janpath Road. There are several good places around Paharganj: **Metropolis**, **Ajay Guest House**, **Anoop**, **Bright**.

Where to Eat

All the large hotels have good restaurants which often feature regional food festival buffets. These can be expensive and there are many options available since almost every residential colony has its own market with eating places.

SOUTH DELHI

Hauz Khas Village Bistro Complex. A variety of restaurants offering Indian, Chinese, Italian and Thai food.
Asian Games Village Complex. The restaurants here are worth trying.

OLD DELHI

Moti Mahal, Netaji Subhash Marg. A famous Delhi restaurant.
Karim's, near Jama Masjid (with a branch at Nizamuddin West). Superb tandoori.
Chor Bazaar, Hotel Broadway. Kashmiri specialities.

AROUND CONNAUGHT PLACE

There are several good restaurants in this area. Try **Nirula's**, **Zen** for Chinese, **El Arab** for Lebanese food, **Wimpy's** for fast-food, **Wengers** for confectionary, snacks and bread. There are also several good local places opposite L-Block.

Shopping

CENTRAL DELHI

Connaught Place, Janpath for Tibetan curio shops and the Central Cottage Industries Emporium opposite the Imperial Hotel, Shankar Market and Bhagat Singh Marg with its row of State Emporia are the main shopping areas of Central Delhi.

NORTH DELHI

Chandni Chowk and the Red Fort area in the north are great for bazaar atmosphere, silver jewellery, wholesale silks, tourist items, some "antiques/ antiquarts" and local sweets and snacks.

SOUTH DELHI

To the south, Sundar Nagar Market, near the zoo, has several art and antique stores. The Hauz Khas Village Complex has many shops, designer outlets, a beauty parlour and health club, and an oddly commercialised ethnic atmosphere which is worth seeing.

DIPLOMATIC AREA

Near this area there is a chic shopping complex called Santushti, run by the Airforce Wives Association. South of this, Yashwant Singh Place, next to Chanakya Cinema, has several shops selling leather and fur items. Sarojini Nagar Market, nearby, is another "colony" market selling many goods including vegetables, household items, export surplus clothes and shoes.

Other "colony" markets worth visiting are South Extension, Defence Colony, Greater Kailash (N and M Block Market), Khan Market and Lajpat Nagar Central Market.

Nightlife

BARS

Broadway Hotel, Asaf Ali Road, **Hotel Marina** and **Alka** at Connaught Place, **Hotel Imperial** on Janpath and all the luxury hotels have bars serving beer, cocktails and foreign liquor – at a price.

DISCOTHEQUES

Discos are still limited to five-star hotels, except **Fireball**, 32nd Milestone on the Delhi-Jaipur Bypass near Gurgaon (Haryana). Entry is normally restricted to members or hotel residents and guests, but sometimes they allow entry with a cover charge.

DANCE, MUSIC, AUDITORIUMS

Current performances are listed in the daily papers and the city magazines, *Delhi Diary*, *City Guide* and *First City*. **Parsi Anjuman Hall**, Bahadur Shah Zafar Marg, tel: 331 7831. Daily folk and classic dance performances, 7pm–8pm.
Hauz Khas Village. Nightly open-air dance performances.
India International Centre, Lodi Estate, tel: 461 9431.
Triveni Theatre, Tansen Marg, tel: 371 8833.
Shri Ram Centre, Safdar Hashmi Road, tel: 371 4307.
Kamani Auditorium, Copernicus Marg, tel: 388084.

Sport

Bowling: Qutab Hotel, off Sri Aurobindo Marg, South Delhi, tel: 660060.
Golf: Delhi Golf Club, Dr Zakir Hussain Marg, tel: 436 2768/436 2235.
Gliding/flying: The Gliding Club, Safdarjung Airport, tel: 461 8271.
Polo/riding: Delhi Polo Club, President's Estate, Rashtrapati Bhawan, tel: 301 5604. Polo season October–March. Riding facilities.
Delhi Riding Club: Safdarjung Road, tel: 301 1891.
Children's Riding Club: tel: 301 2265.
Sailing: Defence Services Sailing Club, tel: 301 9604.
Tennis: Delhi Tennis Association, Africa Avenue, tel: 696 3955.
Swimming: all deluxe and luxury hotels.
Yoga: Sivananda Yoga Vedanta Nataraja Centre, 52 Commercial Centre, East of Kailash, tel: 644 3697.
Central Research Institute for Yoga: 68 Ashok Road, tel: 371 8301.

Dharamsala, Himachal Pradesh

Where to Stay

MODERATE

Glenmoor Cottages, Upper Dharamsala, tel: 4410; fax: 4113. Five self-contained cottages in a forest location.
Surya Resorts, South End, tel: 2768. Modern and comfortable.

BUDGET

HPTDC Bhagsu, tel: 3191. Good value mid-budget rooms.
HPTDC Dhauladar View, near Bus Stand, tel: 2889. Large rooms with bath and balcony, dormitories available. Good restaurant, bar, garden terrace and views.

Hotel Tibet, Bhagsu Road, tel: 2587. Good hotel, excellent restaurant and view of the valley.
Om, near Bus Stand. A few good value budget rooms and a small restaurant.

Where to Eat

Chocolate Log, Jogi Bari Road. Cakes, pies, quiches and other goodies. Roof terrace cafe closes at 6pm.
McLlo, Central Square. Excellent selection of food and beer.

Diu, Gujarat

Where to Stay

MODERATE

Hotel Samrat, Collectorate Road, tel: 2354. Diu's best hotel with a/c rooms with bath and balcony. Good restaurant.
Gangaur Sagar Rest House, Nagoa Beach, tel: 2249. Beachfront hotel and restaurant.
Mozambique, Market Square, tel: 2223. Pleasant rooms in a Portuguese building, restaurant and bar.

BUDGET

Jay Shankar, Jallandar Beach. Simple rooms and a great seafood restaurant.
Hare Krishna Guest House. Located along the road beyond the fish market. Simple, cheap rooms, restaurant.

Gangtok, Sikkim

Where to Stay

EXPENSIVE & MODERATE

Nor-Khill, Stadium Road, tel: 23186. Formerly Chogyal's guest house. Luxury rooms, all amenities including a good restaurant.
Hotel Tashi Delek, Mahatma Gandhi Marg, tel: 22038. Central, luxury hotel complex. Full board only. Multi-cuisine restaurant, roof-top cafe.
Hotel Tibet, Paljor Stadium Road, tel: 22523/23468. Comfortable and friendly. Good Tibetan restaurant.
Hill View, M.G. Road, opposite Tashi Delek. Well located, pleasant rooms and garden.

BUDGET

Green Hotel, M.G. Road. Pleasant, friendly place. Excellent Chinese/Indian/Tibetan restaurant.
Siniolchu Lodge, Enchay, near the Enchay Gompa. The best budget option, worth the extra walk.

Where to Eat

Besides the restaurants mentioned above, try:
Lhappa, Tibet Road, tel: 3002. Bar and restaurant.
Shaepi Restaurant at the Hotel Mayur, Paljor Stadium Road, tel: 22825. Tandoori, Chinese and Sikkimese cuisine.
The Orchid, N.H. 31A, tel: 3151. Good, cheap Chinese and Tibetan food.

Shopping

New Market, M.G. Road. Tibetan curio shops.
Lall Market. The local market.
Paljor Stadium Road. Tibetan and Sikkimese curios.
Directorate of Handicrafts and Handloom. National Highway has a showroom selling carpets and tanka paintings among other things.

Attractions

MUSEUMS

Institute of Tibetology. Large collection of books, rare manuscripts, religious objects. (10am–4pm, closed Sunday).
Orchid Sanctuary, near the Institute above. 200 species of orchid. (April–May, 8am–4pm).

Goa

Where to Stay

EXPENSIVE

Fort Aguada Beach Resort, Sinquerim, tel: 0832-276201; fax: 276 0444/217733. Luxury hotel resort run by the Taj group at the far end of Calangute beach. Choice of rooms or cottages facing the sea, large gardens, pools, restaurants, shops and sports facilities.
Aguada Hermitage, Sinquerim, tel: 0832-276201; fax: 276045. Fifteen luxury villas with an almost Mediterranean ambience located above the lively beach.
Oberoi Bogmalo, Bogmalo, tel: 0834-52191. Situated near Colva Beach, this luxury five-star hotel has restaurants, bars, pool, health club, sun terrace and water sports facilities.
Cidade de Goa, Vainguinim Beach, Dona Paula, tel: 0832-3301-3308; fax: 43303. Designed by Charles Correa, the award-winning Indian architect. This has Goan-style rooms and court laid out to create a village atmosphere with views across the Zuari estuary and Marmagoa harbour. Five-star facilities and pool-side restaurant.
Leela Beach, Mabor Cavelossim, tel: 0834-46263; fax: 246352. Ultra-luxury hotel resort with artificial lake, gardens that extend to the beach, swimming pool, restaurants, bars, shops and water sports facilities.
Ramada Renaissance Resort, Varca, tel: 0834-23611. Modern five-star hotel with sea-facing rooms, restaurants, bar, pool, water sports facilities and a golf course.
Taj Holiday Village, Sinquerim, tel: 0832-75117507. Thirty-five imaginatively-designed cottages in beautiful grounds, with pool and beach.

MODERATE

Hotel Mandovi, Dr D. Bandodkar Road, Panjim, tel: 226270. Old-style, centrally air-conditioned hotel with rooms overlooking the river, shops, pool and travel agent.
Hotel Fidalgo, 18th June Road, Panjim, tel: 226291. Among the oldest of the well-established, centrally located hotels in Panjim. Modern amenities, health club, shops.
Panjim Inn, E-212, 31 Janeiro Road, Fontainhas, Panjim, tel: 226523. Comfortable hotel, originally a Portuguese town house. Rooms with balconies.
Co-Co Banana, near Meena Lobo's restaurant, Calangute Beach. Attractive cottages with bath and balcony that catch the sea breeze. Central garden.
Concha, Umtavaddo, Calangute, tel: 6506. Old-fashioned, elegant colonial house with pleasant rooms, garden and verandahs.
Baia Do Sol, Baga Beach, Calangute, tel: 6084. Popular, clean, with garden. Proximity to local square makes some rooms noisier than others.
Cavala Motel, Calangute Road, tel: 2290. Well appointed rooms with bath and balcony, good restaurant.
Riverside, Baga Beach, tel: 6062. Pleasant, family-run hotel with spacious, clean rooms overlooking the Baga River. Great restaurant. Can be noisy in peak season due to motorbike freaks crossing the adjacent bridge.

Republica, near GTDC Tourist Hostel, Panjim, tel: 224630. Best value for budget travellers. Clean rooms with bath, river views and a common verandah.

Park Lane Lodge, near Chapel of St Sebastian, Panjim, tel: 227154. Old colonial house, friendly atmosphere.

O'Camarao, north of GTDC Tourist Resort, Calangute, tel: 6229. Well-maintained bungalow, clean rooms with balcony, restaurant.

Joanita, Baga Road, Calangute. Clean rooms, pleasant garden.

Nani & Rani's, Baga Beach. Some rooms and a restaurant in the main building. Basic cottages to rent on the beach with common toilets and outdoor shower.

Manali, near Starco's on Anjuna Beach. Basic, clean rooms, common baths, safe-deposit, terrace restaurant. Popular, book in advance.

Where to Eat

Casa Portuguesa, Baga Beach. Charming villa with vaulted ceilings, small verandah, tropical garden, candlelit tables. Traditional Goan food and Portuguese specialities. Open only for dinner.

Valerios, Baga Beach. Elegant, modern restaurant with first-floor roof terrace, sea and river views. In season, live music every Wednesday.

Venite, 31 Janeiro Road, Panjim. Popular seafood restaurant serving Western food, chilled beer and feni. Charming atmosphere.

O'Conqueriro, Porvoim (4km/2 miles from Panjim Bridge). The best of traditional Goan cuisine, seafood and some Portuguese dishes. Popular with locals.

Martin's Beach Corner, Caranzalem, Mandovi. Open-air cafe at the river's edge, famous for its magnificent seafood dishes (crabs, prawns, oysters, fish and roe). Also renowned for its Hollywood clientele (Gregory Peck, Roger Moore).

Tatophani, Baga Road. Western-style cafe/snack bar run by Germans. Great for breakfast, coffee and light lunch. Good shop.

St Anthony's, Baga Beach. One of Goa's best known restaurants. Good food, seafood, beer, music and pleasant ambience.

BUDGET

There are a large number of beach shack restaurants serving extremely cheap, fairly good food with specials chalked on a board. Besides these, there are numerous eating places, try:

Annapurna, Ormuz Road, Panaji. South Indian restaurant on the first floor serving traditional thalis and snacks.

Clisher, near GTDC Tourist Resort, Calangute. Good breakfasts, beer, seafood and sea views.

NV's, South Calangute. Away from the beach, fresh fisherman fare (crab, calamari), generous helpings.

Ram Das Swami, above Ozran, Vagator Beach. Good food, generous portions, great sea view.

Shopping

The shops in Goa are mostly near the beaches offering a range of handicrafts, curios and jewellery from other parts of India. Basic swimwear is available and scarves for beach wraps. Fancy leatherware shops offer a choice of bags and other items.

Beach hawkers selling Rajasthani clothes, scarves and jewellery are a nuisance, but you can haggle with them and obtain a bargain.

The flea market held every Wednesday at Anjuna Beach is the best place to head if in a shopping mode. It will give you an idea of what is available and you may find interesting handmade jewellery, antique silver buckled belts, clothes and swimwear from Bali, homemade cakes, cookies and other goodies.

Gondal, Gujarat
Where to Stay

The Riverside Palace, Gondal, tel: 21950. A converted Maharajahs palace, decorated in period English furniture. Elegant, personal service. Good position for temples and wildlife.

Gopalpur-On-Sea, Orissa
Where to Stay

MODERATE

Oberoi Palm Beach, tel: 068121. Comfortable, self-sufficient luxury cottage complex with lawn, restaurant, bar, jogging track. Beach nearby.

Sea Side Breeze, tel: 0681275. Good mid-budget option on the beach. Large, simple rooms.

BUDGET

Rosalin, tel: 0681271. Near the sea. Small, simple rooms, pleasant restaurant.'

Where to Eat

Mermaid, Hotel Mermaid. Authentic, delicious Bengali specialities. Book in advance.

New Snack Bar, beach view cafe, open until 10pm.

Gwalior, Madhya Pradesh
Where to Stay

EXPENSIVE

Usha Kiran Palace, Jayendraganj, Lakshar, tel: 323213. Formerly the Maharaja's guest house, it is now a luxury hotel managed by the Welcomgroup. Spacious, comfortable rooms with period furnishings overlooking pleasant lawn.

MODERATE

MPTDC Tansen, 6A Gandhi Road, tel: 21568. Large, well-maintained hotel with good restaurant. Book in advance.

BUDGET

Fort View, M.L.B. Road, tel: 23409. Good value option with a choice of simple accommodation.

Bhagwati, Nai Sarak. Central, inexpensive. Views of the fort.

Where to Eat

Budget food options are almost non-existent here. It is safer to eat in the hotels listed above, or try the **India Coffee House** on Station Road for South Indian snacks and good breakfasts.

Guwahati, Assam
Where to Stay

EXPENSIVE & MODERATE

Bellevue, M.G. Road, tel: 40847/35448. Charming, old-fashioned place on a hill away from the bazaar area.

Brahmaputra Ashok, M.G. Road, tel:

41064/35310. Luxury hotel near the river. All amenities including a multi-cuisine restaurant and bar.

Nandan, G.S. Road, tel: 40855/43531. Large hotel opposite Indian Airlines office.

BUDGET

New Strand, G.N.B. Road, Pan Bazaar. Clean, cheap rooms near the railway station.

Tourist Lodge, Station Road. Convenient, basic accommodation.

Railway Retiring Room. Dormitory accommodation can be booked at the enquiry counter.

Where to Eat

Ming Room, Ulabari. Good Chinese food.

Paradise, M.D. Road, Sangamari. Good Assamese food. Lunch specials.

Silver Tulips, S.N.B. Road, Silpukhuri. Good Mughlai cuisine, moderate prices, pleasant atmosphere.

Haridwar, Uttar Pradesh

Where to Stay

Hotel Surprise, Jawalapur-Haridwar Road, tel: 427789. Luxury hotel located well outside the holy city so it is able to sell meat dishes in its restaurant. All modern amenities, pool.

Suvidha, Shravan Nath Nagar, tel: 427423. Comfortable, mid-budget hotel, situated behind the Chitra Talkies cinema, near the river.

U.P. Tourism Rahi Motel, Station Road, tel: 426430. A range of rooms and dormitories set amid pleasant gardens. Centrally located near the bus-stand. Good budget option.

Where to Eat

Chotiwala, Lalta Rao Bridge, Upper Road. Popular since 1937. Famous for pure vegetarian food and thalis.

Ahaar, Railway Road, tel: 427601. Good thalis, Pujabi specialities and Chinese food.

Hassan, Karnataka

Where to Stay

Hassan Ashok (ITDC), Bangalore-Mangalore Road, tel: 68731. Restaurant and bar.

Vaishnavi Lodging, Harsha Mahal Road, tel: 67413. Good budget accommodation with vegetarian restaurant.

Hospet, Karnataka

Where to Stay

Malligi Tourist Home, 6/143 Jambu Natha Road, tel: 8101. Close to M.G. Road. Popular, comfortable hotel, pleasant bar, restaurant and gardens. New annexe. Mid-budget.

Sri Krishna Tourist Home, near Government hospital. Good value Indian-style rooms, vegetarian cafe.

Hyderabad/Secunderabad, Andhra Pradesh

Where to Stay

EXPENSIVE

Oberoi Krishna, Banjara Hills, tel: 222121; fax: 040-223079. Gorgeous hotel designed to blend in with the natural rocks and waterfalls; underground shopping precinct. All five-star amenities.

Welcomgroup Grand Kakatiya Hotel and Towers, tel: 310132; fax: 040-311045. Brand new businessmen's hotel, sleek and efficient. Pool, restaurant, 24-hour coffee shop.

Gateway Banjara, tel: 222222; fax: 222218. Lakeview hotel with all luxury amenities and good restaurants. Owned by the Taj Group which also plans to convert two of the Nizam's residences into romantic holiday lodgings.

MODERATE

Ritz, Hillfort Palace, tel: 233571. Down-at-heel palace with more character than comfort, grand lawns, pool. Good central location.

Parklane, 115 Park Lane, Secunderabad, tel: 84066. Roomy and scrupulously clean with attentive staff. Located in Hyderabad's twin city across the lake.

Baseraa, 168 Devi Road, Secunderabad, tel: 823200. Immaculate a/c rooms make this hotel good value.

Royal Lodge, Nampally High Road, tel: 201194. Situated near the railway station. Good, basic, budget accommodation.

Where to Eat

Banjara, Banjara Hills. Mughlai barbecue is the best in town.

Kamat's. There are several outlets of the Udupi-style vegetarian chain in the city; the best branch is at Ravindrapati. Food at all outlets is inexpensive.

Medina, near Charminar. Hyderabadi cuisine, inexpensive and particularly good.

Palace Heights. Up-market multi-cuisine of standard variety, however the rooftop view is magnificent and the atmosphere opulent.

Attractions

MUSEUMS

Ajanta Pavilion. Copies of Ajanta frescoes and other murals. Gardens.

Archaeological Museum. Sculpture, paintings, arms. Gardens.

Salar Jung Museum. Fabulous one-man collection. Tippu Sultan and Mughal relics.

Indore, Madhya Pradesh

Where to Stay

Indore Manor Hotel, A.B. Road, tel: 31645; fax: 492283. The best hotel in town. Located away from the centre. All amenities, good restaurant, bar and coffee shop.

President, 163 R.N.T. Road, tel: 432858. Ritzy, mid-budget hotel, good vegetarian restaurant, roof-top cafe and health club.

BUDGET

Amrit, 25/6 Chhoti Gwaltoli, tel: 467054. Clean, simple place with spacious rooms, some with a/c.

Purva, 1–4 Dhenu Market, tel: 38554. Clean, good value option. Close to railway station.

Where to Eat

Gypsy, M.G. Road. Modern, Western fast-food place serving burgers, pizzas, ice-creams and confectionery.

Woodlands, Hotel President, 163 R.N.T. Road. Posh restaurant, classy South Indian cuisine.

Status, 565 M.G. Road. Great budget option, good vegetarian food and thalis at lunch. Located below Hotel Purva.

Jaipur, Rajasthan

Where to Stay

EXPENSIVE

Rambagh Palace, Bhawani Singh Road, tel: 75141. The ultimate art deco palace for film-star fantasies.

Posh interiors, health club, squash court and indoor pool. Folklore programmes nightly on fountained lawns. **Jai Mahal Palace**, Jacob Road, Civil Lines, tel: 371616. Another top class Taj Group hotel.

Raj Mahal Palace, Sardar Patel Marg, tel: 521757. The old British Residency converted into a tasteful lodging complete with pool.

MODERATE

In many old towns in Rajasthan, some of the most interesting places to stay are in converted family houses now run as guest houses or small hotels. In Jaipur try:

Bissau Palace, Chandpole Gate, tel: 74191. A grand building with Rajput warrior decor. Gardens, pool, tennis court. Some rooms lack a/c, but with lofty ceilings remain cool.

Narain Niwas, Kanota Bagh, Narain Singh Road, tel: 56129. Roomy and regal, with 19th century royal relics of the Kanota chieftan's family. Vegetarian restaurant, pool.

LMB, Johari Bazaar, tel: 565844. Vegetarian hotel in the walled city.

BUDGET

Diggi Palace, Diggi House, Shivaji Marg, Hospital Road, tel: 374265. Best deal for budget travellers. Beautiful old palace with lawns and a very good terrace restaurant.

Jaipur Inn, Shiv Marg, Bani Park, tel: 66057. Clean rooms and dormitory. Food and camping facilities.

Around Jaipur

Circuit House, Tonk. South of Jaipur, Small, predominantly Muslim town with magnificent museum and library.

Ramgarh Lodge, Jamuva Ramgarh. Overlooking Ramgarh Lake (Jaipur's reservoir), the nine-bedroom lodge is managed and can be booked through the Rambagh Palace in Jaipur.

Samode Palace Hotel, Samode. The palace, which has 20 rooms, is the main attraction of this small village. It contains an excellent Sheesh Mahal (hall of mirrors). Bookings can be made through Samode House, Gangapole, Jaipur 302002.

Shopping

The bazaars of Jaipur reflect the rich culture of Rajasthan with bright, colourful fabrics, handicrafts and cloths.

Look out for the traditional tie-and-dye textiles made by knotting the material and dipping it in dye to form delicate *bandhani* patterns. The block prints of Sanganer, many with *khari* (over-printing with gold), *ajrah* prints from Barmer, *jaajam* prints from Chittor and the floral prints from Bagru can be found in the bazaars in the old city. Rajasthan Government Emporia sell fabric by the yard, or made up into garments and wall hangings.

Jaipur and Sanganer are famous for their "blue pottery". These hand-painted vessels are decorated with floral motifs and geometric patterns in combinations of blue, white and occasionally other colours.

Leather workers using camel and other hides produce a variety of traditional footwear. In Jaipur the cobblers make *mojadis*, soft slippers embroidered with bright colours.

Carpets and *dhurries* are made both for local and export markets. Jewellery can be found in the **Johari Bazaar**. Jaipur has the best selection of *pichwais* or cloth paintings. Engraved brassware, enamel work and inlay is also available.

Warning: The export of ivory in any form and items made with wild animal products is banned.

Jaisalmer, Rajasthan
Where to Stay

Jawahar Niwas Palace, Amar Sagar Road, tel: 2208. Beautiful, old palace converted into an hotel, with spacious rooms, open-air coffee shop, restaurant and billiards room.

Naryan Niwas Palace, Malka Road, tel: 2408. Situated on a hill, the hotel has a pleasant courtyard, restaurant and bar. Atmospheric with ethnic decor.

Naryan Vilas, Malka Road, tel: 2283. Interesting old house, mid-budget accommodation, food facility.

BUDGET

ITDC Moomal Tourist Bungalow, Amar Sagar Road, tel: 2392. Range of clean rooms, some in round huts, with bath. Bar, decent restaurant, dance performances on Sundays.

Where to Eat

Trio, Gandhi Chowk. Good food and live folk music.

Natraj, opposite Salim Singh ki Havelli. Good roof-top restaurant.

Leo, Gadi Sagar Pole. Excellent budget food.

Jammu, Jammu & Kashmir
Where to Stay

EXPENSIVE

Hotel Asia Jammu-Tawi, Nehru Market, tel: 43930. Near the railway station, close to the centre of town. Restaurants, bar, shops, pool, foreign exchange, parking.

Jammu Ashok, opposite Amar Mahal, tel: 47127. A little further from the town. Reasonably good hotel with restaurants, pool and shops.

MODERATE

Cosmopolitan, Virg Marg, tel: 47561. Good mid-budget option with some a/c, restaurant, bar and coffee shop.

Mansar, Denis Gate, tel: 46161. Close to the centre, restaurant and bar.

Jewels, near Jewel cinema. Good choice of rooms, cable TV, fast-food restaurant.

BUDGET

Tawi View, Maheshi Gate, tel: 47301. Rooms with bath, restaurant. Popular.

Aroma, Gumat Bazaar. Very reasonable rooms with bath.

Where to Eat

Bar-e-Kabab. Pleasant outdoor restaurant with entertainment. April–September.

Cosmo, Hotel Cosmopolitan. Chinese and Kashmiri food.

Rachna, Shalimar Road. Good vegetarian food.

Tourist Reception Centre Canteen, Veer Marg. Simple, budget Indian and Continental food.

Jhansi, Uttar Pradesh
Where to Stay

Hotel Sita, Shivpuri Road, tel: 442956. Modern, Westernised hotel, pleasant rooms, good restaurant.

Raj Palace, Shastri Marg, tel: 442554. Near the bus-stand. Decent mid-budget rooms with bath.

Pujan, Gwalior Road, tel: 1737. Pleasant rooms make this a good budget deal.

Where to Eat

Holiday, Shastri Marg. Classy a/c restaurant with good Indian cuisine.

Jodhpur, Rajasthan
Where to Stay

EXPENSIVE

Umaid Bhawan Palace, tel: 22516/22366. Magnificent, expensive hotel with spacious rooms, large gardens, restaurants, bars, underground pool.

MODERATE

Ajit Bhawan, Ajit Colony, tel: 20409. Well-maintained palace converted into an hotel with ethnic "hut" rooms. Good traditional meals. Folk performances.
Adarsh Niwas, Station Road, tel: 26936. Centrally located, comfortable and modern mid-budget option.

BUDGET

Shanti Bhawan, Station Road, tel: 28447. Wide range of rooms. Central.

Where to Eat

Kalinga, near Shanti Bhawan Hotel. Good, inexpensive food.

Kanniyakumari, Tamil Nadu
Where to Stay

TTDC Hotel Tamil Nadu, Seafront, tel: 71229. Wide range of accommodation: cottages, rooms with or without a/c, dormitories. Decent food.

Kangra, Himachal Pradesh
Where to Stay

Palace Motel, Taragarh, tel: Baijnath 018926-34. Formerly a palace, it has a few pleasant rooms with antique furniture. Good restaurant/room service.

Kasauli, Himachal Pradesh
Where to Stay

MODERATE

HPTDC Ros Common, Lower Mall, tel: 2005. Best hotel and restaurant in town, lovely surroundings. Book in advance.

BUDGET

Gian, P.O. Road. Decent, basic budget accommodation.

Where to Eat

For cheap food try the snack stalls in Sadar bazaar.

Khajuraho, Madhya Pradesh
Where to Stay

EXPENSIVE

Hotel Taj Chandela, tel: 2054. The smartest luxury hotel in town with five-star facilities, restaurants, bar, pool.
Jass Oberoi, By-Pass Road, tel: 2085. Classy luxury hotel with all amenities including multi-cuisine restaurant, pool, tennis courts.

MODERATE

Khajuraho Ashok, tel: 2024. Comfortable rooms, efficient service, various amenities and pool.

BUDGET

Harmony, Jain Temple Road, tel: 2135. Simple, clean rooms, pleasant garden and restaurant.
MPTDC Rahil, tel: 2062. Basic rooms, dormitories, cafeteria.

Where to Eat

MODERATE

Lal Bungalow, near museum. Pleasant restaurant in a courtyard, good salads, choice of Indian, Western or Chinese.
Mediterraneo Ristorante Italiano, Jain Temple Road. Pleasant roof-top cafe owned by an Italian/Indian couple. Excellent fresh pasta and other food.

BUDGET

Raja Cafe, Main Square. Popular place with a book and curio shop. Good for beers, snacks and information.
Safari, Jain Temple Road. Western-style food and snacks.

Kodaikanal, Tamil Nadu
Where to Stay

EXPENSIVE

Carlton Hotel, Lake Road, tel: 40056. The best in town. This lakeside colonial house has been converted into a luxury hotel with cottage accommodation. All amenities.

MODERATE

Hilltop Towers, Club Road, tel: 40413.

Near the lake, a good mid-budget option.

BUDGET

Greenland's Youth Hostel, St Mary's Road. The best budget option. Rooms and dormitories, lovely views.

Kota, Rajasthan
Where to Stay

MODERATE

Brijraj Bhawan Palace Hotel, Civil Lines, tel: 25203/23071. A former palace set in its own grounds by the river. Restaurant and room service. Moderate to expensive.

BUDGET

Chambal Tourist Bungalow, Nayapura. An RTDC motel with clean, pleasant rooms and a restaurant.

Kottayam, Kerala
Where to Stay

MODERATE

Vembanad Lake Resort, Kodimatha, tel: 564866. Located 2 km (3 miles) from the town, comfortable cottages in gardens by Lake Vembanad. A good outdoor restaurant with seafood specialities.
KTDC Aiswarya, Thirunakkara, tel: 61256. Pleasant rooms, a/c and cable TV optional. Restaurant.

Kovalam, Kerala
Where to Stay

EXPENSIVE

TDC Ashok, Kovalam, Vizhinjam, tel: 68010.

MODERATE

Sea Rock, near Lighthouse Beach, tel: 422. Good sea-facing rooms, terrace restaurant with fresh seafood.

BUDGET

Seaside Cottages, Lighthouse Beach. Good, basic rooms.

Where to Eat

There are a large number of good, reasonably priced beach restaurants serving fresh seafood and snacks. Music.

Kulu, Himachal Pradesh

Where to Stay

EXPENSIVE

Span Resorts, Kulu-Manali Highway, tel: Katrain 38/40. Luxury rooms in an ashram/resort (Osho/Rajneesh), good food.

MODERATE

Shobla, Dhalpur, tel 2800. Spacious rooms, pleasant lawn, river views, good multi-cuisine restaurant.

BUDGET

Biljeshwar View, Dhalpur. Centrally located, clean rooms, dormitory.
Madhu Chandrika, Lower Dhalpur, tel: 2800. Good budget option with rooms and dormitories. Near bus-stand.

Leh, Ladakh

Where to Stay

EXPENSIVE

Lha-Ri-Mo, tel: 2377. Central deluxe hotel with good views and a restaurant.
Dragon, tel: 339. Comfortable rooms around a courtyard in a mock-traditional building. Good restaurant.

MODERATE

Bijou, Library Road, tel: 2331. Good value accommodation in a traditional Ladakhi house.
Choksar, Library Road, tel: 3626. Another good mid-budget choice.

BUDGET

Oriental, Chamspar Lane. Located below the Shanti Stupa. Excellent option, good food.
Palace View, old town. Basic, clean accommodation.

Where to Eat

Dreamland, Fort Road. Popular restaurant with Tibetan specialities and jasmine tea.
Kyishong, near the main bazaar. A small, good value Tibetan restaurant with decent food.
La Montessori, main bazaar. Good Tibetan food. Budget-friendly.
German Bakery, Karzoo. Homemade bread, cakes and pies. Recommended.

Lucknow, Uttar Pradesh

Where to Stay

MODERATE

Carlton, Shah Najaf Road, tel: 244021. Well-established, legendary hotel with old-fashioned rooms and baths, garden, restaurant and coffee shop.
Charans, 16 Vidhan Sabha Marg, tel: 247219. Choice of mid-budget rooms in quiet, central location.
Clarks Avadh, 8 Mahatma Gandhi Road, tel: 240131. Top luxury hotel with all five-star facilities.

BUDGET

Baba Tourist Lodge, Charbagh Railway Station, tel: 54357. Wide range of rooms from budget with common baths to a/c. Situated next to the railway station.
Chowdhury Lodge, 3 Vidhan Sabha Marg, tel: 241911. Best value budget accommodation, bed-tea service.

Where to Eat

Chef Restaurant, Vidhan Sabha Marg. Good multi-cuisine restaurant, snacks and ice-cream.
Hong Kong, Mahatma Gandhi Road, Hazratganj. Good Chinese food.
Royal Cafe, Hazratganj. Popular multi-cuisine restaurant.

Shopping

Chikan Corner, near the Chota Imambara, Hussainabad. The place to buy ethnic clothes and scarves with traditional Chikan embroidery.
Gangotri, the Uttar Pradesh Government Emporium, Hazratganj. Quality handicrafts/handlooms.
Asghar Ali Mohammed Ali, Aminabad. The place to buy, or try, Lucknow's famous perfume oils (*ittar/attar*) like amber, *khus* and *gulab* (rose).

Madras, Tamil Nadu

Where to Stay

Ambassador Pallara, 53 Monteith Road, tel: 826 8584; fax: 826 8757. Convenient location close to Ana Salai Road and museum. Pool.
Taj Connemara, Binny Road, tel: 852 0123; fax: 8523361. Excellent hotel managed by the Taj Group with all amenities and a very good Chettinad cuisine restaurant.

Taj Fisherman's Cove, Chingleput, at Covelong Beach on the way to Mammallapuram, tel: 04114-6268. If you can afford to commute to Madras this is the ideal place to stay. Lovely beach, good food.
Taj Coromandel Hotel, 17 Nungambakkam High Road, tel: 827827. This may be more luxurious and better on service and food, but being in Madras it does not have the beach-side hotel's atmosphere.
Trident, 1/24 G.S.T. Road, tel: 234 4747; fax: 234 6699. Near the airport. Sleek, modern and efficient. Excellent coffee shop, garden atmosphere.
Welcomgroup Park Sheraton, 132 T.T.K. Road, Alwarpet, tel: 452525. Another sleek, modern and efficient hotel. Superb buffet, possibly the best in the country, certainly the largest.

Where to Eat

EXPENSIVE

Cascade, Nungambakkam. Best Chinese food in town. Prices are steep.
Raintree, Taj Connemara, Binny Road. Open-air ambience is superb in this up-market restaurant serving Chettinad cuisine.
Residency, Park Sheraton, T.T.K. Road. Up-market, but the daily buffet is something to experience.

MODERATE

Bahar, Cathedral Road. The barbecue is the best in town.
Dasa, Anna Salai. Udupi fast-foods in up-market ambience, but at moderate prices.
Imperial, Egmore; **Buhari**, Mount Road and Central Station. A chain serving non-vegetarian Muslim fare with a strong flavour of Kerala and Sri Lanka.
Maratha, Trident Hotel. Best up-market coffee shop in town. Thai fare, South Indian Thalis (good value for money) and varied Continental fare all recommended.
Woodlands Drive-in, Cathedral Road. Set in a horticultural garden. Better on *channa-bhatura* (North Indian fare) than on its own Udupi cooking.

BUDGET

Tic-tac. Tasty and inexpensive Chinese and North Indian food.

Attractions

MUSEUMS & ART GALLERIES

Fort Museum, Fort St George. Good collection of East India Company era exhibits. Interesting collection of old prints and memorabilia of Robert Clive.
Cholamandal Artists' Village, Injambakkam. Artists' co-operative exhibiting modern art and handicrafts.
Modern Art Gallery, Pantheon Road. Indian art collection over the last 100 years.
National Art Gallery, Pantheon Road. Ancient Indian paintings and handicrafts.

Madurai, Tamil Nadu
Where to Stay

EXPENSIVE

Madurai Ashok, Alagarkoil Road, tel: 43531/42531. Luxury hotel, all amenities including pool, bar and foreign exchange facility.
Taj Garda Retreat Pasumalai, tel: 601020/602380; fax: 604004. A company guest house from the days of the Raj, with wonderful views and outstanding gardens. Pool.

MODERATE

Pandyan Hotel, Race Course, Tallakulam, tel: 42470/71. Good mid-budget option with restaurant, bar, exchange and shops.

BUDGET

TTDC Tamil Nadu, Algarkoil Road, tel: 42462 (also on W. Veli Street, tel: 37470). Moderate to inexpensive comfortable rooms, restaurants.
Railway Retiring Rooms. Good value budget rooms on the first floor of the railway station.

Manali, Himachal Pradesh
Where to Stay

EXPENSIVE

Joe Lawrence's, Old Manali Road. Luxury cottages within a colonial campus.
HPTDC Log Huts, tel: 39. Comfortable huts with lounge, kitchen and bath in a pleasant location.

MODERATE

Sunshine, off Old Manali Road. Lovely old-fashioned rooms with fireplaces in a classic colonial wooden building. Food available.
John Banon's, Old Manali Road. Well-established guest house, good rooms, good views, fine food.

BUDGET

Laxmi, Old Manali. Set in an orchard. Good, clean rooms.
Veer, Old Manali. Great value rooms with good views and a garden.

Where to Eat

Tasty, Mount View Hotel. Good Western food.
Mount View, The Mall. Popular restaurant with good Chinese, Japanese and Tibetan food.
Darjeeling, Model Town Road. Good indoor/outdoor cafe.
Shiva Cafe, Old Manali. Popular budget restaurant, plenty of atmosphere and good food.
German Bakery, Mission Road and Old Manali. Western-style pastries, pies, bread and health food.

Mandu, Madhya Pradesh
Where to Stay

MPTDC Tourist Cottages, tel: 32345. Pleasant, spacious rooms with bath and view of the Sagar Talao Tank. Nice open-air restaurant.
Archaeological Survey Rest House, Taveli Mahal. Two good value double rooms, food. Book in advance.
SADA Tourist House, opposite Jama Masjid. Basic, very low budget accommodation.

Mangalore, Karnataka
Where to Stay

Welcomgroup Manjarun, tel: 26502. Pool, bar, restaurant serving Indian and Western food, barbeque, 24-hour coffee shop, foreign exchange.
Summer Sands, tel: 6400. Cottages and rooms built in traditional style with a good multi-cuisine restaurant.

BUDGET

KSTDC Maurya Netravati, near busstand, Lighthouse Hill Road, tel: 411192. Good value budget rooms, restaurant.

Mussoorie, Uttar Pradesh
Where to Stay

EXPENSIVE

Savoy, The Mall, tel: 2010. Well-established, elegant Raj-style hotel in good grounds.

MODERATE

Ratan, Gandhi Chowk, tel: 2719. Good value accommodation, centrally located in the library area.

BUDGET

Shalimar, Charliville Road, tel: 2410. Old-fashioned hotel below the Kempty road. Good value budget choice.

Where to Eat

Clarks, The Mall, Kulri. Good multi-cuisine restaurant and bar with Raj-style ambience.
Tavern, The Mall, Kulri. Popular multi-cuisine restaurant and bar with live band performances during the tourist season.
Whispering Windows, Gandhi Chowk, tel: 2611. A small hotel with a good restaurant and bar.

Mysore, Karnataka
Where to Stay

EXPENSIVE

Lalitha Mahal Palace Hotel, tel: 27650; fax: 33398. Palatial rooms, old-style bathrooms and public facilities, moderate service. Dome modelled on St Paul's cathedral.

MODERATE

Green Hotel, Chittaranjan Palace, 2270 Vinobha Road, tel: 512536; fax: 516139. Charming palace conversion in own gardens. Claims to be world's first hotel to embrace sustainable tourism through energy-saving and equal-opportunity employment policies and by donating profits to Indian charities.
Inn Southern Star, Vinobha Road, tel: 27217/9. A good bet, but short on atmosphere.
Kabini River Lodge, near the Nagarhole National Park. Good quality but much less expensive, a model of what can be done with little resources.

Where to Eat

Kamat's, Jhansi Laxmibai Road. Quality vegetarian food.

Dasprakash, J. Gandhi Square and Yadavagiri Road. Udupi cuisine, *dosais* a speciality.

Metropole, Jhansi Laxmibhai Road. Raj-style Western fare, old-fashioned standards still maintained.

Nainital, Uttar Pradesh
Where to Stay

EXPENSIVE & MODERATE

Hotel Manu Maharani, Grasmere Estate, tel: 2531. The best luxury hotel in town, all modern amenities, bar and a good Szechuan Chinese restaurant.

Vikram Vintage Inn, Mallital, tel: 3177. Elegant rooms in a quiet wooded location, all amenities, billiards and snooker.

Evelyn, The Mall, tel 2457. Well-maintained hotel with great views of the lake. Recommended.

BUDGET

Basera, Mallital. Good budget option situated near the ropeway station.

Youth Hostel, Mallital, tel: 3353. Great value dormitories and a couple of rooms, peaceful location.

Where to Eat

Embassy, The Mall, Mallital. Classy, multi-cuisine restaurant with Mughlai specialities.

Sakley's, The Mall. Good restaurant and bakery/confectionary.

Marino, The Mall. Good, inexpensive vegetarian thalis.

Shiva, Mallital Bazaar. Good, cheap.

Ootacamund (Ooty), Nilgris, Tamil Nadu
Where to Stay

EXPENSIVE

Fernhill Palace, tel: 3910. Reminiscent of the Raj era, this beautiful old palace is set on a large estate with sprawling lawns. It was built in the mid-19th century by the British and is now owned by the Taj Group.

Savoy Hotel, 77 Sylkes Road, tel: 4142. Forty rooms, some in cottages. Evocative of the Raj. Fires in the rooms for cold evenings.

MODERATE

Nilgiri Woodlands, Racecourse Road, tel: 2551. Rooms and dormitories in an old colonial building with a restaurant.

BUDGET

TTDC Hotel Tamil Nadu, above Tourist Office, tel: 4010. Good value rooms, dormitories and restaurant.

YWCA, Ettines Road. Popular for its good value rooms, dormitories and restaurant.

Pondicherry
Where to Stay

Ashok Hotel, Chinakalapet, tel: 854 6068. Seaside location some miles out of Pondicherry on the Auroville side.

Ashram International Guest House, Gingee Salai, near Post Office, tel: 26699. Well-kept, centrally located vegetarian guest house.

Grand Hotel d'Europe, 12 rue Suffren, off Lal Bahadur Street. An old-style hotel with French restaurant.

Pondicherry Ashok, Chinnakalapet, tel: 854160. A new, mid-range hotel.

Sea Side Guest House, 10 Goubert Salai, tel: 26494. Ashram guest house, spotlessly clean with a magnificent view.

Where to Eat

Aurobindo Ashram Guest Houses, Goubert Avenue, Gingee Salai and rue Romain Rolland. Cafeteria-style vegetarian food in ample quantities.

Grand Hotel d'Europe, rue Suffren. Once famous for its French cuisine, vestiges of which still remain.

Transit, rue Romain Rolland. Excellent multi-cuisine restaurant in an area where several small Vietnamese restaurants serve "home-cooked" meals. It has a few French dishes on the menu, but with 24 hours notice will produce a meal comparable to the best in the Grand's heyday.

Port Blair, Andaman Islands
Where to Stay

EXPENSIVE

Andaman Beach Resort, Corbyn's Cove, tel: 21463. A choice of comfortable rooms and cottages set amid beautiful tropical greenery opposite a white-sand beach. Restaurant, bar, TV lounge, table tennis.

Bay Island, Marine Hill, tel: 20881, 21389. Port Blair's best hotel, hewn from exotic timbers. Spacious rooms with balconies overlooking the sea, good restaurant with seafood specialities, decent bar, salt-water swimming pool.

MODERATE

ANTDC Megapode Tourist Home, Haddo, tel: 20207. Choice of rooms and a/c cottages with great sea views, gardens, good food.

Sinclair's Bay View, Corbyn Cove Road, tel: 21159. Clean, comfortable hotel on a cliff overlooking the sea. Restaurant, bar, excellent views.

BUDGET

ANTDC Tourist Guest House, Corbyn's Cove, tel: 20211. It only has four great value rooms so book in advance at the tourist office in town.

Hornbill Nest, near Corbyn's Cove, tel: 20018. Spacious, clean cottages perched on a coastal hill. Good food available if booked in advance.

Youth Hostel, Town Area, tel: 20459. Small, basic and very cheap.

Where to Eat

China Room, near Phoenix Bay Jetty. Excellent Burmese-style seafood at moderate rates is available if booked in advance.

Hotel Ashoka, Gandhi Road. South Indian food, coffee and snacks available all day in this small, basic restaurant.

Sports

Andaman & Nicobar Scuba Diving Society, Bay Island Hotel, Port Blair. Diving facilities, equipment hire and PADI courses.

Pune (Poona), Maharastra
Where to Stay

EXPENSIVE

Blue Diamond, 11 Koregaon Road. Tel: 663775. All luxury amenities, good restaurants, coffee shop, pool and shopping arcade.

ITDC Ashok, 5 University Road, Shivajinagar, tel: 57391, 50463. All comforts, restaurant, coffee shop, bar.

Amir, 15 Connaught Road, tel: 661840. Good mid-budget choice, three restaurants, bar, health club, shops.

BUDGET

Ritz, Connaught Road, tel: 62995. Best budget option, close to the railway station.

Puri, Orissa
Where to Stay

EXPENSIVE

Mayfair Beach Resort, C.T. Road, tel: 4041. Five-star facilities, luxury cottages on the beach, pool, good restaurant. Recommended.

Toshali Sands, Konarak Road, tel: 2888. Located 9km from the town, the hotel has deluxe cottages, pool, garden, gym, sauna and a good restaurant.

MODERATE

Shankar International, C.T. Road, tel: 2696. An older but efficient hotel with a range of rooms, lawn and good sea views.

South East Railway Hotel, C.T. Road, tel: 2063. A relic from the Raj, all traditions intact. Dining room open to non-residents.

BUDGET

Chandara International, C.T. Road, tel: 4117. Excellent facilities for the budget traveller. Clean rooms, dormitories. Great value.

Z (Zed), C.T. Road, tel: 2554. Good value, clean, comfortable rooms, dormitories, TV lounge.

Where to Eat

Mayfair, C.T. Road. Elegant and expensive restaurant with an unusual menu and good food.

Holiday Resort, C.T. Road. Posh hotel restaurant serving excellent Bengali thalis for lunch.

Om, Shankar International, C.T. Road. Small, good restaurant, reasonable prices.

Shopping

Utkalika, Temple Road. Local handicrafts and handloom fabrics.

Surdarshan, Station Road. Traditional stone sculpture.

Holiday Inn, C.T. Road. Local jewellery and fabrics.

Brady's, C.T. Road. Popular with budget travellers.

Quilon, Kerala
Where to Stay

KTDC Yatri Nivas, tel: 78638. Good, basic rooms beside the lake, restaurant, beer bar.

Government Guest House, Ashtamudi Lake, tel: 70356. Formerly the British residency. It has five spacious rooms and serves only breakfast.

Rishikesh, Uttar Pradesh
Where to Stay

Inderlok, Railway Road, tel: 30555. Well-established, central hotel, pleasant rooms, restaurant, terrace garden, foreign exchange.

GMVN Tourist Complex, Rishilok, tel: 30373. Good value mid-budget cottages set in pleasant grounds.

Green Hotel, Swarg Ashram, tel: 31242. Popular budget option with a decent Indian/Chinese restaurant.

Sanchi, Madhya Pradesh
Where to Stay

MPTDC Tourist Lodge, tel: 223. The best accommodation in town. Clean, simple rooms, decent restaurant, gardens. Book in advance.

Railway Retiring Rooms, at the station. Good budget option.

Shimla, Himachal Pradesh
Where to Stay

EXPENSIVE

Woodville. Old-world ambience in a comfortable, classic British house with lawns and badminton court.

Oberoi Clarks, The Mall, Tel: 6091/5. Another beautiful old building renovated to five-star standards.

Chapslee. Very elegant British manor with wonderful suites, period furnishings and antiques, library, card-room, tennis court, croquet lawn.

MODERATE

White, Lakkar Bazaar. Decent, clean rooms with views and TV.

Auckland, tel: 72621. Good, clean, pleasant rooms, some with views.

Shingar. Good value, situated near the Oberoi Clarks.

BUDGET

Dreamland. Rooms with views, hot water, good service.

YMCA. Very popular. Large, clean, old-fashioned rooms, shared baths, dining hall, cable TV. Membership fee.

Where to Eat

Davico's, The Mall. Indian and Western fast food, milk shakes.

Baljees/Fascination, The Mall. Popular snack bar, decent multi-cuisine restaurant.

Choice, Middle Bazaar, just below The Mall. Good budget Chinese food.

Shopping

Maria Bookshop, The Mall. Books, maps and prints.

Himachal Emporium. Local handicrafts and woollens.

The Mall, **Lower Bazaar** and **Lakkar Bazaar** have various shops selling handicrafts, clothes, jewellery.

Sport

Ice-skating rink, below Rivoli Theatre, tel: 3600.

Skiing (January–March). Contact HPTDC for details.

Golf. Nine-hole golf course at Narkhanda.

Fishing. For details and permits contact Assistant Director Fisheries, Khalini, tel: 4732/6985.

Shivpuri, Madhya Pradesh
Where to Stay

MPDTC Tourist Village, tel: 2600. The best option. Comfortable, modern cottages (a/c or plain) on the lakeside, good restaurant and bar. Book in advance.

MPDTC Chinkara Motel, tel: 2297. Small motel on NH3. Simple, clean rooms with bath, food.

Srinagar, Kashmir
Where to Stay

Most foreign tourists prefer to stay in a flat-bottomed, stationary wooden **houseboat**, between 20 metres (65 ft) and 40 metres (130 ft) long, and 3 metres (10 ft) to 6 metres (20 ft) wide.

Each consists of a front veranda, living room, dining room, kitchen, rooftop sun-deck and two or three bedrooms with en suite bath and toilet.

There is a range of categories, each donating a different tariff and level of comfort. The price includes accommodation, meals, tea and transport to and fro, aboard a *shikara*, a slim, elegant boat unique to Kashmir. You will discover that the categories are not rigid and, depending on the owner, some B-class boats are often better maintained than some A-class boats. In addition, intense competition during the peak season means that you may well obtain a lower than expected price at this time.

Bookings can be made at the TRC in Srinagar, but the prices here are the highest. You can try negotiating directly with the touts or owners, or take a *shikara* ride and see for yourself what is worth renting. It is acceptable to transfer from one boat to another if you are unhappy with the service or facilities.

Due to the current political situation in Kashmir many **hotels** have been closed, so it is advisable to contact them first by telephone, or make enquiries at any Jammu & Kashmir Tourism Counter.

EXPENSIVE

Oberoi Palace, Gupkar Road, tel: 71241/71242. Formerly the Maharaja's palace. Beautiful gardens, badminton court and several shops.
Centaur Lake View, Cheshma Shahi, tel: 75631/77601. All amenities including restaurants, coffee shop, health club, pool and sports facilities. (Since 1989 security forces have had a big presence here).

MODERATE

Shahenshah Palace, Boulevard, tel: 71345/71346. Overlooking Dal Lake. Restaurants, coffee shop, pool.
Shah Abbas, Boulevard, tel: 79335/79336. Centrally located with restaurant and coffee shop.
Tramboo Continental, Boulevard, tel: 73914/71718. Good value choice with restaurant.
Welcome, Boulevard, tel: 74104/73467. Another good value option on Dal Lake.
Dar es Salaam, Nagin Road, tel: 77803.

Ahdoo's, Residency Road, tel: 72593. Rooms with bath and TV, good restaurant.

BUDGET

Grand Hotel, Residency Road. Reasonably priced rooms with en suite bathrooms.
Green Acre Guest House, Raj Bagh, tel: 73349. A wide range of rooms in a private residence with garden and good food.
Tourist Reception Centre, Shervani Road, tel: 49554/47756. Good value rooms, but the army might still be in residence.
Youth Hostel, Wazir Bagh. Across the river from the centre of town. Dormitories.

Where to Eat

Ahdoo's Hotel, Residency Road. Excellent Kashmiri specialities and other Indian food. Great value.
Tao Cafe, Residency Road. Chinese food. Popular, with a garden.
Shamyana, Boulevard. Good pizzas, garlic bread.
Alka Salka, Residency Road. Good, pricey Indian and Chinese food.
Lhasa, off Boulevard. Good budget-priced Chinese/Tibetan food.
Glocken Bakery, Dal Gate. Various baked goodies and bread.
Sultan Bakery, near the Glocken Bakery. Recommended.

Shopping

Kashmir Handicrafts Emporium. There are several, the one in the old Residency at the Bund is the largest.
The Boulevard, Dal Lake. A large number of shops.
The Oriental Apiary, between Dal and Nagin Lakes. Excellent range of locally produced honey.

Where to Stay

EXPENSIVE

Parishutham, 55 Grand Anicut Canal Road, tel: 21466. Comfortable, pricey accommodation with cable TV, restaurant, craft shop, swimming pool and foreign exchange.

MODERATE

TTDC Tamil Nadu, Gandhiji Road, tel:

1421. Large and comfortable, with restaurant, bar and garden. Good value.

BUDGET

Railway Retiring Rooms. Six doubles on the first floor of the railway station.

Thrissur/Trichur, Kerala
Where to Stay

Casino, T.B. Road, tel: 24699. Near the railway station. The best hotel in town, mid-budget, restaurant and foreign exchange.
Government Guest House, Palace Road, tel: 20300. Officially for VIPs. Huge suites with balconies. Food available to order in advance.
KTDC Yatri Nivas, off Museum Road, tel: 27383. Good budget option, beer bar.

Tiruchirapalli (Trichy), Tamil Nadu
Where to Stay

Femina. Comfortable rooms, some with balconies, good restaurants, 24-hour coffee shop.
Ashby, 17A Junction Road, tel: 40652. Large rooms with verandahs around a courtyard. Restaurant-cum-bar.

Trivandrum/ Thiruvananthapuram, Kerala
Where to Stay

Luciya Continental, East Fort, tel: 73443. near the railway station, this big mid-budget hotel has modern rooms, restaurant and coffee shop.
Pankaj, M.G. Road, tel: 76667. Another good mid-budget option. Comfortable, modern and with a restaurant.
Yatri Niwas, KTDC Hostel, Thycaud, tel: 64462. Basic accommodation at budget rates. Food.

Udaipur, Rajasthan
Where to Stay

EXPENSIVE

Lake Palace, tel: 23241. Exquisite, romantic, luxurious lakeside hotel with all amenities, pool and lakeview restaurant.

Shiv Niwas Palace, City Palace, tel: 28239; fax: 23823. The magnificent guest apartments of the City Palace have been converted into an exclusive hotel.

MODERATE

Shikarbadi, Goverdhan Vilas, off NH8, tel: 83200/4. Formerly the Maharaja's hunting lodge, this attractive hotel has a restaurant, pool, gardens and deer park.

Anand Bhawan, Fatehsagar Road, tel: 23256/7. Good value. Comfortable rooms, views.

Vadodara/Baroda, Gujarat
Where to Stay

EXPENSIVE

Welcomgroup Vadodara, R.C. Dutta Road, tel: 323232. Gujarat's only five-star hotel, with all amenities.

MODERATE

Rama Inn, Sayaji Gunj, tel: 330131; fax: 331133. Good, mid-budget option, comfortable rooms, restaurants, pool.

BUDGET

Green, R.C. Dutt Road, tel: 323111. Best budget option in an old house with great ambience.

Varanasi (Benares), Uttar Pradesh
Where to Stay

Taj Ganges, Nadesar Palace Grounds, tel: 42481. One of the top hotels in town, a member of the Taj Group. All amenities, two good restaurants, bar and swimming pool.

Clarks, The Mall, Cantt, tel: 46771. Another of the top hotels. Well established, atmospheric, all amenities including pool.

Hotel de Paris, 15 The Mall, Cantt, tel: 46601. First established by a Frenchman in the early 19th century, it has spacious rooms, large gardens and lots of character.

UPTDC Tourist Dak Bungalow, 59 Cantt, tel: 42182. Good value rooms and grounds for campers, food. Musical performances in the evening.

Where to Eat

El Parador, near the water tank, Maldahiya Roadways, tel: 46555. Unusual menu featuring European specialities and good desserts.

Kemps, Parade Kothi, Cantt, near the Tourist Bungalow. Good, reasonably priced Western food.

Sindhi, Bhelupur Thana. Varanasi's traditional pure vegetarian food.

Vishakhapatnam, Andhra Pradesh
Where to Stay

Park Hotel, Beach Road, tel: 54861. The best hotel in town. All amenities, restaurant, bar and access to beach.

Karanths, 33-1-55 Patel Marg, near the railway station, tel: 69347. Immaculate and inexpensive rooms with bath. Good, cheap thali restaurant.

Festivals
Calendar of Events

January

New Year (1 January): Goa, Kerala, the metropolises. Businesses close, parties after midnight.

Muharram: Delhi, Hyderabad, Lucknow. Commemorates martyrdom of the grandson of Prophet Mohammed.

Pongal (Sankranti): Tamil Nadu, Karnataka, Andhra Pradesh. Four-day long harvest festival.

Republic Day (26 January, public holiday): All-India. Spectacular parade in New Delhi.

Basant Panchami: West Bengal, Madhya Pradesh. Hindu festival of learning; kite flying.

February

Desert Festival: Jaisalmer (Rajasthan). Camels, turbans and tourists.

Float Festival: Madurai. Colourful procession of imaginative floats.

February/March

Holi: Northern India. Colours and water are thrown in this boisterous spring celebration lasting until 2am.

March/April

Gangaur: Jaipur, other Rajasthan cities, Bengal and Orissa. Festival of Parvati. Women dress in a blaze of colour.

Carnival: Panaji (Goa). Pre-Lenten celebration; Mardi Gras.

Spring Festival: Kashmir. First blossoms in the almond orchards.

Ugadi (New Year): Andhra, Karnataka, Tamil Nadu. Hindu solar New Year.

April/May

Baisakhi: All-India, Amritsar. Foundation of Sikh brotherhood; a New Year celebration in West Bengal.

Pooram: Trichur. Spectacular elephant procession; fireworks.

Meenakshi Kalyanam: Madurai. Mammoth procession of large temple chariots celebrates the marriage of a god.

Buddha Purnima: Sarnath, Bodhgaya. Marks the birth, enlightenment and death of Lord Buddha.

June/July

Rath Yatra: Puri. Honours Lord Krishna. Parade of huge temple chariots.

July/August

Teej: Rajasthan. Women welcome the monsoon. A time of local fairs.

Amarnath Yatra: Amarnath. A great pilgrimage to an icicle.

Raag Panchami: Jodhpur. Fair and festival honouring a cobra deity.

August/September

Raksha Bandhan: Northern India. Brothers and sisters and platonic friends pledge kinship by the girls tying threads around the boys' wrists.

Independence Day (15 August, public holiday): All-India. Commemorative parades.

Janmashtami: All-India. Birthday of Lord Krishna; dance dramas.

Ganesh Chaturthi: Maharashtra. Festival of Lord Ganesh; fairs and cultural events. In Bombay, parades take the idol of the god for immersion in sea.

Onam: Kerala. Harvest festival; four days of feasting, dancing and "snake" boat races.

Id-ul-Fitur: All-India. Celebrating the end of the month-long Ramzan fast.

September/October

Dussehra (Durga, Pooja, Navarathri): Delhi, Kulu, Mysore, West Bengal, Southern States, Uttar Pradesh. An annual battle between the forces of good and evil is enacted over a 10-day period; dance dramas, burning of effigies, exhibitions.

Gandhi Jayanti (2 October, public holiday): Raj Ghat in Delhi. Birthday of Mahatma Gandhi.

October/November

Diwali: All-India. Festival of lights; fireworks; considered New Year for many people.

Pushkar Fair: Ajmer. Spectacular crowds of pilgrims at the lake; camel fair.

Guru Purab: Amritsar, Patna. The birthday of the founder of the Sikh religion, Guru Nanak.

December

Christmas Day (25 December, public holiday). Goa, Kerala. A Western tradition celebrated in Indian fashion.

Shopping

What to Buy

Leave plenty of space in your luggage for shopping. The assortment of wares is staggering and so are the comparatively low prices.

Places selling handicrafts (of all kinds) are an inevitable first stop for the shopper. These handicrafts are themselves statements of the diversity that is India, and are at the same time products of its remarkably varied and attractive artistic traditions. Nowhere else could such variety exist. Interesting as souvenirs, many are also valuable investments.

Carpets from Kashmir, at the upper end of the the price range, crafted in the Persian tradition, are available in different sizes and knot-counts. Unless you know a lot about carpets, shop at a Government Emporium. Less expensive but still beautiful are rugs and *dhurries* from all over the country. Then there is the huge assortment of precious and semi-precious gem-stones, jewellery set in both gold and silver, traditional as well as modern, chunky or dainty, all at irresistible prices.

Textiles, for which India is justly famous, present a bewildering array of textures, weaves, prints, designs and colours, which would make unusual and attractive dresses, cushion covers or bedspreads. Shawls, rich evening stoles and silk scarves make excellent gifts. Remember that many hotel tailors offer 24-hour tailoring.

Carved figurines of sandalwood and elaborately worked wooden panels from the south make memorable souvenirs. Objects in brass, copper and gun metal, inlaid, enamelled, worked or simply beaten, offer a wide choice.

Exquisite marble inlay work and papier-mâché items with intricate designs are painstakingly crafted in traditions that have existed for centuries. Reproductions of miniature paintings on paper or cloth must be chosen carefully. Look at several before you decide. Leather wallets, shoes and bags, if less exotic, are also good buys. Hand-painted pottery, and cane goods ranging from table mats to furniture, are excellent value. The incredible array of ready-made clothes could make interesting additions to your wardrobe. Antiques and semi-antiques of every kind are tempting, but bear in mind laws governing the export of antiques – and beware of fakes.

With the amazing variety of goods on offer, shopping can be bewildering, so look around before you start buying. For safe shopping, Government Emporia and shops on the Department of Tourism's approved list are recommended.

The Central Cottage Industries and the various State Emporia have branches in major cities. They help make the diversity of Indian wares accessible at central points. If you prefer to wander in the bazaars and bargain, visit these first to get a feel of quality and prices. Be wary of shops to which guides or taxi drivers appear eager to take you. You will pay more to cover their commission. Exports of skins, furs and ivory is either banned or strictly regulated. Remember to get a certificate of legitimate sale and permission for export.

Language

Communication in India, where there are 15 assorted languages and umpteen hundred dialects, is sometimes best accomplished in very simple English. With appropriate local gestures, and the accent modified to the region, this is most likely to be understood.

Yet attempts to speak Hindi, the official tongue, are always appreciated. The language follows regular phonetic pronunciation similar to Spanish, and the letter "h" is almost always silent, except at the beginning of a word. The vocabulary which follows is a very basic beginning. Note that these words will normally appear in the Hindi script, and that their rendition into our alphabet can result in a variety of alternative spellings.

A short list of Traveller's Tamil is included as well. Hindi is less common on the streets of Madras where the elite speak a refined, old-colonial English. A smattering of the local lingo will stand you in good stead all over the south, where Hindi draws baffled stares. The citizens of Calcutta, though they prefer Bengali, usually understand Hindi well, and their English may be better than yours. The same is true in Bombay.

Traveller's Hindi

Good morning	Shubh prabhat
Good night	Shubh ratri
Good	Acha
Very good	Bahut acha

Bad	Bura
Yes	Han
No	Nahi
Perhaps	Shayad
Please	Meherbani se
Thank you	Dhanyavad
Hello/goodbye	Namaste
How are you?	Aap kaise hein
What is your name?	Aap ka naam kya (Aap ka subh naam)
My name is (Elvis)	Meera naam (Elvis) hai
What is the time?	Kya baja hai
Which way to (hotel)	Kis taraf (hotel)
What is that?	Voh kya hai
How much (cost)?	Kitna (kitna paise)
Too much (cost)	Jada hai
Come lower (cost)	Kum karo
Is it possible?	Kya yeh sambhav hai
Go away	Chale jao (*chelo) [*the first is rude]
Hurry up	Jaldi kare
Left	Bai
Right	Dai
Slow down	Aaahista
Stop	Thehariye
How far is?	Kitni dur hai
Here	Yaha
There	Vaha
Now	Abhi
Same	Saman, barabar
Today	Aaj
Week	Saptah
Month	Mahina
Year	Sal
How?	Kaise
What?	Kya
Who?	Kon
Why?	Kyon
Where?	Kaha
When?	Kab
Restaurant	Dhaba
Menu	Minu
Bill, please	Bill lao
Water	Pani
Rice	Chawal
Fruit	Phal
Vegetables	Sabzi
Bread	Chapati
I	Ma
We	Hum
They	Ve
Man	Aadmi
Woman	Ourat
Child	Bacha
Mother	Mata
Father	Pita
Son	Larka
Toilet	Bakhana
Train	Gadi
Joke	Mazak
Prayer	Pratha, puja
Sleep	Sona
Beautiful	Sunder
Excellent (Number One)	Premiere
Shirt	Kamiz
Trousers	Pyjama
Laundry	Dhobi

NUMBERS

1	ek	20	bis
2	do	30	tish
3	teen	40	chalish
4	char	50	pachash
5	panch	60	sahath
6	chhe	70	setur
7	saat	80	aashi
8	aarth	90	numba
9	nau	100	sau
10	das	1000	hazar

Traveller's Tamil

I/me	Naan
You	Nee
Who?	Yaar
When?	Yeppothu
Why?	Ean
What?	Yenna
Yes	Aam
No	Illai
Good	Nallathu
Bad	Kettathu
Excuse me	Manniyungal
How much?	Ennavillai
Thank you	Nandri
Eat	Sappidu
Drink	Kudi
Sleep	Thoongu
Come	Vaa
Go	Po
Stop	Niruthu

NUMBERS

1	onru	6	aaru
2	irandu	7	eezhu
3	moonru	8	ettu
4	naangu	9	ompath
5	ainthu	10	paththu
100	nooru		

Glossary of Common Foods

Common Dishes

Roomali: snack or meal of *rotis* or *parathas*, layered and stuffed with minced meat or *paneer* cheese.

Dal makhni: dish of rich spiced lentils with coriander.

Shahi paneer: cheese in cream and potatoes.

Khatte allo: spiced potato.

Baingan mumtaz: stuffed aubergine.

Firni: a kind of exotic rice pudding served in an earthenware bowl.

Kheer: rich thickened milk with raisins and nuts.

Subze: spiced vegetable dishes.

Rogon josh: curried lamb.

Gushtaba: spicy meat pounded to pâté consistency, formed into balls and simmered in spiced yogurt.

Idlis: steamed rice-cake eaten with fresh coconut chutney.

Sambhar: chilli-laced lentil soup.

Biryani: chicken or lamb in orange-flavoured rice, sprinkled with rose water, almonds and dried fruits.

Tandoori: chicken, meat or fish baked in a clay oven.

Thali: large round metal tray filled with little bowls of boiled rice, lentil curries and several portions of vegetables.

Unleavened Breads

These are baked in a tandoor clay oven.

Chapati: crispy bread.

Romali roti: paper thin bread.

Naan: fluffy, yogurt leavened bread.

Paratha: millet-based, sprinkled with cumin, sesame, caraway, or stuffed with peas, onions or potatoes.

Khulcha bhatura: soft, doughy bread eaten with spicy chick peas.

Dosa: a form of crêpe made from lightly fermented rice flour and stuffed with spiced potato, eaten with fresh coconut chutney and *sambhar*.

Desserts and Confectionary

Kulfi: ice-cream flavoured with cardamom, pistachio nuts and saffron.

Rasgullas: cream cheeseballs in rose syrup.

Burfi: halva sweets covered in wafer-thin silver paper.

Gulab jamun: spongy ground almond balls, served dripping with honeyed syrup.

Jalebi: cartwheel-shaped sweets, served with syrup.

Paan: betel nut and spices wrapped in a betel leaf.

Drinks
Nimbu: lime soda, served sweet, salted or plain.
Lassi: yogurt-based drink.

Further Reading

General Section

History

A Concise History of India, by Francis Watson (Thames and Hudson, London, 1979). Compact and thorough history in readable format, with illustrations and photographs.

A History of India, Volume I, by Romilar Thapar (Pelican, 1980). Recounts from ancient times through to the Delhi sultanate; Volume II, by Perceval Spear, continues from the Moghuls to the murder of Gandhi.

Amritsar: Mrs Gandhi's Last Stand, by Mark Tully and Satish Jacob (Jonathan Cape). Account of Operation Blue Star, the storming of the Sikhs' Golden Temple, and the aftermath which scarred a nation following Indira Gandhi's assassination.

An Introduction to India, by Stanley Wolpert (Viking 1992). Informative account of India's complexities by an American academic.

Freedom at Midnight, by Larry Collins and Dominique Lapierre (Tarang, 1975). Gripping popular history of the birth of the Indian nation.

The Great Moghuls, by Bamber Gascoigne (London, 1971). Well-researched book which describes the dynasty that for two centuries ruled India, in turn both enlightened and decadent, austere and brutal. Sumptuous photographs complement highly readable text.

India, by Barbara Crosette (University of Indiana Press, 1993). Contemporary Indian politics and international relations recounted by *New York Times* correspondent who was on the scene at Rajiv Gandhi's assassination.

The Wonder that Was India, by A.L. Basham (Rupa, Delhi, 1967). Learned historical classic in idiosyncratic, rapturous prose.

Society, Culture and Religion

A Book of India, by B.N. Pandey (Rupa, Delhi, 1982). A real masala mix of philosophies, traveller's notes, poetry, literary trivia, revealing a quixotic India. Recommended.

Changing Village, Changing Life, by Prafulla Mohanti (Viking). Wry account of village life in Orissa.

Freedom in Exile, by Tenzin Gyatso (Rupa, Delhi, 1992; Hodder and Stoughton, London, 1990). Eloquent autobiography of the Tibetan holy man, the 14th Dalai Lama.

In Exile from the Land of the Snows, by John Avedon (Michael Joseph, London, 1984). Moving portrayal of Tibetan struggle and life of exiles in India.

India: A Literary Companion, by Bruce Palling (John Murray, London, 1992). Another compilation of impressions taken from literature, letters and unpublished diaries, skillfully presented.

India File, by Trevor Fishlock (John Murray). Witty observations of a resident British correspondent.

May You Be the Mother of a Hundred Sons, by Elisabeth Bumiller (Penguin). Women's issues tackled head-on, everything from dowries to infanticide, with dozens of poignant interviews.

A Million Mutinies Now, by V.S. Naipul. The scholar seeks his roots and finds a cast of characters not easily pigeonholed. A more positive follow-up to his earlier *India: A Wounded Civilisation*.

The Mind of India, by William Gerber (Arcturus Paperbacks, 1967). Snippets from The Vedas, Buddhism, ancient and medieval commentaries, modern mysticism, all help to understand a Hindu perspective.

The Path of the Mystic Lover, by Bhaskar Bhattacharyya (Destiny/Inner Traditions, Vermont, 1993). Scoundrel/scholar delves into the lyrics of Bengali folk musicians, the Bauls. Obscure, but fascinating. Illustrations more 1960s than tantric.

Plain Tales from the Raj, by Charles Allen (Abacus). First-hand accounts from ex-colonialists.

Travel

A Goddess in the Stones, by Norman Lewis (Pan Macmillan). Intrepid Brit tackles the tribals in Bihar and Orissa. Entertaining.

An Indian Attachment, by Sarah Lloyd (Eland, 1992). Insightful account of a love affair with a Punjabi sikh which lunges the Western woman into a spiral of cultural anxieties.

Chasing the Monsoon, by Alexander Frater (Penguin). A whimsical odyssey which goes up the west coast, into the northeast, and onto the plains, as refreshing as the rains. Recommended.

City of Djinnns (sic), by William Dalrymple. Modern Delhi, with a few forays out of station, is etched with mirth and historical detail. Flawed in parts by callow tone and dubious coincidences, but highly readable.

Three Quarters of a Footprint, by Joe Roberts (Transworld). South and Central India examined by thoughtful, unpretentious Englishman.

Fiction

A River Sutra, by Gita Mehta (Viking, 1993). Gently wrought stories which linger in the imagination.

Midnight's Children, by Salman Rushdie (Jonathan Cape, 1981). Rushdie burst onto the literary scene with this dazzling novel of partition. Sardonic.

Out of India, by Ruth Prawer Jhabvala (Penguin). A collection of strong short stories that amuse and startle.

Pather Panchali, by Bibhutibhushan Banerji (Rupi, Delhi, 1990). Outstanding Indian novel which outdoes the film by Satyajit Ray, depicting richness of spirit amid poverty in Bengal.

The English Teacher, by R.K. Narayan (various editions). Narayan evokes infuriating and endearing characters which inhabit Malgudi, a composite Indian village.

The Thousand Headed Snake, by Anthony Spaeth (Weidenfeld and Nicolson, London, 1993). Second in a South Asian thriller trilogy marked by vivid detail of the Indian background and personalities.

Food, Lingo & Images

Curries and Bugles, by Jennifer Brennan (Penguin, 1992). Legends and tales mixed up with the favourite recipes of Raj-era memsahibs and sahibs.

Hanklyn-Janklin, or a Stranger's Rumble Tumble Guide to some Words, Customs and Quiddities Indian and Indo-British, by Nigel B. Hankin (Banyan Books, New Delhi, 1992). Lives up to its title and is a delightful reference work.

Hobson-Jobson, (Routledge and Kegan

Paul, London), the 1886 glossary on which Hankin modelled his modern etymology. The pair complement one another.

Indian Style, by Suzanne Slesin, Stafford Cliff (Thames and Hudson, 1990). Colour prints of exterior and interior design, in exacting detail, capture the texture of India.

Sadhus, The Holy Men of India, by Rajesh and Ramesh Bedi (New Delhi, 1991). Striking images of Indian ascetics and informed text reveal hidden life of those who renounce the world.

Taj, by Raghu Rai (Delhi, 1988). The ultimate photographic depiction of the world's monument to love. Large format, high impact.

Other Insight Guides

The 190-title *Insight Guides* series and the complementary 110-title *Insight Pocket Guides* series have particularly strong coverage of the Indian subcontinent.

Insight Guide: Rajasthan features full coverage, with insightful essays and stunning photography, of the region that remains many people's first introduction to India.

Insight Guide: Delhi, Jaipur and Agra is the perfect companion for travellers taking the classic tour of India's Golden Triangle.

Insight Guide: South India is a comprehensive guide to the southern states of Andhra Pradesh, Karnataka, Tamil Nadu and Kerala.

Insight Guide: India's Western Himalaya explores the states of Jammu and Kashmir and Himachal Pradesh, a pristine world of cool forested hills and high deserts, towering peaks and rushing rivers.

Insight Guide: Indian Wildlife is an indispensable guide for nature lovers, combining expert text and astonishing photography of the parks and sanctuaries of India, Nepal and Sri Lanka.

Insight Guide: Calcutta reveals the often ignored fascinations of this teeming city, one of the liveliest and warmest in India.

● The Pocket Guide series, designed for readers on a tight schedule, provides carefully timed itineraries and personal recommendations from a local "host". Conveniently portable, they are the next best thing to having your own sympathetic tour guide.

Insight Pocket Guide: New Delhi guides you through the tangled alleys and tamarind tree-lined avenues, recommending the best sights to see, places to eat and things to do.

Insight Pocket Guide: Sikkim, Darjeeling and Kalimpong takes you from the great monasteries to lesser known sights and includes the newly opened treks in this alluring Buddhist Himalayan region.

Art/Photo Credits

Photography by
Ping Amranand 14/15
Apa Photo Library 133, 134
Clair Arni 24
Bruce Bernstein, Courtesy of Princeton Library, NJ 45, 46, 48, 296, 311
Marcello Bertinetti/Apa 124, 176, 178, 184, 201
John Borthwick/Apa 180, 183, 245
A. Cassio/Apa 166, 207
Dhiraj Chawda 144
Gertrud & Helmut Denzau 136/137, 141, 252
D.P.A. – Agrawahl 67, 106, 109, 110, 147
Ashvin Gatha/Apa 130, 289
R.K. Goyal 61, 80, 83, 102, 126, 164L
Hans Höfer 26/27, 198, 255
Luca Invernizzi/Apa 104, 131, 188, 210, 215, 216, 260, 264, 292/293, 301, 317L, 320, 325
Ravi Kaimal 64
Roy Karlsson 269
Wilhelm Klein 44, 47, 49, 79R, 85, 93, 152/153, 154/155, 206, 221, 278L, 232
Rupinder Khulla 312L
Philip Little 278R, 279, 285
Max Lawrence 278L
Lyle Lawson 1, 2, 16/17, 20, 58, 62, 68/69, 105, 108, 112, 113, 132, 138, 146, 150/151, 187R, 191, 196/197, 242, 250, 251, 261, 266, 306, 312R, 323
Craig Lovell 39, 43, 70
Dieter Ludwig 307
Antonio Martinelli 12/13, 84, 87, 94, 100, 148/149, 158/159, 162, 171, 172L, 193, 203, 208, 214, 218/219, 231, 265, 268, 298, 303, 304R, 310, 315
A. Martinelli/R. Meazza 18/19, 31, 75L, 75R, 91, 156, 167, 175, 225, 262/263, 270, 290, 308, 321

Roberto Meazza 11, 72, 82, 169, 187L, 217, 228, 229L, 229R, 230, 235, 237, 277, 280, 284, 316, 317R
Ashvin Mehta 77, 78, 282, 283, 326, 327
D. Messent/Apa 172R, 192, 195, 204, 205, 213, 223, 224, 234, 238, 239, 241, 243, 248, 300, 304L, 313
Roland & Sabrina Michand 71
Fayaz Mir 25
Pramod R. Mistry 135L, 288
Courtesy of Nehru Memorial Museum, New Delhi 50, 51, 52, 53, 54, 55, 56
J.L. Nou 32R, 76R, 89, 96/97, 98, 101, 305, 322
Avinash Pasricha 66, 115, 116, 117L, 118, 256, 259, 287
Aditya Patankar 33, 117R, 128L, 209, 212, 314
Gunter Pfannmuller/Apa 302
Ronnie Pinsler 76L, 79L
Peter Sayle 226, 319, 324
Dr Geethi Sen 28, 32L, 35, 36, 41, 121, 123, 128R, 274
Toby Neil Sinclair 140, 179
Jeanine Siniscal 60, 164R, 240, 247, 253, 258
Clark Stede 233
Hashim Tyabji/Fotomedia 142
Paul Van Reil 135R
Joseph A. Viesti/Apa 168

Maps Berndtson & Berndtson

Visual Consultant V. Barl

Index

371